"Creative, hopeful, audacious. Here is a book that the city building professions have been, unknowingly, waiting for. Transcending technical and policy 'fixes,' this book addresses the cultural and spiritual dimensions of shaping cities as if people, land, and nature were sacred. An impressive, pluriversal collection of essays, asking arguably *the* most important question of our era: what will it take to build seven generation cities?"

Leonie Sandercock, *FRSC, Professor in Community Planning, University of British Columbia, Canada*

"*Sacred Civics* offers a forward-looking framework that re-imagines what our cities can be if we change our mindset to a more relational one. Through the voices of scholars and practitioners, the book gives a blueprint for how to put into practice the transformative ideas and principles so well articulated here. A wonderful achievement."

Sheila R. Foster, *Professor at Georgetown University, USA*

"The old metaphors for cities have run dry. Cities as machines or technologies or mechanisms aren't getting us anywhere. They aren't computers … they aren't smart. But they are systems that are built and managed by communities of humans and their non-human allies. As such, the values that we bear in mind as we do the work of city-ing matters. The work that we do together matters. It should be seen as sacred. Even the act of figuring out what this means is something that we should do together, and as such is a sacred process. This book ties many of the relevant threads together into the pattern we need for doing the work of cities in the 21st century. It liberates us from the mechanistic models of the past. It liberates us to figure out what's next for cities. Those of us who work to build just cities and communities need this book."

Nigel Jacob, *Co-Founder, Boston Mayor's Office of New Urban Mechanics, USA*

"Nature and the sacred have long been banished from the city. Yet can cities become the site of wisdom, wholeness, and healing? This is the urgent question this unique and wonderfully creative volume tackles by weaving together indigenous ontologies, the relational turn in urban studies, and decoloniality to persuasively develop the principles of 'sacred civics' and 'seven generation cities' as the foundation for a substantial rethinking of city building and the democratization of city futures. Chung-Tiam-Fook, Agyeman, and Engle have assembled a truly outstanding and diverse group of indigenous and nonindigenous writers and artists, including some of today's leading scholars in urban studies, to offer us a cogent framework of urban design as a praxis for the just co-existence of all within a living cosmos. Their call for a relational accountability for the urban worlds we design, grounded on a renewed Earth spirituality and a paradigm of interdependence and care, couldn't be timelier. Along the way, readers are invited to inspiring and rigorous analyses on the implications of such rethinking for commons, property, governance, nature, and the economy. The book will be of great value to urban planners and designers as well as to scholars and students in Indigenous and decolonial studies and those concerned with urban natures, transitions, pluriversality, and the sacred."

Arturo Escobar, *Professor of Anthropology Emeritus, University of North Carolina, USA*

"Cities need big ideas to fill small spaces. This book reveals how life's details might better correspond with life's broader sources to create healthier urban futures. I am impressed with the rich and varied angles of vision found in *Sacred Civics*. The book is practical and poetic. It cultivates hope even as it recognizes the significant challenges we face."

John Borrows, *Canada Research Chair in Indigenous Law, University of Victoria, Canada*

SACRED CIVICS

Sacred Civics argues that societal transformation requires that spirituality and sacred values are essential to reimagining patterns of how we live, organize and govern ourselves, determine and distribute wealth, inhabit and design cities, and construct relationships with others and with nature.

The book brings together transdisciplinary and global academics, professionals, and activists from a range of backgrounds to question assumptions that are fused deep into the code of how societies operate, and to draw on extraordinary wisdom from ancient Indigenous traditions; to social and political movements like Black Lives Matter, the commons, and wellbeing economies; to technologies for participatory futures where people collaborate to reimagine and change culture. Looking at cities and human settlements as the sites of transformation, the book focuses on values, commons, and wisdom to demonstrate that how we choose to live together—to recognize interdependencies, to build, grow, create, and love—matters.

Using multiple methodologies to integrate varied knowledge forms and practices, this truly ground-breaking volume includes contributions from renowned and rising voices. *Sacred Civics* is a must-read for anyone interested in intersectional discussions on social justice, inclusivity, participatory design, healthy communities, and future cities.

Jayne Engle, PhD, is an urbanist, strategist, co-creator of social change initiatives, and Adjunct Professor of Urban Planning at McGill University, Canada. She built a civic innovation portfolio with the McConnell Foundation in Canada and has worked globally bridging local participatory practice and research with long-range structural transformation.

Julian Agyeman is Professor of Urban and Environmental Policy and Planning, and Fletcher Professor of Rhetoric and Debate at Tufts University, Medford, MA, USA. He is the originator of the concept of "just sustainabilities," which explores the intersecting goals of social justice and environmental sustainability.

Tanya Chung-Tiam-Fook is Director of Research & Academic Programs at the Centre for Indigenous Innovation and Technology, Toronto, Canada, and author of *Civic-Indigenous Relationships in the Era of Truth and Reconciliation* (2021) and *Transformational Processes for Community-Focused Adaptation and Social Change* (2015).

ROUTLEDGE EQUITY, JUSTICE AND THE SUSTAINABLE CITY

Series editors: Julian Agyeman and Stephen Zavestoski

This series positions equity and justice as central elements of the transition toward sustainable cities. The series introduces critical perspectives and new approaches to the practice and theory of urban planning and policy that ask how the world's cities can become 'greener' while becoming more fair, equitable and just.

The *Routledge Equity Justice and the Sustainable City* series addresses sustainable city trends in the global North and South and investigates them for their potential to ensure a transition to urban sustainability that is equitable and just for all. These trends include municipal climate action plans; resource scarcity as tipping points into a vortex of urban dysfunction; inclusive urbanization; "complete streets" as a tool for realizing more "livable cities"; the use of information and analytics toward the creation of "smart cities".

The series welcomes submissions for high-level cutting-edge research books that push thinking about sustainability, cities, justice and equity in new directions by challenging current conceptualizations and developing new ones. The series offers theoretical, methodological, and empirical advances that can be used by professionals and as supplementary reading in courses in urban geography, urban sociology, urban policy, environment and sustainability, development studies, planning, and a wide range of academic disciplines.

The Green City and Social Injustice
21 Tales from North America and Europe
Edited by Isabelle Anguelovski and James J. T. Connolly

Sacred Civics
Building Seven Generation Cities
Edited by Jayne Engle, Julian Agyeman, and Tanya Chung-Tiam-Fook

For more information about this series, please visit: www.routledge.com/Routledge-Equity-Justice-and-the-Sustainable-City-series/book-series/EJSC

SACRED CIVICS

Building Seven Generation Cities

Edited by Jayne Engle, Julian Agyeman,
and Tanya Chung-Tiam-Fook

Routledge
Taylor & Francis Group
LONDON AND NEW YORK

earthscan
from Routledge

Cover graphic: Paul Messer, with artistic inspiration from Catherine Tàmmaro
Chapter glyph artwork: Catherine Tàmmaro

First published 2022
by Routledge
4 Park Square, Milton Park, Abingdon, Oxon OX14 4RN

and by Routledge
605 Third Avenue, New York, NY 10158

Routledge is an imprint of the Taylor & Francis Group, an informa business

British Library Cataloguing-in-Publication Data
A catalogue record for this book is available from the British Library

Library of Congress Cataloging-in-Publication Data
A catalog record has been requested for this book

ISBN: 978-1-032-05910-5 (hbk)
ISBN: 978-1-032-05911-2 (pbk)
ISBN: 978-1-003-19981-6 (ebk)

DOI: 10.4324/9781003199816

Typeset in Bembo
by Newgen Publishing UK

to city dwellers everywhere

We need to take responsibility for our future. Those of us alive right now are the only people who can fight against the present dangers; the only people who can build the communities, norms and institutions that will safeguard our future. Whether we are remembered as the generation who turned the corner to a bright and secure future, or not remembered at all, comes down to whether we rise to meet these challenges.

Toby Ord, The Precipice: Existential risk and the future of humanity (2020, 188)

CONTENTS

ILLUSTRATIONS

Figures

Tables

CONTRIBUTORS

Julian Agyeman is Professor of Urban and Environmental Policy and Planning, and Fletcher Professor of Rhetoric and Debate at Tufts University, Medford, MA, USA.

Michel Bauwens is Founder of the P2P Foundation, an observatory on commoning and peer production and is the co-author of *P2P, A Commons Manifesto*. Based in Thailand, he has crafted Transition Plans for the city of Ghent and for Ecuador in 2014. Since 2019 he has been advisor to SMart.coop, a labor mutual.

Kofi Boone is Professor of Landscape Architecture and Environmental Planning at NC State University, USA.

Tessy Britton is a social systems designer and founder of Participatory City, UK. She believes that inclusive participation, built around people and everyday life, has the potential to be the single most important opportunity we have to solving the many challenges being faced in cities across the world.

Fang-Jui "Fang-Raye" Chang is Strategic Designer at Dark Matter Labs, UK, and author of *Radicle Civics—Unconstituting Society* (2022).

Tanya Chung-Tiam-Fook is Director of Research & Academic Programs at the Centre for Indigenous Innovation and Technology, Toronto, Canada.

Jayne Engle, PhD, is an urbanist, strategist, co-creator of social change initiatives, and Adjunct Professor of Urban Planning at McGill University, Canada.

Gorka Espiau is Director of the Agirre Lehendakaria Center for Social and Political Studies (University of the Basque Country, Spain).

Pamela Glode-Desrochers is Executive Director of the Mi'kmaw Native Friendship Society and Vice President of the National Association of Friendship Centres in Canada.

Ginger Gosnell-Myers is of Nisga'a and Kwakwak'awakw heritage and is Simon Fraser University's first Indigenous Fellow at the Morris J. Wosk Centre for Dialogue in Vancouver where she focuses on urban Indigenous policy and planning in Canada, and author of *Co-creating the Cities We Deserve through Indigenous Knowledge* (2022).

Indy Johar is Executive Director at Dark Matter Labs, UK, and author of *Radicle Civics— Unconstituting Society* (2022).

Rok Kranjc is a sustainability transitions researcher at the Institute for Ecology, Slovenia, and a translator and editor at Institute ČKZ. He is the founder of Futurescraft, a design studio for experiential futures and games about post-capitalist economies. He is affiliated with the P2P Foundation and Participatory Futures Global Swarm.

Aarathi Krishnan specializes in strategic and applied foresight for the humanitarian and development sector. She is an affiliate at Berkman Klein Centre for Internet and Society at Harvard University as well as 2020–2022 Technology and Human Rights Fellow at the Harvard Carr Centre for Technology and Human Rights.

Deborah McGregor is Associate Professor and the Canada Research Chair in Indigenous Environmental Justice at York University in Canada. She is the co-author of *Reconciling Relationships with the Land through Land Acknowledgements.*

Itziar Moreno is Co-Director of the Agirre Lehendakaria Center for Social and Political Studies (University of the Basque Country, Spain).

Emma Nelson is a recent graduate of York University's Master of Environmental Studies program in Canada and the co-author of *Reconciling Relationships with the Land through Land Acknowledgements.*

Kathy Peach is Director of the Centre for Collective Intelligence Design at Nesta, the UK's innovation foundation. Recent publications include *Collective Crisis Intelligence for Frontline Humanitarian Response* (2021), *Collective Intelligence for Sustainable Development* (2021), and *Our Futures: By the People, for the People* (2019).

Edgar Pieterse is the Director of the African Centre for Cities at the University of Cape Town, South Africa. He is holder of the South African Research Chair in Urban Policy.

Jose Ramos is an action researcher, futurist and social innovator with a focus on the commons. He is Director for Action Foresight and Futures Lab; Co-editor of the *Journal of Futures Studies*; Co-Founder of the Participatory Futures Global Swarm, and Adjunct Senior Lecturer at the University of the Sunshine Coast, Australia.

AbdouMaliq Simone is Senior Professorial Fellow at the Urban Institute, University of Cape Town and Honorary Professor at the African Centre for Cities, University of Cape Town, South Africa.

Laurie Smith is Senior Foresight Lead at Nesta, UK. Recent publications include *Innovation Sweet Spots* (2021), *Exploring a Hunch* (2020), *There Will Be No Back to Normal* (2020), and *Our Futures: By the People, for the People* (2019).

Jennie C. Stephens is Professor of Sustainability Science and Policy and Director of Northeastern University's School of Public Policy & Urban Affairs in Boston, USA, and author of *Diversifying Power: Why We Need Antiracist, Feminist Leadership on Climate and Energy* (2021).

Yvonne Takau is a recent graduate of the Master of Planning program at the University of Otago, New Zealand. She is of Tongan descent and currently works as a planner at Aukaha in Dunedin, New Zealand, supporting the aspirations of Kāi Tahu in the natural and built environments of the Otago Region.

Catherine Tàmmaro, Wyandot (Toronto, Canada) has a decades-long history of multidisciplinary art-making. Catherine works with many agencies, city-wide and beyond to advise and facilitate art-making/teaching workshops and ceremony, and maintains her own art practice.

Michelle Thompson-Fawcett is Professor in the School of Geography, University of Otago, New Zealand. She teaches and researches in geography and urban planning, with a focus on fostering Indigenous sovereignty by realizing culturally sustainable environmental futures. Michelle is of Ngāti Whātua descent.

PREFACE

> It is a long road heading toward that new and better world for all beings. Do we even dare to dream city-civics can be built on a foundational understanding of Sacred Natural Law? … We must hold on tight to raise that vision of reworlding in the newly born Sacred Civics movement.
>
> *Catherine Tàmmaro, Wyandot Small Turtle Clan FaithKeeper and artist*

In light of a long and tangled history of injustice and mistrust, how can we work together to create reciprocal and conscientious forms of city building, urban land stewardship, and civic engagement across our cities, communities, institutions, and systems that will help us move toward more equitable and generative relationships, and mutually valuable outcomes? This is a core question motivating this collaborative book. We are convinced that the scale of transformation required to move forward in this epochal period in history calls for seeing our cities anew and through a relationality and futures lens. We refer to these cities of the future as "seven generation cities."

Seven generation cities are based on the Seventh Generation Principle, which is emblematic of Indigenous philosophy, ceremony, and natural law. This principle has lived through the teachings and lifeways of a multiplicity of Indigenous Nations across Turtle Island, Latin America, and the Caribbean, and is derived from the Gayanashagowa or Great Law of Peace/ Great Binding Law, the Constitution of the Haudenosaunee Five Nations Confederacy (later six Nations)[1] that was passed down by Peacemaker.

The Gayanashagowa forms the governance, ceremonial, spiritual, and social foundations of the Haudenosaunee Peoples, and the Seventh Generation Principle particularly articulates this ancient philosophy:

> In our every deliberation, we must consider the impact of our decisions on the next seven generations.
>
> The thickness of your skin shall be seven spans—which is to say that you shall be proof against anger, offensive actions and criticism. Your heart shall be filled with peace and good will and your mind filled with a yearning for the welfare of the people of the

Confederacy. With endless patience you shall carry out your duty and your firmness shall be tempered with tenderness for your people. Neither anger nor fury shall find lodgement in your mind and all your words and actions shall be marked with calm deliberation. In all of your deliberations in the Confederate Council, in your efforts at law making, in all your official acts, self-interest shall be cast into oblivion. Cast not over your shoulder behind you the warnings of the nephews and nieces should they chide you for any error or wrong you may do, but return to the way of the Great Law which is just and right. Look and listen for the welfare of the whole people and have always in view not only the present but also the coming generations, even those whose faces are yet beneath the surface of the ground—the unborn of the future Nation.[2]

A sacred philosophy and pillar of governance for many Indigenous Nations, the Seventh Generation Principle has also inspired broader contemporary thinking and policy on sustainability, especially regarding long-term decisions about harvesting and use of lands, waters, and natural resources. It requires us to be more truthful about the world we are leaving behind, and more generous, intuitive, and futures-minded in our city building and reworlding for current and subsequent generations.

Models of sacred civics leadership can co-create seven generation cities that require each of us to be caring and responsible stewards of the lands and waters at the foundation of cities, and accountable to future generations in our thinking, decisions, and actions.

Our Positionalities

Tanya Chung-Tiam-Fook

Having grown up predominantly in Toronto, I feel humbled and privileged to be a visitor and conscious steward in the sacred homelands of the Michi-saagiig of the Credit First Nation and the traditional territories of the Wendat, Anishinaabeg, and Haudenoshaunee confederacies. My Akawaio Indigenous and mixed ancestry from Guyana and the Netherlands, combined with interdisciplinary and international experiences, enable me to bring multifaceted and intersectional perspectives and sensibilities to my scholarship and praxis. My passion, and most important role, is to bridge worlds: cultural and ecological realms, Indigenous and Western paradigms, and global North and South, through pathways of reciprocity, Two-Eyed Seeing, compassion, collaboration, (re)storying, and reworlding.

Julian Agyeman

I am of mixed British/Ghanaian (Ashanti) heritage and grew up in Northern England. I was educated and worked in Britain before emigrating to the USA in 1998. I now live in Cambridge, Massachusetts, and work at Tufts University, which is located on colonized Wôpanâak (Wampanoag) and Massa-adchu-es-et (Massachusett) traditional territory. I'm a critical urban planning scholar who is trying to close the gap between belonging in the city, and what cities are becoming, using the lens of just sustainabilities, defined as: "the need to ensure a better quality of life for all, now and into the future, in a just and equitable manner, while living within the limits of supporting ecosystems."

Jayne Engle

A descendant of settlers from Europe, I grew up on a farm in Pennsylvania on traditional unceded homelands of the Susquehannock Peoples. My family's custom of welcoming people seeking refuge from conflict zones and difficult home environments shaped my worldview. As an adult, I've worked globally, including as a participatory city planner in the USA, Canada and Western Europe; in regional policy and economic transition with the Peace Corps in Eastern Europe after the fall of the Soviet empire; and as a participatory researcher in Haiti following the devastating earthquake of 2010. I now live with my two children on the island of Tiohtià:ke, also called Montreal. As a city planner and builder, I'm committed to urban system transformations for the long term that are radically inclusive, decolonizing, and ennobling.

Notes

1 Also known as the Iroquois Confederacy, arguably the oldest living participatory democracy in the world.
2 The Council of the Great Peace. (No official date but conjectured by Haudenosaunee historians to be written sometime between AD 1142 and 1500.) The Great Binding Law/Gayanashagowa, the Constitution of the Five Nations Confederacy.

GRATITUDE

We are deeply grateful to all the people who made this book possible. To Grace Harrison, Rosie Anderson, and Matthew Shobbrook at Routledge for their belief in this project and willingness to see things differently. To Paul Messer for design contributions and to Maria Turner and Leanne Ridgeway for editing support. To Rachel Brunner for outstanding administration, research, and editing support throughout the entire book project.

We are deeply grateful to the contributing authors who inspire us and from whom we learned a great deal. Special thanks to Catherine Tàmmaro for artistic inspiration and chapter glyphs, and for wise and generous counsel throughout the project.

Gratitude to our Ancestors and future Ancestors and to the many teachers, Elders, and city builders of all ages from whom we draw strength and courage. And to our families in all their forms. Thank you.

INTRODUCTION

1

IMAGINE SHAPING CITIES AS IF PEOPLE, LAND, AND NATURE WERE SACRED

Jayne Engle, Julian Agyeman, and Tanya Chung-Tiam-Fook

> The sacred is all around us, always. The sacred is in each of our bodies, a miracle of life and water and earth. It is present in every object we touch, every wall and window we somehow believe separates us from our Mother. We each hold the beauty of creation in every fiber of our being. We are never far from the answer to the problem we have created—it is within each of us.
>
> *Tara Houska*[1]

Our greatest challenges are not scientific or technological; they are deeper than that—they are spiritual and cultural. Imagine shaping cities as if peoples, lands, and natures were sacred. What if each person were seen as inherently worthy of dignity, empathy, respect, and a life of flourishing? And what if the infrastructures of food, transport, housing, and other civic, cultural, and economic systems were conceived to be in relationships of reciprocity with underlying natural ecosystems, which are essential for all life?

The motivation for this book is that recognizing peoples, lands, and natures as sacred lays the foundations for building equitable and regenerative cities where both present and future generations can thrive. All sorts of possibilities flow from such a recognition, which would mean improving upon how we construct places, shape civic infrastructures, systems, and economies, and how we organize and govern ourselves.

What do we mean by Sacred Civics?

The word "sacred" evokes many understandings, depending on context and tradition.[2] For purposes of this book, sacred is not about formal religion or its manifestations.[3] Rather, we intend a recognition of the sacred, or spiritual, as a divine or mystical force within all living beings. By sacred we mean unique, intrinsically worthy of respect and dignity, relational, life-giving and sustaining, and defiant of commodification. Practically, sacred relates to a sense of connection between people and with nature, a shared sense of purpose and meaning that

DOI: 10.4324/9781003199816-2

flows from that, and which translates to a shared sense of how to coexist: living better together in the shared space of cities. People, land, and nature in all forms, are considered sacred, worthy of merit, and having agency.

Civics in this book means "of the city," and specifically of the peoples and life forms who live in proximity within place-based communities. A sacred civics, then, would engender a sense of belonging, and have us collectively shape cities and communities as life-centered places, where local residents shape what the city can become, building just and inclusive, regenerative economies for the long term, where we can individually and collectively flourish.

We expect sacred civics as a discourse and practice to grow, expand and evolve over time. The following are initial ideas for deconstructing and grounding sacred civics in order to transcend current patterns and forge a culture of reciprocity.

Deconstructing. Sacred civics invites us to question why cities exist and to deconstruct assumptions about how we build them and why. As a practice, it involves deep listening, unlearning and relearning, and daring to challenge and change dominant paradigms. As Indigenous law scholar John Borrows said: "The sacred when it comes into the human community is about our deliberation ... our listening to one another—it's conjunctions, it's trying to conjugate life in a way that helps us to open to the possibility of human form and behavior."[4]

City building, according to a sacred civics, is transformational work, as it recognizes the persistent paradigms of colonialism[5] and imperialism, the horrific legacies and ongoing vestiges of genocide, enslavement of peoples and natures, systemic racism, ecocide, and oppression in all forms. It commits to upending extractive values and incentives (whether intentional or unintentional) which serve to concentrate wealth accumulation in the hands of the few while perpetuating inequality for current and future generations, and that destroy the natural systems we depend upon for life.

Grounding. Sacred civics means deep care for the common good for all peoples and entails a sacred responsibility to look after each other, and nature, in perpetuity. It demands cultivating a sense of purpose greater than ourselves that expands across space and time. Sacred civics applies a relational worldview to city building that sees cities as complex organisms comprising social-ecological systems and webs of relationships. It is grounded in an earth spirituality, which is to "take into account the wellbeing, integrity, and even the dignity, of all beings, and not treat them as mere 'resources'" (Eisenstein 2019, 158). This spirituality draws on Indigenous teachings and worldviews and recognizes the agency of people and nature.[6] The Seven Sacred Teachings (also called Grandmother/Grandfather Teachings) of many Indigenous cultures hold that the virtues of love, truth, bravery, humility, honesty, respect, and wisdom, are the basis to guide responsible individual behavior in support of healthy community life. Sacred civics invites cultivating everyday spirituality in the realm of the city—the search for wholeness, connectedness, balance, and healing, and is a commitment to practicing reconciliation and reciprocity among peoples and with Earth. Practically, sacred civics would have us reimagine patterns of how we house, feed, and govern ourselves, determine and distribute wealth, inhabit and design cities, and construct relationships with others and with nature.[7] It would give expression to biophilia through human–nature collaborations[8] and the infrastructuring needed to support that.

While sacred civics is inherently a place-based practice, its ideas and philosophical underpinnings draw from transdisciplinary literatures across geographic regions. From urban planning, we draw particular inspiration from traditions of insurgent, radical, decolonial, and progressive planning, including the works of Leonie Sandercock (2003); Faranak Miraftab

(2009; 2017); Victoria Beard (2003); John Friedmann (1987; 2011); Libby Porter (2010; 2020); Ananya Roy (2011); Julian Agyeman (2003; 2013); AbdouMaliq Simone (2001); Edgar Pieterse (Simone and Pieterse 2018); and Vanessa Watson (2009). We draw as well on philosophies of social ecology (Bookchin 1995) and of development economics (Sen 1999) and sacred economics (Eisenstein 2021), of the commons (e.g., Ostrom 1990; Foster and Iaione 2015 and Bollier and Helfrich 2019), and quite significantly on Indigenous authors, such as John Borrows (2019); Sherri Mitchell (2018); Robin Wall Kimmerer (2015); Carol Ann Hilton (2021); Michelle Thompson-Fawcett and Quigg (2017); Thompson-Fawcett, Ruru, and Tipa (2017); Thompson-Fawcett and Freeman (2006) and Blair Stonechild (2020).

Sacred civics is also inspired by practices from the field of transition design (Tonkinwise 2015), ecological design (Benyus 1997; Watson 2019) and futuring (Fry 2015), as well as the public intellectual traditions of Naomi Klein (2014; 2019), Achille Mbembe (2021), and David Suzuki (2007). There is strong resonance with the anthropological notion of pluriversality (Escobar 2018; 2020; Vasudevan and Vovoa 2021) in the pathway it foretells, whereby a homogenous, globalized, dominant city building paradigm gives rise to a civics that makes visible spirit of place and spirit of people who inhabit the worlds within cities, past, present, and future.

Transcending. The dominant narrative of cities as separate from nature reproduces itself in cultural artifacts, including on screens and in books. It pervades cognitive models across traditions, and even futurists rarely represent cities in decades and centuries to come with nature as having any agency. And while there are wonderful exceptions to this lack of urban–nature imaginary, they are notable for their relatively small number.[9] Sacred civics is intended as a galvanizing invitation and a cultivation of capability to transcend the persistent, cultural narrative of separation and its continued reproduction in the space and imaginaries of cities. In his works on the pluriverse,[10] anthropologist Arturo Escobar evokes the Zapatista Movement's notion of "a world where many worlds fit" and draws out principles for transition (re)design that support the idea of partially connected but radically different worlds, that would relocalize and communalize social life, and enable autopoiesis (self-creation of living systems). These notions help transcend myths of separation such as city/nature and materiality/spirituality, yet real-world examples of city building enactment at scale are still few.[11]

In spite of their standing as the largest system that humans make, cities lack transcendent metaphors. The technocratic tendency to reduce cities to categorization by issue, sector, discipline, or component parts helps with analysis, study, and prediction, but does little to create collective imagination and raise expectations about how differently cities could be conceived. Some recent exceptions include city building in Afrofuturism, such as Wakanda in the Marvel Black Panther films. The world building of Wakanda invites imagining what a city and civilization that escaped colonialism and external imperialism could look like. Such transcendent metaphors for city building could be developed, such as cities as vast human–nature collaborations, mini-planet worlds, or giant living, breathing beings. Various digital technologies and other creative arts can be brought to bear in helping to collectively imagine and shape reworlding of cities. There is transformational possibility for harnessing new and/or revitalized ancient technologies to serve a sacred civics ethos. Bringing a sacred civics sensibility to new technologies to heighten awareness of spiritual and cultural dimensions is an important part of what is needed. Participatory futuring, discussed later, provides promising ways to democratize city reworlding and to catalyze collective wisdom and imagination with artists, technologists, and communities.

Reciprocating. Sacred civics holds that those of us alive now on Earth have a sacred responsibility to leave the planet in a healthier condition than we found her, so that she can continue to sustain life in all forms for generations and millennia to come. Conscious and responsible planning means use and stewardship[12] of Earth's gifts, ensuring that we never take more than we need, and that we always give back. This is what we mean by reciprocity. In practice, reciprocity must be the foundation of structural decisions about institutions and places, and also everyday decisions about what we build, and how we choose to live, work, give, share, and relate in the communities and cities we call home. But how will we know if we are making progress in reciprocity, and working toward a sacred civics, for that matter?

These emergent, transformative concepts require different knowledges, and ways of understanding success, measuring progress, and holding ourselves accountable. By definition, the notion "sacred" defies conventional measurement which tends to reduce value to financialization. It is critical to develop alternative ways of gauging advancement toward a sacred civics and to establish proxies for assessment. Because the aims of sacred civics are bold and ambitious with long-term, common-good outcomes, we propose a way to gauge progress is the application of a sacred civics lens to investment, infrastructure, and institutional decisions, that adheres to accountabilities of the health of all people, across boundaries and into the future, and the health of Mother Earth and the materials crafted from her bounty.[13] Proxies established can inform emergent learning and an adaptive approach to ongoing decision-making.

These accountabilities are incredibly ambitious and raise more questions than they answer, but how can we expect anything less of ourselves if we are to be good and wise Ancestors? An excellent scale at which to see and gauge progress is that of communities and cities. In local worlds, adhering to these accountabilities would be transformative; it could evolve our notions of a social contract, which is an abstract, citizen–state relationship, to one of sacred covenants in place-based systems, between people, and with Earth, across geographies and time.

Bringing into Ceremony

It is important to acknowledge the Faith Keepers, Knowledge Keepers, Elders, and community leaders from spiritual and cultural lineages all over the world whose ceremonial and cultural leadership and work are central to city building and placekeeping[14]/placemaking. They provide teachings, protocols, wise counsel, world-bridging, and continuity between past, present, and future generations that give civics meaning and life. How much more conscious, inclusive, enduring, and grounded in relationships with land, place, and community would our city building be if our collective work was guided by protocols such as Land Acknowledgements and responsibilities and accountabilities to all peoples, future generations, and the Earth? Acknowledging the lands, first peoples and complex relationality of the urban places where we live, connect and work, for example, and the learnings, creations, innovations, and collective wisdom left by those who came before us, is a powerful way of connecting our words and actions within sacred space.

Core Arguments of the Sacred Civics Thesis

Three core arguments underlie our sacred civics thesis: (1) cities are critical sites of societal transformation; (2) holism, including attention to the sacred, is needed to help upend dominant patterns that shape current city building; and (3) enacting a sacred civics means honoring higher order responsibilities and accountabilities.

1. **Cities are critical sites of societal transformation and civilizational change.**
    Cities have evolved as the largest sets of systems shaped by humans. And while the largest cities on the planet together occupy just 1–3 percent of the Earth's land surface, each one is a whole world in itself, and contains multiple worlds within it—a pluriverse of sorts.[15] The worlds within cities are shaped by people and all life that sustains them. West refers to cities as "emergent complex adaptive social network systems resulting from the continuous interactions among their inhabitants, enhanced and facilitated by the feedback mechanisms provided by urban life" (West 2018, 253). West refers to our epoch as the "Urbanocene," the period that began with the industrial revolution, characterized by the exponential growth in size and number of cities. Cities are the crucible of modern civilization—centers of power and hubs of innovation, education, creativity and conviviality—and they are also sites of extreme and proximate inequality, material poverty, social isolation, oppression, disease, and consumption of energy and resources. Given that the majority of people on the planet live in cities—a trend that is expected to continue for the foreseeable future, especially in the Global South—there is a pressing need to reconsider how we build them. In short, "the future of humanity and the long-term sustainability of the planet are inextricably linked to the fate of our cities" (West 2018, 214). If societal transformation is to manifest, it must be tangible in the largest sets of systems that humans have collectively built.

2. **Holism is foundational to evolving social constructions and upending assumptions in dominant worldviews that currently shape most city building.**
    Seeing holistically—that is, understanding people and cities as multitudes of interdependent and complex systems, and with attention to spirituality and the sacred—can unlock a different set of city building pathways. Such a holism comprises intellectual, physical, emotional, and spiritual dimensions of people, and recognizes inherent kinship, equality of all people, and relationality of all life; and that everything besides sacred natural laws is socially constructed, and therefore in the realm of possibility to change. Adding the spiritual, or sacred, dimension represents the potential that people, cities, and societies have capabilities to transform and transcend that which exists. For diverse Indigenous and land-based Peoples, the sacred dimension is not an addition, but rather something inherent to building social institutions and community.

    The level of consciousness that sacred civics invites is not reducible to siloed progress or addressing problems with single-point solutions. It requires holistic system thinking and system innovation as well as awareness of inherent holism of people and interrelationships between people and place. The places where we live are embedded in—and rely on—natural systems which provide the gifts offered by ecosystems that support human survival and flourishing. From the air we breathe, the water we drink, and the soil in which we grow food. If we are not in conscious and reciprocal relationships with the land in our patterns of living, our making of housing and urban development, and in the ways we work and grow our livelihoods, then we will not be healing and regenerating Earth in ways fit for future generations. These patterns and habits start where we live, and in our inhabiting holism within ourselves and the systems within which we are nested.

Figure 1.1 provides a conceptual diagram for understanding sacred civics and bringing it into being. The inner circle is inspired by dimensions of holistic life that are often present in Indigenous teachings and other cultural traditions: intellectual, emotional, physical, and spiritual. We make the case for bringing this holistic sensibility to bear in city shaping and placekeeping, where spirituality and the sacred have rarely been valued within mainstream interpretations. Our use of the term "spirituality" does not necessarily refer to formal religion or its urban manifestations, but rather to constructing cities with a sense of the sacred and spiritual that recognize the inherent dignity, worth, agency, and energy of all people and of nature across space and time. It also recognizes that the human spirit needs wisdom, knowledge, connectivity with nature, and love to thrive, and that cities, as the sites where most humans live, ought to provide everyday expression of these for everyone.

The second nested circle of Figure 1.1 shows the fundamentals of sacred civics transformations: value(s), commons, and wisdom, described below. Outside the circles are the accountabilities for future-fit institutions, which we turn to next.

3. **Enacting a sacred civics invites an ennobling of city builders and placekeepers to honor higher order responsibilities and accountabilities.**

A sacred civics ethos ennobles people to honor sacred responsibilities of care for one another and all life. This means a different set of accountabilities must be built into governments, institutions, and systems in order for them to be fit for the future. These include accountability to all people, including future generations, and to Earth and that which is made from her gifts.

Accountability to all Peoples. Currently, governments answer to a subset of people; in liberal democracies, this subset consists of voters and special interest groups. Others, like children, migrant workers, and people in prison, have little to no say. We also need to be accountable for extraction and externalities beyond political boundaries. The obscene inequalities within and between cities and countries must be acknowledged and acted upon through local and global expressions and coalitions of solidarity—and proxies for accountability to it—if we are to heal and move forward as a species.

Accountability to Future Generations. The origins of democracy enshrined accountability to future generations, a commitment that has fallen away over the past several hundred years. Societies are currently handcuffed by the hegemony of short-termism, characteristic of political election cycles and quarterly corporate logics. If we are to be accountable to generations not yet born we need long-termism in policy, funding, and investment decisions, and new forms of engagement and proxies for accountability, such as civic assemblies with representation of future peoples.

Accountability to Earth. Most constitutions and legal systems acknowledge rights of persons and corporations, but not the inherent rights of nature. Indigenous governments are an exception; a healthy and generative relationship with nature is considered a sacred responsibility of people. Being in a respectful and reciprocal relationship with Earth and having accountability for healthy ecosystems is essential if we are to mitigate disastrous climate impacts, stop biodiversity loss, and also stop exceeding other planetary boundaries. Cities have a critical role to play in this given that their ecological footprints extend well beyond political and geographical borders.

Accountability for the Designed World. Addressing material life cycles, reducing or eliminating extraction of resources and their transportation, and building an economy that is circular are essential to restoring and regenerating Earth's systems. Cities can reimagine our relationships by what we make—including buildings, products, plastics, and electronics—while building new economies based on wealth-sharing, collaboration, growing, and production at neighborhood and city levels.

How do we translate these accountabilities to the city level? There are myriad ways, from enacting statutes of Rights of Nature and Rights of Future Generations, to ecological footprint analysis, mapping, and measuring city flows and their externalities; participatory budgeting for ecological transition; city commitments to produce nearly all that they consume; and applying decision filters to infrastructure investment decisions that honor higher order accountabilities with appropriate and robust proxies.[16] Additional ways are explored throughout the book.

Valuing and Commoning with Wisdom: Fundamentals for Sacred Civics Transformations

Shifting to a sacred civics requires at least three transformations: (1) evolving societal systems to value the common good; (2) developing stronger cultures of commoning and collective action; and (3) cultivating and practicing wisdom that opens pathways to creating healthy cities for the long term—what we call seven generation cities. Value(s), commons, and wisdom are

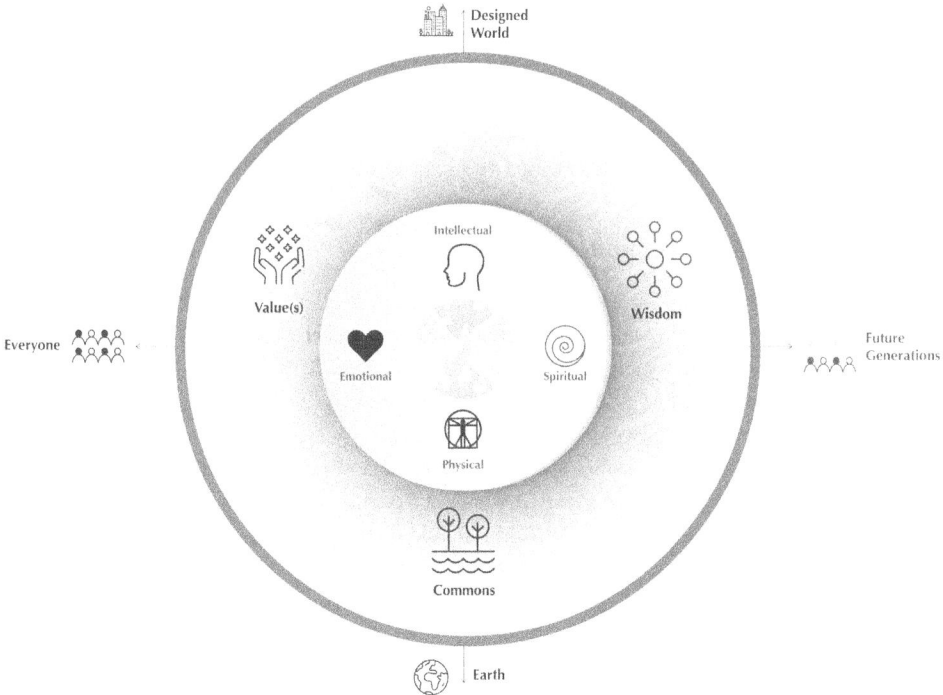

FIGURE 1.1 Cultivating sacred civics: Valuing and commoning with wisdom and related accountabilities

dimensions of transformation, and they can also be nested. That is, sacred civics can be seen as an invitation to value the wisdom of the commons and commoning.

We discuss these dimensions below and chapter authors refer to these themes throughout the book. As a preface, we question several assumptions that have become part of the societal DNA of modern/colonial economic and political systems, even though they are social constructions and therefore possible to challenge and change. The following three are ubiquitous in our current globalized societies to the extent that they are often mistaken for natural law and seen as impossible to change.

Assumption Bust 1: Ownership/Property

The right to private ownership, particularly of land, is sacrosanct in many societies. But in the world we need to create, should this be the case? Or should land be self-sovereign, like air and water arguably are? How can we rethink property, land rights and legal systems that underpin how cities are built? What collective ownership, guardianship and stewardship models of land, products, and companies can we scale or create anew? We also need to ask, who owns the city and its component parts, and why? If the answer is that all residents have a stake and responsibility, then how can we re-conceive ownership?[17]

Assumption Bust 2: Role of Corporations

What should the role of the corporation be in today's world? Should we expect shareholder interest to give way to public interest? (And what does public interest mean?) What about data and digital rights/sovereignties? Who should own or steward data, and who should get to use which data for which purposes? Should we expect private technologies such as smart phones, digital media platforms, and applications to actually be good for us, for our children, for democracy? How can we invent institutions and regulatory systems in parallel with new technologies to strengthen civic democracy and data sovereignty, and build trust?

Assumption Bust 3: Sovereignties

Political boundaries of nation-states have been constructed from various circumstances of history, often forcibly by war or peace treaties. They are inherently unjust and fraught with collective action problems, such as adherence to the transnational targets set in the Paris Agreement on climate change. They also disrupt the natural formations of landscapes, and the movement and behavioral ecology of diverse species. We need to question existing sovereignties and jurisdictions of political and other powers. An ecosystem view, for example, might have watersheds or biomes and their agents as the basis for governance and sovereignty. In a similar vein, Indigenous Nation maps, like that of Turtle Island,[18] have overlapping boundaries.

There is also a great deal of dissonance between sovereignty and solidarity. COVID-19 vaccines are a case in point. Nation-states' actions are based on a set of interests that run counter to vaccine equity from a global perspective. This has significant implications for our future, even if rational from a short-term national perspective. And at the city level, jurisdiction issues are frequent impediments to positive change, as cities often lack jurisdiction over policy and investment decisions for critical infrastructure.

Valuing: Evolving Common-Good Worldviews

> The function of Aboriginal values and customs is to maintain the relationships that hold creation together.
>
> *Leroy Little Bear*

At the heart of current societal crises is the Western addiction to a certain worldview of globalism that stands in opposition to the global solidarity, or internationalism, that flows from common-good or pluriversal worldviews. This worldview is the primary ideology of the dominant political and financial establishment and it runs so deeply in our societal systems, that often people believe that the dominant economic system is value-free or value-neutral, which dismisses the central role of genocide, slavery, and colonialism in its evolution over the past five hundred years or so.[19]

The nation-state political system also runs counter to global solidarity. "To care about the fate of the common good … is what democracy requires,"[20] said Michael Sandel; it cannot be border-restricted as such limitations are a vestige of colonialism and ongoing imperialism. The axiology of the modern/dominant worldview has power, speed, efficiency, and productivity as its *summum bonum*. In contrast, a common-good worldview places human equality, flourishing, and regenerative nature as the apex.

Axiology matters, because it determines behavior, attitudes, thought, and action. As economist Joseph Stiglitz said, "you can make money destroying the world … and there's something wrong with that."[21] Currently, the tectonic plates of irreconcilable worldviews are crashing, and the wreckage is rapidly exacerbating human inequality and ecological disaster. Science fiction author Kim Stanley Robinson put it like this:

> It is not true that leaving finance to the market will arrange everything well, as the past 40 years have shown. The market systemically misprices things by way of improper discounting of the future, false externalities and many other predatory miscalculations, which have led to gross inequality and biosphere destruction. And yet right now it's the way of the world, the law of the land. Capital invests in the highest rate of return, that's what the market requires.[22]

So what values and new value creation models and understandings could most effectively shape our relationships to one another and to nature?

We need to evolve worldviews that foster core values of promoting human dignity, of respecting and being in reciprocity with nature, and of nurturing and regenerating the commons. Several chapters in this book show clear pathways and possibilities for doing this. Even in our current economic system, the root source of value is nature, and destroying her, as we are currently doing, will lead to the system imploding.

"Property will cost us the earth"[23]

The persistent legacy of colonial systems has divided land into pieces in ways that create and perpetuate structural inequality. From an ecological perspective, it is as absurd to assume the right to owning land as it is to owning air or water. Why do we continue to reproduce extractive, colonial land ownership systems that concentrate wealth and power? This will likely need to change if we are to build equal societies and be good stewards of nature. Evolving a common-good worldview would mean breaking up the system of massive private ownership and wealth accumulation in the hands of a few. In our current urban economics regime, private owners of land and property in cities accumulate wealth through the labor of those who pay rents and through the benefit of all in the city who contribute to value by living, working, and transacting in close proximity. Urban land ownership could be thought of as a monopoly of access in this sense. It is a model that is inherently unjust and by design, it exacerbates inequality over time. As John Ralston Saul put it, "the crude European concept of ownership [involves] a great deal of control with very little responsibility."[24] Property ownership is seen as a sacred right by many, which causes direct conflict with the accountabilities mentioned above, and with that which is just, now, and for future generations, and planetary health.

Sacred Values

Economist Thomas Picketty (2020) argues that "ownership societies" justify inequality in part through a "quasi-sacralization" of property rights, that is, as if the unfortunate outcomes of disparities of wealth and power that come from property ownership are an externality resulting from a higher good. Similar logics helped create conditions for big tech platforms to gain their monopolistic power. When private wealth is seen to contribute to a greater good, far too many deep and extensive societal externalities are simply accepted. Our laws, regulations, and institutions currently significantly lag capabilities to advance in parallel with the societal bads of our economic systems.

Building better civic futures will require changing our understanding about value and how it is created, extracted, and distributed. It will mean adding sacred values to the equation, which are visceral and tied to humanity and all life. Sacred values include freedom, capabilities, health, nature, equality, trust, participation, honor, justice, respect, care, honesty, humility, love, compassion, cooperation, courage, friendship, interdependence, commitment, responsibility, and sharing. They reflect rights to voice, difference, human flourishing, and the city, and the rights of nature and future generations. Sacred values hold transcendent significance. They are often non-negotiable and protected from trade-offs with non-sacred values (e.g., money), because they tap into ethical principles and spiritual values.

People sometimes risk their lives for sacred values, and they are among the most important values for communities. While it may seem obvious that people, land, and nature should be considered in sacred value systems, the dominant global economic system has been built on extraction, and, in many ways, enslavement of these through legacies of colonialism and imperialism. The persistence of this system is in evidence throughout the landscapes, institutions, and infrastructures of our cities. Applying a sacred civics lens to major institutional and infrastructural investment decisions could address this. A challenge of sacred values, however, is that they tend to defy conventional (financialized) measurement. No one can precisely define or measure justice, democracy, security, freedom, truth, or love, or any value. But if no one speaks up for them, if systems aren't designed to (re)produce them, if we don't have dialogue about them and their presence or absence, they risk ceasing to exist.

Value questions that arise in a sacred civics context, include: If we built economies to value human flourishing for all on a healthy planet and for the long term, how would that translate to the civic realm and urban economic geographies? How could we value the care and creativity that people contribute to their communities, and build local circular economies of care, production, and stewardship of life?[25] How should we organize and govern ourselves for our great social, ecological, and economic transitions?

Commoning: Reconceiving who Owns the City

It is clear that the current dominant institutions of state and market are not the answer, either alone or together. Their logics lead to extraction of systems that need to be regenerated (such as nature), and to either further privatization or nationalization, neither of which provide adequate incentives or means for collective stewardship of community and natural assets. The notion of the commons has evolved as a school of thought with many different branches, and which provides institutional arrangements and practices for societal transition. Commons have existed since time immemorial as malleable social relationships in place-based communities. Long before the social construction of property ownership and property rights, people have collaborated and coordinated to devise arrangements for how they share, manage, and contribute to collective goods and resources. And people and communities continue to do so today outside of strict government and market paradigms.

Today, commoning is a transformative concept, as a form of social practice and organization and also as an ethic and a platform for reimagining how we live and work together, locally and globally (not to mention a way to bust the assumptions above!). At its heart, the commons is "both collective and non-commodified—off-limits to the logic of market exchange and market valuations" (Harvey 2012, 124–125). Elinor Ostrom won a Nobel Prize in Economics in 2009 for her extensive study of real-world scenarios of commons-based stewardship in which small communities around the globe have devised ways to successfully manage common resources like grazing land, forests, and irrigation waters. Other authors with recent books and papers on the commons include Sheila Foster, Christian Iaione, David Bollier, and Michel Bauwens, and many more include commons notions in their works, including in this book.[26]

The term "commons" goes under other names in some cultures, and it is also a contested term. Many Indigenous Peoples and other ancient place-based cultures, for example, do not use the terms "commons" and "commoning," but have similar concepts and systems for collective stewardship and guardianship of lands, water resources, data/knowledge, cultural productions, and wealth-sharing. And some Indigenous activists criticize urban commons initiatives, groups, and advocates for not acknowledging the Indigenous homelands/treaty lands that the commons occur upon, or consulting with contemporary treaty holders. As such, the commons are naturalized as settler spaces. Similar contentions exist around open data and Indigenous knowledges and data. We recognize this problematization and welcome further development and evolution of the concept and framing over time.

Enabling the Commons

The commons provides a set of ways to think about and reorganize for transformation in spatial and digital realms. Some promising pathways to imagine commoning with a sacred civics lens are set out below, and organized under headings of scale, institutions, and mindsets. Fundamental questions that underlie this inquiry include: What if the city were understood as a shared system provisioning for the good of all, in current and future generations? How could we better share and care for civic assets and commons such as air, land, and water, city infrastructures and our data? What if a viable land base in cities was restored to urban Indigenous communities and other racialized and displaced peoples, in order to support all facets of their social wellbeing? How could we law together at city level to bring out what is noble in people? Could commons-based governance models provide a hybrid arrangement of state, market, and civil society to strengthen local democracy and build civic trust?

Scale. Practices of commoning can be applied at any scale, from global to local. At one end of that spectrum, global commons law was created to protect certain areas of Earth (e.g., Antarctica, the high seas, the seabed, and the atmosphere) for all humanity and future generations, and deliberately not restricted to nation-state boundaries or interests (Garcia 2021). At the other end of the scale are specific place- and neighborhood-based commons forms. The idea of micro-treaties with the Earth, is one example, whereby a human guardian or steward is in a treaty relationship with land, with responsibility for care and reciprocity, rather than in a fee simple ownership position which consists of a bundle of rights to extract value from a parcel.[27] Most people live in between these two scales, that is, in cities.

The city has emerged in recent years as a critical site for commoning. By commons of the city, we mean collective assets and resources (or gifts), including land, infrastructure, goods and services, and also intangible assets of culture and spirit of place. Commoning is not new in cities, which are by definition places of coexisting and continually negotiating life and relationality in shared space. And while state and market mediate a great deal of contemporary urban life, residents are often involved outside those realms in co-creating shared lives (e.g., community gardens, bike sharing, collective cooking). At the neighborhood scale, commons-based organizing often involves building participatory ecosystems and movements, even if they are not called that. Sheila Foster and Christian Iaione have done seminal work on the city as a commons, including adapting Elinor Ostrom's institutional design principles for the commons to the city context.[28,29]

A number of cities have adopted extensive urban commoning plans, including Ghent, Seoul, and Sydney.[30] Barcelona has been a leader in applying commons principles to the city's digital realm, which means data are seen as collectively produced public assets to be owned, managed, and distributed for the common good.[31] Together with New York and Amsterdam, Barcelona has built on this work to create the network of Cities for Digital Rights, a group which now has more than 50 member cities.[32]

Commons applications in both spatial and digital realms of cities holds tremendous potential, particularly in thinking about how smart city approaches can serve the common good by increasing equality, building civic trust, and regenerating nature for climate, biodiversity, and health outcomes. We can imagine, for example, how differently the failed Sidewalk Labs Quayside Project proposal with Waterfront Toronto could have gone if it had been constructed within a commons ethos. Perhaps it is utopian to imagine parent company Alphabet subordinating market interests for common-good outcomes, but it feels like a missed opportunity. Radical interpretations of urban economics to create shared value and truly affordable housing would have been possible if governments and civic leaders had invented institutions in parallel with the technologies in ways that would strengthen local democracy and contribute to the health and vitality of communities and ecosystems. That is the opportunity for truly smart cities.

We are now in an age in which cities everywhere are facing increasing resilience challenges, and building robust civic commons will be critical in addressing them. In times of disaster, mutual aid groups (a kind of commons) can do what the market and state cannot, for example, "caremongering" groups that developed in response to the COVID-19 pandemic provided solace and care to members at the community level. These commons are more humane, trusted, legitimate, adaptive, participatory, and rooted in place. They open possibilities for people and communities to connect in more holistic ways, and have the power to address physical, emotional, intellectual, and spiritual needs.

In the face of continually evolving emergencies, such as housing crises, a commons approach could also help to create more perpetual affordability mechanisms and collective ownership or stewardship models of property and of companies. For if the answer to the question, "who owns the city?" is that we all do, it means that we have collective responsibility as stewards of our collective rights to the city. This reframing opens beautiful opportunities for how we choose to value and share gifts of nature, and how people cultivate more meaningful and convivial ways of living and working together.

Institutions. Our hypothesis is that ecosystems, social movements, and other commons-based mechanisms are becoming more effective organizing forces than individual organizations, for strengthening local democracy and enabling more equitable and regenerative local provisioning. But what are the institutional arrangements that might make this work?

> Commons-based institutions are characterized by a move away from a vertically (top-down) oriented world to a horizontally organized one in which the state, citizens, and a variety of other actors collaborate and take responsibility for common resources.
>
> *Foster and Iaione 2015, 336*

In many fundamental ways, our largest institutions and governments are not built for the age of long emergencies we now inhabit.[33] Systemic societal dissonance is increasing with the visibility of obscene and growing inequality among people in an economy that rewards extraction and unfettered private wealth accumulation. Most policy interventions are mere band-aids to the growing problems. The deep change needed is unlikely to grow from institutions that were built for a different era and with logics of colonialism and systemic racism that perpetuate the problems that plague humanity and the planet today. Societal institutional innovation is needed that will support collaboration among people to take responsibility for building better lives for all on a healthy planet. Commoning is necessarily a part of this.

Promising possibilities for transforming existing institutions or creating new ones to enable commoning are happening from global to local scales. Global commons law, referred to earlier, is unique in ascribing rights and duties to humanity and individuals (including Indigenous Peoples) rather than single nation-states (Garcia 2021). Similarly, in Anishinaabe governance practice, people have a duty "to law" together, which means continually negotiating in dialogue with each other and nature to resolve issues and make collective decisions. The growing field of global commons law has as its purpose "intergenerational guardianship of the human heritage" (Garcia 2021, 17) rather than satisfaction of individual nation-state interests. The underlying philosophy that can be applied to other institutions is that, unlike state interests, governing the commons is shaped by higher aims and serves specific purposes that transcend national boundaries and considerations. Well, isn't that what is needed? Shouldn't that be part of our collective sacred duty to future generations?

A number of commons-enabling institutions, platforms and networks operate at local level across the world and as digital platforms. These tend to be independent of state and market, though some are hybrid or have links to either or both, and they entail policy, regulatory, legal, and financial mechanisms coming into play. Examples include the Office of Civic Imagination in Bologna, Italy; the LabGov Harlem E-project (a community-owned edge cloud computing architecture in New York); worker cooperatives in Cleveland, USA, Preston, UK, and the Basque Country, Spain; and the Village Community Movement and Sharing City platform of Seoul, South Korea.[34] Another way of manifesting commons-based relationships is through perpetual people–nature collaborations.[35]

Tools that are changing systems to enable commoning include mutual credit, cooperative finance, mutual aid societies, insurance, community land trusts, community supported agriculture, time banking, and platform cooperatives.[36] More recently, the world of Web3, blockchains, cryptocurrencies, NFTs (non-fungible tokens), and DAOs (decentralized autonomous organizations) is also quickly evolving and will likely grow as an important source of commoning tools.

We see tremendous potential for more robust connections between commons-based institutions, movements, and technologies across the globe. A global commons platform could link a critical mass of these, possibly in coordination with existing networks of cities which are already transforming systems, and have similarly aligned values, such as C40 Cities, Mayors Organized for Reparations and Equity (MORE), Mayors for a Guaranteed Income (MGI), the Global Parliament of Mayors, Transition Towns, and other global resilient cities networks.

Mindsets. Shifting systems and institutions to enable commoning also requires shifts in mindsets, consciousness, values, and, ultimately, narratives. Commons invite transcending how we currently organize and govern ourselves. A starting point for commons consciousness involves seeing land more as a bundle of relationships and responsibilities, rather than as private property that bestows a bundle of rights. Such an ethos is consistent with diverse Indigenous traditions and values, and is also communicated in the Land Back movement.[37] Various African and Afro-descendant philosophies, and many others, also have deep cultural relationships with nature and social systems that are consistent with commoning, but don't necessarily use that term. Examples include "Ubuntu" in various African traditions and "Konbit" in Haiti.[38]

Regarding language, the term "commons" itself can be a barrier. While it is well theorized in academic circles, it does not resonate in some cultures' vernacular. On the ground in the USA, for example, some practitioners found that the term "co-cities" is more understandable and resonant, and more easily interpreted as residents co-creating and co-governing shared resources and assets.[39]

Whatever the language, communities are increasingly seeing the transformative possibility of the commons and commoning as a means to enable community agency and create tools to organize differently for a better, more inclusive urban life for everyone, and which places reciprocity with nature at the heart. The commons, and specifically thinking in terms of the city as a commons, and adapting global commons law to local contexts, represent potential for mission-level building as part of a sacred civics.

Awakening the Wisdom of the Commons

How can collective wisdom be cultivated to realize such visions for a sacred civics embeddedness in city building that would harness value of the commons in the interest of public good for all life and into the future?

Wisdom is a complex topic, which does not provide for a singular, essentialized way of seeing and addressing challenges. Awakening wisdom begins with acknowledgment of the wisdom of Earth and all her landscapes and beings. Earth teaches people the gift of wisdom when we learn to be rooted in place, in presence, and in relationship. We understand wisdom not as a state to achieve but rather a presence of (inter and trans)being with other human and more-than-human beings and the animacy of place (or pulse of life), that must be continually nurtured with reciprocity and care. Wisdom is sometimes conflated with intelligence, but it is much more; it adds layers of meaning, spirituality, kinship, phenomenology, intuition, and emotionality to cognition. Indigenous social entrepreneur Nadine St-Louis once wrote:

> The emotional, spiritual, cognitive and physical dimensions of knowledge are common in Indigenous epistemologies … while colonial constructs have prioritized corporations, consumerism and individual wealth, which results in poverty and social isolation.[40]

How can we change fundamental aspects of dominant cultures which are not wise? How can we be practical about wisdom and apply it to transformation? Wisdom is a vast topic which we approach with humility and even some trepidation, not least because we cannot begin to do it justice in this brief section. We broach it here because we see cultivation and enactment of collective wisdom as critical, particularly because in many ways the wisdom of humanity seems to be growing little, if at all, and it lags dangerously behind our power.[41]

Wisdom Grandfather/Sacred Teaching

Nibwaakaawin (Wisdom) teaches us that to live life based on our unique gifts is to live wisely. Look, listen and learn. Observe your life and the lives of others. By watching and listening, you can learn everything you need to know. Knowledge can be learned. Wisdom must be lived. Live and learn. Look into any clear lake. You do not see your reflection. You see that of those who came before you—the Ancestors. Through All Your Relations and this Teaching of Wisdom, you will come to use your gift to direct your life's journey. Do not live based on what you wish you were. Live in honour of what you are. If you have been given the gift of song, then sing. If yours is the gift of dance, then dance.

Inspired by Seven Sacred Teachings of White Buffalo Calf Woman (Bouchard, Jones, Martin et al. 2009)

Wisdom of Practical, Embodied, Relational, and Multiple Knowledges

For purposes of this book, we are interested in wisdom that can manifest from practical, embodied, relational, and multiple place-based knowledges, as well as experiential, intuitive, and other ways of knowing that go beyond the Western-scientific, instrumental-rationality which is but one paradigm. We are inspired by collective wisdom cultivations and expressions such as ubuntu,[42] buen vivir and sumak kawsay,[43] Etuaptmumk/Two-Eyed Seeing,[44] and in co-creation with artists.[45] We note as well that varied traditions and disciplines have associated wisdom directly with love.[46] And some traditions see an inherent relationship between spirituality and wisdom.

Indigenous scholar Blair Stonechild offers this vision:

> Had humanity's growth taken place according to spiritual wisdom and had knowledge and technological development occurred carefully over thousands of years rather than a few feverish centuries, humanity would have created a brilliant and durable civilization in which peace, harmony, and happiness thrive. Entire sciences and technologies would have to be assessed in terms of determining their wisdom—what the impacts are on human and natural welfare and whether they are beneficial for future generations.
>
> *Stonechild 2020, 247*

And John Borrows refers to the gift of wisdom as "an expansion of ourselves and our relationships with others."[47]

Wisdom is connected to how we understand rationality, which over the past couple of centuries in the Western world, including in city planning theory, has evolved narrowly as an instrumental-rationality. Much earlier, Aristotle espoused value-rationality, which centers understandings of power, relationality, and values that then inform scientific analysis of instrumental-rationality. This idea of practical wisdom or *phronesis* is the least known of Aristotle's three ways of knowing.[48] Value-rationality is the underlying logic of phronetic social science, which focuses on agency-structure dynamics in local, practical knowledges, and addresses questions from community perspectives: Where are we going as a community (and society)? Is it desirable? What power dynamics are at play? What should be done about it, and what should *we* do?

"The goal of the phronetic approach becomes one of contributing to society's capacity for value-rational deliberation and action" (Flyvbjerg 2001, 167). The collective learning and action brought to bear through such inquiry creates conditions for cultivating collective wisdom. In a sacred civics, we imagine bringing a value-rational approach to city building that centers the Seven Sacred Teachings for city building for the next seven generations.

Wisdom in Lawing Together

Legal traditions of the First Nations, in particular those of Anishinaabe, tend to focus on responsibilities to the collective through individual virtues gifted to peoples by Creator: love, truth, bravery, humility, honesty, respect, and wisdom (Borrows 2019). This represents a cosmovision in which individual behaviors contribute to social good. It is notable that European legal traditions tend to focus on rights of the collective which are social virtues—liberty, security, equality, freedom—and these have individual benefits. The Anishinaabe worldview involves "pro-social individual virtues" and the European traditions tend toward "pro-individual social virtues."[49]

In many First Nations' traditions, law is a verb, and people have responsibility to law together. Constitutions and law are living institutions, ever evolving. In his book, *Law's Indigenous Ethics*, John Borrows discusses the Seven Sacred Teachings—Love, Truth, Bravery, Humility, Wisdom, Honesty, and Respect—which are the principles of Anishinaabe law (Borrows 2019). The book's thesis is that people's lives could be much better if we embodied the Seven Teachings within all our laws. In a sacred civics, an inquiry is how to apply these more fully in city building decisions. Devising policies, systems, and practices that apply the Seven Sacred Teachings is a key collective wisdom opportunity for us as city builders.

How do we bring sacred values to bear in how we law together? Rights of Nature and Rights of Future Generations statutes provide pathways. They help us question basic Western assumptions, such as: Should people have the right to own land, or does the land own us? Are rivers and other natural assets resources to consume or our relations? How would we coproduce city life and economies if the Seven Teachings were the guiding, sacred values, and the basis for creating value? One of the questions of a sacred civics is how can we apply these teachings in city building decisions?

How would we coproduce city life and economies if the Seven Teachings were our guiding, sacred values? Wisdom and spirituality have not, historically, been core in city planning discourses and practices. Sacred civics thus invites transcending current city-making paradigms. Can cities themselves develop capabilities for transcendence in the ways that human beings can? How can we evolve collective consciousness and commitment to aims higher than ourselves, to what biologist E. O. Wilson called in his quote a "sacred narrative"?

> People need a sacred narrative. They must have a sense of larger purpose, in one form or another, however intellectualized. They will find a way to keep ancestral spirits alive.

Devising policies, systems, and practices that apply the Seven Sacred Teachings is a key collective wisdom opportunity for us as city builders. What would it mean to bring (collective) wisdom to the center of city building? Some questions that arise include:

- What are the physical, digital, and social infrastructures needed so that children in seven generations will thrive in just, radically inclusive, caring, and regenerative cities?
- What if we applied lenses of common good for current and future generations and reciprocity with Earth to decisions about building infrastructure and institutions?

These are questions with both societal and philosophical implications, and we daily enact individual and collective responses to them in conscious and unconscious ways. A starting point of wisdom is consciousness including consciousness of what we are not seeing and understanding and acting upon. Will those of us alive now have the wisdom to build seven generation cities?

Organization of the Book

In the first two chapters, the editors provide frameworks for cultivating a sacred civics and for imagining possibilities to awaken seven generation cities. This introduction provides a theoretical and practical transdisciplinary grounding that challenges assumptions about dominant city building paradigms of globalized cities and invites other ways of futuring together. Chapter 2 extends the thesis with original instructions as a gateway to identifying seven foundational keys for seven generation cities, along with seven pathways of praxis for moving into this radical way of reworlding that embraces and nourishes all peoples, lands, and ways of being, knowing, and creating.

The rest of the book is organized in parts of Space, Time, Agency, and Togetherness. We perceive and imagine the world through space and time, and we think and act and take responsibility as individuals and collectively. Though there are not fixed lines between these elements of space, time, agency, and togetherness, we have organized the remaining chapters in this way to give structure to the volume—and ensure attention to—each dimension, while recognizing their interdependencies.

Space

The site is to the city what the cell is to the body.

Through a sacred civics lens, spaces and places are precious, imbued with meaning and spirit, and non-commodifiable. This ethos clashes with dominant urban land economies, which have largely been built on logics of colonialism, private ownership, rights of extraction, and concentrated wealth accumulation for a few. Works in this section provide glimpses of both oppressive past legacies and current day improvisations required of so many for survival, as well as imaginaries for what cities could be, and the potential of urban land to have agency in co-creating very different urban relationalities.

Chapter 3: Honouring the Sacred in Cities: Indigenous Teachings for City Building

By Tanya Chung-Tiam-Fook

Through the lens of two prophecies, Tanya Chung-Tiam-Fook demonstrates how Urban Indigenous Peoples across Canada are working to decolonize and reclaim cities and public spaces to imagine and self-determine the worlds they want to live within. She describes how civic institutions can make cities more inclusive of Indigenous models and practices through genuine forms of community-engaged planning and co-design; creating synergy between the cultural values, protocols and technologies that have sustained Indigenous societies for thousands of years, and contemporary forms of social and technological innovation. Being conscious and responsible city builders is good medicine for urban communities, ecologies, and public spaces, and lays a spiritual foundation for seven generation cities.

Chapter 4: The Black Commons: A Framework for Recognition, Reconciliation, Reparations

By Julian Agyeman and Kofi Boone

In their chapter, Julian Agyeman and Kofi Boone situate the Black Commons in the context of Amartya Sen's concept of capabilities which shows the need for Black communities to build new kinds of wealth and wellbeing that can support their ability to thrive. Through analyzing historic strategies of the Black Commons, Agyeman and Boone argue that these Commons offer a foundation for sharing the values of mutual aid together with information sharing and building community sustainability. The concept of a Black Commons is expanded to include many cooperative forms of ownership, even extending into digital forms of production.

Agyeman and Boon apply these ideas to equitable strategies for overcoming current racial justice challenges including the need for recognition, reconciliation, and reparations to compensate Black communities seeking to be made whole and sustainable.

Chapter 5: (Un)situated Improvisation

By AbdouMaliq Simone

AbdouMaliq Simone's chapter addresses critical and growing issues regarding the mismatch of masses of people subject to precariousness and extraction of existing power structures and elites, the financialization of urban life, and the growing divide this represents for megacities everywhere. Simone shows how trajectories of urban change in cities such as Jakarta exert a substantial unsettling force that not only resituates residents across a wider space but also induces a more provisional, temporary orientation to practices of inhabitation. Beyond accelerated circulation of bodies, goods, experience, and information, increasing numbers of residents hedge their bets, avoiding firm commitments to place and occupation, while also systematically attempting to expand their exposure to the wider urban context. Engaging some of the practices of outward movement employed by youth in Jakarta's working-class urban core, the chapter considers the configuration of collective life on the run.

Chapter 6: Co-creating the Cities We Deserve through Indigenous Knowledge

By Ginger Gosnell-Myers

Ginger Gosnell-Myers argues that if urban cities represent the identity of modern civilization and the power of that civilization, then the erasure of Indigenous Peoples and Indigenous knowledge from cities is a perfect illustration of contemporary colonization in modern form. In an era of truth and reconciliation, Indigenous urban planners are pushing back in resistance to this contemporary colonization to create the conditions for an Indigenous cultural comeback in every neighborhood, bike path, and downtown core. Through every installation of Indigenous public art, incorporation of Indigenous design into a building, or daylighting Indigenous knowledge on how the lands and waters sustained life for millennia before settlers bulldozed and renamed it all, this chapter shows how cities are being engaged on a new path with Indigenous urban planners and communities demonstrating what respectful and meaningful reconciliation can be.

Time

> The teachings of our Elders are not about the past but about the future.
>
> *Douglas Cardinal*[50]

Time is the most frequently used noun in the English language. Perhaps an indication of the stifling tyranny of now that most of us are caught in due to increasingly short attention spans, short-term political cycles, market-driven logics, and for many, precarious work that makes food on the table and shelter overhead prevailing concerns for daily survival. While full presence in the now for mindfulness is healthy, the tyranny of now can mean too little time and energy are invested in manifesting flows of memory and imagination which open up possibilities to be in relation with the wisdom of Ancestors, the lives all around us, and those of future generations. Practices of foresight, Land Acknowledgement, social innovation, and transition design, and insurgent urban planning can enable collectively facing histories and ongoing cultures of violence, racism, and colonialism in order to reveal imaginaries of future possibilities, and write new narratives about what cities can be.

Chapter 7: Unsettling the Coloniality of Foresight

By Aarathi Krishnan

We are accountable for the futures we create. In her chapter, Aarathi Krishnan argues that the practice of foresight is not neutral but is conditioned by our cultural values, our economic systems and our capacity for collective imagination. She presents an emergent approach to the decoloniality of foresight that requires us to interrogate and repair the deep systemic levels of oppressions that have marginalized and minoritized so many. It requires us to consider justice in the governance of our futures so that we are not locking those that are often missed from these conversations into future indebtedness or inequity. It ensures that the responsibilities of intended and unintended consequences of actions are embedded into design, decision-making and governance processes so our reimaginations of societies, economies, governments, and cities are spaces of safety and flourishing for all, and not just some.

Chapter 8: Inhabiting the Edge

By Edgar Pieterse

Edgar Pieterse's chapter engages with the depth and effects of spatial inequality in Cape Town. He reflects on learnings derived from a series of design studios organized by the African Centre for Cities over the past decade and focused on addressing the racialized spatial dynamics of the city. Pieterse describes an emergent thought experiment to figure out how to institutionalize these conversations in the form of a multi-dimensional innovation cluster of initiatives called "the Edge." The initiatives include a museum, urban science hub, green economy incubator focused on Black entrepreneurs, and youth outreach. For the Edge Innovation Cluster to work it must engage the complex and multivalent spirit of the city, scarred by colonialism, dispossession and intergenerational violence, with an eye on animating a more inclusive current of civic spirituality and social justice. Eight principles are explored to animate what the connective tissue of the Edge Innovation Cluster could become. Pieterse concludes with a description of a process to foster a novel culture of engagement and listening around the initiatives' elements and animating principles.

Chapter 9: Reconciling Relationships with the Land through Land Acknowledgements

By Deborah McGregor and Emma Nelson

One of the limitations of conventional Canadian conceptions of reconciliation is the underlying assumption that reconciliation applies, virtually exclusively, to relationships among peoples. Deborah McGregor and Emma Nelson, an Anishinaabe scholar and a settler planner respectively, claim that the Indigenous conception of reconciliation extends beyond peoples to the natural world and is informed by direct relationships to the Land. They explain how Land, Spirit and relationships have endured through time and can offer profound insights if one can learn to relate to the People and Land. McGregor and Nelson embrace the themes of values, commons, and wisdom as they investigate this question through an examination of the Land Acknowledgement and provide strong recommendations for practice and teaching, and implications for institutional policy.

Chapter 10: Urban Planning Oscillations: Seeking a Tongan Way before and after the 2006 Riots

By Yvonne Takau and Michelle Thompson-Fawcett

In Tonga, upholding anga fakatonga (the Tongan way of life) is a defining feature reinforced over the last 200+ years of relations with the West. Key values of honoring family, faka'apa'apa (respect for seniority), loto to (humility), and collectivity continue to shape the way the nation operates. Unlike most other Pacific nations, Tonga managed to remain sovereign, then gained independence from protectorate status under Britain in 1970. In their chapter, Yvonne Takau and Michelle Thompson-Fawcett describe the lingering impacts of colonial interventions and Tonga's reactions to them in urban, administrative, and governance arrangements. Takau and Thompson-Fawcett appraise the urban context and potential of the Tongan city of Nuku'alofa, hinging around the 2006 democracy riots in the city. They explain that while there is still much to be achieved in urban planning, it is important in a Tongan context to keep perspective, avoid hastiness, and maintain a posture of gratitude while looking to the future: oua lau e kafo kae lau e lava: stay positive and count your blessings.

Agency

> Transformation is not accomplished by tentative wading at the edge.
>
> *Robin Wall Kimmerer (2015, 88)*

Agency is the power of all people to co-create society. Everyday embodied experiences and expressions of agency are directly relational to the spaces we inhabit, and are mediated by constructions of social infrastructure and the memory and history of land and nature that give us life. That people and nature have agency is not about isolationism, but rather about justice. And collective agency in a sacred civics is integral; values of social justice, feminism, participation, and antiracism are core and cannot be separated from policy making, whether about climate, technology, transportation, or other urban fields.

Chapter 11: Social Infrastructure for Our Times: Building Participatory Systems that Value the Creativity of Everyone

By Jayne Engle, Tessy Britton, and Pamela Glode-Desrochers

In their chapter, Jayne Engle, Tessy Britton, and Pamela Glode-Desrochers introduce social infrastructure as the spaces, facilities, services, systems, and platforms that foster civic interactions and help individuals, families, groups, and communities meet their social needs, maximize their potential for flourishing, and improve community wellbeing, vitality, and resilience. They explain that social infrastructure becomes participatory when people have agency to contribute their creativity to building collective action projects and collective imagination for the future. Their chapter addresses the questions: Why does (participatory) social infrastructure matter, and what are we learning about the potential of the participatory city approach as a critical infrastructure to enable local and societal change? We explore participatory systems initiatives underway in the UK and Canada that model what societal change can look like when we build regenerative, circular, wellbeing economies from the neighborhood up. Engle, Britton, and Desrochers discuss progress and limitations of current work underway, as well as intentions for future-building, scaling and research.

Chapter 12: The Ceremony of Reclaiming Agency through Wonder

By Catherine Tàmmaro

Catherine Tàmmaro's chapter invites us into a time and space not of critical mind, but of dwelling mind, and powerfully evokes a sense of wonder and depth. This chapter explores sacred connectedness of spirit as it moves us toward sovereignty and agency within and without. Tàmmaro illustrates how our bodies are connected to Mother Earth, Father Sky, Elder Brother Sun, and Grandmother Moon. The wisdom of ancestral knowledge Tàmmaro brings as a practiced Elder is woven throughout as she presents themes of time from the ancient past of the lands and Ancestors within it, and the sense that they are ever present with us and in the city. She invites us to dream of city-civics built on a foundational understanding of Sacred Natural Law, and a letting go of old notions of inequality. She invites us to shift our mindset from Taking to Thanking, from War to Peace and from Commodification to Resonance and Reverence.

Chapter 13: Feminist, Antiracist Values for Climate Justice: Moving beyond Climate Isolationism

By Jennie C. Stephens

In her chapter, Jennie Stephens argues that the injustices of the climate crisis require societal transformation, a great reset that involves a restructuring, reclaiming, and resisting of the concentration of wealth and power. She makes a critical argument regarding the need to move beyond climate isolationism to climate justice, which would center value on social justice, feminism, and antiracist values in climate policy. This chapter reviews the inadequacy and dangers of climate isolationism, and explores why feminist and antiracist values are essential for transformation. Stephens calls for more consistent and intentional consideration of power and power dynamics as well as different forms of wisdom and knowledge to empower more transformative and inclusive climate decision-making by shifting from climate isolationism to climate justice.

Togetherness

We were born at just the right moment to help change everything.

Eric Holthaus[51]

City building involves continually negotiating coexistence and co-creation in shared urban space, and it has the potential to foster togetherness, inclusivity, and regeneration if we understand the city as a commons where people share resources, care for each other, and make kin with all forms of life. Cultures of commoning and participatory futuring can help to construct the collective narratives and radicle/radical imagination and possibilities that enable social and system transformations.

Chapter 14: Participatory Futures: Reimagining the City Together

By Kathy Peach and Laurie Smith

Kathy Peach and Laurie Smith argue that overcoming the complex challenges we face in our cities won't happen unless we democratize futures thinking and create new platforms for public imagination. They weave values of togetherness and participation for healthy, democratic future-building throughout their chapter as a response to the current practice of thinking about the future being dominated by a small group of academics, consultants, government foresight teams, and large organizations. Democratizing futures means creating new capacity among many more diverse people to explore and articulate their alternative and desirable visions of the future. This is anticipatory democracy, not the extractive surveying of needs and wants against a narrowly prescribed set of options that characterizes many public engagement exercises. Showcasing a range of examples of participatory futures methods from around the world, this chapter highlights the role of new digital technologies and techniques from art, design, and theater in creating these new platforms for public imagination.

Chapter 15: Basque Civics

By Gorka Espiau and Itziar Moreno

At the end of the 1970s, the Basque Country, home to one of the oldest Indigenous cultures in Europe, was emerging from 40 years of dictatorship in which any expression of local culture had been repressed. The area was experiencing an industrial collapse that generated high unemployment and an international image directly associated with terrorist violence. In this chapter, Gorka Espiau and Itziar Moreno draw attention to the values of equality and solidarity and common-good narratives that created conditions for transformation in the Basque Country. Despite the circumstances in the 1970s, Bilbao and Basque society managed to transform its economy and industrial base. Espiau and Moreno describe how the Basque Country now leads international rankings in advanced manufacturing, education, and health care, and has also generated a balanced distribution of wealth. Their article shares some of the key elements that made this extraordinary civic transformation possible.

Chapter 16: Commons Economies in Action: Mutualizing Urban Provisioning Systems

By Michel Bauwens, Rok Kranjc, and Jose Ramos

In this chapter, Michel Bauwens, Rok Kranjc, and Jose Ramos set out a promising commons-centric model of resource-sharing, contributive economics and cooperative, polygovernance. They examine the latest in urban commons developments which serve as both an accessible introduction to the fundamental concepts used to describe contemporary urban commons and commoning, and as an overview of recent experiences of cities interested in promoting models of public-commons cooperation and governance where these cities have adapted them through a variety of collaborative protocols, institutional designs, and social innovations. The authors make the case for cosmolocal production, a planetary mutualization of knowledge and alternative mode of production, in which localities benefit from and contribute to others at the global scale through open design and open knowledge infrastructures, fueled and guided by new types of contributive economy and thermodynamic accounting. In this way, readers have at their disposal both a local and global overview of key developments, proposed institutional adaptations, possible futures and potential facilitating actions to co-design multi-generational good lives within urban, and regional to planetary boundaries, by harnessing the latent potentialities of the commons as a form of social organization.

Chapter 17: Radicle Civics—Unconstituting Society: Building 21st-Century Civic Infrastructures

By Fang-Jui "Fang-Raye" Chang and Indy Johar

In Radicle Civics, Fang-Raye Chang and Indy Johar explore alternative pathways of organizing the future, based on distributed agency and a superdiverse public, which challenges concentrations of both power and responsibility. They seek to draw out the roots of our future societies, expanding the horizon of both the possible and necessary. This future is explored from the perspective of recognizing we exist in an unbounded world that will be inhabited by diverse autonomous agents, be they humans, future humans, and non-humans (trees, rivers, mountains, etc.). Chang and Johar describe a future that invites us to unconstitute and reconstitute society, embrace emerging possibilities to build on new practice of civic institutional infrastructures, and enable all beings to thrive in a safe and just space.

Notes

1 Quote from Sacred Resistance chapter by Tara Houska (2020, 218–219) in Johnson and Wilkinson (2020, 213–219).
2 We recognize "sacred" can be a dangerous word, as it can be used or appropriated in ways that lead to shutting down dialogue. We come to this exploration from a place of humility and respect, mystery and wonder.
3 "Sacred" in this book is not primarily about formal religion. References to "sacred commons" and "spiritual infrastructure" are provided in C. L. Bombino (2017), "Sacred Commons: Building both physical and spiritual infrastructure in America": http://irfalliance.org/.
4 From a lecture by John Borrows at McGill University, 2019.
5 References to colonialism include settler–colonialism as one variant of colonialism.
6 The agency of nature can manifest, for example, through "rights of nature" statutes, such as in Ecuador, Bolivia, and New Zealand, and in municipalities including Pittsburgh. See the Global Alliance for the Rights of Nature for more on the rights of nature movement and legal and jurisdictional applications: www.therightsofnature.org.

7 A number of discussions, talks, and essays helped lay the ground for "sacred civics" framing and this collection, which aims to bridge worlds and ways of thinking, doing, and being. Some of the specific ideas, projects and convenings that led to this are set out in Dark Matter Labs (2020a; 2020b); Engle (2019; 2020; 2021); and Engle, Johar, and Ryan (2020).

8 Astbury (2015).

9 Examples of works that evoke urban–nature imaginaries for future cities include: *Ecocities: Rebuilding cities in balance with nature* (Register 2006); *City Futures in the Age of a Changing Climate* (Fry 2015); and films, *Black Panther* and *2067*.

10 *Designs for the Pluriverse: Radical interdependence, autonomy, and the making of worlds* (Escobar 2018) and *Pluriversal Politics: The real and the possible* (Escobar 2020). Interestingly, Escobar refers frequently to communities and the communal in these works, yet rarely to cities.

11 Vasudevan and Novoa (2021) set foundations for expanding pluriversality in urban planning scholarship, creative methodologies, and community-based approaches (or "local worlding"), making links to traditions of insurgent planning, radical planning, and decolonialism, such as works by Leonie Sandercock, Faranak Miraftab, Victoria Beard, John Friedmann, Libby Porter, Ananya Roy, Vanessa Watson, and Oren Yiftachel.

12 The language and cultural understanding of "stewardship" is contested. For a problematization of stewardship, see Weber (2015).

13 Accountabilities to all people, future generations, Earth, and the designed world: described in Engle, Johar, and Ryan (2020).

14 "Placekeeping" is a reframing of the more commonly known term "placemaking" from an Indigenous lens of holism and relationality. Building on the understanding of placemaking as a process where people collectively reimagine and shape public spaces in order to maximize shared value, *placekeeping* conceives of place (and the land that provides a foundation for place) as having inherent being and agency. As people, we can hold place, be caretakers and stewards of place, and form relationships to place. For Indigenous peoples, place is both the setting and co-creator of our being in the world, ancestry and memories, stories and ceremonies, languages, land stewardship, cultural paradigms, and social identities (Chung-Tiam-Fook 2020a).

15 The term "pluriverse" has come into more frequent usage in works by Arturo Escobar (2020; 2018). It centers relationality and an orientation of collective good and the agency of people in reshaping through transition design. It draws from Indigenous traditions and movements, especially the Zapatistas of Chiapas.

16 Some such measures and proxies are being developed by: Center for Democratic and Environmental Rights (rights of nature): www.centerforenvironmentalrights.org/; Fab City (city production and consumption): https://fab.city/; Doughnut Economics Action Lab (meeting social foundations within planetary limits): https://doughnuteconomics.org/; and City of Montreal (participatory budgeting for social and ecological transition): www.makingmtl.ca/participatorybudget.

17 Some questions around land ownership and stewardship are addressed beautifully in *Micro-treaties with the Earth*, by Jonathan Lapalme and Marie-Sophie Banville, Dark Matter Labs (2020b).

18 Map of Indigenous nations, including of Turtle Island, the Indigenous name for the land mass also known as North America: https://native-land.ca/.

19 Kehinde Andrews (2021) makes the case that the ongoing legacies and racism of genocide, slavery, and colonialism persist and manifest today in what he calls "The New Age of Empire."

20 Michael Sandel in an interview with John Ralston Saul, discussing Sandel (2021).

21 Joseph Stiglitz in an interview with Leilani Farha in the film, PUSH, 2019.

22 Kim Stanley Robinson in the *Financial Times*, August 20th, 2021.

23 Quote by Andreas Malm in a blog, www.versobooks.com/blogs/4985-property-does-not-stand-above-the-earth, January 27th, 2021.

24 John Ralston Saul (2014, 62).

25 Examples that invite a different way to understand and transform our understanding of value include well-being economies and doughnut economics. For more on well-being economies, see

https://weall.org and Katherine Trebeck (2019), and for doughnut economics, see https://doughn uteconomics.org and Kate Raworth (2018). The City of Amsterdam is one of a growing number of places that are adapting doughnut economics to the city scale: https://time.com/5930093/amster dam-doughnut-economics/.

26 Some additional references that elucidate the commons and commoning include: *Co-Cities*, by Sheila Foster and Christian Iaione (2022); *Designing Regenerative Cultures*, by Daniel Wahl (2016); *Sharing Cities*, by Duncan McLaren and Julian Agyeman (2015); *Free Fair and Alive*, by David Bollier and Silke Helfrich (2019); and *Assembly*, by Michael Hardt and Antonio Negri (2017).

27 See Dark Matter Labs (2020b).

28 The discourse of the "city as a commons" is grounded in Foster and Iaione's seminal paper (2015) of same name. Right to the city and spatial justice movements are foundational, including Lefebvre (1996), David Harvey (e.g., 2012; 2014), and Edward Soja (2010).

29 Foster and Iaione (2018). Ostrom in the City: Design principles and practices for the urban commons. In Cole, Hudson, and Rosenbloom, eds. *The Routledge Handbook of the Study of the Commons.*

30 Ghent commons transition plan: https://stad.gent/en/city-government/ghent-commons-city/ commons-transition-plan-ghent; Seoul sharing city plan: http://english.seoul.go.kr/policy/key-policies/city-initiatives/1-sharing-city/; Sydney commons transition plan: https://drive.google. com/file/d/1TxN4-XFORuS6i_xgL0QhLyWODXXWS6zx/view.

31 By Francesca Bria, Our Data is Valuable: Here's how we can take that value back. *The Guardian.* April 5th, 2018.

32 Cities for Digital Rights: https://citiesfordigitalrights.org/.

33 Toby Ord (2020, 195) argues in *The Precipice: Existential risk and the future of humanity*, that "we can't rely on our current intuitions and institutions that have evolved to deal with small- or medium-scale risks," as our systems of organizations, norms and laws that handle risk have not been built for the extensive existential risks the world now faces.

34 See Co-cities web site: http://commoning.city/.

35 People–nature collaborations are described in Janice Astbury's PhD thesis, University of Manchester, 2015.

36 *The Alternative UK* (2020). "From TINA (there is no alternative) to TAPAS (there are plenty of alternatives!). Commons, and commoning, just keeps on bubbling up." www.thealternative.org.uk/ dailyalternative/2020/5/30/tina-tacos-commons-bubblng-up.

37 #LandBack is an Indigenous-led movement. To learn more, see three short documentary films, produced with support of the David Suzuki Foundation: https://davidsuzuki.org/what-you-can-do/what-is-land-back/.

38 For Ubuntu and commons thinking, see Shumba (2011). Commons thinking, ecological intelligence and the ethical and moral framework of Ubuntu: an imperative for sustainable development. *Journal of Media and Communications Studies* 3(3): 84. For more on Haitian Konbit, see Robillard (2013). *Konbit: finding Haitian solidarity in modern times.* Master's thesis. Future Generations.

39 Principal investigators of the Co-Cities Project are Sheila Foster and Christian Iaione: http:// commoning.city/.

40 Email from Nadine St-Louis to Jayne Engle, August 2019.

41 This is the thesis of Toby Ord's book, *The Precipice: Existential risk and the future of humanity* (2020).

42 Ubuntu is an African philosophy and form of humanism often expressed in the phrase, "I am because of who we all are."

43 The Republic of Ecuador (2010). *National Plan for Good Living 2009–2013: Building a Plurinational and Intercultural State*, SENPLADES. *Sumak Kawsay* is a cultural syllogism in Kichwa (Ecuador)/ Quechua (Perú) meaning "the plentiful life." It refers to a philosophy of life based on ancestral Indigenous knowledge and practices, where *ayllu* (family–community) coexists in harmony with the *pacha* through certain principles and values.

44 Bartlett, C., M. Marshall, and A. Marshall. (2012).

45 See Collective Wisdom, by Cizek and Uricchio (2019).

46 Several to note: bell hooks (2021), adrienne maree brown (2017), and Bertrand Russell, who in 1959 near the end of his life, responded to the question, what would you say to future generations?, with: "to love is wise, to hate is foolish."

47 See Borrows (2019, 175).

48 Aristotle considered three ways of knowing: episteme (scientific knowledge), techne (knowledge of craft), and phronesis (ethical knowledge and practical wisdom). Phronesis has been the least explored and emphasized in the development of Western academic and cultural practices.

49 From the Preface of Borrows (2019, 22–23), written by Andrew Stewart.

50 Quote by Douglas Cardinal in his talk "Indigenizing Cities: Honouring the Truth and Reconciling for a Collaborative Future," Future Cities Canada Speaker Series, July 3rd, 2019.

51 Quote by Eric Holthaus in "How did a small town in Canada become one of the hottest places on Earth?" in *The Guardian*, June 30th, 2021.

References

Agyeman, J. (2013). *Introducing just sustainabilities: Policy, planning and practice*. Zed Books.

Agyeman, J., R. Doyle Bullard, and B. Evans, eds. (2003). *Just sustainabilities: Development in an unequal world*. MIT Press.

Andrews, K. (2021). *The new age of empire: How racism and colonialism continue to rule the world*. Bold Type Books.

Astbury, J. (2015). *Inviting landscapes: Resilience through engaging citizens with urban nature*. PhD thesis, University of Manchester.

Bartlett, C., M. Marshall, and A. Marshall. (2012). Two-Eyed Seeing and other lessons learned within a co-learning journey of bringing together Indigenous and mainstream knowledges and ways of knowing. *Journal of Environmental Studies and Sciences* 2(4): 331–340.

Beard, V. A. (2003). Learning radical planning: The power of collective action. *Planning Theory* 2(1), 13–35.

Benyus, J. M. (1997). *Biomimicry: Innovation inspired by nature*. Harper.

Bollier, D. and S. Helfrich. (2019). *Free, fair, & alive: The insurgent power of the commons*. New Society.

Bombino, C. L. (2017), Sacred Commons: Building both physical and spiritual infrastructure in America. *Institutional Religious Freedom Alliance*: http://irfalliance.org/.

Bookchin, M. (1995). *From urbanization to cities: Toward a new politics of citizenship*. rev. ed. Cassell.

Bookchin, M. (2005). *The ecology of freedom: The emergence and dissolution of hierarchy*. AK Press.

Borrows, J. (2019). *Law's Indigenous ethics*. University of Toronto Press.

Bouchard, D., J. Jones, J. Martin, K. Cameron, Swampfox, and N. Jones. (2009). *The seven sacred teachings of White Buffalo Calf Woman = Niizhwaaswi aanike'iniwendiwin: waabishiki mashkode bizhikiins ikwe*. MTW Publishers.

brown, a. m. (2017). *Emergent strategy: Shaping change, changing worlds* (Reprint ed.). AK Press.

Chung-Tiam-Fook, T. (2020a). *Re-imagining new urban futures through Indigenous placekeeping*. Future Cities Canada. May 13th, 2020. https://futurecitiescanada.ca/stories/re-imagining-new-urban-futures-through-indigenous-placekeeping/.

Chung-Tiam-Fook, T. (2020b). From smart cities to regenerative cities. *Municipal World* 130(11): 9–11.

Cizek, K. and W. Uricchio. (2019). *Collective wisdom field study: Co-creating media within communities, across disciplines and with algorithms*. Co-Creation Studio at MIT Open Documentary Lab. MIT Works in Progress.

Dark Matter Labs (2020a). *Civic-Indigenous 7.0: Seven points of convergence towards civic and Indigenous futures*. Medium. Written by Lapalme, J. and M.-S. Banville, in collaboration with J. Borrows, McConnell Foundation, and others. January 22nd, 2020. https://medium.com/cities-for-people/civic-indigenous-7-0-ec3a9104901b.

Dark Matter Labs (2020b). *Property rights/property wrongs: Micro-treaties with the Earth*. Medium. Written by Lapalme, J. and M.-S. Banville, with foreword by J. Borrows, and in collaboration with McConnell

Foundation. September 14th, 2020. https://provocations.darkmatterlabs.org/property-rights-prope rty-wrongs-micro-treaties-with-the-earth-9b1ca44b4df.

Ecuador, Republic of (2010). *National plan for good living 2009–2013: Building a plurinational and intercultural state*. SENPLADES.

Eisenstein, C. (2019) Earth spirituality. In *Pluriverse: A post-development dictionary*, edited by A. Kothari, A. Salleh, A. Escobar, F. Demaria, and A. Acosta. Tulika Books.

Eisenstein, C. (2021). *Sacred economics, revised: Money, gift & society in the age of transition* (Revised ed.). North Atlantic Books.

Engle, J. (2019). Some thoughts on valuing the sacred in the city. Part of an essay collection curated by N. Ahmed, M. Claudel Z. Ebrahim, C. Pandolfi, and B. Wylie. *Some Thoughts*. November 19th. https://medium.com/cities-for-people/sacred-civics-ee4564c77092.

Engle, J. (2020). Sacred Civics: Valuing what matters in cities. *Provisions: Observing and archiving COVID-19. The Site Magazine*. www.thesitemagazine.com/jayne-engle.

Engle, J. (2021). *Sacred civics: What could it mean to build seven generation cities?* [podcast and video]. Cities@Tufts, Virtual Colloquium. February 16th. https://www.shareable.net/sacred-civics-seven-generation-cities/.

Engle, J., I. Johar, and A. Ryan. (2020). *The emergence room: Accountabilities needed for future-fit institutions*. Medium. October 19th, 2020. https://medium.com/@JayneEngle/the-emergence-room-82a15 1ec6737?p=82a151ec6737.

Escobar, A. (2018). *Designs for the pluriverse: Radical interdependence, autonomy, and the making of worlds (New ecologies for the twenty-first century)*. Duke University Press.

Escobar, A. (2020). *Pluriversal politics: The real and the possible (Latin America in translation)*. Duke University Press.

Flyvbjerg, B. (2001). *Making social science matter: Why social inquiry fails and how it can succeed again* (1st ed.). Cambridge University Press.

Foster, S. R. and C. Iaione (2015). The city as a commons. *Yale Law & Policy Review* 34(2): 281.

Foster, S. R. and C. Iaione (2018). Ostrom in the city: Design principles and practices for the urban commons. In *Routledge handbook of the study of the commons*, edited by D. Cole, B. Hudson, and J. Rosenbloom. Routledge.

Foster, S. R. and C. Iaione (2022). *Co-Cities: Innovative Transitions Toward Just and Self-Sustaining Communities*. MIT Press.

Friedmann, J. (1987). *Planning in the public domain*. Princeton University Press.

Friedmann, J. (2011). *Insurgencies: Essays in planning theory* (RTPI Library Series, 1st ed.). Routledge.

Fry, T. (2015). *City futures in the age of a changing climate*. Routledge.

Garcia, D. (2021). Global commons law: Norms to safeguard the planet and humanity's heritage. *International Relations* 35(3): 422–445.

Hardt, M. and A. Negri (2017). *Assembly*. Oxford University Press.

Harvey, D. (2012). *Rebel cities: From the right to the city to the urban revolution*. Verso.

Harvey, D. (2014). *Seventeen Contradictions and the End of Capitalism*. Oxford University Press.

Hilton, C. A. (2021). *Indigenomics: Taking a seat at the economic table*. New Society Publishers.

hooks, b. (2021). *All about love*. Harper.

Houska, T. (Zhaabowekwe, Couchiching First Nation). (2020). Sacred Resistance. In *All we can save: Truth, courage, and solutions for the climate crisis*, edited by A. E. Johnson and K. K. Wilkinson. One World.

Johnson A. E. and K. K. Wilkinson, eds. (2020). *All we can save: Truth, courage, and solutions for the climate crisis*. One World.

Kimmerer, R.W. (2015). *Braiding sweetgrass: Indigenous wisdom, scientific knowledge and the teachings of plants* (First Paperback ed.). Milkweed Editions.

Klein, N. (2014). *This changes everything: Capitalism vs. the climate*. Alfred A. Knopf.

Klein, N. (2019). *On fire: The (burning) case for a green new deal*. Simon & Schuster.

Lefebvre, H. (1996). The right to the city. *Writings on cities*. Wiley.

Mbembe, A. (2021). Out of the dark night. Columbia University Press.

McLaren, D. and J. Agyeman (2015). *Sharing cities: A case for truly smart and sustainable cities*. MIT Press.

Miraftab, F. (2009). Insurgent planning: Situating radical planning in the global south. *Planning Theory* 8(1): 32–50.

Miraftab, F. (2017). Insurgent practices and decolonization of future(s). In *The Routledge handbook of planning theory* (1st ed.), edited by M. Gunder, A. Madanipour, and V. Watson. Routledge.

Mitchell, S. (2018). *Sacred instructions: Indigenous wisdom for living spirit-based change*. North Atlantic Books.

Ord, T. (2020). *The precipice: Existential risk and the future of humanity*. Hachette Books.

Ostrom, E. (1990). *Governing the commons: The evolution of institutions for collective action*. Cambridge University Press.

Picketty, T. (2020). *Capital and ideology*. Harvard University Press.

Porter, L. (2010). *Unlearning the colonial cultures of planning*. Routledge.

Porter, L. (2020). Indigenous cities. In *Understanding urbanism* (1st ed.), edited by D. Rogers, A. Keane, T. Alizadeh, and J. Nelson. Palgrave Macmillan: pp. 15–26.

Raworth, K. (2018). *Doughnut economics: Seven ways to think like a 21st-century economist*. Chelsea Green Publishing.

Register, R. (2006). *Ecocities: Rebuilding cities in balance with nature*. New Society.

Robillard, L. (2013). *Konbit: Finding Haitian solidarity in modern times*. Master's thesis, Future Generations.

Roy, A. (2011). Slumdog cities: Rethinking subaltern urbanism. *International Journal of Urban and Regional Research* 35(2): 223–238.

Sandel, M. J. (2021). *Tyranny of merit*. Picador Paper.

Sandercock, L. (2003). *Cosmopolis II: Mongrel cities of the 21st century* (2nd ed.). Continuum.

Saul, J. R. (2014). *The comeback*. Penguin.

Sen, A. (1999). *Development as freedom*. 1st ed. Alfred A. Knopf.

Shumba, O. (2011). Commons thinking, ecological intelligence and the ethical and moral framework of Ubuntu: An imperative for sustainable development. *Journal of Media and Communications Studies* 3(3): 84.

Simone, A. (2001). On the worlding of African cities. *African Studies Review* 44(2): 15–41.

Simone, A. and E. Pieterse. (2018). *New urban worlds: Inhabiting dissonant times*. John Wiley & Sons.

Soja, E. W. (2010). *Seeking spatial justice*. Globalization and Community Series. University of Minnesota Press.

Stonechild, B. A. (2020). *Loss of Indigenous Eden and the fall of spirituality* (Illustrated ed.). University of Regina Press.

Suzuki, D., A. McConnell, and A. Mason. (2007). *The sacred balance: Rediscovering our place in nature* (3rd ed.). Greystone Books.

Thompson-Fawcett, M. and R. Quigg. (2017). Identity, place, and the (cultural) wellbeing of Indigenous children. In *Children's health and wellbeing in urban environments*, edited by C. R. Ergler, R. Kearns, and K. Witten. (Routledge Geographies of Health Series). Routledge: p. 223.

Thompson-Fawcett, M. (Ngāti Whātua), J. Ruru (Ngāti Raukawa ki Waikato, Ngāi Ranginui ki Tauranga, Ngāti Maniapoto), and G. Tipa (Ngāi Tahu). (2017). Indigenous resource management plans: Transporting non-Indigenous people into the Indigenous world. *Planning Practice and Research* 32(3): 259–273.

Thompson-Fawcett, M. and C. Freeman. (eds.). (2006). *Living together: Towards inclusive communities*. Otago University Press.

Tonkinwise, C. (2015). Design for transitions—from and to what? *Design Philosophy Papers* 13(1): 85–92.

Trebeck, K. and J. Williams. (2019). *The economics of arrival: Ideas for a grown-up economy* (1st ed.). Policy Press.

Vasudevan, R. and E. M. Novoa. (2021). Pluriversal planning scholarship: Embracing multiplicity and situated knowledges in community-based approaches. *Planning Theory*, 21(1): 77–100.

Wahl, D. C. (2016). *Designing regenerative cultures*. Triarchy Press.

Watson, J. (2019). *Lo-TEK: Design by radical Indigenism*. Taschen.

Watson, V. (2009). Seeing from the South: Refocusing urban planning on the globe's central urban issues. *Urban Studies* 46(11): 2259–2275.

Weber, A. (2015). Reality as commons: A poetics of participation for the anthropocene. In *Patterns of commoning*, edited by D. Bollier and S. Helfrich. Common Strategies Group in cooperation with Off the Common Books: pp. 369–391.

West, G. (2018). *Scale: The universal laws of life, growth, and death in organisms, cities, and companies* (Reprint ed.). Penguin Books.

2

AWAKENING SEVEN GENERATION CITIES

Tanya Chung-Tiam-Fook, Jayne Engle, and Julian Agyeman

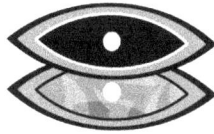

Original Instructions for Awakening Seven Generation Cities

Indigenous origin stories and original instructions inspire and serve as a compass for our sacred civics foundational keys. Nation states and cities also hold origin stories[1] that are most often told through the singular lens of the colonizers and/or dominant politico-economic ideologies, while erasing the stories and experiences of the peoples and lands whose very gifts, labors, and lives form the foundation—and often the heart—of cities. Cities originate from accreting layers of multiple, collective, and divergent "truths," worldviews, narratives, and aspirations that shift over time and space and manifest in the public spaces, buildings, institutions, and arteries of commerce, trade, mobility, and connectivity of urban centers. By working to liberate cities from centuries of colonial legacies and impacts on peoples and natures, and the straitjacket of neoliberal urbanism that increasingly works to transform complex, pluriversal urban worlds into commodities ruled by the dictates of technocratic-economic systems and elites—we can begin to also recover and give momentum to the many intermingling values, wisdoms, and stories that constitute the heart—and future reworlding— of cities.

Seven Foundational Keys to Unlock Imaginaries and Possibilities

Our diverse communities, cultures, and ecologies hold a wealth of interwoven stories that constitute the heart and soul of cities. These stories animate landscapes, physical structures, social and sacred infrastructures, and multiple generations of people; and if we are open to receiving, they provide an orientation for how our collective dreams and gifts can activate more democratic, equitable, and sustainable futures for the next seven generations. Guiding and breathing life and possibility into pathways of transformative praxis and the co-creation of seven generation cities are seven interrelated, foundational sacred civics keys: relationality, agency, reciprocity, decoloniality, spirituality, responsibility, and pluriversality.

Relationality. At their core, cities are built from our social relationships to land, community, and place, transformed over time by how those relationships and their underlying values

DOI: 10.4324/9781003199816-3

evolve. Understanding our complex and multiple relationships and perceptions of place and land enables a more critical and layered engagement with urban systems, spaces, and ecologies, and it enables our ability to reimagine those beyond our own human-centered existentiality, consciousness, rights, needs, desires, and actions. Relationality with place can be manifest through intentional land acknowledgments and cultivating cities of reconciliation backboned by the principles of the United Nations Declaration on the Rights of Indigenous Peoples.

Agency. Cities are not just a human construct; they are alive, sensate, and enact collective forms of agency manifesting through the self-determination of each person, community, collective, and institution to think, dream, co-create, act, protest, embody, transform, and demand justice and positive social change. Cities are also activated by the agency of the lands and beings that support and sustain them. As hubs of life and embodied experiences and expressions of agency, cities can activate the collective values of a sacred civics: belonging, justice, equity, and sovereignty for all peoples, the Earth, and future generations with relation to all spheres (e.g., health, food, climate, technology) and across sectors (e.g., institutions, investments, and infrastructures). Individual and collective agency of people and nature can make for more effective collective action, such as through enactments and codifications of rights of nature and civic assemblies.

Reciprocity. One of our greatest responsibilities as humans within our nexus of relationships with the lands and more-than-human kin we live among in cities is the dynamic of reciprocity and gift-sharing. Reciprocity shifts the prevalent anthropocentric logic of unfettered, unilateral extraction, accumulation, and consumption into a genuine sense of accountability to and reconciliation with the Earth. Reciprocity is about an ethical and equitable exchange of gifts: between humans and the Earth; and between people. As people, we are dependent on and benefit from the Earth's bounty in immeasurable ways but while those gifts are freely given, there are associated teachings and responsibilities that we must learn to put into action better. Reciprocity can show up through, for example, transitioning capital and investment models; responsible harvesting, regenerative agriculture and land restoration; and modifying urban planning pedagogies, methodologies, and practices.

Decoloniality. Decoloniality is a monumental commitment. It requires local and global solidarity and long-term action to decenter and dismantle the dominance and damage of coloniality in all of its logics, ontological and paradigmatic underpinnings, matrices of power, and extractive, subjugating relationships, including in urban planning, governance, finance, and regulation. The legacies and impacts of colonialism continually reproduce throughout society. Despite the diversity of ethno-cultural, spiritual and geographic lineages, citizenry, and influences within cities of all sizes, there has been a systematic and systemic denial of the rights, perspectives, and ways of being and doing of Indigenous, Black and other racialized and marginalized communities regarding access to the spaces, social infrastructures, planning, and decisions that impact their communities and heritage. Coloniality and racial capitalist systems have oppressed and often erased the presence and expressions of creativity, placekeeping, and innovation by Indigenous, Black, and People of Color in public spaces and civic institutions throughout cities globally. Decolonizing city building needs to be at the heart of societal transition.

Spirituality. Becoming more conscious, intentional, and deeply engaged city dwellers, stewards, and builders from a sacred civics lens requires seeing the city as a living matrix of social-ecological relationships constituted from the many parts that include land and nature, people, and institutions. Grounding and enlivening the city organism and the creative and innovative forces, infrastructures, and institutions that drive urban life, are the spiritual relationships and values that interconnect the human, ecological, and sacred dimensions of the city through embodied experiences and expressions of reciprocity and accountability for the wellbeing, integrity, and justice of all beings and future generations. While each person has their own understanding of spirit/spirituality and sacred relationships, knowledge, and practice, as residents and city builders, we are all called upon to live in ways that coexist with and are in reciprocity with all peoples and the Earth. In addition, we are called upon to be more reflective about: the purpose of cities and who/what they are built for; who is validated and who is marginalized through urban systems and why; the logics and structures driving the divides and barriers that make urban life untenable for many people and other beings; and the policy levers and societal transformations to create more inclusive, caring, just, and sustainable cities for all beings now and into the future. Opportunities for everyday expression of spirituality are possible through sacred and ceremonial spaces, including those that recognize Indigenous or cultural ancestry of place and land, and invite spiritual and ceremonial practices of Faith Keepers, Knowledge Keepers, Elders, and healers as central elements of placekeeping and city building.

Responsibility. From planetary to personal, we each carry ethical, cultural and sacred responsibilities to the Earth, our fellow humans and future generations that are key to sustaining our own lives, and the complex webs of biotic and social life in which we participate. When we perceive the Earth's abundance as gifts and not as commodities, our relationship to the Earth is transformed from human-centric need, extraction, and consumption to one of respect, kinship and reciprocity—including our sense of responsibilities to live in balance with and steward the natural systems and beings with whom we share the world. As self-sovereign beings living in the interdependent and densely networked social-ecological systems that cities represent, each person is called upon in the spirit and sacred responsibilities of relationality, agency, reciprocity, decoloniality, care, and stewardship—to live as if the future generations of all life matter. While we are intricately dependent on the gifts of natural systems, and the social and civic infrastructures within cities, the values of self-responsibility and self-sufficiency are core to realizing our capabilities to thrive as individuals, communities, and institutions. Although traditional holders of power and responsibility in the political, regulatory, economic, and planning realms of cities are governments, banks, industry, and corporations, they are often not the main agents of innovation, creativity, and positive social change. We need to reimagine more primary leadership roles and responsibilities for the network of residents, practitioners, creators, youth, Knowledge Keepers, and scholars who are courageously and boldly reinventing cities, often from the bottom up—as well as investments, policy lenses, and infrastructures that can effectively and sustainably work to manifest their visions and initiatives from now into the future.

Pluriversality. Pluriversality recognizes worlds within which many worlds are present. It invites us to reimagine cities as constellations of placeworlds where diverse peoples' values, sacred foundations, relationships, creations, and innovations are the building materials for a plurality of futures. Positive images based on cultural values and narratives in particular can enable powerful future imaginaries, helping to catalyze social change and overcome internalized logics and beliefs that create barriers to change. Pluriversality enables cosmolocal production whereby place-based communities and initiatives collaboratively contribute to and benefit from multiple, interacting sources of shared or open design, technology, innovation, storytelling, knowledge and cultural productions, and services and resources. These mutualistic forms of sharing gifts across a cosmos or pluriverse of placeworlds can transform damaging status quo logics into exciting and generative new cultural, economic, social, and political models for cities. Through reworlding, urban Indigenous, Black and other historic-ally marginalized peoples are reimagining and activating their own futures, as well as reshaping the cultural and natural worlds within cities through transformative frameworks and calls to action on truth and reconciliation, reparations policies, rights and justice-based movements and models, land stewardship and guardianship regimes and community land trusts, participatory social infrastructures, braided knowledges and technologies, reconciliation and regenerative economies, civic transformation, buen vivir and kawsay sacha (living forest), Te Aranga Māori Design Principles, and equity and radical inclusion. These and many other possibilities have the ability to set new pathways out of coloniality and structurally unjust systems; ennoble and enable multiple peoples, natures, worldviews, and stories in cities; and create synergies across placeworlds and forms of reworlding.

Pathways of Praxis to Awaken Seven Generation Cities

How do we move forward together in these times of flux, uncertainty, crisis, hope, and transformation? When brought to bear together in our mindsets, behaviors, and institutions, the seven keys above can unlock pathways of praxis for seven generation cities. Based on wisdoms and cultures of commoning, Indigenous-inspired teachings, Afrofuturisms and other traditions, we can learn to invest in and care for natural and built civic assets of cities as what are today shared homelands for most of humanity. The following pathways of praxis can help bring the foundational keys to civic life. The outcry and increasing momentum—particularly by younger generations—for social, ecological, and climate justice; radical inclusivity and self-determination; and transformative systems and paradigmatic change in cities across the globe is manifesting in tangible ways through inspiring forms of embodiment and action. We've grouped these as seven pathways of praxis.

1. Becoming Good Ancestors

Imagining cities of the future as hubs of creativity, innovation, conviviality, wellbeing, and prosperity for forthcoming generations of peoples and natures, how can we work together to build reciprocal and conscientious forms of city building, urban land stewardship, and civic engagement that contribute to the enduring vitality of cities? As descendants, we can learn to be good ancestors by maintaining the original instructions and sacred duties that our diverse cultural ancestors enacted through their sacred roles and responsibilities. Being conscious and responsible caretakers of the Earth, placekeepers, and city builders is good medicine for urban communities, ecologies, and public spaces, and lays a spiritual foundation for seven generation cities.

2. Reconstituting Sovereignties and Treaties, and Lawing Together

Since time immemorial, Indigenous Nations around the world have exercised their inherent rights, responsibilities, and legal and governance traditions as the original sovereign nations over the lands and natural abundance of their territories. Their diverse ways of visioning and law making were and continue to be guided by the natural laws of the land and all aspects

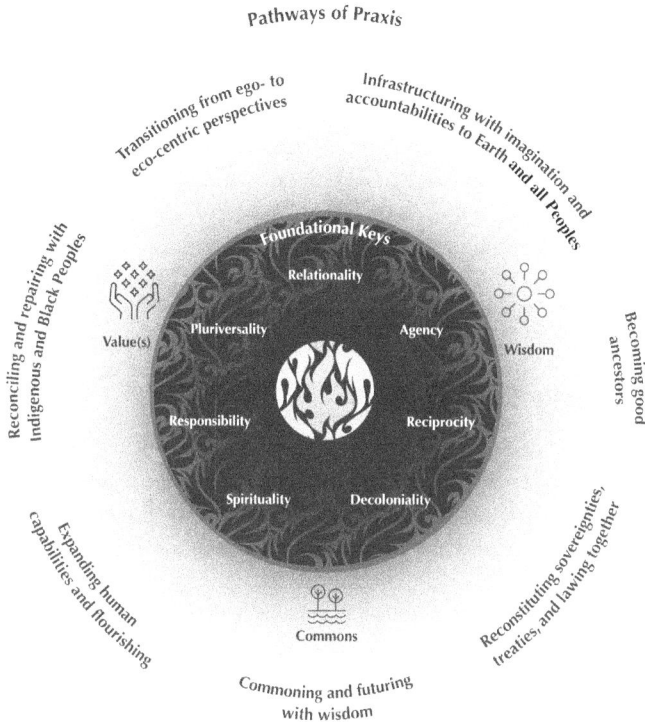

FIGURE 2.1 Awakening seven generation cities: foundational keys and pathways of praxis

of life, including water and land stewardship, food, health and medicine, education, and economy. Shared leadership and decision-making processes and structures, and distribution of roles and responsibilities vary depending on the particular cultural and governance traditions of each Indigenous Nation. Indigenous lifeways, rights and relationships of reciprocity with land (as opposed to unilateral land use) and land guardianship (not ownership) need to be better recognized and embedded within settler governments as foundational to transformative reconciliation processes and public policy more generally.

3. Commoning and Futuring with Wisdom

When we strip away the status quo conventions that define current urban development, we see that cities are living, thriving organisms interconnected through a mycorrhizal-type network of relationships and flows that enliven and sustain natural and civic systems. If we recognize the agency, inherent rights, and sovereignties of natural systems, then the concept of human ownership and control of these life systems and beings becomes untenable. Through a sacred civics lens, city-organisms comprise many diverse social, digital, and infrastructural commons that should be accessible to all residents, and collectively stewarded and governed through participatory frameworks and according to commonly developed rules and protocols. While natural, social, and digital commons provide many resources or gifts for communities and cities, they must be activated through the social relations of decoloniality, social and ecological justice, and participatory community action and governance. Indigenous perspectives on commoning bring us to the heart of collective guardianship and property regimes, placekeeping and the interconnected relationships that bind people to land and place, and to a stewardship community. Commons thinking and practices mirror the principles embodied by Indigenous treaties and covenants, Afro-diasporic models for mutual aid and cooperatives, and many diverse cultural examples of collective property regimes, farming cooperatives, community land stewardship, and knowledge and data commons. As such, commoning provides a culturally relevant model for restoring a land base in cities to urban Indigenous, Black and other racialized and displaced peoples, in order to support all facets of their wellbeing.

4.   *Expanding Human Capabilities and Flourishing*

Obscene inequality in cities is rising. Even in countries highly ranked on indices such as the United Nations Human Development Index (HDI), there is still a high level of spatial inequality within most cities. Many factors contribute to this, including the increasing financialization of urban life, and the dissonance of the logics of government actors whose rational interests are typically to keep expectations low among their constituencies. That said, a growing number of visionary possibilities can address these challenges, such as establishing new shared value creation models, such as the Black Commons, and decolonized foresight and participatory futures practices. To counter the financialization and dissonance in ways that support human capabilities and flourishing new local governance mechanisms are needed such as civic assemblies and mayors or commissions for the future (e.g., a city-based adaptation of the Wales Future Generations Commission). Such examples can test new cosmolocal value creation models and provide for positive improvisation to enable co-creation of new or renewed social covenants and operating systems (the crowdsourced constitution of Mexico City is but one example of this).

5.   *Reconciling and Repairing with Indigenous and Black Peoples*

In the spheres of urban planning, placekeeping, tech, and innovation, movements are growing to ensure Indigenous cultures, approaches, and futures are reflected through city building, design, and the innovation economy driven by the commitment of Indigenous practitioners and ally institutions to advancing reconciliation. Aligned movements among Black-led groups are also burgeoning across the world including #BlackLivesMatter (BLM), which grew significantly during the pandemic period and following the police killings of George Floyd, Breonna Taylor, and too many others. Alongside these movements, there are growing responses and calls for increasing efforts of reconciliation and reparations with Indigenous and Black Peoples. Mechanisms include City of Reconciliation frameworks (e.g., City of Vancouver), adoption by governments of the United Nations Declaration of Rights of Indigenous Peoples, and Truth and Reconciliation Commissions (such as in South Africa and Canada). In the US context, reconciliation is being pursued by Black communities as a critical strategy toward reckoning by the US state regarding structural racism and racial violence. US President Biden's recent Infrastructure Bill, for example, has invested specific funds to remove racist infrastructures, and a number of city mayors joined forces in 2021 to create a network of Mayors Organized for Reparations and Equity (MORE).

6. *Transitioning from Ego- to Eco-centric Perspectives*

Anthropocentric narratives of human mastery and dominance relative to the natural world are deeply ingrained in urban systems. Cities have largely been shaped by the social, political, and ecological realities of distinctly human worlds, privileging resource-dependent corporate interests and technological innovation often at great cost to the health and integrity of ecological and climate systems. How do we decenter "human" in urban policy so that there is a more integrated and holistic eco-centric[2] focus on cities as whole social-ecological systems, comprising a complex, interconnected multiplicity of natural systems? Nature-inspired and biomimetic design and infrastructure can revitalize and hybridize innovations based on ancient or emerging technologies from around the world. Cities can be designed to resemble and function like extensions of the natural world of which they are part, with healthy organs, arteries, and connective tissue. Cree Elder, architect and city planner Douglas Cardinal and other renowned Indigenous architects and designers have created exquisite works that emulate natural landscapes and communities they reside within; are energy and water efficient, and re-presence cultural values, identities, and practices.[3]

7. *Infrastructuring with Imagination and Accountabilities to Earth and all Peoples across Time*

Societies and civilizations live or die by the infrastructure they build. Many infrastructures are no longer fit for purpose, and in some cases, they are on the brink of collapse. What are the social, ecological, cultural, economic, physical, and institutional infrastructures that we need to create and build for this new age? And how can they be built in ways that exemplify global solidarity? It is rare for modern cities to build with imaginaries that extend for seven generations or with a sense of responsibility to the many billions of people who will, hopefully, dwell here in the future. Cosmolocal infrastructuring provides a vision and mechanisms for collectively solving mutual sustainability problems through the means of planetary mutualization of knowledge in which local places contribute to and benefit from other communities' sharing open knowledge, technologies, design, and hardware. Infrastructuring with imagination through working with artists and others on participatory futures processes has great potential for producing decolonized and wise strategic foresight practices. Assessing infrastructure investments through lenses of climate justice, future generations, and feminist and decolonizing values will be foundational to building seven generation cities. In a similar vein, wellbeing cities is growing as a rubric to center infrastructures of deep care for the common good. Transforming urban commons infrastructures—social, physical, and digital—to improve wellbeing, compassion, care, shared wealth, and participation in deep democracy exemplifies sacred civics in action. Critical questions to address in assessing how to build forward include: What does decolonized, emancipatory social and civic infrastructure look like? What learning, scaling, and financing architectures are needed to build more robust and systemic social infrastructure for seven generations that communities anywhere can adapt to their contexts?

Looking Forward: Elders Are the Nurturers and Youth are the Builders of our Futures

> Like Grandmother Toad we must rise with that rich black earth in our little fist. That handful of good earth, we cannot let stream through our fingers and wash away. We

must hold on tight to raise that vision of reworlding in the newly born Sacred Civics Movement. We must plant the seeds in our governmental bodies and foster them, carry them through to harvest to be put through like ceremony in the next cycle of growth.

Catherine Tàmmaro (chapter 12, this volume)

How to leverage civic assets in ways that dismantle systemic barriers and unlock diverse human capabilities?[4] How can cities forge transition pathways to mobilize needed systemic and place-based social, ecological, and technological change? How can seven generation cities transform our relationship to Earth from one of rampant extraction to one of kinship and reciprocal generosity through the embedding and activation of sacred civics keys and pathways for praxis? The reflections and actions shared across the following chapters come from many parts of the world, and they share fundamental commonalities as to what a good life and well-being entail: reciprocal gift-sharing between human and more-than-human beings, community and interdependence, sovereignty and participatory democracy, and transformative shifts in urban systems, institutions, investments, and infrastructures to secure the common good for all.

Co-creating sacred civics imaginaries for cities of the future invites birthing of a sacred civics movement nourished by collective belief that social change movements and commons-based systems are effective organizing forces for cultivating relationships of reciprocal gift-sharing, strengthening local democracy and enabling more equitable and regenerative local provisioning. Imagining futures collectively can be unifying and galvanizing, to elevate communities' collective action capabilities and to transcend their contestations.

As taught through the stories and prophecies of the Ancestors, times of crisis compel us to recover and rebuild or transform what is broken. Anishinaabe Elders from the Great Lakes Region of Turtle Island foretold this time of the Seventh Fire and looked forward to lighting the Eighth Fire with two paths in front of humanity: one well worn, marred by greed and industry and without wisdom or respect for life; the other less worn, spiritual, respectful of all life, ecologically healthy, and enduring. As we work toward recovery and civic transformation, our opportunity is to be more truthful about the world as it is, and to be regenerative and seven generations-minded in reimagining cities. Indigenous and other lifeways of the pluriverse are being recovered and revitalized and shared with peoples around the world. Based on teachings of Algonquin Elder and spiritual and environmental leader William Commanda, Penawapskewi writer and lawyer Sherri Mitchell reflects on the spiritually significant moment at the closing of this generation: "Every time we share those teachings and walk upon the path, we are kindling the Eighth Fire and moving toward peace and harmony and the renewal of the Earth."[5]

As the crashing of irreconcilable worldviews becomes more evident in this epochal moment, may we harness collective wisdom and seize the possibility to light the Eighth Fire, and build cities where children in seven generations will thrive.

Notes

1 Gómez-Mont, G. (2021) What—and who—is a city for? *Policy Opinions*. https://policyoptions.irpp.org/magazines/august-2021/what-and-who-is-a-city-for/.

2 Rowe, S. (1994). Ecocentrism: the Chord that Harmonizes Humans and Earth. *The Trumpeter*, 11(2).

3 See also Watson, J. (2019). *Lo-TEK: Design by Radical Indigenism*. Taschen.

4 Sen, A. (2001). *Development as freedom*. New York: Oxford University Press.
5 Mitchell, S. (2018). *Sacred Instructions: Indigenous Wisdom for Living Spirit-Based Change*. North Atlantic Books.

References

Gómez-Mont, G. (2021) What—and who—is a city for? *Policy Opinions*. https://policyoptions.irpp.org/magazines/august-2021/what-and-who-is-a-city-for/.

Mitchell, S. (2018). *Sacred Instructions: Indigenous Wisdom for Living Spirit-Based Change*. North Atlantic Books.

Rowe, S. (1994). Ecocentrism: the Chord that Harmonizes Humans and Earth. *The Trumpeter*, 11(2).

Sen, A. (2001). *Development as freedom*. Oxford University Press.

Watson, J. (2019). *Lo-TEK: Design by Radical Indigenism*. Taschen.

PART I

Space

3

HONOURING THE SACRED IN CITIES

Indigenous Teachings for City Building

Tanya Chung-Tiam-Fook

A Time of Transformational Shifting

Within their collective memory, most Indigenous cultures hold allegorical prophecies[1] about a time of darkness and uncertainty that precipitates a deep transformational shift in the ecological, spiritual, philosophical, epistemic, and cultural foundations of society, leading to a period of deep reflection and accountability by the Peoples for their actions and how they impact the land and the future generations. It is also a time of awakening in the Peoples of their sacred relationships and covenants with the Earth and all beings, and their duties to cultivate and activate their spiritual, cultural, and ecological understanding and responsibilities. According to our Elders, Knowledge Keepers, and the Ancestors, the darkness is not a malevolent force but rather, a manifestation of the collective pain, trauma, fear, and ignorance that have not yet been brought into consciousness and integrated into our collective wholeness.

Colonial capitalist systems around the world have fundamentally transformed people's relationships with the Earth, as well as global social, economic, and political systems and institutions. Over the past several centuries, capitalist forms of land ownership and use, economic growth, extractive resource development, agriculture, health care, production, trade, consumption, science, and technology have become extremely unsustainable, unhealthy and inequitable for our social and ecological systems. Our dominant modes of living and producing have brought a prolonged period of intensifying darkness and physical, emotional, spiritual, and psychological distress for many impacted communities.

Consequently, the Earth's systems and beings have borne levels of devastation and suffering that are pushing many ecological and human communities over their threshold for adaptation and resilience. This time of shadow is a threshold to important environmental, social, and internal shifts, and often amplified with disasters caused by extreme weather events, and massive health crises such as the COVID-19 pandemic. Such crises cause not only pain and loss to many families and societies around the world, but also cascading economic, mental wellness, social, and political impacts that reverberate into the forthcoming generation(s).

DOI: 10.4324/9781003199816-5

In a spirit of rebirth and renewal, the prophecies also foretell these times of uncertainty and distress are when the richest teachings, self-discoveries and transformations can occur at individual and collective levels. Collective reflection and truth-telling about the brokenness and inherent flaws within our national and global systems and paradigms have been happening at an unprecedented level throughout media platforms and boardrooms everywhere. People are looking more than ever for values and models that connect us to one another and to place; and that hold the promise of building a more regenerative and life-sustaining world.

Two iconic prophecies from the Northern and Southern hemispheres that encapsulate an archetypal awakening of sacred energy and consciousness through both the deep transformational shift happening in our planet and global society, and the path to transformative reconciliation for Indigenous and settler peoples are: the story of the Harpy Eagle and the Condor from Indigenous lineages in the Amazonian and Andean regions of South America, and the Anishinaabe prophecy of the Seven Fires from Turtle Island.

The *Harpy Eagle and the Condor Prophecy*[2] is an allegory of long ago when human societies split into two divergent paths—that of the Eagle and that of the Condor. The path of the Harpy Eagle is the path of the mind, of the industrial, and of masculine energy. The path of the Condor is the path of heart, of intuition, and of feminine energy. Despite their differences, the two pathways are complementary, symbiotic, and interconnected—similar to the Harpy Eagle and Condor who soar together in the same sky and in both the forest and mountain landscapes. In this way, the Peoples of the Harpy Eagle and those of the Condor will be able to create a new level of consciousness for humanity if they activate this potential and ensure that a new consciousness is allowed to arise.

After more than 500 years of conquest and colonialism in Turtle Island and Abya Yala (North and South America), many Indigenous Peoples across the Americas are working in partnership to fulfill the prophecy of the (Harpy) Eagle and the Condor, including a 2015 gathering of diverse Indigenous women leaders in New York who joined in ceremony and signed a historic *Treaty in Defense of Mother Earth* (Indigenous Women of the Americas 2015). The Treaty states:

> As Indigenous Women of the Americas, we understand the responsibilities toward the sacred system of life given to us by the Creator to protect the territorial integrity of Mother Earth and Indigenous Peoples. These responsibilities include the safety, health and wellbeing of our children and those yet to come, as well as the children of all of our non-human relatives, the seeds of the plants and those unseen.
>
> *Indigenous Women of the Americas 2015*

The *Seven Fires Prophecy* tells of seven prophets who came to the Anishinaabeg and told them of their journey into the future, marked by seven sacred fires. The story is quite detailed and portends of events that Indigenous Peoples have witnessed and experienced from the creation of Turtle Island to the present-day impacts of settler colonialism and the global capitalist system. However, during this time, the Peoples would awaken from this time of illusion and suffering, retracing their steps to recover the gifts of the original instructions, stories, and teachings from the Creator that had been left on the path. William Commanda, late Anishinaabe Elder and holder of the Seven Fires Wampum belt shared this version:

A New People would emerge. They would retrace their steps to find the wisdom that was left by the side of the trail long ago. Their steps would take them to the Elders, who they would ask to guide them on their journey … There will be an awakening of the people, and the sacred fire will again be lit. At this time, the light-skinned race will be given a choice between two roads. One road is the road of greed and technology without wisdom or respect for life … The other road is spirituality, a slower path that includes respect for all living things. If we choose the spiritual path, we can light yet another fire, an Eighth Fire, and begin an extended period of Peace and healthy growth.

Commanda 1997

I share calls to action and transformational change interpretations of the spiritual teachings and featured in this chapter from my role as a conscious steward of the urban lands, waters, and places with immense humility and recognition of the ancestral and contemporary Indigenous knowledges and practices that inspire and enrich my own thinking. My lineages include: Akawaio from Guyana; Dutch–Romani from the Netherlands; and Fukien from southern China. Born to immigrant parents, I am a transplant and settler within the homelands of the Anishinaabeg, Wendat and, Haudenosaunee confederacies, governed by the Dish With One Spoon Wampum covenant in the place now known as Toronto.

The Indigenous Soul of Modern Cities

Contrary to industrial and commercial histories and visions of city building, cities are not created from capital, bricks, and mortar. At their core, they are built from our relationships to land, community, and place, transformed over time by how those relationships and their underlying values evolve. Unfortunately, many natural and built spaces and place names in cities across Turtle Island bear little resemblance to the original languages, ecological landscapes, and features upon which they are built.

Wetlands and watercourses have often been diverted, dammed, dredged, or artificially created. Wild landscapes like forests have long been fragmented and sculpted into parks and trails; or cleared and covered with asphalt, concrete, and built structures. Indigenous place names have been Anglicized or Gallicized from their original languages, or names have been changed altogether—changing or erasing the original meaning rooted in First Peoples' languages, relationships with and perceptions of the lands and places where they lived, seeded lands with crops and stories, harvested food, navigated trade and hunting routes, and held gatherings and ceremony.

Although these transformations were driven by the colonial interest to build settler cities as a marker of material and commercial progress—in Canada, they were grafted upon the ancestral territories and permanent or seasonal use sites of First Nations, Inuit and Métis Nations. As part of our collective placekeeping, city building and reconciliation work in cities, it is immensely important that we honour the Indigenous lineage of and vibrant contributions to municipalities, and develop an expanded vision of what a city means today, and for the next seven generations.

In 2021, more than 80 percent of Indigenous Peoples in Canada call cities home, and are active in every sector of society and the economy. As such, urban hubs across Canada are in fact not settler cities, but *Indigenous* cities. In fact, the urban reserves of: Muskeg Lake Cree

Nation and Roseau River First Nation (two of many under the Treaty Land Entitlement Framework Agreements) in Saskatchewan and Manitoba; Squamish, Musqueam, and Tsleil-Waututh Nations in British Columbia; St. Mary's First Nation in New Brunswick; and the Yellowknife Denes in Northwest Territories are some examples of First Nations that are within or adjacent to major municipalities.

Yet despite this, settler urban planning and policy processes often sought to erase, dispossess, and dismiss Indigenous rights, presence, and expressions of placekeeping in public spaces and civic institutions throughout Canada's cities. In response, urban Indigenous and ally collectives and organizations have been working to unsettle built and natural commons and reclaim public spaces around settler cities. As part of this decolonizing work and reclaiming Indigenous rights to the city and models of city building, is the imperative for both Indigenous Peoples and civic allies to dismantle an entrenched colonial settler worldview in policies and practices, thereby creating space for Indigenous and other worldviews and forms of placekeeping.

Indigenous city building also extends to rural and remote Indigenous communities in that many Indigenous Nations and regional Indigenous organizations provide governance, social, health, public infrastructure, and environmental services that are similar to municipalities—albeit different in scale and approach. For Indigenous Nations, the path toward the resurgence of peoples' sovereignty and self-governance centres on increased self-sufficiency for their communities and bridging systemic divides by closing gaps in data and digital infrastructure; health and social services; and opportunities in economic development and educational and entrepreneurship advancement.

In particular, there is a lot of momentum among Indigenous business and community leaders to restore, build, and strengthen Indigenous economies and reconciliation economies aligned with the wisdom of traditional Indigenous economic models, relationships with the Earth and community, and Indigenous cultural and humanistic values.[3] A reconciliation economy is a promising model for advancing Indigenous economic and social development in all spheres of wellbeing, and enabling the equitable distribution and sustainable management of a community's or city's natural and economic wealth among Indigenous and non-Indigenous Peoples.

As the First Peoples of their respective lands, the Ancestors of contemporary Indigenous Nations built vibrant settlements, governance structures, housing, land and water stewardship, and food production technologies, and social and health systems. They were the original placekeepers and city builders, artists, planners, innovators, scientists, and architects. Indigenous models have transformed natural environments and urban landscapes and embody connectivity to land and place, kinship, holism, sovereignty, vitality, and cultural continuity.

As Indigenous urbanism and models for planning, placekeeping, urban land stewardship, and governance emerge more within mainstream spaces, there is a growing shift in consciousness, values, and models toward greater inclusiveness, humanism, and relationality. Such shifting will hopefully shake governments and institutions out of their status quo complacency and power structures while also laying the foundation for Indigenous-informed futures for cities.

Critical self-reflection by settler governments and institutions of structural inequities, epistemic racism, policy biases, and blind spots, especially those that privilege dominant settler views and reproduce unequal power dynamics and exclusionary practices, is the only way to disrupt status quo patterns and inequitable practices. When dominant paradigmatic assumptions are challenged in an honest and reflective way, there is the possibility of transforming dominant narratives into multiple place-based narratives grounded in the situated experiences and practices of diverse peoples. A number of core actions are needed for such transformation to implant in a way that is sustainable and aligned with urban Indigenous sovereignty and futures. These actions are at the heart of a more genuine process of decolonization and transformative reconciliation and are commonly asserted across the Indigenous worlds in Canada, USA, Australia, and Aotearoa/New Zealand:

- Honouring and integrating Indigenous sovereignty in all Indigenous–settler relationships and engagement with Indigenous Peoples;
- Restoring land rights and access to Indigenous Nations and Peoples (including urban contexts);
- Recovering the health and wellbeing of rural and urban ecosystems and species; and
- Righting Indigenous–settler relationships and building a regenerative reconciliation economy based on collaborative and equitable sharing and stewardship of the abundance of Turtle Island across Indigenous and settler societies (Manuel and Derrickson 2017).

Anishinaabe arts journalist and Chair of the Canada Council of the Arts Jesse Wente advises that the recognition of sovereignty, restoring land, and rebuilding a reconciliation economy together is the only recipe for system-level reconciliation. He states that this is the "promise of realizing a new and regenerative relationship that our future generations can be proud of" (Wente 2021).

Politics and Sacredness of Urban Space and Place

Space

While many urban spaces within natural, social, and built places and landscapes in cities are open to the public and are intended as civic commons for all residents to live, work, play, celebrate, and engage, they have often been designed and planned in ways that privilege the worldviews and rights of access of particular settler groups above those of urban Indigenous and racialized communities. A key element of urban planning and city building is for civic leaders to work with Indigenous partners to decolonize public spaces by addressing and dismantling the settler colonial histories, policies and practices that have marginalized or erased Indigenous Peoples from those spaces. Concurrent to decolonizing space and place is for civic institutions to learn from and champion Indigenous transformations of those spaces to reflect the myriad forms and expressions of Indigenous culture, urbanism, and decolonial action.

There are infinite ways to understand, inhabit, decolonize, and Indigenize space beyond the three-dimensional understanding of *physical* space measured by Euclidean geometry or the distance between waypoints in cartographic space. For Indigenous Peoples, perceptions of space have taken on political, legal and regulatory, ethical and sacred dimensions that determine for whom space is activated and under what conditions.

Indigenous space has a multitude of meanings but it often refers to how an Indigenous Community creates and sustains Indigenous geographies—in cities and civic spaces that have been dominated by settler influence—through diverse placekeeping activities such as place-naming, ceremony and cultural practice, artistic and design, land stewardship, planning, and resistance. Indigenous space is also a reflection of kinship, culture, community, and an extension of ceremony and connection with the natural world. Public spaces or civic commons are renegotiated and transformed by Indigenous practitioners as sites alive with Indigenous physical, cultural, and spiritual presence.

Another conceptualization and practice of Indigenous space relates to place and Indigenous urbanism. The idea of "homelands" for Indigenous Peoples often refers to ancestral and treaty lands in rural areas but the overlap between modern cities and Indigenous territories—and the reality that approximately 80 percent of people call cities home—means that urban areas are also Indigenous homelands. Non-Indigenous people often perceive Indigenous presence in cities as transient and incongruent with static ideas and assumptions of Indigenous culture. As such, civic institutions must expand their understanding of both cities and urbanism to include Indigenous city building and placekeeping models of reimagining urban spaces and environments through planning, design, arts, ceremony, activism, and scholarship.

S*acred* space is perhaps the most integral to diverse Indigenous ways of being in the world as it is often anchored in ceremony, cultural and creative expression, and relationships to the Earth, the Ancestors, and the Elders and Knowledge Keepers. Sacred sites are often animate and spiritually alive places attached to particular land or water stewardship practices, cultural and ontological beliefs, myths, ceremonies, symbolism, protocols, and practices that protect and sustain peoples and their lands.

Within an area or public space, there may be a designated sacred space for Indigenous Peoples to practice ceremony and spiritual or religious devotion such as a longhouse, wigwam, teepee, teaching or healing/sweat lodge, totem pole, medicinal garden, smudging area, church, and space on the land or by the water. These are spaces and moments when Indigenous Peoples are able to: connect with identity and lineage; feel a sense of deep belonging and relationship and kinship with Creation; and envision future journeys and future generations.

Ethical space (Ermine 2007) is an encounter between the distinct (and often opposing) worldviews of Indigenous and settler groups, where the space created in the middle enables respectful, cooperative, and collaborative engagement. The intersection between their respective systems of knowledge, governance, science, law, economics, culture, and spirituality can be quite fragile and often fraught with the weight of history and future expectations. Indigenous-led ethical standards in research and data governance; and more equitable rules of engagement with the inherent Aboriginal Rights and Treaty Rights provisions under Canadian Law (and especially landmark Supreme Court decisions) have provided an ethical space as a framework for dialogue and intercultural communication between Indigenous Nations and settler governments, institutions, and practitioners.

Place

Before we look at the social, built, and imagined places within cities, we must look at the land that forms the foundation and life support system for communities and institutions. Place, and the land it occurs upon, are alive, sensate, and possess agency. For Indigenous Peoples, the natural world is perceived as a world of self-sovereign entities that have inherent rights, wellbeing and personhood to be honoured and protected by human societies and laws. Although natural laws have existed in many Indigenous and other ancient cultures for millennia, there has been a growing movement in modern times to advocate for and enshrine legal provisions and treaties regarding the personhood and inherent rights of landscapes and species in many countries including Ecuador, Bolivia, Canada, USA, Aotearoa/New Zealand, India, and Uganda.

To really know and understand a place i.e., its energy, social and ecological memory, stories, and the imprint of its inhabitants, requires that we peel back the layers to learn about the peoples, beings, and spirit that live there. The cultural, ecological, socioeconomic, and political contexts of resident and visitor communities shape the character and development of a place. For Indigenous Peoples, place is both the setting and co-creator of our being in the world—it is about recovery and internal (re)connections, relationships, journeys to self, land, clan/kin, culture, and community. In the aliveness of place and the lands that nourish it, there is sacred energy and the imprint of those who came before—the Ancestors. Even in the middle of a large city, place and its connection to the living Earth and to the peoples who keep place and hold space, has much wisdom and memory to teach us when we learn to be rooted in place, in presence, and in relationship.

Relational acknowledgement of place and land through a grounding in cultural protocol, land stewardship, and ceremony transforms that space into something both tangible and sacred; past and present. By learning and honouring the original caretakers, contemporary stewards, and future generations, we can honour the lineage of place. Within my own ancestral Akawaio and syncretic Caribbean traditions of honouring the animacy and life-giving energies of the lands, waters, and more-than-human kin, there is an understanding that akwalu (sacred force) animates all living beings and bonds us to the Imawariton (Ancestors); (A)Maiko', Piyai'ma and Rato (classes of Master spirits of natural landscapes); and Makunaima (Creator). All natural and spiritual beings are ascribed personhood, and exist in a non-linear, circular continuum of akwalu and a'kwari̵ (soul), between matter and spirit; life and after-life.

Relationship to place can also be a fraught and painful concept for urban Indigenous Peoples as many share a history of removal, dispersal, and dislocation from family, origin nation/community, homelands, language, and cultural traditions through state instruments of genocide and assimilation. Like seeds on the wind, many of our Ancestors were either stolen or had to migrate for opportunities, far from their lands and communities—their families fragmented, and their futures uncertain. Having to take root and adapt to new places and cultures; and their Indigenous identity marginalized or even denied makes connection to place more complex and necessitates an anchoring in identity, community, land, and cultural practice within urban hubs. For Indigenous Peoples who do not have a continuous shelter or safe housing, this connection and identity shifts in place more frequently. Despite the often disjointed and traumatic paths that bring Indigenous Peoples to cities, the land and relations (human and more-than-human) continue to be home, as beautifully captured by the Anishinaabe oral teaching that the land and animals are of our first family.[4]

Reworlding and Commoning in Shared Space

A good place to start discussion of civic–Indigenous relationships is through the lens of Indigenous inherent rights and the treaties that govern many cities under both Indigenous natural law and Aboriginal Law under the Charter of Canada. Indigenous Peoples view treaties as sacred covenants between the peoples and the Creator, which include the land, water, animal and plant relations, the Ancestors, and future generations. The Dish With One Spoon Wampum agreement[5] between the Anishinaabe Three Fires Confederacy (Ojibwe,

Odawa, and Potawatomi Nations) and Haudenosaunee Confederacy (Mohawk, Oneida, Onondaga, Cayuga, Seneca, and Tuscarora) is the most well-known internation "one-dish alliances." Treaties also constitute ongoing agreements between First Nations and the settler governments of what is now Canada.

Treaty processes were grounded in the worldviews, languages, knowledge systems, and governance structures of the nations involved, and they were governed by their natural laws and their values of justice, peace, respect, reciprocity, and accountability. As with most teachings and practices of the Indigenous world, relationships are central to treaties and other forms of agreements. Relationships between sovereign nations; between people and natural relations; and between people and the Creator, and the spirit world. Renewal and other ceremonial processes were paramount in maintaining agreements (Simpson 2008).

As immensely important as political treaties between sovereign Indigenous nations and the nation of Canada continue to be with respect to recognizing the inherent, unextinguishable rights of Indigenous Peoples in our modern cities and provinces/territories, it is the spirit of treaties that are at the heart of our roles and responsibilities as both Indigenous and settler peoples. Although these agreements were political and diplomatic in nature, they "were also sacred, made in the presence of the spiritual world and solemnized in ceremony" (Simpson 2008, 29).

The sacred relations, obligations, and responsibilities by Indigenous Nations vis-à-vis the lands, beings, rights, and cultural institutions that treaties protect are honoured by Indigenous Community through the elements of natural laws, sacred values, ceremony, cultural and land-based teachings, governance, and conscientious relationships. Indigenous treaties and other covenants are intended to be alive for as long as the living Earth flourishes. For the future of cities and the ways we conceive of and practise sharing space in those cities, it is incumbent on municipalities, civic institutions, and diverse communities to not only acknowledge treaties with Indigenous nations in symbolic ways such as land acknowledgements or as an element of colonial history, but to really understand and commit to the deeper, ongoing relational and sacred agreement of what it means to live on treaty lands and/or Indigenous homelands.

The public natural and built spaces of the civic commons have often been designed and planned in ways that are more accessible to and representative of the preferences of socio-economic and ethno-cultural groups that are relatively more privileged economically vis-à-vis Indigenous and racialized communities. Moreover, those who advocate for, plan, design, and program the civic commons often fail to acknowledge that urban commons occur on stolen Indigenous lands, or consult with the rights and aspirations of urban Indigenous Peoples and the original treaty holders (Hardison 2006). They also do not acknowledge the many different types of commons regimes that exist—in particular, that civic commons run by municipalities, conservancies, and settler institutions are rarely similar to commons models envisioned and activated by Indigenous cultures (past or present).

A truth that is often challenging for city builders to understand is that while Indigenous and non-Indigenous Peoples coexist in places and lands in cities, the way each group inhabits and keeps place reflects fundamentally different worldviews and are rarely common with each other (Porter and Barry 2016). In these ways, civic commons become naturalized settler spaces and can be complicit in producing and maintaining coloniality and forms of injustice (Fortier 2017; Barker 2009). In thinking about civic commons and the act of commoning,

Indigenous perspectives bring us to the heart of collective guardianship/property regimes, placekeeping, and the interconnected relationships that bind people to land and place, and to a stewardship community.

Commoning is premised on a network of relationships, shared responsibilities and agreements, and collaborative practices and decision-making among groups of people. These values mirror Indigenous treaties on Turtle Island. The Dish With One Spoon covenant and other "one-dish treaties," invite us to equitably share and responsibly steward the lands and natural abundance of the Great Lakes region; eating from a common dish, sharing one spoon, and only taking what each one needs. No knife should be used as there should be no conflict or violence; everyone has an equal right to eat from the dish or harvest from the land's bounty. The sacred principles and spirit of treaties like the Dish With One Spoon Wampum connect people to the Creator, to the land, to one another, and to future generations.

This current era of truth-telling, reckoning, and reconciliation for the unimaginable injustice, trauma, violence, and destruction of life perpetrated by colonial and state agents against Indigenous and Afro-descended Peoples, and many other racialized and marginalized communities—calls on all of us to look deeply at the ruptures in our systems and social fabric for new (or revitalized) values- and rights-based models for collective guardianship and commoning. The added layers of threat multipliers such as climate change and a global pandemic add to the urgency of reworlding seven generations cities of the future. Based on the wisdom of Indigenous-inspired teachings and other humanistic models for commoning, relationality, and building compassionate and just systems for all peoples, we can learn to invest in and care for the natural and built civic assets on Indigenous homelands that we share in common.

Although our systems and institutions have been reticent to confront the Eurocentric coloniality very much part of the DNA of the state of Canada, it is important to recognize that many Canadians (including newcomers), are also eager for a reset in worldview and rebuilding relationships. They understand that it is in the best interest of all peoples and institutions across the country that we confront the shadows of the past and present through truth-telling and restoration of what has been taken and denied, opening spaces for new futures for Indigenous and non-Indigenous Peoples. That desire for deep change and agency held by diverse peoples across Canada can be mobilized to support Indigenous communities and Indigenous models in engaging governments and institutions, and transforming cities for future generations.

Indigenous Reworlding of Civic Spaces and Futures

Indigenous futures within urban settings imagine what life will be over the long term for Indigenous Peoples in cities—including the next seven generations. This concept of a future imaginary draws on a synergy between ancient cultural values, principles, technologies, laws, and forms of governance that have sustained Indigenous societies for thousands of years, and contemporary forms of social, land-based, and technological innovation.[6] To create new pathways and new futures that are self-determined and self-reliant, Elders often encourage us to look back to our cultural teachings, values, and practices so that we can move forward. While Elders are invaluable stewards of their respective cultural and spiritual traditions, they are also the midwives and nurturers of Indigenous futures.

Mainstream city building, planning, and innovation designs and activations in urban public spaces are rarely developed in collaboration and co-design with Indigenous practitioners and community and thus reflect the dominant settler worldview and agenda of municipal and civic decision makers and practitioners. In contrast, Indigenous Peoples' understandings of and approaches to planning and urban placekeeping are incredibly diverse and encompass the multifaceted relationships of peoples with their landscapes, and multiple expressions of what it means to be an Indigenous person in a mixed society. Placekeeping is about sharing our shared histories that have often been deliberately erased; harnessing the wisdom and history of our Ancestors to reawaken Indigenous markers of place, and re-presence Indigenous Peoples and cultures.

Urban Indigenous practitioners and organizations across Canada are working to decolonize and reclaim public spaces to imagine and self-determine the worlds they want to live within and the stories they want to share. Civic institutions can make cities more inclusive of Indigenous cultural, governance, and innovation models through genuine forms of community-engaged planning and co-design, weaving in accountability to lands and to future generations. A telling indicator of how far into the journey of decolonization, transformative reconciliation, and democratizing a city has travelled with Indigenous Peoples is when Indigenous youth can see clearly the breadth of their cultures and identities in the urban landscape and design.

Reworlding or reimagining the places and spaces they inhabit as Indigenous Peoples, and the underlying settler paradigms that dominate them, opens up a multiplicity of ways for them to be, know, and do in cities and such ways connect them to their Indigeneity, community, Ancestors, and the land. Through reworlding, Indigenous Peoples are also imagining and activating their own futures, as well as reshaping the landscapes and futures of the cities they call home.

For Indigenous Peoples, sovereignty is the act of having rights to land relationship and guardianship, knowledge, culture and language, governance, foodways, and social well-being. The recognition and embedding of these rights within government and civic policy and practice is foundational to a more realistic and transformative reconciliation process in Canada. Another core element of reconciliation—and sustainable Indigenous futures—is the restoration of a viable land base to urban Indigenous communities that would support housing needs, growing wild foods and medicinal plants, demonstrations of social innovation and land stewardship in action, ceremony, art-making, and other expressions of placekeeping.

In particular, sustainable foodways and food sovereignty for Indigenous Peoples in cities have been an ongoing challenge for communities across the country, from Vancouver to Iqaluit to Toronto. A dedicated urban land base for growing and harvesting healthy foods through long-evolved ancient agricultural technologies would enable diverse community members to live in healthy, sustainable and cooperative ways—thereby strengthening their self-reliance and autonomy.

Indigenous governments and innovation leaders across Canada and globally are transforming their communities to be more self-sustaining and to become leaders in clean energy and nature-inspired technologies and designs, often integrating Indigenous and Western technologies and design principles. These innovations model exciting and viable solutions to the complex environmental, health, and socioeconomic challenges facing cities. Broad examples from the diverse forms of urban Indigenous placekeeping and social innovation embody the lands, cultural motifs, and spirit of the Nations. These include ceremony, traditional healing and teaching lodges, landscape and culturally inspired architecture, and community-led social infrastructure. Such examples can be supportive spaces for caring and co-creating, artistic creations, Indigenous planning and urbanism, Earth working and food sovereignty, and land and water guardianship.

Indigenous science, technological, and infrastructural innovation excellence demonstrated across sectors and professional fields is on par with large municipalities, and is being harnessed by urban Indigenous practitioners to transform cities for the next seven generations. Examples include: land-based and climate research and science institutes, community broadband networks, LEED (Leadership in Energy and Environmental Design) green building design and green infrastructures, e-health and education platforms, digital-based guardian stewardship, blockchain-enabled data sovereignty and community-backed assets, Artificial Intelligence-powered virtual Indigenous futurism and language revitalization, net-zero housing innovation, LED (light-emitting diode) vertical farms, and culturally informed smartphone apps for safe food harvesting, mental wellness, and accessibility.

Connecting Cities to the Lands that Give Them Life

Spiritual teachings and metaphors across many cultural lineages act as rich and timeless tools that orient societies regarding their existence within the cosmos; nature of being in the world; nature of knowing, knowledge base, and forms of knowledge sharing; interconnected relationships with all beings and landscapes; and capacity to adapt to and transform knowledges, systems, and technologies in synchronicity with changes in their natural and social environments.

A similar philosophy and teaching moves through diverse Indigenous cultures about the extended web of kinship relations that interconnects all human and more-than-human natural and spiritual beings. Our interconnectedness with the natural world and everything in the universe links us in moral and ethical ways to all other beings and compels us to live by certain values, teachings, roles, and responsibilities. Our Ancestors knew their sacred roles and responsibilities in Creation and we are learning to be good ancestors by maintaining those original instructions and sacred duties. Being conscious and responsible caretakers of the Earth, placekeepers, and city builders is good medicine for urban communities, ecologies, and public spaces, and lays a spiritual foundation for seven generation cites.

Let us imagine for a moment, a network of human settlements that are each a thriving hub of life, sacred energy, interconnectivity, cooperation, innovation, and creative and (re) productive activities aligned with the systems and rhythms of nature. These urban hubs would be based on regenerative economies, linked to human and ecological wellbeing and capable of adaptive learning and self-renewal in their capital flows, resources, and networks. Neighbourhoods and communities interlinked locally and regionally/globally through a complex web of social and ecological connective tissue sustain diverse peoples, ecosystems, social systems, and future generations. Such communities are rooted in abundance, gifting, reciprocity, commoning, providing for future generations, and innovative practices inspired by the Earth.

This is how many Indigenous and ancient land-based societies existed prior to colonial contact and it is a model that continues to inspire and be at the foundation of many contemporary Indigenous and non-Indigenous communities around the world. Reimagining cities as abundant, regenerative, and influenced by Indigenous cultures means realizing our vital connections to the land base that nourishes and sustains us. How can we work together to build a permanent relationship between the built structures of cities and the urban ecosystems that give cities life (Jamieson 2015)? Urban ecosystems are the life sustainers in our cities, generously providing the hydration, nourishment, medicine, recreation, and grounding to support our physical, emotional, spiritual, and mental wellbeing.

A very innovative and hopeful way out of contemporary crises such as climate change, the COVID-19 pandemic, and structural inequality for our global society may well be to look back to ancient technologies, and design and planning practices so that we can look forward by creating regenerative cities of the future. Such cities are designed to resemble and function like extensions of the natural world and are led by Indigenous matrilineal governance, as described by Cree Elder and distinguished architect Douglas Cardinal.[7] Cities are living, sacred organisms sustaining life. They link ecosystems and human communities; comprise healthy institutional organs, terrestrial, and wetland arteries, and a soul that nourishes all ways of being, knowing, and creating.

In her talk on Indigenizing Cities, Mohawk visionary and lawyer Roberta Jamieson (Jamieson 2015) calls on Indigenous and non-Indigenous Peoples to create Wampum Cities whereby urban areas become places for all peoples to coexist and flourish together in shared space, according to their own worldviews, practices, and aspirations. Such places are where Indigenous and diverse peoples' values, sacred foundations, creations, and innovations are understood and honoured as inspiring models for cities of the future. Seven generations cities have the potential to be grounded in sacred energy and intention; (re)generative economies and innovations; natural and humane laws; matriarchal and collaborative forms of governance; interconnected landscapes and systems; caring and resilient communities; beautiful diversity and wellbeing of *all* communities; and accountability to those generations which came before and those yet to come.

Notes

1 Prophecy is used here with some fluidity as it does not necessarily denote an event unfolding in the linear progression of historical time. Instead, Indigenous stories and prophecies witness/foretell of events and realities that are perceived to occur in cyclical and synchronic time, or simultaneously.

2 While there are many versions of this prophecy and the origins, lineage and evolution are unclear, I refer to a version known to exist prior to European contact. It speaks of the ways of the harpy eagle (native to the tropical forests of the Amazon region) and the ways of the condor (native to the Sierra or Andean Mountain range). This is not the version that evolved in recent times to integrate concepts of North/South dichotomies and reconciliation, and their respective archetypal and geographical resonances.

3 The Indigenomics Institute is a leading Indigenous economic advisory for Indigenous communities, public governments, and the private sector. http://indigenomicsinstitute.com/indigenomics-institute/.

4 Shared by Naveau, N. (p.c. 2020).

5 The Dish With One Spoon Wampum represents a formal peace agreement ensuring mutual benefit to all parties and extends to all other Indigenous nations and settlers who arrived in the area around the Great Lakes region. It reflects the principles that were given to the Haudenosaunee by the Peacemaker in the Kaienerekowa (Great Law of Peace), stating that Nation leaders should eat from this common dish, sharing one spoon and only taking what each one needs.

6 See Initiative for Indigenous Futures https://indigenousfutures.net/; and Centre for Indigenous Futures www.concordia.ca/campaign/priorities/indigenous-futures.html.
7 Cardinal, D. (2019). p.c.

References

Barker, A. J. (2009). The contemporary reality of Canadian imperialism, settler colonialism, and the hybrid colonial state. *The American Indian Quarterly* 33(3): 325–351.

Cardinal, D. (2019). "Indigenizing Cities: Honouring the Truth and Reconciling for a Collaborative Future," TD Future Cities Speakers Series.

Commanda, W. (1997). Aboriginal Learning Network Constituency Meeting of Elders, policymakers, and academics, Aylmer, Québec. www.youtube.com/watch?v=xanNCAJuzgA.

Ermine, W. (2007). Ethical space of engagement. *Indigenous Law Journal: Looking Forward: Paths to a New Relationship* 6(1): 193–203.

Fortier, C. (2017). *Unsettling the commons: Social movements within, against, and beyond settler colonialism.* Arbeiter Ring Publishing.

Hardison, P. *Indigenous Peoples and the Commons.* On the Commons, November 20th, 2006. www.onthecommons.org/indigenous-peoples-and-commons#sthash.BJAjNFvm.dpbs.

Indigenous Women of the Americas (2015). *Treaty in Defense of Mother Earth.* https://amazonwatch.org/assets/files/2015-09-28-defenders-of-mother-earth-treaty.pdf.

Jamieson, R. (2015). The key to making a city more Indigenous, keynote address presented at the *Walrus Talks*, Calgary. www.youtube.com/watch?v=H0r-oxXfHYI.

Manuel, A. and Grand Chief Ronald Derrickson. (2017). *The reconciliation manifesto: Recovering the land, rebuilding the economy.* James Lorimer and Company.

Porter, L. and J. Barry. (2016). *Planning for coexistence? Recognizing Indigenous rights through land-use planning in Canada and Australia.* Routledge.

Simpson, L. (2008). Looking after Gdoo-naaganinaa: Precolonial Nishnaabeg diplomatic and treaty relationships, *Wicazo Sa Review* 23(2): 29–42.

Wente, J. (2021). A story of joy: Reducing the harm so we can heal, online lecture presented at Vancouver Island University's annual *Indigenous Speakers Series* in partnership with Canadian Broadcasting Corporation (CBC) IDEAS.

4

THE BLACK COMMONS

A Framework for Recognition, Reconciliation, Reparations

Julian Agyeman and Kofi Boone

Setting the Stage: Coalescences

In September 2021, we are, in the USA, reflecting on a series of intersecting crises whose roots can be traced back to the colonialist and White Supremacist ideologies of slavery. Clint Smith's (2021) magisterial *How the Word Is Passed: A Reckoning with the History of Slavery Across America* lays out, across generations, the story of how slavery has been, and continues to be, central in shaping US collective history, and the histories of ourselves. The crises are intersecting in the sense that they are coalescing around the core issue of race, as many issues do in the USA.

We are, as of September 2021, beginning to emerge from a global pandemic. This period, marked by over 18 months of quarantines around the world, has forced critical reflection on the systems we have grown accustomed to for sustaining our lives. In both a global and US context, the COVID-19 pandemic response revealed and deepened profound societal disparities, inequities, and injustices. The murder of George Floyd by Minneapolis Police Officer Derek Chauvin in May 2020 (largely experienced through viewing a brutally visceral viral video) drove communities around the world, from Bristol, UK, to Sydney, Australia, into massive shows of outrage and protest. Additionally, we are recognizing the 100th anniversary of the 1921 Tulsa Massacre, a mass murder of Black people and their hopes and dreams, alongside the destruction of property in the city's Greenwood District, also known as The Black Wall Street.

All of these events, and others too many to mention that fly under the (social) media radar, have centered the persistence of systemic racism, inequality, and inequity throughout US society, as well as providing the impetus for grassroots, values-driven collective action to fill gaps that have been exacerbated by neoliberal rollbacks in government programs. The COVID-19 pandemic revealed US and global systemic inequities resulting in high infection

DOI: 10.4324/9781003199816-6

and death rates, as well as low health care access rates in Black, Indigenous and low-income communities. In response, we have witnessed "caremongering," communities mobilizing and forming systems of mutual aid to provide everything from childcare, to food and mobility access.

The murder of George Floyd propelled #BlackLivesMatter (BLM) into a major global social movement and the long-standing issues of lack of police accountability and the possibility of restorative justice to the forefront, providing national political pressure for criminal justice oversight and reform. And although acknowledging a seminal event from a different era, the increasing recognition of the horror of the Tulsa Massacre has also provided a boost toward thinking about a more equitable society. Each of these events, and the legacies of slavery that underpin them, on their own have had a devastating effect on US equity and justice issues, and which cumulatively, have been catastrophic. It is therefore legitimate to ask, as we do in this chapter, where we are today as a society, and what, if any, are the green shoots of optimism?

In this chapter we situate the Black Commons in the context of Sen's (1999; 2009) concept of capabilities which we see as the need for Black communities to build new kinds of wealth and wellbeing that can support our ability to thrive. We discuss definitions of growth, wealth, and wellbeing and argue for a reclamation of the idea of *Commonwealth* as a way of enabling human capabilities instead of extractive, consumption-based measures of wealth. We review historic precedents to the Black Commons including Black and Black-serving Cooperatives and Community Land Trusts (CLTs) and argue that they offer a foundation for sharing the values of mutual aid together with information sharing and building community sustainability. Thus, we argue, pooling individual resources into a common resource—a commons—was a strategy deployed by Black communities in the USA historically.

Since 2018, the Black Commons has been promoted by The Schumacher Center in the USA as a means of dismantling barriers to Black land ownership through the networked use of CLTs, and the creation of a just and regenerative economy (Witt 2018). The concept of a Black Commons can be expanded, as we do in this chapter, to include many cooperative forms of ownership, even extending into digital forms of production. We apply these ideas to equitable strategies for overcoming current racial justice challenges including the need for *recognition* of previous harms done, *reconciliation* with affected groups, and eventually *reparations* to compensate Black communities seeking to be made whole and sustainable.

Positionality Statement

We write this chapter as two African diasporic scholars who were born on both sides of the Atlantic Ocean; Julian in the UK, Kofi, in the USA. We acknowledge that we are settlers on Turtle Island, on a part also known as the USA. We are professors in Urban Planning (Julian) and Landscape Architecture (Kofi) at private (Julian) and public (Kofi) US universities. We are Black men who have worked our entire careers to transform how our disciplines address deep-seated inequities and injustices in planning and landscape with approaches that demonstrate the need to center equity and justice in commonly held notions of sustainability. In the pursuit of this key objective, we have had to grapple, personally and professionally, with many of the traumatic events of recent history. On a basic level, we acknowledge that our embodied experiences as Black men tie us to the ability of Black people to self-define and protect ourselves from external harms. The general lack of public protections from the harms of racial capitalism, settler/colonialism, and slavery through police brutality and mass incarceration have resulted in Black (and Indigenous) community identity formation that has relied on internal, communal, and mutual support. This includes building wealth in an exploitative capitalist structure; even in periods of extreme material deprivation.

Background and Theory

Wellbeing, a high quality of life for all, now and into the future, especially among those most disadvantaged in the US and elsewhere, is essential in achieving *just sustainabilities* (Agyeman 2013). Conventional economic growth, predicated on racial capitalism and resource extractivism, cannot be relied upon to deliver this for a number of reasons. First, there is increasing and serious doubt over the ability of the economy to continue to generate rates of growth adequate to allow for population growth and consumption increases (Harvey 2011). Second, there are potentially serious limits to the growth model arising from environmental factors (most notably the climate crisis). Finally, there is little evidence of a sustained relationship between economic growth as currently measured by Gross Domestic Product (GDP), and wellbeing, especially at higher levels of income and consumption, as was demonstrated in 1995, in the influential article by Cobb et al. in *The Atlantic*: "If the GDP Is Up, Why Is America Down?".

Institutions respond to the indicators they measure: politicians routinely promise GDP growth, call it "progress," and seek to deliver it regardless of the environmental or social consequences. In the USA and elsewhere, the beneficiaries of "growth" are typically the more affluent, while those who suffer the consequences in terms of environmental and social injustices are typically poor and Black, as evidenced by the growth of the Civil Rights Movement-aligned environmental and economic justice movements. A wide range of alternative indicators to GDP have been suggested, ones that attempt to measure what really matters to people. Typically, they either adjust economic measures such as the Index of Sustainable Economic Welfare (ISEW) (Jackson et al. 1997) or the Genuine Progress Indicator (GPI) (Cobb et al. 1999), or combine economic indicators with others, such as health and education, which affect Black lives disproportionately, to create a composite indicator such as the Human Development Index (HDI) (Klugman 2010). The ISEW adjusts GDP to take account of defensive expenditures on environmental protection and health care, and to value leisure and unpaid work (primarily carried out by women in the home). Some countries, notably New Zealand, are moving from solely measuring economic production to measuring people's wellbeing as well (Roy 2019).

Sen (1999; 2009) reminds us that justice is measured in more than consumption or even wellbeing. It is measured in *capabilities* and *freedoms* too. He also points out that with freedoms come accountabilities—in this case justifying state intervention, which has been rolled back, as a result of over 40 years of neoliberalism. The capabilities approach sees people as assets rather than burdens, invests in their capacities, and uses peer-support networks in addition to professionals, to transfer knowledge and capabilities. Further, Kretzmann and McKnight's (2005) development of the Community Asset Mapping process emphasizes documenting community relationships and potentials and was an intentional counter to the definition of assets and wealth solely as material possessions . Brown's Emergent Strategy goes further to challenge people to do assessments that include emotional and spiritual measures ranging from the personal to global scales (Brown 2017).

Clearly, for Black, communities of color, and low-income communities, for whom wealth accumulation has been a struggle either because of the theft of their land, home, and other resources, or because they've been deprived of the access, capabilities, and opportunities needed to accumulate intergenerational wealth, issues such as wellbeing, capabilities, and freedoms are critical. We would argue, through the idea of the Black Commons, that both these, and individual, collective, and intergenerational wealth accumulation are possible.

The term "Commonwealth" is most often used in a political sense and as a way of describing the political affiliation of a state or nation. In the case of the USA, scholars theorize that places like Virginia, Pennsylvania, and Massachusetts chose to self-identify as Commonwealths and states as a means of further distancing themselves from the monarchy from which they separated. However, the definition of "Commonwealth" has changed over time and Kohn's (2016) argument for the idea of an urban commonwealth aligns with some of the positions of this chapter. In *The Death and Life of the Urban Commonwealth*, Kohn questions why social goods need to be directly connected to the benefits of private property ownership and extends the definition of "commonwealth" to those social goods held in common. Social justice advocates argue that social goods shouldn't be distributed solely based on wealth gained from private property and wealth. Linking Kohn and Sen's ideas on social goods and capabilities, could result in a further redefinition of "commonwealth." Leveraging social goods held in common to resource the capabilities of Black communities, is not an idea without precedent.

The Commons

The term "commons" is used to describe a wide array of shared resources ranging from natural resources to digital information. Commons is an English word describing shared resources with equal interest (or stake) by each stakeholder. It derives from the Latin word *res communis*, used by the Roman empire to distinguish resources that were for everyone. The concept predates the English take on it, and can be found in many cultures around the world. But the role of England and Europe in establishing settler colonial land uses and patterns that treated land as property gives a focus to the use of the term "commons." From its beginnings, not all things were held in common. And the commons existed in the context of private property rights.

"The Tragedy of the Commons" is a well-known Malthusian critique of the commons (Hardin 1968). Hardin argued that in the absence of strong social controls and governance, shared resources become exploited by individual self-interests until they collapse. This concept had an impact on broader conversations about the need for strong top-down governance and penalties to prevent individual exploitation of shared resources. However, Ostrom, and many others, have rebuked Hardin's assumptions as Hobbesian and Malthusian, and presented numerous examples of local communities effectively managing shared resources without Hardin's heavy-handed prerequisites (Ostrom 1992). Not only are local communities capable of avoiding the depletion of shared resources without formal governance, their effectiveness demonstrates the ability of communities to engage in polycentric forms of organization infused with shared values and beliefs and not just laws and regulations. The Feminist Commons Movement emerged as a way to liberate women by uncoupling gendered definitions of work and household responsibilities from mainstream norms and processes.

Black Fugitivity and the Black Commons

Since European colonialism and the Transatlantic Slave Trade, African people and their descendants have grappled with maintaining and transforming their own identities within dehumanizing structures imposed by White Supremacist policies and actions. This has been reflected in open conflict and acts of rebellion against their oppressors. But this is also inclusive of countless acts of resistance where people engaged in activities that are reflective of a collective "dream of being elsewhere" (Hartman 2007). Harney and Moten (2013) have characterized the sum of these large and small acts of resistance as "Black Fugitivity" and in pursuit of life outside of the pathologies associated with Blackness in a settler colonial state. These acts included the fusions of imposed Christian faith with African traditions, sustaining African culinary traits in the Americas, and countless other attempts for self-definition embedded in the daily lives of the enslaved.

Concepts of shared land and property extended from this impulse to make spaces outside of Black pathologies. In one definition of the Black Commons, the commons was the place-based setting enabling these activities. The Black Commons, in a US context, has been discussed in historical context, but has garnered more attention since the 2000s. Roane (2018) situates it as a place of Black community engagement with practices sustaining Black cultural, material, and spiritual needs in the midst of the horrors of slavery. He cites the Yam Grounds as an early precedent focusing on the survival needs of enslaved Africans in early America. The grounds were subsistence agricultural plots created by enslaved African people within plantations as places where information, traditions, and other spiritual and material resources were shared. The Jamaican social theorist Sylvia Wynter (1971) called Yam Grounds "The Plot." Wynter has explained how these parcels of land were transformed into spiritual, communal areas where enslaved people could establish their own social order, sustain traditional African folklore and foodways—growing yams, cassava, and sweet potatoes.

The connection between food, land, power, spirituality, and cultural survival was subversive in its nature. By appropriating physical space to support collective growing practices within the heart of the brutal constraints of slavery (the plantation), Black people also demonstrated the need for common, shared mental, and spiritual space to enable their survival and resistance. Herbalism, medicine and midwifery, and other African American healing practices were seen as acts of resistance that were "intimately tied to religion and community," according to historian Sharla M. Fett (2000).

Following the end of the American Civil War in 1865, Reconstruction involved sweeping policy and resource redistribution strategies that included the Federal taking of land formerly held by members of the Confederacy and redistributing them to Black people. This program, often referred to erroneously as "40 acres and a mule" was fraught with crippling bureaucratic complexity and faced intense resistance by White southerners. Despite the hostile environment, Black people did acquire land, including land in what is now known as Oklahoma, and other parts of the American West.

Savi Horne, Executive Director of the Land Loss Prevention Project suggests that Black people in the USA during this time were trying to maintain pre-colonial African land rights traditions by continuing the practice of heir rights (Mendelson 2018). Heir rights mean that when a landowner dies, land ownership is divided evenly between all of the living heirs. However, this practice does not align with American legal land rights protections. Additionally, racial intimidation and White violence often prevented Black landowners from formally documenting their land rights or wills (if they had them). The lack of deeds and wills directly contributed to devastating Black land loss a century later. Today, Black farmers own less than 2 percent of all of the nation's farms, down from 14 percent in 1920, because of decades of racial violence and unfair lending and land ownership policies, translating into a land value loss of USD $1 trillion.

Reconstruction policies had uneven effectiveness and even those gains for Black people were contingent on Union soldiers occupying wide swathes of the American South to enforce societal change. President Andrew Johnson overrode Reconstruction policies and ordered the Federal government to return confiscated land to their original owners. Many other Reconstruction policies were ended and with the Compromise of 1877 and the removal of Union soldiers from the American South, Reconstruction ended, giving way to the Jim Crow Era, where state and local laws enforced racial segregation, especially in the Southern States, and elsewhere within the USA.

Black Cooperatives

Faced with legalized state and local racial discrimination, as well as the threat of lynching and White violence, Black people still pursued land, development, and settlements throughout the later 19th and early 20th centuries; much of which reflected the components of the Black Commons (Figure 4.1). Black churches and religious institutions were formed across the country. Many Black churches became places where communities pooled resources for shared benefit ranging from mutual aid and building funds, to the purchase of land. Nembhard (2014) catalogs the rapid expansion of these cooperatives acknowledging the critical role of research by WEB DuBois in codifying methods and promoting cooperatives as a cornerstone of Black community empowerment in the Jim Crow Era. This accelerated during "The Great Migration"; an era from 1916–1970, in which six million Black people migrated from the Jim Crow South to fast growing northern cities such as New York City, Chicago, Detroit, Los Angeles, Philadelphia, Pittsburgh, Cleveland, Baltimore, and Washington, D.C.

Black business districts emerged across the country in no small part due to the success of cooperative thinking and practice. The most famous, the Greenwood District of Tulsa Oklahoma, was, at its height, the most successful Black business district in the country and housed cooperative enterprises. The infamous Tulsa Race Riot of 1921 carried out by racist White residents of Tulsa resulted in the destruction of the Greenwood District and the murder of hundreds of Black people. However, it is important to note that the moniker "Black Wall Street" was not conferred to this district before the massacre; it received that title after thousands of Black people from across the country donated to the surviving Greenwood business owners who rebuilt the district after the riot. The Greenwood District was not the only Black Wall Street; another existed in Downtown Durham, North Carolina. Parrish Street was the home of North Carolina Mutual Life Insurance Company and Mechanics and Farmers Bank. Collectively, both businesses were key institutions resourcing Black cooperatives across the country and employing the most Black people in the country until the mid-20th century.

CAPABILITIES

FREEDOMS

FREEDOMS

INVESTMENTS

INVESTMENTS

"Commonwealth"

Social Goods held in
Common

INVESTMENTS

CAPABILITIES

CAPABILITIES

FREEDOMS

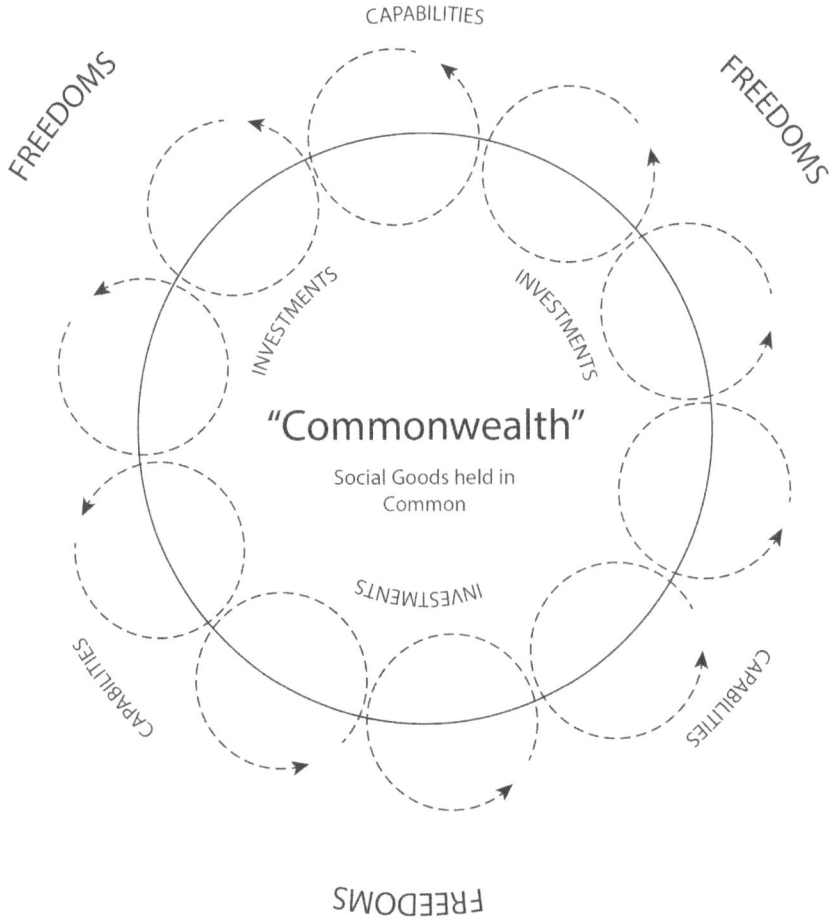

FIGURE 4.1 Components of the Black Commons

A Contemporary Form of Cooperation: Community Land Trusts

The land trust model is not unique to the concept of the Black Commons. It has appeared over time, and in different cultural contexts. Ebenezer Howard's (1898) *Garden Cities of Tomorrow*, theorized about the land trust as a means of social reform and provided allotments to working class people in England. In an American context, land trusts were first executed by White social reformers in northern states like New York and Ohio as a counterpoint to the exploitative land practices of industrial capitalists.

But in the context of the Black Commons, the formalization of CLTs in the USA is directly tied to the extension of the goals of the Modern Civil Rights Movement. Fannie Lou Hamer, leader of the Mississippi Freedom Party, envisioned cooperative ownership of livestock and land as a means of elevating the poorest Black Mississippians out of poverty. She and others created a "Pig Bank" where farmers could receive pigs, breed them, and return the piglets to a collective pool for others. This expanded into Mississippi Freedom Farms; 680 acres of land in rural Mississippi being owned and held in trust and used for living and working by Black farmers. The trust was conceived as a means of separating the cost of land ownership from the potential to gain resources from its cultivation. This land trust did not come to pass. But in southwest Georgia, Civil Rights pioneers Charles Sherrod and Robert Swann showed that CLTs were a means to move forward within the goals of economic justice, particularly in Black communities. In 1967, they and others formed the Schumacher Center for a New Economics and issued the first formal CLT policy. Today, it remains the foundation for countless CLTs across the country.

Out of this came the Schumacher Center's proposal, The Black Commons (Witt 2018). It puts forth an ambitious strategy for greatly expanding the scale and impact CLTs can have on Black communities. They propose a national entity acting as a fiduciary for non-contiguous land donations to a national trust. Often CLTs are controlled by local boards. In this approach, those local boards would need to coordinate in a national network and participate in collaboration with the national fiduciary institution. The land loss challenges that have already afflicted rural Black communities are being magnified in the current wave of rapid urbanization, city growth, and gentrification/displacement. Extending and connecting the CLT model, along with solidarity economy initiatives as described in regard to local food systems in Boston, by Loh and Agyeman (2018), could have far-reaching positive impacts by bringing the benefits of collective land ownership to scale with countervailing capitalist efforts.

Perhaps the foremost example of CLTs and the Black Commons, is The Dudley Street Neighborhood Initiative (DSNI) which straddles the Roxbury–Dorchester line in Boston, MA. DSNI is an excellent example of what can happen when non-profit organizations understand that the framing of their activism should be proactive and based on a vision of place as a commons. In fact, the center of the neighborhood is called *Dudley Town Common*. This is a vision that sees not "community deficits" but rather "community assets," and capabilities, in Sen's (2009) sense. Medoff and Sklar (1994), who chronicled the DSNI effort in their book "Streets of Hope," call this "holistic development": a combination of human, economic, and environmental development.

DSNI's 34-member board of directors is diverse, with equal representation of the community's four major cultures (and therefore historical narratives of place): African American, Cape Verdean, Latinx, and White. It works to implement resident-driven plans with partners including community development corporations (CDCs), other non-profit organizations and religious institutions serving the neighborhood, banks, government agencies, businesses, and foundations. It was formed in 1984 when residents of the Dudley Street area came together out of fear and anger to revive their neighborhood, which was nearly devastated by arson, disinvestment, neglect, and redlining practices, and to protect it from outside speculators. DSNI is the only community-based non-profit organization in the USA that has been granted eminent domain authority over abandoned land within its boundaries. However, it soon realized that retaining community-driven development would not be sufficient to halt the kind of gentrification that displaces residents in other parts of Boston. DSNI's solution was the creation of a CLT, Dudley Neighbors, Inc. (DNI), which uses a 99-year ground lease[1] that restricts resale prices in order to keep the land available for affordable housing. It protects 30 acres of community-controlled land with 98 permanently affordable homes, urban farm sites, parks and open space, and commercial properties for use by local small businesses, non-profit organizations, and affordable rental housing providers.

Another contemporary example of a Black CLT includes Seattle's Africatown CLT ("We are here not for income, but for outcome"). It was developed to acquire, steward, and develop the land assets needed for the Black/African diaspora community to grow and thrive in place in Seattle's rapidly gentrifying Central District. It also supports other individuals and organizations in retaining and developing land. In June 2020, the City announced it would transfer a decommissioned fire station to the Africatown CLT, saying "we understand the urgency behind making bold investments in the Black community and increasing community ownership of land" (Roseland and Boone 2020). The building is slated to become the William Grose Center for Enterprise and Cultural Innovation, a long-planned incubator for Black-owned businesses. The development could include meeting rooms, technology labs, and maker spaces, along with up to 20 units of housing for young adults.

Roseland and Boone (2020) note that "as cities reflect on their roles in perpetuating institutional racism and what they can do to relieve it, they can use their zoning laws and negotiating power to support CLTs, as one way to keep housing affordable and benefit minority communities." There are now roughly 225–280 CLTs in the USA (not all Black-focused), which include 15,000 home ownership units and 20,000 rental units. Incentivizing this cooperative development, New York City passed a bill in 2017 exempting CLTs from certain taxes and in 2019, Houston announced a plan to use a CLT to develop 1,000 affordable units.

It would be remiss of us not to mention another form of cooperation and commons: the digital commons. Organizations such as #BlackLivesMatter and the Movement for Black Lives are demonstrating a renewed vigor around collective action and a blueprint for how this can be achieved in a digital age. At the same time, Black Americans are also forging a "cultural commons" through events such as DJ D-Nice's Club Quarantine—a hugely popular online dance party. Club Quarantine's success indicates the potential for using online platforms to facilitate community building, pointing toward future economic cooperation.

Recognition, Reconciliation and … Reparations?

The previous eras we have described show how the adaptive/coping mechanisms of Black people working in common have been used to claim spaces, sustain spirituality, gain wealth and political power, and build social cohesion. How can these ideas and mechanisms be used to build equitable strategies for overcoming our current, pressing racial justice challenges? Here we focus on the three Rs: the need for *recognition* of previous harms done, the need for *reconciliation* with affected groups, and eventually some form of *reparations* to compensate Black communities seeking to be made whole and sustainable.

Recognition

Increasingly important is the concept of recognition: recognizing and respecting another human, their status, and rights. A similar concept is that of a Land Acknowledgment with respect to Indigenous lands. Clearly, in the context of this chapter, recognition, first, of Black trauma as we have described it, and second, the varied concerns and barriers Black people face in participating in traditional economic activity, is critical. Broader examples of recent US-inspired, but now international justice movements focused on recognition include #BlackLivesMatter, the #NeverAgain movement fighting gun violence in the USA, and the #MeToo movement that promotes gender equality and campaigns against sexual harassment.

After taking office, US President Joseph Biden issued an Executive Order On Advancing Racial Equity and Support for Underserved Communities Through the Federal Government (White House 2021). This Executive Order, a form of recognition, requests that all Federal agencies develop racial equity assessments and measures within a year of the Order. This Order does not solely focus on Black people and communities. Instead, it aggregates Black communities into "underserved communities"; "populations sharing a particular characteristic, as well as geographic communities, that have been systematically denied a full opportunity to participate in aspects of economic, social, and civic life." The move made by the Executive branch of the US government to recognize Racial Equity at the community scale is unprecedented. The Executive Order recognizes systemic inequities and the role government resources play in sustaining them. However, the Executive Order's focus on "equality of opportunity" in some ways distances the effort from *equity*: explicitly connecting contemporary strategies to the specific historical context of Black community underdevelopment.

Reconciliation[2]

Once a harmed group has been recognized, as Biden's Executive Order does, the process of reconciliation can start. The exact line between reconciliation and reparations can be blurred, but we want to offer up the USD $1.2 trillion Infrastructure Bill pending before Congress, with USD $550 billion in new spending, as a form of reconciliation. Roads, bridges, expanding rail and public transit networks, improving water infrastructure, upgrading electric power grids, improving broadband networks, replacing lead pipes, and boosting traffic safety are all important. However, it is in the specific funds to remove racist infrastructures—such as the highways that were built with the *specific intention* of isolating Black neighborhoods, that we find the truest alignment with the notion of reconciliation. But, although Biden has proposed USD $20 billion for reconnecting neighborhoods isolated by historical federal highway construction, the bill delivered only USD $1 billion for these efforts—enough to help only a few places.

In 2014 Rochester, New York, the city buried nearly a mile of the Inner Loop East, which served as a barrier, isolating the city's downtown from Black neighborhoods. Since then, the city has reconnected streets that were divided by the highway, making the neighborhood whole again. Other cities that have removed or are removing highways dividing Black neighborhoods from other amenities include Cincinnati, Chattanooga, Detroit, Houston, Miami, New Orleans, and St. Paul.

The challenge with many of these efforts is that, although reconciliation via physical infrastructure is advancing, reconciliation to mitigate economic exploitation manifesting in gentrification and displacement is not. The ties between public investment and its impact on rising adjacent private property values is well known. In New Orleans, grassroots resistance to plans for converting part of Claibourne Avenue in the Treme neighborhood from elevated urban freeway to at-grade boulevard was driven by the lack of provisions protecting the community from the real estate speculation and gentrification that can happen after freeway removal (Reckdahl 2018). The next frontier of reconciliation could be to learn from the legacies of cooperatives, CLTs, and other approaches to building local community organization and wealth in the face of transformative infrastructure investments.

Reparations

There is much debate over the nature, extent, type, and eligibility for reparations which, for the purposes of this chapter, we are characterizing through Sen's capabilities theory as *restoring and sustaining the capability to succeed*. MORE (Mayors Organized for Reparations and Equity) is a mayoral coalition that believes "cities can—and should—act as laboratories for bold ideas that can be transformative for racial and economic justice on a larger scale, and demonstrate for the country how to pursue and improve initiatives that take a reparatory approach to confronting and dismantling structural and institutional racism." Three cities, Evanston, IL, Providence, RI, and Asheville, NC, have begun exploring what this might look like. The mayors of the latter two cities are MORE members.

Evanston will pay reparations available to eligible Black residents for what it describes as harm caused by "discriminatory housing policies and practices and inaction on the city's part." The program is believed to be the first of its kind in the USA and is seen by advocates as a potential national model. Providence has released a "truth-telling" report representing the first phase of a three-phase initiative announced by Mayor Jorge Elorza in July 2020. It chronicles the history of racial injustice against Black and Indigenous People over 400 years, as a first step toward understanding how best to provide reparations to those communities for the trauma they've suffered. In June 2021, Asheville City Council voted to appropriate USD $2.1 million of the proceeds from the sale of City-owned land at 172 and 174 South Charlotte Street to fund community reparations. A portion of this property includes land the City purchased in the 1970s through Urban Renewal of East End/Valley Street.

The Asheville case reveals the limits of existing political and economic structures in conceiving and achieving reparations. Their plan has been criticized locally as a rebranding of existing policy initiatives already within existing structures of power. Allocating funds from the sale of publicly owned parcels is a good first step in developing a sustainable resource base from which to support reparative work. However, the sum is minuscule in the face of historic harms done to Black communities in Asheville, especially through urban renewal and freeway construction. Current proponents of reparations are moving their claims up, from equity, to justice, to liberation. As a process of resourcing structures that are designed to help harmed Black communities succeed now, current efforts at reparations clearly have a long way to go to define, nurture, and sustain Black capabilities and longer-term wellbeing.

While cities are a natural scale for reparations, companies such as Tacoma's Sacred Design Lab can lead the way. As part of their collective liberation efforts, they have committed to a reparational payment of 24.4 percent to all contractors and employees who are descended from African people who were enslaved in the USA and Caribbean.

The Black Commons: Scaling Up, Scaling Out, Scaling Deep

In the face of centuries of oppression, exploitation, and violence, but also moments of progress and reform, how can we learn from the rich legacy of Black community building as a means to inform the broader project of forming a Black Commons?

In late 2021, there are place-based "islands" of good practice as we showed above, but they are interspersed within seas of indifference. There are concerned groups of mayors, such as MORE, but again, they are in a minority. But there are many governments around the country, such as Seattle, using racial equity screens to ensure that their policy and planning centers these issues. There are non-profit organizations such as Boston's DSNI, or Atlanta's Partnership for Southern Equity working toward the goal of a Black Commons, even if this is implicit, rather than explicit in their work.

Clearly, a bold vision for a thriving and enduring Black Commons would connect this good, already existing, community-based work, bringing it to light, to a wider audience. Perhaps a Black Commons Working Group, building on the Schumacher Center and MORE's work, made up of representatives from city governments and major non-profit organizations could look at what it would take, financially and institutionally, to scale these ideas up such that they affect laws, policies, and institutions; impact more cities and more people, and moreover, change cultural values, beliefs, and ultimately hearts and minds (Moore, Riddell, and Vocisano 2015).

Ultimately however, the Black Commons, in addition to the work suggested above, also requires a nationwide process that begins with a national conversation on recognition, reconciliation, and reparations which would be, in effect, a truth and reconciliation process such as those held in South Africa and Canada. In light of the "culture wars" raging in the USA, we don't see this happening within the next few years. However, the goals of treating each other in humane ways, being empathetic to the needs of others, and affording each other the dignity of personhood are more important than ever, in personal, policy, and political realms.

Notes

1 Terms such as these represent a real forward step compared to what is currently available, but clearly fall far short of Seven Generation Cities' thinking that we highlight in this book.
2 We recognize that "reconciliation" has a particular meaning in South Africa and Canada where there have been Truth & Reconciliation Commissions.

References

Agyeman, J. (2013). *Introducing just sustainabilities: Policy, planning and practice*. Zed Books.

Brown, A. (2017). *Emergent strategy: Shaping change, changing worlds*. AK Press.

Cobb C., G. S. Goodman, and M. Wackernagel. (1999). *Why bigger isn't better: The genuine progress indicator—1999 update*. Redefining Progress.

Fett, S. M. (2000). *Working cures: Healing, health, and power on Southern Slave Plantations*. UNC Press.

Hardin, G. (1968). The tragedy of the commons. *Science* 162(3859): 1243–1248.

Harney, S. and Moten, F. (2013). *The undercommons: Fugitive planning & Black study*. Autonomedia.

Hartman, S. V. (2007). *Lose your mother: A journey along the Atlantic slave route*. Farrar, Straus and Giroux.

Harvey, D. (2011) *The enigma of capital and the crises of capitalism*. Revised edition. Profile.

Howard, E. (1898). *Garden cities of to-morrow*. Swan Sonnenschein & Co.

Jackson, T., N. Marks, J. Ralls, and S. Stymne. (1997). *An index of sustainable economic welfare for the UK 1950–1996*. Centre for Environmental Strategy, University of Surrey.

Klugman, J. (2010). *Human Development Report 2010: 20th anniversary edition. The Real Wealth of Nations: Pathways to human development*. United Nations Development Programme (UNDP).

Kohn, M. (2016). *The death and life of the urban commonwealth*. Oxford University Press.

Kretzmann, J. and J. McKnight J. (2005). *Discovering community power: A guide to mobilizing local assets and your organization's capacity*. Asset-Based Community Development (ABCD) Institute.

Loh, P. and J. Agyeman. (2018). Urban food sharing and the emerging Boston food solidarity economy. *Geoforum* 99: 213–222. https://doi.org/10.1016/j.geoforum.2018.08.017

Medoff, P. and H. Sklar. (1994). *Streets of hope: The fall and rise of an urban neighborhood*. South End Press.

Mendelson, S. (2018). Pursuing social justice on the farm with Savi Horne and the Land Loss Prevention Project. *Good Food Jobs*. November 20, 2018. www.goodfoodjobs.com/blog/pursuing-social-justice-on-the-farm-with-savi-horne-and-the-land-loss-prevention-project/.

Moore, M., D. Riddell, and D Vocisano. (2015). Scaling out, scaling up, scaling deep: Advancing systemic social innovation and the learning processes to support it. *The Journal of Corporate Citizenship* 58: 67–84. www.jstor.org/stable/jcorpciti.58.67.

Nembhard, J. G. (2014). *Collective courage: A history of African American cooperative economic thought and practice*. The Pennsylvania State Press.

Ostrom, E. (1992). Governing the Commons: The evolution of institutions for collective action, *Natural Resources Journal* 32(2): 415.

Reckdahl, K. (2018). A divided neighborhood comes together under an elevated expressway. *Next City*. August 20, 2018. https://nextcity.org/features/view/a-divided-neighborhood-comes-together-under-an-elevated-expressway.

Roane, J. T. (2018). Plotting the Black Commons. *Souls* 20(3): 239–266. https://doi.org/10.1080/10999949.2018.1532757.

Roseland, M. and C. Boone. (2020). Community land trusts could help heal segregated cities. *The Conversation*, September 10, 2020. https://theconversation.com/community-land-trusts-could-help-heal-segregated-cities-144708.

Roy, E. (2019). New Zealand's world-first "wellbeing" budget to focus on poverty and mental health. *The Guardian*. May 14, 2009. www.theguardian.com/world/2019/may/14/new-zealands-world-first-wellbeing-budget-to-focus-on-poverty-and-mental-health.

Sen, A. (1999). *Development as freedom*. Alfred A. Knopf.

Sen, A. (2009). *The idea of justice*. Allen Lane.

Smith, C. (2021). *How the word is passed: A reckoning with the history of slavery across America*. Little, Brown and Company.

The White House. (2021). *Executive order on advancing racial equity and support for underserved communities through the Federal Government*. January 20, 2021. www.whitehouse.gov/briefing-room/presidential-actions/2021/01/20/executive-order-advancing-racial-equity-and-support-for-underserved-communities-through-the-federal-government/.

Witt, S. (2018). Proposal for a "Black Commons." *Schumacher Center for a New Economics*. January 2018. https://centerforneweconomics.org/wp-content/uploads/2018/01/Proposal-w-summary-Black-Commons-.pdf.

Wynter, S. (1971). Novel and history, plot and plantation. *Savacou* 5: 95–102.

5

(UN)SITUATED IMPROVISATION

AbdouMaliq Simone

Unsettled Arrangement

This chapter is an attempt to address a critical question of contemporary urban living across many regions of the so-called Global South: What does it mean for inhabitants to collaborate, to operate in some semblance of collectivity as they spend more of their time in motion? Drawing upon an ethnographic vignette from Jakarta, I think through this question with some local idioms that point to the quasi-sacral dimensions of shifting the capacity to witness, to see anew where one has come from, and to extend the capacities of that place through particular practices of movement.

Our imaginations of collective life tend to gravitate toward people gathered together in place, or tied together in complementary actions with a simultaneity that approximates the sense of such gathering. Such imaginations still inform the activation of political technologies and their tropes of democratic deliberation, consensus, where everyone plays their part for the attainment of shared political goals.

But as the trajectories of urban life's transformation increasingly alter the very underpinnings of the collective sociality with which we are familiar, there is a need to supplement these conventional understandings with notions of more feral, dispersed, and provisional collectivities whose forms and objectives are not settled as urban inhabitants increasingly live through structurally unsettling situations in unsettled ways (Berlant 2016; Jensen 2015; Escobar 2008; Esteva 2015; Moten and Harney 2013). Here, rather than cultivating lives worth living *in place*, increasing numbers of residents in the Global South are, for the moment, investing in lives *out of place*, prioritizing the elaboration of itineraries of circulating through the urban. This is not just movement here to there, but ways of moving through different spaces, experiences, people, and possibilities. The objective is to defer definitive emplacement in specific territories, in order to piece together contexts in which to operate—to generate income, acquire different kinds of knowledge, take advantage of particular institutional and social affordances, to avoid excessive obligations and dependencies (Furniss 2016; Clare 2019). We seek to discover how to move around particular urban regions, or among them, in order to best situate oneself in order to take advantage of the right opportunity at the right time. This is an

DOI: 10.4324/9781003199816-7

opportunity that is not so much planned for, not so much the function of mapping or even anticipation, but concretized only through actually moving around, or rather, circulating (Caldeira 2012; Fallov, Jørgensen, and Knudsen 2013).

This does not mean that the aspiration of a settled life is any less important. Rather, just not for now. While there remains a need to have a place to sleep, anchor children and schooling, "park" aged parents, store things, and fulfill the bureaucratic necessities of having an address, the aim is often to fulfill these functions with a minimal level of investment and commitment. This is not to shed the responsibilities of social reproduction or to concentrate it within the scope of a particular number or kind of household members, but an orientation that disperses the household across multiple sites and social networks, where each site operates as a hedge against the insufficiencies of the others, or conversely, as ways in which to extend the potentialities incumbent in any one location.

De Boeck and Baloji (2016) describe how poor families in Kinshasa speculate on where the city is headed by investing in small parcels of land often great distances apart, and that require inordinate amounts of labor in order to access and manage. Given all the things that households have to attend to in order to evaluate the efficacy of any livelihood strategy or social arrangement, "bad" decisions or placing "all of one's eggs in one basket" risk a failure more debilitative than perhaps was once the case. Calculating how particular kinds of work address particular kinds of living arrangements, transportation costs, domestic consumptions, investment in education, health coverage, untoward social exposure, local political atmospheres, and care infrastructures often lead households not to balance out expenditures in a single location, but to extend household functioning across a variety of spaces in order to facilitate access, forge complementarity among diverse livelihood activities, and reduce costs (Yotebieng and Forcone 2018; Kopper 2019).

While Southern urban contexts have long been replete with extended household systems, with their circulation of members, collaborative economic arrangement and support systems, these entailed the multiplicity of nodes largely consolidated within specific places. Children would be sent to live with an uncle or aunt, for example, whose official residency enabled them to access better schools or employment. Cycles of visitation and gathering were critical aspects for the exchange of information and support. Additionally, extended families were often rooted all together in specific locations that enabled them to consolidate businesses availed to multiple family members and exert significant influence in the governance of local affairs. While such arrangements certainly endure, individual families tend to extend their own operations across multiple territories, which often is occasioned by the dissipation of substantive extended family ties. Here, mutual kinship obligations become oppressive burdens and overwhelm the economic capacities of particular family networks. Particularly as land politics become increasingly cutthroat and dispossessing, family conflicts around land and property generate rifts not easily repaired (Plueckhahn and Bayartsetseg 2018).

The dispersals of households have clear impacts on collective life, as households face both reduced time and resources to commit to developing locally based solidarities and neighborhood relations. While such practices may remain incumbent to the roles of particular household members, who may continue to participate in local religious and social institutions, savings clubs, and support networks, these often deeply gendered roles inevitably have to be counterbalanced with the increased labor intensity of a household management that is extended across a plurality of situations and challenges. The intensified complexity of everyday exigencies subjects local institutions to more individualized instrumentalities—i.e., the ways in which individuals engage collective experiences as a means of furthering particular agendas and self-aggrandizement (Gago 2017; Gandolfo 2018; Thieme 2018).

Additionally, the hard-won struggles of some urban residents to concretize their rights to settlement, formalize land tenure, own a house, and be full citizens of a particular urban locality have often meant their emplacement in locations of urban regions far from where the "economic action" is now located, or within built environments that remain under-serviced, under-repaired, and which exude the atmosphere of being marginal to the life of the city. In such instances, a younger generation of residents is increasingly disinterested to stay put. Without the means to definitively relocate to other parts of the city, the original residence is maintained simply as a place from which to launch repeated forays elsewhere, thus imbuing those original places with a heightened sense of provisionality.

In part, this emphasis on circulation and extending households is based purely on volition. It emanates from the sense that no matter how valuable and familiar particular living situations might be, they will soon prove inadequate to what is required to sustain urban residence. But often, residents are unclear about what exactly will be required, unclear about exactly where things are headed. While in the past many residents have sold land holdings in the urban core, taken part of the money and invested in locations in the urban periphery while retaining the rest to either invest in other kinds of assets or to establish savings, sometimes for the first time, there has been a shift in emphasis in recent years toward deferring such decisions. In part, this is because the promise of new, well-serviced settlements at the periphery have never materialized, often rapidly deteriorate, or prove untenable in terms of managing transportation needs, Additionally, the trajectory of substantive opportunity and economic growth follow corridors that end up circumventing many of these peripheral developments (Keil 2018).

Even in more stable, middle-class-oriented neighborhoods, pressures of various sorts impinge upon the confidence of residents. Here, historically, households forewent holding on to long traditions of making-do, of the rambunctious, irreverent sociality that characterized everyday relations, the wheeling and dealing that composed specific domains and practices of work and accumulation in favor of the modes of respectability that were proffered as the tickets to middle class attainment. Organizing life around heteronormative, nuclear families ensuring the proper upbringing and education of children and the performance of disciplined comportment that reigned in the more carnivalesque features of everyday sentience were the signs of eligibility for accumulation. But after several generations of such respectability, manifested in measured moves to urban suburbs, while grandparents remained in the original neighborhoods, and the consolidation of middle-class status—often through jobs in public bureaucracies—there is anxiety about what all of this respectability and accumulation really means. Through a multiplicity of small trading activities, micro-investments, and improvised social gathering, many of those who left these urban core districts, return to it as a space of play and operations. While there may be no place to reside, or only places of temporary stay in the majority of residential buildings now converted to hostels, they are engaged as arenas of recouping the transgressive behaviors that were relinquished, recuperating sensibilities of disregard to property, to careers, to status, which are now seen as tactical advantages to identify new ways of being in cities where steady employment wanes, costs increase, and general dissatisfaction grows.

Extracting the Collective

It is important to keep in mind how many residents have been pushed to the limits, pushed out of familiar ways of working, pushed out of their homes and neighborhoods. Collective life is then also pushed, extended beyond the configuration of defined entities. In response, residents may have continuously *pushed* their particular agendas and aspirations, but were willing to be indifferent to them as well (Tadiar 2013).

This is because endurance was an atmosphere of abiding, of a willingness to "stand by" various trajectories of possible futures. "Stand by," both in the sense of waiting to see how things unfolded as well as a commitment to see through various initiatives to improve livelihoods and environment; a willingness to operate "in reserve," prepared to make something out of dispositions seemingly out of their control (Escobar 2018).

A process of extracting from popular collective efforts is increasingly enacted through technical operations. These are all of the specific interventions that impact directly on the "sensibility" of the overall environment, generating a subjectivity that is not bound to any particular subject or clear-cut representations of what is going on. It is aimed, for example, at how and where people walk, the loads and occupations that buildings can bear, the way spaces are designed to frame particular ways of seeing and paying attention, densities of sound that obscure or heighten discernment, and goods that are shifted across locations, and types of consumption (McFarlane 2016). What transpires is an "unmaking" materialized by taking the ways people speak, the kinds of buildings they live in, the corridors along which they move, the codes by which they manage various relations, the sacrifices they make to get ahead, the risks they take in order to ensure opportunities become probabilities. These probabilities are then to be addressed by specific media content, policy, political messages, or social engineering (Beller 2018).

In many ways, Jakarta reflects the convergence of all of these considerations. Everyday life proceeds within a multiplicity of apparently contradictory trajectories. The complexities of managing inhabitation within narrowing bounds of available support and upon terrain subjected to intense environmental crises, massive overbuilding, seemingly unlimited territorial expansion, and patchworked governance, propel many households into identifications with the more conservative forms of Islam. A preponderant image is that of the "happy Muslim family"—incessantly documented with Instagram photos and WhatsApp testimonials. Well-educated women consign themselves to domestic kitchen enterprises, contributing to an almost infinite inventory of online sales of baked goods. The actual loss of household income through subtracting larger numbers of women from the labor market is compensated by attempts to reduce household expenditures, the ramifications of which can be felt across the urban economy. Through other trajectories, the less Islamically inclined—not in terms of religious devotion but in the adherence to specific lifestyles—are ensconced in an interminable restlessness, often holding down multiple jobs, participating in scams, taking on subcontracts and freelance work, and moving across various improvised gatherings at 7–11 shops, coffee houses, and informal eating places late into the night amidst various compositions of friends, strangers, and associates in an often frenzied process of scheming, plotting, and exchanging.

Circulations across the Belt Black

At Jakarta's vast and increasingly dense peripheries, the contiguities of discrepant spatial functions and built environments largely remain unrelated, in contrast to the thick social relations-based economies of popular districts in the urban core. It is the various itineraries of circulation across these discrepant spaces that largely bestows some measure of coherence—i.e., the lines drawn between migrant hostels, agricultural workers, fabricators of everyday items, scavengers, security guards, and retail workers that forge temporary complicities to forge local economies based on moving things around and repurposing the large volumes of underused or dilapidating spaces for "hit-and-run" operations of all kinds.

Disparate tenure regimes, fragmented governance structures, competing "mafia" organizations, and vast amounts of foreign direct investment into mega-residential developments and industrial zones often remain unsettled in terms of how they actually function, as if they exist in parallel universes. Many of these projects remain under-utilized or their efficacy seems only to exist on paper. In these peripheries or urban extensions, residents seem to continuously hunt for new partners, new games, and rarely settle into specific jurisdictions, constituencies, or styles of work. Collective organizations rely upon constant improvisation that enables them to raise money for a particular charitable event, that forces through the repair of leaking roofs in migrant dorms, eliminates shakedowns of workers on payday, or manages to convert an unused shophouse into a temporary day-care center. But these are largely one-off victories, just effective enough to carry them through to the next problem, but without altering the overall scheme of things.

In contrast to the past, when young people held on to any job or vocation they could find, there is an inclination now toward the temporary. If things don't look to be heading in preferred directions; if there doesn't seem to be real prospects for advancement, the youth tend to move on, look elsewhere, as they circulate through various types of employment, accruing what they can in terms of skills and contacts, and then trying to marshal them into advanced credibility somewhere else. Charting the itineraries of scores of young people from the "black belt" of Jakarta's urban core—i.e., the popular districts of Tanah Tinggi, Kampung Rawa, and Galur, with whom I have worked for over a decade, there are discernible patterns of circulation focused on *spiraling*. Most of the time, it is young men that venture out of these districts, but increasingly young women are also part of this pattern. Often, they will pick a nearby commercial center, shopping mall, market, or small industrial zone where casual jobs can often be found, along with a bed in a boarding house. They, too, will assess the opportunities offered to them in whatever job they have chosen to do, and in particular, pay attention to what others around them have to say. Usually, they will take up residence within a short radius of their home but often temporarily settling in a district close to where their home is located.

They experiment with living in the variety of outskirt locations relative to their original home. They familiarize themselves with the area and then venture further into more unfamiliar terrains. Such behavior means that they initially stay close to home without necessarily being easily located by family or associates. In the process they cross paths with others who have their own itineraries. It is at these encounters where conflicts might sometimes occur, where the women's efforts to secure temporary residence become intensely competitive. Unlike gang conflicts that focus on the consolidation and defense of territory, the women's conflicts are focused on their schedules, their ability to secure temporary circuits of passage, and of young people literally caught in a crossfire of competing aspirations as they attempt to secure temporary ways to keep going.

In Jakarta jargon, *spiral* refers to sex without commitment—a connotation anchored in reference to IUD contraception. Extending the notion of the spiral as sex without commitment, spiral here is a way of accumulating jobs, money, experience, and information without commitment. It is a way to venture into the wider world where the real opportunities may be found. But it is never clear exactly *where* they are to be found. More importantly, such opportunities, whatever they are, are not to be approached head-on, but rather in a more indirect way. It is about trying to have a broad perspective on things, and this is based on looking at the familiar terrain from different angles, and then making the immediately unfamiliar more familiar as one heads outward. It doesn't mean that the youth from these districts only navigate the city in this manner, or that they will live their lives by this kind of circumnavigation alone. To spiral is one of many ways of doing things. But in Jakarta an entire infrastructure has grown around it, a practice of mobility supported by cheap boarding house rooms and food stalls, cheap places to hear the conversations of strangers, to be enticed into various schemes and projects that mostly never materialize but which also never cease to be offered and tried out. At the same time these practices are seen less as individual projects but rather as a collective, even civic responsibility. They encapsulate not only their own aspirations but those of their "hoods."

Indrawan:

> At first I was delivering pampers (drug packets) for the cops because they had me boxed in with some fake charges and it was part of them trying to break up this Kota Paris [*district in Tangi Tinggi*] operation, and one of the sub-bosses decided to try and make an example out of me so I had to leave, but meanwhile I had learned a little bit of the cop's operations around the area and managed to rip off a pretty big supply of stuff that I could sell to raise some money, and then there were these guys in the market of Johar Bahru who were selling in their clothes stall, so I helped them set up a delivery service and got rewarded with managing another cellphone store they rented. I didn't know much about phones or anything but I started to practice and found all of the ways you can put things on the internet to sell and stuff, so after a while I finally made it to the Ambassador (large electronic market) where they make all kinds of prototypes on cheap software, and then I was going around helping small shops install the stuff.

It is well known that Indonesians are the world's most prolific users of social media, and for these youths, the constant use of WhatsApp and Instagram provides a medium that continually repositions their physical location to align with the oscillating networks of contacts, gossip, advice, and images. As their bodies literally circulate across Jakarta, their texts and photos circulate back and forth, opening up beckoned calls for returns back home where situations have changed, invitations to join parties which have been quickly organized, or warnings to take detours around hot spots which might be best avoided at that particular time. More importantly, such media fuels conversations which can cover a multitude of disparate topics including politics, ghosts, genetics, spaceships, microchips, Muslim minutia, porn sex, automated vehicles, medical cures, and housing finance.

The youth hesitate; they wait, but not for long, just long enough to build up enough confidence to make the next move without overwhelming themselves with anxiety, without rushing home. It doesn't mean that they don't know how to play their part when they need to, play being the youth from the black belt who know where the drugs are, know the police that can be bought off, know where to get discount prices for almost anything, or know where to get things fixed cheaply.

This performance comes in handy when they find themselves hanging out in some of Jakarta's key gravitational nodes—such as the strategically located and super heterogeneously mixed housing project, Kalibata City, with its scores of coffee shops and small eating places. This is where journalists, artists, non-governmental organizations (NGO) staff, designers, freelance workers, musicians, and young aspiring entrepreneurs often converge, where they tirelessly gather to propose different projects, moneymaking schemes, and DIY urban interventions, and where the particular capacities of the black belt often come in handy in order to keep costs down or acquire something to lure investors, grease wheels, facilitate favorable outcomes.

But again, black belt youth do not want to get stuck in this role; they don't want to be simply adjuncts to the competencies of others. But through these professionals and hipsters, they learn more about where the venues of value are located. Afterward, some may pour over YouTube videos learning the vernaculars of particular ascendant trades, such as baristas, apartment brokers, or app designers. Most will never secure something in these areas but the attempt trying is added to an expanding repertoire of knowledge exhibited in some of the most menial jobs to their advantage as everyone in Jakarta appears increasingly restless to do something more with what they have. There are, for example, youths who end up as sales clerks or porters in the massive retail markets, who quickly demonstrate how stall owners, distributors, fabricators, and contractors can maximize their yield. While they, themselves, may never become the big players in the marketing game, they demonstrate a particular acuity in manipulating small differences, know how to rescale their poor wages in such a way as to increase their free time and access to other opportunities.

While this incessant self-refashioning through circulation may reiterate the familiar neo-liberal game of constantly having to improve oneself, what's different here is that the spiraling is also a matter of collective positions, of knowing how to be part of an assembly of contacts and friends that one has gathered along the itineraries of movement and where one has also been the target of such gathering. The spiral is about knowing how to make the *shift*, which in Islamic vernaculars of *hijra*, becomes a religious responsibility to move the terms of one's life so that the place where one comes from—one's extended family and community—might be availed a different, perhaps better world in which to operate. This shift, through the practice of the spiral then comes to represent a distribution of care, information exchange, locational advantages, points of access, refuge, and destination. None of these are ever fixed over time, but still make up a matrix of resourcefulness that may not restructure the conditions of precarious work and life, but constitute a hedge against it, a way of enduring with it. Importantly, it means that the black belt doesn't remain simply a swathe of defined territory, a simmering mass of uncertain density awaiting implosion and subsequent urban regeneration that the majority of inhabitants will never be a part of.

While *spiraling* points to a medium of collective life in circulation, *compression* indicates a mode of collectivity within the context of provisional settlement. Within the uncertain, intermediary spaces of facing unsettling conditions in places of origin or long-term attachment and deferring definitive resettlement as something that is more widely considered as premature and fraught with risk, Jakartans come to hedge this dilemma through investments in "affordable" apartments in large vertical complexes. These usually are no larger than 42 square-meter spaces that average around USD $60,000, usually settled by around 20 separate financing arrangements so as to accommodate a wide variety of incomes and repayment schedules. The bulk of apartments are conventionally sold prior to construction. Around half of the units sold are intended for onward rental, and of those that will be owner inhabited, another half of these are intended only for short-term residence.

In the actual day-to-day operations of many of these vertical living situations, so many different realities, games, authorities, distribution systems, pricing allotment, and servicing practices are at play, compressed into an appearance of relative homogeneity and standard-ization, that it becomes nearly impossible to detect which of the many facets, logics, and operating procedures are activated at any particular time. While residents may basically share the same "platform" of residency, and come to know each other as "neighbors," there are so many different "regimes" underlining this residency, that forging a sense of common purpose is difficult. The reality that constitutes the particularities of each neighbor's tenancy may be so markedly different as to attenuate any practical sense of commonality. Or, it simply points to a locus of commonality based on common exposure to a situation where the prospects of a shared existence are modified by the workings of a multiple of specific arrangements whose actual compositions are not easily decipherable.

For most Jakartans who acquire these apartments, they are not mostly seen as a destination. But at the same time, what they might lead to is also not clear. The acquisition, whether lived in or not, whether rented long term or on a daily basis, is experienced as a kind of holding pattern. This holding pattern is underwritten by arrangements, financing, and governance that in many ways is itself a holding pattern. As an abruption of clear genealogy, so many different realities are compressed into these projects that not only are empirical investigations always being thrown off track, but any semblance of collective life always entails the need for improvised arrangements across heterogeneities that are not afforded any contractual basis of settling into definitive patterns of association and exerting impact. Individual buildings will have their own WhatsApp groups to act as bulletin boards, mobilize complaints about bad services, or attempt to exert some kind of regulatory framework for dealing with various problems. Resident committees will be formed to deal with issues of security and moral turpitude, or organize events and various support systems. But in terms of engaging the fundamental structures informing residency, the bulk of collective actions remain rooted in highly (un)situated improvised arrangements that seek to capitalize, compensate for, under-mine, or strengthen the highly particular conditionalities that underpin each individual residency, themselves never clearly stabilized. Collective life here is a circulation through differing circumstances, compressed in ways that render the specificities simply as incompar-able specificities.

Conclusion

If work was once generated through spatial enrichments of urban inhabitation—i.e., residents interconnecting different activities, needs, aspirations, and spaces—as these possibilities through residency decline, more intentional mobilizations of effort will have to be generated. Mobilization of available assets and skills—in training, care, repair, and service provision—will be required. Rehabilitation and retrofitting of spatial assets, local environmental and commu-nity management, and various forms of service provision are areas to be developed.

But these efforts must not simply view the collective formations emanating from circu-lation and provisionality as a problem to be solved, to be settled once and for all. Just as the very ethos of popular economies attempts to think through the conditions and potentials of the operations of any discrete experimental, alternative-seeking activity in terms of the conditions and operations of others, the structural conditions informing circulation are not rectified through forcing through emplacement. It entails the imagination and governance of territories in motion, finding ways to take seriously the perceptions of residents who are in motion, and to find multiple instances where the operational landscapes and modes of inhabitation that do not correspond to administrative geographies of the present can be mapped with them—where the very acts of understanding become the occasion for new collective ventures. It entails identifying forms of participation, provisioning, and regulation capable of more judiciously anticipating and specifying the urban futures, whose uncertainties now largely occasion the circulations that attempt to hedge against them.

References

Beller, J. (2018). *The message is murder: Substrates of computational capital.* Pluto Press.

Berlant, L. (2016). The commons: Infrastructures for troubling times. *Environment and Planning D: Society and Space* 34(3): 393–419.

Caldeira, T. (2012). Imprinting and moving around: New visibilities and configurations of public space in São Paulo. *Public Culture* 24(2): 385–419.

Clare, N. (2019). Composing the social factory: An autonomist urban geography of Buenos Aires. *Environment and Planning D: Society and Space* 37(2): 255–275.

De Boeck, F. and S. Baloji. (2016). *Suturing the city. Living together in Congo's urban worlds.* Autograph.

Escobar, A. (2008). *Territories of difference: Place, movements, life, redes.* Duke University Press.

Escobar, A. (2018). *Designs for the pluriverse.* Duke University Press.

Esteva, G. (2015). Enclosing the enclosers: Autonomous experiences from the grassroots – Beyond development, globalization and postmodernity. In *The anomie of the Earth. Philosophy, politics, and autonomy in Europe and the Americas,* edited by F. Luisetti, J. Pickles, and W. Kaiser, pp. 71–92. Duke University Press.

Fallov, M. A., Jørgensen, A., and L. Knudsen. (2013). Mobile forms of belonging. *Mobilities* 8(4): 467–486.

Furniss, J. (2016). Postrevolutionary land encroachments in Cairo: Rhizomatic urban space making and the line of flight from illegality. *Singapore Journal of Tropical Geography* 37(3): 310–329.

Gago, V. (2017). *Neoliberalism from below: Popular pragmatics and Baroque economies.* Duke University Press.

Gandolfo, D. (2018). Lumpen politics? A day in "El Hueco." *Comparative Studies in Society and History* 60(3): 511–538.

Jensen, C. B. (2015). Experimenting with political materials: Environmental infrastructures and ontological transformations. *Distinktion: Journal of Social Theory* 16(1): 17–30.

Keil, R. (2018). Extended urbanization, "disjunct fragments" and global suburbanisms *Environmental and Planning D: Society and Space* 36(3): 494–511.

Kopper, M. (2019). Porous infrastructures and the politics of upward mobility in Brazil's public housing. *Economic Anthropology* 6(1): 73–85.

McFarlane, C. (2016). The geographies of urban density: Topology, politics and the city. *Progress in Human Geography* 40(5): 629–648.

Moten, F. and S. Harney. (2013). *The undercommons: Fugitive planning and Black study.* Minor Compositions/Autonomedia.

Plueckhahn, R. and T. Bayartsetseg. (2018). Negotiation, social indebtedness, and the making of urban economies in Ulaanbaatar. *Central Asian Survey* 37(3): 438–456.

Tadiar, N. X. M. (2013). Life-times of disposability within global neoliberliasm. *Social Text* 31(2): 19–48.

Thieme, T. (2018). The hustle economy: Rethinking geographies of informality and getting by. *Progress in Human Geography* 42(4): 529–548.

Yotebieng, K. and T. Forcone. (2018). The household in flux: Plasticity complicates the unit of analysis. *Anthropology in Action* 25(3): 13–22.

6

CO-CREATING THE CITIES WE DESERVE THROUGH INDIGENOUS KNOWLEDGE

Ginger Gosnell-Myers

Introduction

If urban cities represent the identity of modern civilization and the power of that civilization, then the erasure of Indigenous Peoples and Indigenous knowledge from cities is a perfect illustration of contemporary colonization in modern form. In an era of truth and reconciliation, Indigenous urban planners, and policy makers are pushing back in resistance to this contemporary colonization to create the conditions for an Indigenous cultural comeback in every neighbourhood, bike path, and downtown core. Through every new installation of Indigenous public art, incorporation of Indigenous design into a new building, or daylighting Indigenous knowledge for sustainability plans on how the lands and waters sustained life for millennia before settlers bulldozed and renamed it all—Indigenous urban planners and policy makers are ensuring that the next generation of city dwellers understand that they reside on ancient lands by building Indigenous knowledge into all aspects of city planning.

When you think about Indigenizing cities, what comes to mind? Perhaps it is the poetic, connected, and powerful Indigenous art forms. It could be the growing awareness of the history of colonization of Indigenous nations, or the thousands of children who were taken away to Indian Residential Schools where the conditions were brutal and inhumane. Whatever is top of mind, there is an awareness that there is still much to discover when it comes to Indigenous Peoples, culture, identity, history, deep knowledge, and connection to these lands and waters. This is a perfect illustration of the current intersection of Indigenous Peoples and city building.

What does this mean for city officials looking to ensure that the next generation of urban dwellers have an innate understanding of why reconciliation and creating space that reflects Indigenous knowledge matter? And similarly, how can they ensure that space created within institutions helps staff to learn about the hidden history of colonization; why healing and cultural revitalization matters for Indigenous communities? How can they support learnings about the rich and diverse aspects of Indigenous knowledge? How can cities create space for Indigenous identity to be reflected in all aspects of the public built form, or rename places

DOI: 10.4324/9781003199816-8

currently honouring the architects of colonization to instead honour Indigenous names? And most importantly, how can space be created for systemic change within cities, recognizing that many current policies reinforce white supremacy and Indigenous erasure? There is a future where Indigeneity is easily articulated throughout city planning, but we need to create space for this dialogue to happen.

Before We Can Move Forward, We Have to Look Back

Indigeneity throughout cities has been excluded or marginalized by design. Early settlement of cities first grew around local Indigenous communities, then actively started to push Indigenous Peoples out of their communities to outskirt locations. Indigenous place names, sites of cultural and spiritual significance within cities were renamed after predominantly Eurocentric settlers as a means to entrench their legacy as city founders. This continues to be reinforced today—references to the history of cities centres on settler activities while leaving out details, names, or connections of Indigenous nations. Indigenous families were forcibly removed from their homes and displaced for urban development; sometimes multiple times over as new settler plans looked to expand. The process of city building in North America has been violent, and has wiped out any trace of the Indigenous Peoples who occupied and cared for those lands for thousands of years, while city planners over many generations have engaged in furthering the larger goals of cultural genocide in the name of urban progress. Indigenous Peoples have been physically removed and erased from history to become non-existent within cities and are largely invisible within their homelands.

When examining colonization in contemporary city planning and urban policy making, there remains an attitude of manifest destiny in taking the lands by any means to plan cities that reinforce Eurocentric or culturally neutral identities—approaches that erase Indigenous Peoples and knowledge from the landscape. This is compounded by the lack of relationships cities have with Indigenous communities and a general lack of willingness to explore what cities can do to support Indigenous communities. Because of this, city planning and policy making deserves critical thought, and no practice or process should remain as it is or go unchallenged.

There is much learning to be gained through thinking critically about the impact city planning has on either supporting Indigenous identity or erasing it. These insights are key to informing what actions cities can take to build Indigenous knowledge into their practices. One may assume that the answers to the meaningful Indigenization of cities can be found in some exotic location halfway around the world, and while there is inspiration to be found (ahem—Auckland, New Zealand), the reality is that cities need to begin their reconciliation efforts by looking in their backyard. City officials who want to create an authentic, unique, urban identity through Indigenous culture and knowledge will come to realize it is a collaborative process, co-created with Indigenous communities, led by Indigenous planners.

In Canada, it is largely the municipality (city) that is responsible for determining the design and identity goals of the city. What modern cities look like today was decided once upon a time by mostly male, white, urban planners who were keen to imprint their colonially inspired or culturally neutral designs all over their city. Have you ever travelled to Europe and wished your city back home reflected that richness of culture? (I studied in Italy for a summer. That country routinely brought me to tears with its culturally rich beauty. It also made it hard to look at my city without feeling a deep sense of loss by the complete subjugation of Indigenous cultures.)

When it comes to city policies, especially those that provide direction around design, naming, arts, heritage, and culture—we should think of them as outdated and needing to be updated—because they are. Indigenous Peoples are not the only cultural communities absent from the urban landscape. Black, Chinese, Filipino, Japanese, Latinx communities—just to name a few—are also not represented in any equitable manner. Imagine how powerful a city that embraced all its cultures respectfully would look and feel? Cities are ultimately places of cultural collection and its planned redistribution as decided by elected representatives, is lobbied through various cultural and political groups, and finally determined through the actions of city planners. This is why building place-based planning into city processes is so vital.

Stories of Place Rooted in Indigenous Knowledge Are Foundational to Indigenizing Cities

Integrating Indigenous culture into cities has primarily focused on Indigenous art, which is a beautiful way to showcase culture and is certainly an important visible outcome. However, inclusion of Indigenous perspectives into city projects must go beyond the standard "decoration-only" approach and include innovative ways of demonstrating that local Indigenous nations have always been the original stewards of these lands.

Here are *some* examples of what this can look like:

• Incorporation into city projects' values and principles;
• Architectural design into buildings, landscape;
• Incorporating historical and contemporary stories into a site;
• Street (re)naming and place naming;
• Environmental stewardship considerations;
• Protocol exploration—what does it mean to design layered cultural significance into sites?

At the same time, it is important to recognize how the sharing of any Indigenous cultural, historical, and ecological knowledge of surrounding lands and waters, especially when done by Elders, must benefit those Indigenous communities and ensure that this intergenerational knowledge sharing be part of any planning process.

To only create learning processes on Indigenous cultural, historical, or ecological knowledge for city officials or designers only is not inclusive—we must find ways to share these learning opportunities more widely. Indigenous Peoples are vocally stating their desire to see urban residents learn about their history and deep connection to these lands. At the same time, Indigenous cultural leaders are working hard to ensure that their own community members have access to learning opportunities on their histories, stories, and traditional ecological knowledge. Much of Indigenous culture and language has been eroded due to the devastating impacts of colonization and the Indian Residential Schools. Knowing this, it becomes more critical that both Indigenous Peoples and urban residents be provided with opportunities to learn about the cultural history and traditional ecological knowledge of these lands and waters.

Building up this knowledge base will take time and must take into consideration the complexity of Indigenous communities: iterate that there are many family stories of place and time rather than the more convenient approach to learning from a handful of individuals from the Indigenous nation who are deemed to represent the collective. Indigenous stories are layered and nuanced, and to access them requires trust and relationship building. Not all stories are meant for public consumption—being prepared to take the time to understand this and to co-create new ways to share this knowledge through a range of city projects is reconciliation in action.

It is only through learning about these unique cultures, stories, and histories that widespread respect for Indigenous Peoples can grow. It is only through gaining new insight about these lands through an Indigenous worldview that a future for meaningful reconciliation can really emerge. It will be a complex journey to navigate such learnings. There is then one more key area that must be understood.

Urban Indigenous Communities Are Different to Local Indigenous Communities

There is another Indigenous population within cities that must also be considered in city planning: the urban Indigenous population. These are Indigenous People whose traditional homelands are elsewhere, and who do not have inherent Indigenous rights or title to the lands of the city in which they now live. Indigenous People decide to move to cities for many reasons: Work, education, family, urban life. Many urban Indigenous People consider the city to be their home, and we now see multiple generations of urban Indigenous families raised in cities, while keeping connections to their family back in their homelands. In Canada, the majority of all Indigenous Peoples are considered urban and reside in both large and small urban centres.

Knowledge of the larger urban Indigenous Community has been lacking within local governments who see Indigenous issues as outside their jurisdiction. While contemporary urban Indigenous life has found ways to grow over time, this community has remained invisible to city leaders. Narratives of Indigenous Peoples in cities have been kept in a "no longer here" past tense or worse, have only focused on harmful activities rooted in poverty or stemming from the devastating impacts of Indian Residential Schools. This deficit lens has impacted how decisions regarding urban Indigenous People within cities have been made.

In 2010, the ground-breaking Environics Urban Aboriginal Peoples Study (UAPS) (Environics Institute 2010), the largest national research of its kind in Canada explored the identities, values, experiences, and aspirations of Indigenous People living in 11 major cities and pushed back against the misconceptions held to that point. This was a research project, the implementation of which, I led, collecting the voices of over 2,500 Indigenous participants who responded to 150 questions. The UAPS research found that the urban Indigenous population was a permanent population, not just "passing through," that the majority of urban Indigenous People considered the city to be their home, felt they could make a positive impact, and had aspirations for a good life for themselves and future generations.

The UAPS also found that culture was a vital aspect of a healthy, successful life for urban Indigenous Peoples. Those who felt a strong connection to their culture (demonstrated through knowledge of their family tree) were more likely to say they were happy in their life, had a post-secondary degree or were in the process of completing their education goals, and were more likely to volunteer, vote in elections, and could see themselves advancing in their career. Cultural knowledge and connections were clearly an essential factor. Those Indigenous People who did not have a connection to their culture through knowledge of their family tree were less likely to identify with these positive life features and were also younger in age—there was a generation gap in cultural knowledge. When asked if they wanted to learn more about their culture, the answer was a resounding "yes" along with the recognition that opportunities to connect with their culture had not been presented before.

Indigenous cultures, once targeted by government policies for eradication—later identified by the Truth and Reconciliation Commission as acts of "cultural genocide"—are very important for Indigenous People living in cities. When it comes to urban Indigenous planning, it's about creating opportunities for intergenerational cultural sharing in order for Indigenous self-determination to be expressed in as many ways as possible.

In Canadian cities, where more than half of Indigenous Peoples now live, there is an economy of scale in larger urban centres where tens of thousands of Indigenous Peoples are trailblazing contemporary expressions of identity and using arts, music, fashion, thought leadership, environmental and sustainability advocacy, education, and sporting opportunities to create vibrant urban Indigenous communities. These efforts are providing cities with an electrifying new scene that welcomes all, connecting everyone to Indigenous knowledge through contemporary Indigenous innovation and expression. The challenge for cities is how to ensure that these communities are finally recognized, reflected, and supported. This is where I need to start my personal reflections on these issues based on my work to date.

A Personal Reflection

Since the early 2000s, I have been creating research and policy solutions aimed at understanding and supporting Indigenous communities within cities. I remember early on in my career how alienated urban Indigenous Peoples were from government and First Nations political discourse. There was a sense that Indigenous People in cities were not worth supporting, and this was demonstrated by the lack of investment in understanding urban Indigenous issues beyond that of simply looking at homelessness.

Politically, First Nations and urban Indigenous advocacy groups at the national level consistently fought over "who speaks for and represents Indigenous peoples outside of First Nations reserves." All levels of Canadian government—Federal, Provincial, and Municipal—seemed not to mind this infighting. It was just one more matter they wouldn't have to deal with and they chose to ignore the seemingly unimportant policy gap and let it fall between the cracks without giving it much thought.

As a young Nisga'a and Kwakwaka'wakw woman who had made the city her home, I watched the disorganization of the urban Indigenous political scene and recognized that those who suffered were ordinary Indigenous People and families. Who we were and what we aspired to achieve went unnoticed and was not questioned. When attention *was* given, it usually focused on the negative, the result of which would embed harsh stereotypes. Any urban Indigenous-community building efforts underway were created without much external support. Municipalities seemed uninterested in acknowledging the potential roles of Indigenous People in cities. I often heard, "it's outside our jurisdiction—it's a federal responsibility." Moreover, philanthropic organizations did not support Indigenous Peoples in cities.

It felt like we, the urban Indigenous Community in cities, were on our own. It was just us and our local Friendship Centre.

Fast forward to the present day, and so much has changed in a short while. From 2008 to 2011, I led the implementation of the Environics Urban Aboriginal Peoples Study, which not only demonstrated the vital importance of Indigenous culture but uncovered so many (dare I say) humanizing insights of the identities, values, experiences, and aspirations of Indigenous People in cities. Not only were urban Indigenous populations a significant policy gap at any government level, but they were largely invisible communities within cities, whether they were local First Nations who had resided on their homelands for millennia and watched settler cities grow around them, or Indigenous Peoples who had moved to the city for work, education, or family.

As we were undertaking the UAPS survey and asking Indigenous Peoples about their aspirations for themselves and their families, we received feedback that the survey was the first time that anyone had ever asked them about their hopes for their future. That was a revelation for me: It had highlighted the need to identify the aspirations we have as Indigenous Peoples in cities and to ensure that any initiatives at the policy level incorporated this important consideration. We cannot build or create without knowing what we aspire to as a community. Without knowing these aspirations any policy efforts undertaken were limited, paternalistic, and prescriptive. In other words, they continued to entrench a colonial "we know best" attitude over Indigenous self-determination. If cities were places to support modern cultural vitality, it was quite the opposite for Indigenous Peoples. We had to work twice as hard to create the sense of community that we needed—and deserved.

How to Begin to Address Reconciliation within a Large City

In 2013, I joined the City of Vancouver to undertake hosting the Truth and Reconciliation Commission and the historic *Walk for Reconciliation* by Reconciliation Canada. That same year, Vancouver proclaimed a "Year of Reconciliation 2013–2014," challenged cities across Canada to do the same, and engaged Vancouverites and City staff in a year-long effort to learn about the history of colonization and the government-sanctioned Indian Residential Schools.

Concurrently, I led a city-wide policy and service review that evolved into the creation of a *City of Reconciliation Framework* that ushered in systemic change within all city departments to ensure that the City of Vancouver found new ways to conduct its work in acknowledgement of the unceded Musqueam, Squamish, and Tsleil-Waututh Nation homelands on which it is situated. Within five years, close to 100 new initiatives and policy changes were implemented that ensured reconciliation was reflected as a core value throughout the City. So much space was created for systemic change—it was breathtaking.

Municipalities aren't known for being a place of innovation with regard to Indigenous rights recognition. But we moved forward with our commitments, within our jurisdiction to act, guided by the City of Reconciliation Framework.

There were three foundational pillars of the *City of Reconciliation Framework* (City of Vancouver 2014):

* Cultural Competency: All City staff should have access and opportunity to learn about the history of Indigenous Peoples, starting with the acknowledgement of the history of

residential schools and the impact of harm from the loss of land and culture. City staff should provide access and opportunities for Indigenous Vancouverites to engage in City businesses and services;

- Strengthening Relations: Continue building and strengthening relationships with Musqueam, Squamish, and Tsleil-Waututh Nations, and Vancouver's urban Indigenous community with a focus on the Metro Vancouver Aboriginal Executive Council;
- Effective Decision-making: Enhancing how the City of Vancouver works with First Nations and urban Indigenous communities, conducting work differently and taking thoughtful risks, making exceptions to normal processes that still align within the City mandate, while having better alignment with First Nations and urban Indigenous priorities.

In order to help guide this new way of city planning and policy making, a long-term vision was developed:

> As a City of Reconciliation, the City of Vancouver will form a sustained relationship of mutual respect and understanding with local First Nations and the Urban Indigenous community, including key agencies, to incorporate a First Nations and Urban Indigenous perspective into the work undertaken and decisions made by the City of Vancouver and, ultimately, to provide services that benefit members of these communities.

We found that having the framework was not sufficient enough direction for staff to move toward the type of systemic change needed to facilitate reconciliation, and thus, *long-term goals* were developed in 2015 which provided clarity, guidance, and accountability for all City departments to integrate into their workplans:

- Strengthen Local First Nations and Urban Aboriginal Relations;
- Promote Aboriginal Peoples Arts, Culture, Awareness and Understanding;
- Incorporate First Nations and Urban Aboriginal Perspectives for Effective City Services.

Some of the many initiatives created and supported through the *City of Reconciliation Framework* included those outlined in the box below.

CITY OF RECONCILIATION SAMPLE OF CROSS-DEPARTMENTAL OUTCOMES

- Two Indigenous health, healing, and wellness centres were built and supported through grants from the city, and partnerships with urban Indigenous service providers;
- Implementation of the Truth and Reconciliation Calls to Action report which identified that 28 of the 94 calls to action were actionable through 59 city initiatives aligned under three themes: Healthy Communities and Wellness; Achieving Indigenous Human Rights and Recognition; and Advancing Awareness, Knowledge, and Capacity;
- The City released the Aboriginal Health, Healing, and Wellness in the Downtown Eastside (DTES) Study, which identified the critical role that access to traditional

and culturally appropriate health care practices play in supporting the well-being of Indigenous People;

- Vancouver's 2017 Canada 150+ program included reconciliation as a key theme and hosted three signature events: The Gathering of Canoes, the Drum is Calling Festival (Canada's largest Indigenous music and arts festival) and Walk for Reconciliation (over 50,000 participated);
- The development of Archaeology policies and creation of Chance Find Management training for Engineering operations were introduced—both in collaboration with local First Nations;
- An online three-module course for City staff focused on Reconciliation and Indigenous Peoples, as well as in-person cultural competency training offered to thousands of city staff in all departments;
- Eligibility criteria in all grant programs was expanded to include local First Nations (City of Vancouver 2017).

The *City of Reconciliation Framework* was not to be a "cookie cutter" prescriptive set of policies or programs. Rather, it was to focus on the important elements of what the United Nations Declaration on the Rights of Indigenous Peoples and the Truth and Reconciliation Commission's Calls to Actions outlined, and we used them to provide direction and policy alignment. We empowered staff to respond to a respectful government-to-government working relationship. It provided the City of Vancouver and First Nations the time to create municipal tools, along with the training staff needed to undertake it well.

Vancouver's *City of Reconciliation Framework* wasn't about a government trying to just "deal" with Indigenous rights. It was about creating a pathway forward, together. It set the City of Vancouver on the path to reconciliation. The real work took place in every department, based on working alongside First Nations and the urban Indigenous community, and ensuring that there was collaborative agreement on the next steps and objectives.

GINGER'S GUIDANCE FOR CITY OFFICIALS

- Acknowledge the Indigenous community in the way they want to be acknowledged. Recognize them in the way they want to be recognized. And know the key differences between First Nations and urban Indigenous communities;
- Planning must consider inequities between the City and Indigenous communities, and must take account of the time and capacity involved in planning processes on both sides;
- If you can't break your own policies, you're not going to see the change you want to see. Decolonization is a long-term process meant to completely disrupt and dismantle an unjust system—the system in which we are operating today;
- Be prepared to feel like you're making it all up. International best practices will only get you so far. Localized investment requires relationship building and at the end of the day, you need to figure out what that actually looks like to make the relationship work. It will take time;

> - Without trust between the City and Indigenous community, any efforts are probably going to fail;
> - It's important to try, fail, learn, try again. And again. And again.
>
> Ultimately, it's about creating space within a process normally closed off to Indigenous communities, then finding ways to honour Indigenous voices within processes that have been absent of cultural perspectives.

Yes – this IS special treatment for Indigenous communities. Righting historic injustices and cultural genocide requires it.

Yes, there is still a long way to go. But that's the nature of meaningful reconciliation. It will take time and involve all of us to get it right. When I left the City of Vancouver, I shared this message with my Facebook contacts to summarize how I saw my efforts unfold and the space created in the process:

> I've spent the past 5 years in an important position to create a bridge with the Indigenous community, something that wasn't clearly understood at a municipal level when I started. Reconciliation was adopted as the approach we needed to take to determine what we needed to do. It helped us see and has taken us far!
>
> To the first government to proclaim a Year of Reconciliation, to creating a workable framework to become the world's first City of Reconciliation. To officially acknowledging that Vancouver was on unceded Musqueam, Squamish, and Tsleil-Waututh homelands. And committing to systems and policy change—all City departments had to create a work plan that responded to our City of Reconciliation goals.
>
> This was where much of my work was, with taking a policy or process full of red tape, understanding where we needed to go, breaking the barriers, and then figuring out how to do the work. My favourite sayings were "We are figuring this out as we go along", and "Even if we make mistakes, we are learning". Some things we could change fast. Others, still working on it. But staff know the status quo is not an option if it is a detriment to who we are as a City of Reconciliation, and that was often frustrating to point out but also incredibly hopeful because change was and is occurring.
>
> I worked with every single department, every day, on over 100 City initiatives in identifying what we needed to do and how we needed to do it. And when we were ready to listen and learn and made space within our policies to change, we then took these projects to the Nations, or to the Urban Indigenous Peoples Advisory Committee, or to the Metro Vancouver Aboriginal Executive Council to set new direction, priorities, and to co-develop next steps and a long-term approach. These initiatives are changing the culture of the organization and giving new options and perspectives for how Vancouver as a City will be. There is so much space created right now … thinking back on everything and looking at where this is going—it literally takes my breath away. I won't and can't go into details, there's too much. Starting things, stopping things, predicting then pivoting, pushing, pulling, cajoling, inspiring, supporting, editing, saying maybe – yeah let's do it, jumping then leaping, falling then getting back up again and again …

Many lessons have been learned along the way about Indigenous Peoples in cities that requires thoughtful investigation and dialogue. Cities in Canada have been able to reflect in their policies the learnings from the Environics Urban Aboriginal Peoples Study and have seen the success of the City of Vancouver's commitment to reconciliation and followed Vancouver's leadership. It is still, however, early days in understanding the goals of reconciliation at a municipal level, and what this inspires for new aspirations in city building.

The Path Forward

Cities and municipal governments in Canada have had a hands-off approach when it comes to Indigenous community relations, often leaving matters that involve Indigenous Peoples to federal and provincial governments. This "not my jurisdiction" approach has created an environment in which cities have conducted their business over many generations without any regard for Indigenous communities. City staff have not been expected to consider Indigenous Peoples within their planning processes, would develop heritage designations without any regard for recognizing Indigenous forms of heritage, and would create urban identities for neighbourhoods and parks that excluded Indigenous knowledge. Cities have existed as places of innovation, culture, and economic activity but have reinforced the erasure of Indigenous Peoples.

Since release of the TRC Calls to Action, there has been a growing movement to ensure Indigenous history and culture is reflected through city planning, driven by their commitment to advancing reconciliation. This is a new goal of cities across the country—to acknowledge the truth of these lands having always been the unceded homelands of Indigenous Peoples and co-creating a city and urban identity that benefits all.

New Zealand as a country is moving forward on their reconciliation journey as well. They are co-creating a national identity that is rooted in Māori culture and language. Much of it stems from Māori activism in the late 1970s for New Zealand to promote their language. In 1987 Māori was recognized as an official language of the country. Many cultural institutions have grown from this and there are now a couple of generations that are benefiting from this national recognition and respect for Māori culture. Because of this, it could be said that a goal of the Māori peoples is for all New Zealanders to have Māori pride through respectful rights and knowledge recognition.

You can see it, it's visible, from architecture with Māori design, to Māori place names being recognized, to having significant representation in elected positions in government, and also incorporating the Haka as a sports team tradition. This is identifying New Zealand as a unique place on earth, and they are co-creating a country and identity that benefits all and connects everyone to the land they share through Indigenous knowledge. This is what respectful and meaningful reconciliation can be.

Māori leadership in planning and design have created the Te Aranga Design Principles which set the standard for what Indigenous design in the built form should strive to understand and reflect locally. City building and place making across New Zealand is providing us with the greatest contemporary examples of Indigenous identity within cities, and anyone interested in urban Indigeneity must look to Māori leadership for inspiration.

How we get from here to there requires us to not treat Indigenization of cities or reconciliation as a time defined program. If we are going to move forward as a society in a truthful way, we all need to know whose lands these have always been—we need to understand the deep-rooted connection Indigenous Peoples have to this earth, and we need to learn from that knowledge, especially in the midst of a climate emergency and ongoing sustainability plans that will determine how we need to change in order to support ecosystem health. Cities are positioning themselves to be significant responders to climate change, as they should—but if Indigenous knowledge isn't reflected in those plans, I fear we will reinforce colonization through new forms of erasure of Indigenous People's roles as stewards and key knowledge holders of these lands and waters.

While I'm proud of my efforts and the space I've created to change the discourse on the Indigenization of cities in Vancouver and across Canada, there is still so much work and learning to do. My aspirations for city life are based on experiencing Indigenous knowledge in all aspects of urban living. I want people to know the stories of these lands from Indigenous perspectives— to see an Indigenous person as a future City Manager or Mayor of Vancouver. I see so much potential through Indigenous leadership being truly respected and embraced throughout cities. Will I see this in my lifetime? I'm not sure, but I have hope.

References

City of Vancouver. (2014). *City of Vancouver.* Retrieved from City of Reconciliation framework: https://council.vancouver.ca/20141028/documents/rr1.pdf.

City of Vancouver. (2017). *City of Vancouver.* Retrieved from City of Reconciliation update: https://council.vancouver.ca/20171213/documents/cfsc1.pdf.

Environics Institute. (2010). *Urban Aboriginal Peoples study*. Environics Institute.

PART II

Time

7

UNSETTLING THE COLONIALITY OF FORESIGHT

Aarathi Krishnan

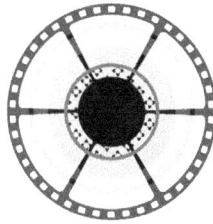

Who Controls the Imaginations of Our Futures?

My name is Aarathi Krishnan. I am Malaysian. I am Australian. I am of Indian heritage and of two different castes. I have lived in many countries, and I currently live on ancestral Lenape homelands now known as New York. I am an immigrant. I am a cis woman of colour. I have multiplicities of identities that don't fit perfectly into a checkbox, nor do I want them to. I stand here on the shoulders of everyone that has come before me, and I have an obligation to all who will come after me. I have worked in humanitarian and development aid for almost two decades and now research how technology futures might be more ethical as it intersects with the humanitarian system. My work is at the intersection of humanitarian and development aid, strategic foresight, and complexity.

The common threads throughout my career are the questions: *How do we serve all of humanity without bringing the inequities of our past into our futures? How do we avoid flattening people's identities into stereotypical ideas of who they are and what they desire so that when they most need the best of humanity, they feel safe and seen in the support being offered to them?* This isn't merely a technical pursuit, but a deeply personal one, driven by the notion that people who look like me, who come from the communities I come from—my grandparents and great grandparents—are often denied voice. We are spoken *on behalf of* when it comes to the choices available to us for our futures and our children's and grandchildren's futures. It is in this vein that I ask these questions. As complexity and uncertainty recasts our understanding of ourselves and our place in the world, it also provokes new answers to the question: *What does it mean to be human in these 21st-century futures?*

Our world is in a liminal place—that space between one form of existence and the next. As we strive now to redesign our places of living and belonging, of redesigning cities and civic spaces, how do we ensure that the designs of these new spaces are not relegated to the imaginations and actions of a few? How do we reimagine our futures weaving in the principles of Sacred Civics such that *wisdom, commons, and our values* guide the tools and approaches we draw on? The rallying call of 2020 and 2021 has been that we must "build back better" to "new normal"—*a Great Reset* recognising that our commons have fundamentally and irrevocably

DOI: 10.4324/9781003199816-10

shifted and our futures are complex and uncertain. The challenge that we face as humanity in this transition, is how we steward our planet and our people well—not just for ourselves today but for current and future generations. We must—all of us—ask ourselves one fundamental question: What kind of ancestors do we want to be? It is the answer to this question that will determine the actions we choose to take today.

As Kathy Peach (2019) notes: "Overall, the future is dominated by privileged white men." Our global systems exist within complex, interlocking imperial formations. *The fundamental practice of foresight* is the process of imagining and designing what our futures can and should be. This process has predominantly been constructed in communities that uphold pockets of monopolies, capitalism, power, and privilege that shape our views of what is possible. What this does, whether implicitly or unconsciously, is reinforce dominant, hegemonic narratives that assume:

- The experiences of all people, of all civil society, is homogenous;
- The singular Global North values that underpin such futures are the only ones that all people aspire to, regardless of their lives or their physical, mental, cultural, societal, economic, or geographic bearings;
- Power dynamics will continue to be affirmed in the hands of those that currently hold it, without considering the cascading impacts of policy decisions on those that are most affected by it.

> We are in an imagination battle. Imagination turns brown bombers into terrorists and white bombers into mentally ill victims. Imagination gives us borders, gives us superiority, gives us race as an indicator of ability. I often feel I am trapped inside someone else's capability. I often feel I am trapped inside someone else's imagination, and I must engage my own imagination in order to break free.
>
> *adrienne maree brown*

As we draw on new tools and approaches to help in our reimaginations, this chapter argues, as the quote by adrienne maree brown's (2017) illustrates, that traditional, hegemonic approaches to foresight are not adequate. This chapter posits that these tools, as they are today, need further expansion for the types of complexities we are facing. It provides a brief description of strategic foresight and how it has traditionally been utilised. It further posits that the baseline of foresight is coloniality and that this very baseline is also its fault line. Coloniality narrows analysis to what is merely plausible, possible, preferable, and probable, rather than futures that are just and equitable. Finally, this chapter puts forward an emergent approach to a new decolonial model of foresight that works to liberate our futures so our reimaginations of societies, economies, governments, and cities are spaces of safety and flourishing for all, not just for some. This chapter puts these arguments forward through the three pillars of Sacred Civics: wisdom, values, and commons, all of which are based in decoloniality.

Understanding Strategic Foresight and its Fault Lines

Strategic foresight is a multi-dimensional approach aimed at driving strategic transformation and anticipation to guide future-oriented decisions and planning. It is the discipline of exploring the future to anticipate changes, develop possible transition pathways, and to withstand shocks to "help us act in the present to shape the future we want," (European Commission 2020). It is not about predicting the future, but rather exploring different possible alternatives of how the future might unfold and how our world might be affected today. Formal foresight practices emerged in the 20th century through military practice, consumer marketing, and science and technology (Careful Industries 2021). Royal Dutch Shell is most often cited as an example of early foresight methodology development. As described by the Asia–Pacific Center for Security Studies, "[s]ince the 1970s, they [Royal Dutch Shell] have explored alternative scenarios of the future to help leaders make better decisions," (Canyon 2018). As a practice, it attempts to blend imaginations of what the future might be with action in the present that requires changes in policies, practices, culture, and investments that governments, institutions, and societies need to adopt.

But, these realms of imaginings and design of democracy, progress, social good, and what it means to thrive have traditionally followed a static, rigid view of these ideas, steeped in pillars of a Northern-dominated world order. Official reports about the future put forward ideas about how the world might evolve. Research on the future of work greatly influences how governments and powerful corporations consider the evolutions that we are experiencing (PwC 2018). We limit the possibilities of what might evolve in our world to four binary scenarios, as if these scenarios are the only things available to all of us, without considering the interconnectedness of risk and complexity that drive how human beings live (ARUP 2019). The very practice of foresight can be steeped in bias and surface-level rhetoric without interrogating what is needed for us to change and adapt to an uncertain world. As Rachel Coldicutt explains, "partly because of its origins, there is a tendency for formal foresight to be 'top down,' reinforcing the requirements of those with existing power … and is often characterized by trust in the inevitability of technological innovation." As a result, these futures can easily be "mistaken as self-evident truths" (Careful Industries 2021).

What is the result of futures that become a singular truth? The systems and frameworks that have served us to date may have improved outcomes for many but haven't done so equally and have been at significant cost. The global COVID-19 pandemic showed in harsh light the fundamental cracks in our global systems and structures. Our systems, our societies, our actions, and our behaviours were a million wounds in a structural ecosystem that was rupturing at its sides. The system has now blown wide open, revealing to humanity's collective shame the ways in which we have all failed: to lift people out of poverty; to make health care sustainable and accessible; to safeguard our planet; to make the world more equal, just, and safe. We have failed, not because the challenges were impossible to solve, but because of our collective lethargy and apathy to truly reimagine a completely different status quo.

> The measures against the #Coronavirus pandemic are made by and for those parts of the world that can afford to retreat in individualism. But for millions of people around the world there's no such thing as socially distancing yourself.
>
> *OluTimehin Adegbeye*

These singular truths for the future result in policy design that is created with very narrow ideas about humanity. We saw this in pandemic policies designed for wealthy countries and blindly rolled out across the world as the quote above by OluTimehin Adegbeye (2020) illustrates. These policies were not designed with consideration for migrant workers or for communities that are unable to socially distance (Kugler and Shakti 2020; Adegbeye 2020).

The poor, the uninsured, the disenfranchised, the information-poor, and the less mobile are bearing the brunt.

To design anew, we must ask ourselves how humanity arrived at this unique point in time. What systems corral how humanity exists? How do they play out in people's experiences and why? Quite often, those that utilise foresight approaches in change efforts assume emancipation and liberation through *systems transformation and reimagination*. They leave out a critical understanding of history, power, and who is deliberately unseen or exploited. Without this analysis, the use of hegemonic foresight might paradoxically expose or expand harm on marginalised minoritised constituents.

Coloniality—Understanding what Precedes to Inform, Situate, and Construct Knowledge of the Future

Hillary Cottam (2021) argues in her publication, *The Radical Way*, that "deeper change does not start with improvement of what is existing, but rather asks a bigger question of what is needed now to flourish." To truly flourish, we cannot design futures that merely replicate or reinforce existing and past inequalities; we must address why and how those inequalities exist in the first place.

One of the reasons for grave inequality is due to historic colonialism and how it manifests in ongoing agony today. The act of colonialism, or colonisation, removes power from the colonised, dispossesses and transfers economic resources, and removes culture in the name of "civility." Colonialism isn't just physical; it is also mental and metaphysical. Colonisers impose their assessment of the value of people, resources, and land. The axiology of coloniality, explained by Arum Linh, is how (colonisers) impose their assessment of the value of the people, resources, and land that become embedded in the institution that then creates the nation-state in settler colonialism. "All of the established laws, policies, institutions, and governance structures are based on those beliefs that were brought upon contact" (Linh 2020).

Coloniality presents itself in a matrix of power that operates through control or hegemony over the economy, including land, labour, and natural resources; authority; gender and sexuality; and subjectivity and knowledge (Martinot 2004). Coloniality was presented to the world as "modernisation" but this was at grave expense to freedom, justice, equality, and a homogenous world view. The ideas of modernity that resulted—such as nation-states, citizenship, and democracy, come as a result of this domination (Grosfoguel 2011). How we then conceive and transfer knowledge, as well as what knowledge we see as credible and valid are also based on these colonial beliefs. How we exist within these structures and how we interpret reality is deeply influenced by colonisation as well. All of these come together to create a narrative that defines how "normal" is understood (Linh 2020).

A colonial relationship is hierarchical, extractive, and exploitative. It produces uneven consequences and malevolent paternalisms. Colonial relationships create presumed superiority and infertility, also known as hierarchies, between colonising and colonised people and places. They are extractive as the uneven consequences of colonialism are felt across the entire system. The *malevolent paternalism* of colonial relations means that solutions are always proffered in the name of and for the good of the colonised; yet the colonised themselves are not recognised as full and legitimate participants in producing those solutions.

So, Is Foresight Colonial?

Foresight approaches have traditionally been homogenous in their design and thinking. Born from an ideology of a dominant Western perspective, the roots of strategic foresight have maintained its homogeneity regardless of how and where it is applied. Essentially, it has been *to look to the future to anticipate what might be coming and be better prepared*. It draws on the principles of thinking in causal and strategic ways, extrapolation, and imagination. It is also fundamentally based on the idea that all people have the same access and the same ways of thinking about the future. In doing so, futures and foresight specialists have *recreated in their own image*.

How is the future talked about in vulnerable contexts such as when people juggle crippling poverty or feel unsafe; in contexts where young people do not feel that they have full agency over their own decisions; where family, culture, and religious obligation play a greater role in how their lives play out? What about spaces where indigenous culture and history were over-taken by capitalist labour markers of progress—whose visions of the future ought to prevail? *How do we talk about long-term possibilities when desperation is a fundamental baseline in people's lives?* Do we consider these issues when we design ideas about the future?

The practice of foresight is not neutral. It is conditioned by our positionality, cultural values, our economic systems, and our capacity for collective imagination. Are we chasing only one idea of what being "progressed" looks like? Do we end up replicating versions of ourselves or the stories we want to tell? The recent Technology Futures Report 2021, for example, put forward different scenarios of technology futures but did not include any aspects of whom these types of futures were privileging, or who would be dispossessed. Nor did it include any ethical considerations of the types of futures these ideas might bring for-ward (World Economic Forum and Deloitte 2021). Without further critical analysis, it was launched through arguably powerful platforms as an "inevitable truth." Foresight can frame our choices and help us choose the pathways ahead of us; however, the more rigid our dependence, the finer the line becomes between foresight seduction and foresight coercion. We end up gently bending our choices, our perspectives, and our sense of ourselves to fit these rigid frames—reducing the breadth of our humanity to those templates that are designed and understood by a privileged few.

Though foresight and social change practitioners might speak and work on transformation and paradigm shifts with their best intentions, such work rarely involves a challenge to the fundamental centrality of the status quo. Part of this reason is that current foresight approaches do not challenge linear and historical ideas of (a) what it takes for change to happen, and (b) how risk and harm might evolve. Instead, foresight approaches constrain future possibil-ities to current, narrow assumptions of power and static ideas of harm. Ironically then, it is this linearity that limits our imaginations that other possible futures could be *tangibly* created and have very different outcomes for current power structures.

For truly equitable futures, the coloniality of foresight must be unsettled. This requires going beyond rhetoric and narratives. Unsettling coloniality does not merely mean to tokenistically include historically oppressed, excluded, and impacted communities. Instead, the methods and approaches used must fundamentally de-centre coloniality and simplistic solutionism; centre justice and equity; and actively work to mitigate harm, now and into the future. Current emerging practices on the decolonisation of foresight focus on participation and inclusion, collective visioning, and futures literacy. Though these are wonderful efforts, we must amplify and evolve this further. Decolonisation is not a metaphor, as Tuck and Yang (2012) argue, meant to replace diversity and inclusion measures or social justice efforts. Without a deep interrogation behind the motives and approaches behind the practice of fore-sight, claims of "participatory futures," "democratising futures," or "decolonising futures" act as a cover for essentially continued Anglo–European coloniality. As Ahmed Ansari argues, "mere representation doesn't necessarily equate to radical alterity." (Raval 2021). If we retain these imaginations and ideas of our futures as an existential reflection or conceptual phil-osophy, we fail to understand that which created the million systemic wounds that our world is suffering from today.

The decoloniality of foresight requires us to interrogate and repair the deep systemic levels of oppressions that have marginalised and minoritised so many of us. It requires us to consider justice in the governance of our futures and our commons, so we are not locking those that are often missed from these conversations into future indebtedness or inequity. It must restore, elevate, renew, acknowledge, and validate the multiplicity of lives, lived experiences, culture, and knowledge; at the same time, it must de-centre hetero/cis-normativity, hierarchies, and structural racial privilege. Most importantly, it must decolonise our minds so we can embrace and draw on the ideas that (a) many different philosophies and principles are valid—a plur-alistic approach; and (b) multiple truths can exist at the same time, experienced by different people in different ways—a multiverse.

When decolonial practice is applied to foresight, we challenge the normative ways in which we are encouraged to think. It opens our minds to the notions that add more critical nuanced analysis into our imaginings. Where the Deloitte Technology Futures report (2021) drew on technical signals and drivers, a decolonial foresight approach can interrogate political and capitalist ideology through the lens of those most impacted by these approaches. The recent Think South report analysed the meaning and impact of data colonialism and technological sovereignty through the lens of Global South communities to challenge the notion that futures are unidimensional (Mhlambi, Freuler, and Ricaurte 2019). Decolonial foresight can also help us expand on how we think about development more broadly. Buen Vivir has done exactly this through critically examining the discourse of sustainable development. The concept and lived practice is based on a "decolonial stance drawing on a new form of ethics that balances quality of life, democratization of the state and concern with biocentric ideals" and goes beyond putting a dollar figure on national well-being (Salazar 2015).

Transformation for social good in the 21st century will only be effective if it is based on systemic interrogation that denies normative static frameworks and linear methodologies designed on outdated assumptions. This transformation must pull out systemic inequality and bias, be representative of all peoples and futures, and link to strategic reform. More than this, who gets to be part of the process and *how it influences decision-making* is just as important as the outcome. If the COVID-19 pandemic has taught us anything, it is how we seek a *fundamental transformation* of our ways of living and being. To truly break from the shackles of our past, we need the imaginations, hopes, and dreams of a new world.

Hope is a radical act. It is what makes us cross seas, skies, take risks, and jump without safety nets when the journey and arrival might endanger safety and might diminish us. We are propelled forward by the hope for a better future for our children and our grandchildren but hope by itself is not enough. We must translate this hope into action that befits the types of resets we need in the redesign of new commons, values, and wisdoms.

Unsettling the Coloniality of Foresight

If the practice of strategic foresight is left to its current set of frameworks and approaches, it will merely relegate to its most simplistic form. As it exists today, strategic foresight is no longer adequate to tackle the complex futures that humanity faces. Our models of governance and strategic design require a broader evolution to consider the "sexual, gender, spiritual, epistemic, economic, political, linguistic, aesthetic, pedagogical and racial hierarchies of the 'modern/colonial, western-centric, Christian-centric, capitalist/patriarchal world-system'" (Grosfoguel 2011). Linearity and hegemony are the cripplers of our futures. As Audrey Lorde (1984) argues "What does it mean when tools of a racist patriarchy are used to examine the fruits of that same patriarchy? It means that only the narrowest perimeters of change are possible and allowable." Futures frameworks that push one dominant narrative limit our questioning of whether global poverty measures have considered colonial history, implications on inequality from brutal economic policies, or planetary implications from industrialisation. It reinforces future progress as singular, linear spectrums that build on the trajectories of our history and assumes that those ideas of progress are what everyone must aspire to in the future. It reinforces power imbalances and excludes those that don't have the same kind of access to participate. It can result in crippling inaction if reimagination is not systematically linked to levers for societal, political, and institutional transformations.

To evolve the practice of foresight, we must elevate factors of privileging forces and analyse bias hot spots and flows of power. We can then see and understand systemic oppression and stop making blind assumptions about how those most impacted will be affected. We must also challenge our baseline assumptions about these approaches and embed new elements that speak to the multiplicity of futures that is available to all of us. Doing so allows foresight to be optimised for human and planetary well-being, narrows the gap of agony, and provides a "dividend" to historically excluded and oppressed communities.

> Imagination is one of the spoils of colonization, which in many ways is claiming who gets to imagine the future for a given geography. Losing our imagination is a symptom of trauma. Reclaiming the right to dream the future, strengthening the muscle to imagine together as Black people, is a revolutionary decolonizing activity.
>
> *adrienne maree brown*

Foresight models baselined in decolonial theory interrogates patterns of power that shape our intellectual, political, economic, and social world as adrienne maree brown (2017) illustrates above. By embedding a decolonial critical approach within the technical practice of foresight, structural and systemic transformation efforts can ensure that the impacts of past inequalities and harm will not hinder historically oppressed communities' ability to flourish in the long term, rather than just to survive in the short term. Incorporating these interrogations elevates current decolonisation of futures approaches from collective and participatory visioning to linking more intentionally to systems transformation efforts.

The focus on decoloniality provides a set of approaches that go *beyond* diversity, inclusion, and empowerment, and arguably do not *influence* or *guide* decision-making and priority setting. A decolonial approach turns us "towards a pluriversal epistemology of the future that, unlike universalism, acknowledges and supports a wider radius of socio-political, ecological, cultural and economic needs" (Mohamed, Png, and Isaac 2020). Utilising a decolonial basis shifts the knowledge sources and experiences we draw on in the very *design and decision-making* that foresight models underpin and ensures that we consider the multiplicity of ways in which issues of equity, justice, rights, fairness, harm, and agency are experienced the world over. Baselining decoloniality allows us to shift current models that are beset with calls for participation and inclusion but still centre decision-making on a normative and power-centralised status quo.

Decolonial foresight can intentionally help design flourishing futures for us. By utilising a decolonial model into our reimagining and redesign efforts, we can:

- Interrogate Future of Work analysis beyond just the automation of jobs, to determine how it can translate into more dignified work;
- Redesign cities, not just with "smart cities" ideals or green initiatives in mind, but rather designing for safety and inclusion for all, including populations that are not normally considered in design considerations (i.e. the unhoused, differently abled, LGBTIQ, ethnic groups, etc).
- Reimagine migration policies, not just to curb migration, but rather make all people feel that they *belong* in a city;
- Reframe discussions about future generations beyond just the ability to move across borders, but rather such that their identities are not diminished in the spaces they choose to reside in;
- Create climate-resilient cities of the future that cater cool spaces for communities that can't afford access to the costs of cooling;
- Expand our notions for cities of the future to include humanitarian considerations for displaced populations beyond makeshift spaces;
- Elevate future pandemic policies to go beyond tech solutionism and consider how those that don't have access to the same types of technology, don't speak the main language of a country or city, or might be undocumented or unsure may still be able to access information and services without discrimination or bias.

Our futures do not have to be echoes of our past. I believe the hope we foster can allow us to be radical in our imaginations. But hope by itself doesn't result in transformation. If redesigned civics are truly what we seek, we must intentionally design and evolve all our current models and frameworks, so they are fit for the types of futures we want to bring forward. As Sabelo Ndlovu-Gatsheni puts it, can we see decolonisation as a process of our "rehumanization—which is a fundamental planetary project"? (Omanga 2020). Unsettling the coloniality of foresight is an act of resistance. It is an act of resistance to the shackles that have held humanity back from evolving our potential of how we live with each other and with our planet. It is an act of resistance to the continued practice of designing for privilege rather than for equity and justice.

A New Model of Systemic Decolonial Foresight

This chapter posits an *emergent* framework of decolonial foresight that aims to dismantle harmful power asymmetries and concepts of knowledge. It is modelled on the following question: how do we stop locking people into future harm, indebtedness, or future inequity?

This framework is based on the following considerations:

- Foresight approaches must be integrated with complexity and systems analysis;
- The structural and systemic forms of oppression and inequity need to be recognised and designed out of our futures. We cannot do this without understanding our history and the roles we have implicitly or explicitly played;
- Just as rights are not static, neither is harm. What is the *current and future* theory of harm that might arise out of a solution/intervention?
- How might we actually *undo* the systems of oppression that have served only a select privileged few?
- What might be the impact of the solution/intervention on future generations and on our planet? *How* might this impact be understood and experienced by different groups of people across the world?
- What are the values and risks of new preferred futures on the models, structures, frameworks, and institutions in which we operate?
- Will the assumptions we make that continue to centre the status quo and its corresponding business models result as a continued fault line?

This emergent decolonial foresight framework is aimed at taking designer and foresight specialists through a set of principles that can be applied to any element of a systems redesign process, from redesigning cities to governance systems. The model draws on the Sacred Civics principles of wisdom, values, and commons to help in the reimagination of policy and redesign efforts.

The framework acts as a compass, not a checkbox, to allow for emergence and relationality.

A set of principles by itself cannot be our solution. To be transformative requires practitioners, policymakers, designers, and funders to consider:

- The interconnectedness of different drivers of risk that might amplify or impede city redesign efforts;
- Complementing the framework with analysis on trade-offs that must be incorporated into redesign;
- The transition processes for new roles and new structures that might emerge;
- The underlying assumptions of design efforts so that they don't turn into fault lines.

Conclusion

Anil Dash (2016) wrote that "We are accountable for the communities we create … Our communities are defined by the worst things we permit to happen. What we allow tells the world who we are." Extending this further, *we are accountable for the futures we create.* Foresight models and practitioners that work to transform systems, places, and institutions for *good* cannot absolve ourselves of the responsibilities of the intended and unintended consequences of our actions in the short *and* long term. If our actions enable negative outcomes in the future, then our very actions are a fallacy in the name of social justice and social good. To ensure that we don't continuously relegate our responsibilities for the impacts our solutions have downstream on minoritised populations, current efforts must shift to critical foresight and decolonial approaches.

TABLE 7.1 Current approaches to foresight versus systemic decolonial approaches of foresight

Current approaches to foresight	*Systemic decolonial approaches of foresight*
Tight circles of "recognised" expertise:	**Recognising positionality:**
Foresight sees similarity in expertise and little recognition of non-academically qualified practitioners or people with lived experience. Recent years have seen a birth of practitioners from the Global South though epistemology of practice remains largely the same. Reflection of positionality, privilege or bias in facilitation approaches and practices is missing. Selin (2008) puts forward the argument that foresight methods have their own schemes on what counts as anticipatory knowledge and specifies through which channels such knowledge should be generated and shared. These futures then get accepted as "official futures" without nuance and become self-fulfilling (Careful Industries 2021).	When the same groups of "experts" facilitate foresight processes and workshops, we continue the same epistemology of knowledge and learning. Whether consciously or unconsciously, we recreate in our own image. Recognising the positionality of facilitation and decision-making within our wider metropolis allows an assessment on impacts of bias or privilege.
Narrow epistemology:	**Legitimacy in pluriversality:**
The frameworks behind foresight tools and approaches have hardly evolved over the last few decades. Though recent years have seen expansion of epistemology in terms of storytelling and concepts of time, this has not translated in a legitimate way to mainstream curricula.	Utilising a wider range of knowledge sources and experiences legitimises a multiplicity of conceptual models and prevents the replication of an echo-chamber worldview via limited perspectives that do not account for normative and cultural realities. The addition of perspective allows us to recognise that multiple truths and multiple realities exist at the same time and are seen, experienced, imagined and lived by different groups of people even within similar contexts. Pluriversality gives socio-political and ecological momentum to affect relationality in literacy and challenges Eurocentric pedagogy that does not reflect realities the world over (Perry 2020).
	As Arturo Escobar argues in *Design for the Pluriverse*: we must liberate the imagination to enable other definitions of possible futures (Escobar 2018).
The four Ps of futures:	**Expansion to five Ps of futures:**
The baseline of all foresight models draws on the four Ps of futures: possible, preferable, plausible, and probable.	Adding in an additional P for Perspective. The five Ps are no longer adequate for two reasons: (1) its terminology is not easily understood by all peoples; and (2) it misses the additional layer of *perspective*: "whose perspective do these four Ps privilege?"[1]

TABLE 7.1 Cont.

Current approaches to foresight	*Systemic decolonial approaches of foresight*
Binary impact assessments:	**Privileging forces:**
Current tools for impact/implication analysis do not build in any rigorous, explicit, intersectional analysis of structural or systemic inequity. This results in future designs replicating inequalities of the past.	An analysis of privileging forces: patriarchy, race/ethnicity, colonialism/paternalism, hetero/cis-normativity, classism/class privilege, ableism, and ageism, to interrogate impacts of futures design (Arcaro 2021).
Participatory engagement:	**Participatory decision-making:**
In an effort to bring diversity and inclusion into futures practice, we have seen a small rise of participatory futures practices engage a wider range of civil society (Peach 2019). Whilst this is a welcomed approach, participatory approaches are not enough by themselves. The issue behind participatory approaches isn't the lack of "listening" to diverse voices, but rather the influence that those alternative points of view have over decision-making.	Participatory decision-making is intentionally designed to seek out alternative points of view and ideas that feed into foresight models, and then design pathways for such points of view and ideas to *influence* decision-making. This ensures that we move beyond "diversity and inclusion" or "participation" as a metric for mitigating bias. It also creates clear, transparent mechanisms that ensure the inclusion of historically excluded, impacted populations to *influence* decision-making.
Hegemonic language:	**Democratising language:**
Futures and foresight tools use the same language regardless of whether it resonates with people the world over or influences their cultural mental models. The same terms are used to describe approaches and methods regardless of whether it is understood or embraced, or even whether the term exists in other languages. When language and terms are not understood, it becomes a form of exclusionary privilege.	When the language of knowledge is so out of touch and reach for much of the world and we dismiss people's ability to understand it, we fail to recognise the fundamental factors needed in democratisation: resonance, understanding, and embracing. Democratising the language of futures to be accessible allows all people to represent their knowledge in ways that best speak to them.
Siloed linearity:	**Complexity and non-linearity:**
Current futures tools are ironically linear. Tools such as future cones, future wheels, and scenarios can end up creating "general" futures without a nuanced analysis of the complexity and systems in which those futures exist.	Systemic decolonial approaches of foresight blend systems analysis and complexity modelling to analyse tension points within systems, hot spots of power and bias, and potentialities for systemic failure.
Simplistic solutionism and constructed representation:	**Objective truth and relational ethics** (Birhane 2021)**:**
Problem identification in futures and foresight approaches tends to be minimal, based on the perspectives of who is in the room. This often results in solutionism that narrowly focuses on what appears to be an obvious issue with some degree of certainty.	Assessing patterns across a wider range of contextual social, technical, economic, and historical systems, norms, and structures to understand *why* rather than blindly and simplistically designing technical solutions and systems based on singular or similar representations.

(continued)

TABLE 7.1 Cont.

Current approaches to foresight	Systemic decolonial approaches of foresight
Future impact assessment:	**Future harm assessment:**
Current approaches to impacts/implications assessments tend to be general without an explicit analysis on how harm or impact might be expanded in the future.	Focusing on future harm expands the range of criteria for assessment including plausible, possible, and probable future harms, dispossession, and impacts that might arise on historically excluded and oppressed communities and their future generations.
Collective visioning:	**Transparent privilege and dispossession:**
Current visioning focuses on getting to a consensus of a COLLECTIVE probable vision of the future, regardless of what the multiplicity, nuanced, *preferable* future might be.	Transparent privilege and dispossession assess whose futures are privileged and whose are dispossessed in decision-making, and the risk of such an assessment in the short- and long-term horizon.

The decolonial foresight framework is firmly grounded on the rights and equity of impacted, minoritised populations that are often left out of redesign considerations and are relegated as passive beneficiaries of the system, rather than as active agents. Anasuya Sengupta once put forward the following provocation: "that Wakanda isn't just the idea of what *could* be, but also a reminder of a past possibility—if we are to consider what was taken away" (Sengupta, Mhlambi, Zolli, and Krishnan 2021).

Let us not sleepwalk into unjust, inequitable futures. As bell hooks (1990) so eloquently argued:

> Am I educating the colonizer/oppressor class so that they can exert better control? … If we do not interrogate our motives, the direction of our work, continually, we risk furthering a discourse on difference and otherness that not only marginalizes people of color but actively eliminates the need for our presence.

Note

1 In conversation with Mansi Parikh and Wayne Pan—Diaspora Futures Collective—August 18th, 2021.

References

Adegbeye, O. T. (2020). Why social distancing won't work for us. *The Correspondent*. March 27, 2020. https://thecorrespondent.com/378/why-social-distancing-wont-work-for-us/50039243100-5409cfb5.

Arcaro, T. (2021). Critical Hydra Theory. Aid Worker Voices. *Elon University*. July 17, 2021. https://blogs.elon.edu/aidworkervoices/?p=1848.

ARUP. (2019). 2050 Scenarios: four plausible futures. *ARUP*. www.arup.com/perspectives/publications/research/section/2050-scenarios-four-plausible-futures.

Birhane, A. (2021) *Algorithmic Injustice: a relational ethics approach*, CellPress Open Access.

Brown, A. M. (2017) *Emergent Strategy: Shaping Change, Changing Worlds,* AK Press.

Canyon, D. (2018). Simplifying Complexity with Strategic Foresight and Scenario Planning. Occasional Paper. *Daniel K. Inouye Asia-Pacific Center for Security Studies.* October 2018. https://apcss.org/nexus_articles/simplifying-complexity-with-strategic-foresight-and-scenario-planning/.

Careful Industries. (2021). "What is Foresight?" A Constellation of Possible Futures. The Civil Society Foresight Observatory Discovery Report. *Careful Industries.* August 2021. www.careful.industries/foresight-observatory/discovery-report/what-is-foresight#footnote12.

Cottam, H. (2021). The Radical Way shifting the social paradigm. *Hilary Cottam Blog.* May 13, 2021. www.hilarycottam.com/the-radical-way_shifting-the-social-paradigm/.

Dash, A. (2016). The Immortal Myths About Online Abuse. Humane Tech. *Medium.* May 27th, 2016. https://medium.com/humane-tech/the-immortal-myths-about-online-abuse-a156e3370aee.

European Commission. (2020). "What is Strategic Foresight?" Strategic Foresight. *European Commission.* Webpage. https://ec.europa.eu/info/strategy/strategic-planning/strategic-foresight_en.

Grosfoguel, R. (2011). Decolonizing post-colonial studies and paradigms of political-economy: transmodernity, decolonial thinking, and global coloniality; *TRANSMODERNITY: Journal of Peripheral Cultural Production of the Luso-Hispanic World* 1(1). https://dialogoglobal.com/texts/grosfoguel/Grosfoguel-Decolonizing-Pol-Econ-and-Postcolonial.pdf.

hooks, b. (1990). *Yearning: Race, Gender and Cultural Politics.* South End Press.

Kugler, M. and S. Shakti. (2020). The Impact of COVID-19 and the policy response in India. Future Development. *Brookings.* July 13th, 2020. www.brookings.edu/blog/future-development/2020/07/13/the-impact-of-covid-19-and-the-policy-response-in-india/.

Linh, A. (2020). What Decolonising Digital Rights Looks Like. *Digital Freedom Fund.* April 6th, 2020. https://digitalfreedomfund.org/author/aurum-linh/.

Lorde, A. (1984) "The Master's Tools Will Never Dismantle the Master's House." *Sister Outsider: Essays and Speeches.* Crossing Press. 110–114.

Martinot, S. (2004). The Coloniality of Power: Notes Toward De-Colonization. *The Center for Global Justice.* www.globaljusticecenter.org/papers/coloniality-power-notes-toward-de-colonization.

Mhlambi, S, J. O. Freuler, and P. Ricaurte. (2019). Think South. Reimagining the Internet. *EDIGS: Emerging Digital Issues in the Global South working group.* October 1st, 2019. https://archive.org/details/think_south_2019/page/n5/mode/2up.

Mohamed, S., M.. Png, and W. Isaac. (2020). Decolonial AI: Decolonial theory as socio-technical foresight in artificial intelligence. *Philosophy and Technology* 405. https://arxiv.org/abs/2007.04068.

Omanga, D. (2020). Decolonization, Decoloniality, and the Future of African Studies: A Conversation with Dr. Sabelo Ndlovu-Gatsheni. *Items: Insights from the Social Sciences.* January 14th, 2020. https://items.ssrc.org/from-our-programs/decolonization-decoloniality-and-the-future-of-african-studies-a-conversation-with-dr-sabelo-ndlovu-gatsheni/.

Peach, K. (2019). New platforms for public imagination. *Blogs, Nesta,* May 24th, 2019. www.nesta.org.uk/blog/new-platforms-public-imagination/.

Perry, M. (2020). Pluriversal Literacies: Affect and Relationality in Vulnerable Times. *Reading Research Quarterly* 56 (2): 293–309. doi:10.1002/rrq.312.

PwC. (2018). Workforce of the future: The competing forces shaping 2030. *PwC.* www.pwc.com/gx/en/services/people-organisation/publications/workforce-of-the-future.html.

Raval, N. (2021). A New AI Lexicon: Modernity + Coloniality, The constitution, scale, and many dimensions of the modern/colonial world-system. A New AI Lexicon. *Medium.* July 28th, 2021. https://medium.com/a-new-ai-lexicon/a-new-ai-lexicon-modernity-coloniality-7f6979ffbe82.

Salazar, J. F. (2015). Buen Vivir: South America's rethinking of the future we want. *The Conversation.* July 23rd, 2015. https://theconversation.com/buen-vivir-south-americas-rethinking-of-the-future-we-want-44507.

Selin, C. (2008). The Sociology of the Future: Tracing Stories of Technology and Time. *Sociology Compass* 2 (6):1878–1895. September 2008. DOI:10.1111/j.1751-9020.2008.00147.x.

Sengupta, A., Mhlambi, S., Zolli, A., and Aarathi Ratha Krishnan. (2021). Foresight and Decolonial Humanitarian Tech Ethics. Video & Podcast: A New Digital Humanism. *Berkman Klein Center for*

Internet & Society at Harvard University. May 7th, 2021. https://cyber.harvard.edu/events/foresight-and-decolonial-humanitarian-tech-ethics.

Tuck, E. and K. Wayne Yang. (2012). Decolonization is not a metaphor. *Decolonization: Indigeneity, Education & Society*, Vol.1, No. 1, 2012, pp. 1–40. https://clas.osu.edu/sites/clas.osu.edu/files/Tuck%20and%20Yang%202012%20Decolonization%20is%20not%20a%20metaphor.pdf.

World Economic Forum and Deloitte. (2021). Technology Futures Report 2021: Projecting the possible. Navigating what's next. *World Economic Forum*. April 5th, 2021. www.weforum.org/reports/technology-futures-projecting-the-possible-navigating-whats-next.

8

INHABITING THE EDGE

Edgar Pieterse

Cape Town is ranked as the eighth most violent city in the world (Cape Town 2020). I am not surprised. Between February 25th, and March 4th, 2021, 14 murders took place, including that of two police officers and a few teenagers killed in a drive-by shooting incident in Mitchell's Plain, a sprawling working-class suburb of the city (Stoltz 2021).

In the wake of this spate of gang-related violence meted out by young black men against other black bodies, the usual ineffectual political fanfare ensues. The national minister of police decrees that the army should be deployed, implying that a heavy-handed armed response is the most effective remedy. Residents want more visible policing and local politicians want to deploy technological solutions such as CCTV cameras and audio detection of gunshots through a system called ShotSpotter Flex. In the plume of public attention and outrage, some might make the throwaway comment about possible root causes for the epidemic of violence. But by and large, the focus remains on more uniforms and guns, until the intensity subsides—only for the cycle to flare up again within a few days or weeks. Meanwhile, the systemic causes of large-scale youth unemployment, poor educational achievements, harsh living conditions and relentless cultural denigration hardly ever gets addressed. This dysfunctionality has been going on for a long time (Pinnock 1997). The spiritual and psychic implications are almost unfathomable. However, I suspect that the extremely high incidence of intra-family sexual violence that have roots in intergenerational trauma is an important symptom of these societal scars. There is considerable South African literature and discourse that explores the concept of woundedness which serves as a shorthand to capture the enduring effects of intergenerational trauma on individuals, communities, and places—inducing a panoply of wicked problems (Manda 2014; Mogape 2020).

I was born and grew up in two hardcore working-class neighborhoods in greater Cape Town—Elsies River and Uitsig—that remain at the epicenter of the kinds of routine violence intimated. I navigated my walks to school, friends, church, corner shops, and wasteland-like play areas with an ingrained vigilance to always read the street. Thus, even though I am now comfortably ensconced in a leafy suburb, worlds away from the violence that structures the atmosphere of working-class neighborhoods across the city, I cannot but feel the implications of the context and backstories that envelop the reported deaths and injuries. Also, a lot of

DOI: 10.4324/9781003199816-11

the research undertaken by the African Centre for Cities (ACC) where I am based is in these communities. It is this tightly woven web of anger, anxiety, fear, and frustration that compels me to imagine possible alternatives, or at least entry points into alternative pathways that young black people can explore—signaling a break with the fate of histories marked by exploitation and routine denigration of being.

As an urbanist, I am fated to think spatially about these conditions and their potential remedies. Cape Town is uniquely endowed with incredible natural assets that translate into a picturesque playground for well-heeled tourists and the upper middle-class who can enjoy exquisite cuisine, breathtaking landscapes, opulent mansions, and just about any consumerist fantasy they can afford. However, for the majority of the city's residents, the daily reality is the extreme opposite of enclave opulence. Barren, sandy landscapes dominate streetscapes. Housing is small and overcrowded and often filled with both dread and laughter. Dread flows from the foreboding specter of erratic gendered violence, and laughter comes from the endless capacity for humor characteristic of working-class lifeworlds manifest through linguistic elasticity. Access to basic services is intermittent or completely absent, especially for the 18 percent of households (272,000) who live in shack structures.[1] In other words, Cape Town is the preeminent case study of urban inequality, cultural erasure, and environmental injustice that intersect in the homes and streets of working-class neighborhoods.

The roots of spatial inequality can be traced to the original colonial incursion in 1652 and the subsequent experiments in urban regulation and management that were all a dress rehearsal for full-blown Apartheid urban planning and governance, introduced in the 1950s and consolidated through market-driven real estate logics in more recent times. The net effect is intergenerational dispossession for black families and intergenerational wealth creation for white families and businesses, both actively structured and stimulated by state practices. It is this cumulative legacy that has proven immovable in the democratic era since 1994, despite a raft of radical democratic laws and policies. Paradoxically, redistributive housing and infrastructure policies served to exacerbate spatial inequality for reasons that I have documented elsewhere (Pieterse 2019; Pieterse and Cirolia 2016).

Interestingly, religious belief has served to both facilitate these structures of rule, and inform various forms of overt and tacit resistance. Indeed, religious ideology and beliefs played a central role in these regimes of exploitation, enrolment, and adaptation. South Africa is a predominantly religious society. Less than 8 percent identify as agnostic or do not believe in anything in particular. More than 84 percent of the population identify as Christian and the remainder is either Muslim or Hindu. However, most Christians belong to African Independent Churches that are not a product of missionary efforts. Their theology is syncretic, incorporating indigenous spiritual beliefs and rituals that have strong echoes with other indigenous belief systems pertaining to ancestors and relations with nature (Cultural Atlas n.d.).

One of the effects of engineered racialized inequality is that the Apartheid project produced a strange spatial tapestry marked by sharp delineations between land uses, classes, and of course, racial groups. Railway lines, highways, secondary roads, and industrial areas all perform as physical barriers to distinguish and prevent cross-pollination. Due to the market-driven logics of both public and private housing markets, these distinctions were further entrenched in the democratic era.

However, there is an opportunity for radical transformation to be found in this spatial tapestry. Along the railway lines and key road arteries across the city, for example, substantial buffer zones exist alongside, creating opportunities for new residential and economic typologies that can also reinforce corridors for increased public transport. These new typologies can potentially be radically mixed-income (incorporating large income bands), include social infrastructure such as crèches, schools, and primary health care facilities, alongside quality public space and opportunities for small businesses. The buffer zones and liminal spaces are untapped opportunities to insinuate nature-based placemaking interventions.

Another example is the ample green and open space pockets that characterize middle-class and upper middle-class suburbs across the city. These spaces are ripe for the insertion of affordable housing opportunities for working-class families, along with a mix of uses. The number of housing opportunities that could be supplied in these locations rank well above 100,000 but it would obviously require steadfast political leadership and frontal engagement with widespread NIMBY-ism (not-in-my-backyard).

Alongside these geographies allowing spatial insertion of new ways of city and community building, Cape Town is also marked by extensive opportunities for more environmentally sound and regenerative forms of development. This ranges from the cleaning and regeneration of extensive river systems and wetlands to the introduction of low-carbon construction materials (using redeployed alien vegetation) and improving densities and the footprint of the public transport systems. Both streams of urban innovation—new housing typologies and the adoption of sustainable infrastructure models—can further be conceptualized as a means to address the crushing problem of unemployment. Close to 64 percent of youth, between 15 and 24 years old, is unemployed, according to official data (South Africa unemployment 2021).

There is a whole new economic system to be grown through a reimagination of the built environment and the "performance" of routine investments that are made to grow the city and attend to its maintenance and retrofitting requirements. In fact, I am certain that the only sliver of hope for young black citizens in the city is a radical expansion of the green economy through a transition to sustainable and green infrastructures. These conclusions derive from a series of projects that I have curated on the spatial inheritances of Cape Town and potential alternative futures. The question that arises is this: Where will the innovation come from to figure out how a transition to sustainable infrastructures can be ensured—in ways that are labor intensive, restorative for peace and wellbeing, and enable experimentation with a collective city identity? The remainder of this chapter sets out a thought/practice experiment—the Edge Innovation Cluster—that I am feeding into various institutional folds and networks of the city, building on its precedent, the Integration Syndicate.[2]

The Edge Innovation Cluster—Grounded Imaginary

Opportunistic Provocation

Cape Town's public sphere is marked by a macabre fatalism. Almost everyone across the political spectrum agrees that the inherited legacy of racialized discrimination and exploitation has established a series of logics that reinscribe racialized class-based exclusion. State policies all decry the continued legacies of spatial apartheid and its educational and economic consequences, yet these self-same policies are complicit in reproducing the status quo. Interest groups representing middle-class residents also acknowledge that something must be done to correct historical injustices, as long as it does not involve allowing poorer households living within their suburban boundaries. Social movements campaign for radical social inclusion and their tactics range from direct action to targeted occupations of public facilities to draw attention to the housing crises but they remain marginal in terms of effective political power.

As a result, there is a continuous "rediscovery" of apartheid spatial ghosts, but a shrug-of-the-shoulders resignation follows because we don't really know how to reverse the path-dependent flow of history. Nor can we expect the market to act against its own interest, or that of the businesses and households who buttress the municipal tax base. One of the key challenges is to find public policy hooks upon which to hang a more ambitious agenda, espe-cially one that can activate a fresh cultural imaginary about ways to escape the trap of self-ful-filling fatalism that nothing can really change. How to do this remains opaque but I am keen to set in motion a series of discussions and explorations to distill a fresh synthesis based on the inputs and imaginaries of many Capetonians who share my concerns. The Edge Innovation Cluster as a concept is an institutional imaginary in the making to stage the necessary explora-tory conversations.

It builds on several explorations since the 2010s. In 2014, for example, ACC initiated, with the New Town Institute, a design studio on the implications of pursuing increased densifi-cation in three kinds of urban fabric in Cape Town: informal settlement context; brownfield post-industrial areas; and a greenfield site where the land was predominantly in public own-ership (Provoost 2015).

These research and design speculations fed into a substantial exhibition on Cape Town that I co-curated from December 2014 to January 2015 with Tau Tavengwa, called *City Desired*.[3] The greenfield site that was explored is an amalgamation of publicly owned land that covers a ribbon of substantial land parcels that buttress a river system in the city. It is also the geograph-ical center of the city, a veritable combination of dead spaces and buffer zones designed to keep racial groups and classes apart and distant (see Figure 8.1). The idea of reimagining this leftover zone as more than just dead space, potentially even the hub of a regeneration zone of metropolitan significance, was not lost on us.

We sought to capitalize on two imperatives. First, the metropolitan and provincial gov-ernment had already designated one component of the zone—the Two Rivers Urban Park (TRUP)—as a priority site for development that could achieve broader goals of restitching the city. We wanted to latch onto this opportunity and preempt the planning ambition of the masterplan that would inevitably be produced by a private planning firm in the city.[4] Our studio proposed a major ecological intervention to clean and regenerate the river systems while making room for labor-intensive opportunities on the banks and introducing wetland ponds to enhance natural filtration. Furthermore, the rivers would be made much more accessible and public by deploying natural water-management techniques that would effect-ively create a major public park of metropolitan significance. Since the park is at the physical crossroads of working-class neighborhoods such as Langa, Bokmakierie, Maitland Garden Village, and middle-class areas such as Mowbray, Pinelands, and Observatory, there would be an obvious opportunity for greater social interaction, especially if cultural and social pro-gramming were to be instantiated. These interactions would take place in a site that is still considered sacred by various First Nations groups.

This is not the occasion to reflect on the impacts of the above speculation, or lack thereof. I will, however, fast-forward a few years from that speculative exercise to 2019 when the Western Cape and City of Cape Town governments published a draft development frame-work for the TRUP and nearby Ndabeni elements of the territory that was the subject of the

1	NDABENI	6	MOWBRAY GOLF COURSE	11	PAARDEN EILAND	16	RONDEBOSCH
2	MAITLAND GARDEN VILLAGE	7	ATHLONE TRANSFER STATION	12	KENSINGTON	17	ATHLONE
3	RAAPENBERG BIRD SANCTUARY	8	LANGA	13	SALT RIVER	18	METROPOLITAN TRAINLINE
4	VINCENT PALLOTTI HOSPITAL	9	BOKMAKIERIE	14	OBSERVATORY	19	WASTE WATER TREATMENT PLANT
5	BLACK RIVER	10	PINELANDS	15	MOWBRAY	20	N2 HIGHWAY

FIGURE 8.1 Map of Density Syndicate research site in context of Cape Town

Density Syndicate's design experiment. Figure 8.2 is a summary extract of the plan and reflects the anticipated future uses of the site, and constitutes the second imperative.

The governmental proposals were underwhelming and failed to appreciate the metropolitan significance of the location of the area and the grander ambitions it could fulfill. The purple

1   NEW URBAN INFILL
2   GENERAL INDUSTRIAL DEVELOPMENT
3   MIXED USE INTENSIFICATION
4   LOCAL AREA ACTIVITY CORRIDOR INCLUDING MIXED USE
5   REGIONAL SPORTS FACILITY RELATING TO THE LIESBEEK CORRIDOR

FIGURE 8.2 Development typology for the Two Rivers Urban Park study area (City of Cape Town 2019)

zone, for example, which is earmarked for general industrial development fails to optimize this site for large-scale (high-density) affordable rental, student, and private housing. Since the surrounds of the site are predominantly industrial, it is one of the few well-located nodes in the core part of Cape Town (within 8 km of the traditional central business district) where one can consider high-rise typologies. The zone earmarked for "mixed-use intensification" (number 3) is already mixed use but not particularly open to the public or inclusive. Most importantly, a very small zone is designated with "new urban infill" (area 1 in Figure 8.2), which is code for housing. Given the scale of housing deficits in Cape Town and the urgency to produce more mixed-income residential stock, this is not nearly ambitious enough.

In confronting the societal crises of unemployment, deep inequality, pervasive patterns of social violence, and cultural conflict, I felt there was an opportunity to resignify this area through an ambitious catalytic program of interdependent projects clustered together. It needs to be an intervention that can find resonance and support across all the many divides in the city—class, political ideology, race, and so forth. The remainder of the chapter spells out this proposition for the Edge Innovation Cluster. The conclusion will contextualize how it is being taken forward.

Projected Program Elements

At its most ambitious, a multidimensional cluster of activities is envisaged that includes the arts, culture, research on urban sustainability innovations, incubating businesses geared for the green economy, and a vibrant youth outreach program. By colocating such a diverse program of work, it can induce ambitious synergies and achieve metropolitan, continental, and global impact. It can also restore faith that it is possible to execute important public-interest initiatives that enjoy the support of all sectors of society. The point being that, as an upper middle-income country, South Africa does have a considerable infrastructure of research centers, museums, youth centers and so forth. However, typically these institutions underperform due to limited budgets for programming and a lack of dynamic interaction between organizations, which is typically the frisson zone that generates creativity.

The success of the program will depend on an institutional framework that allows each component to have relative autonomy, succeed on its own terms, and find inspiration through strategic articulation with the other elements. Overall, the Edge Program glue will be a set of *animating principles* that inform the priorities and programming of each organizational component. Innovation will be driven forward by fostering projects that take the following principles seriously. The design assumption is that this will induce an intellectual, cultural, and spiritual milieu of radical openness, reciprocity, and solidarity. An elaboration of each principle is called for.

Animating Principles for the Edge Innovation Cluster

Engage the Past, Present and Future in One Conceptual Breath

South African society is deeply conservative and enjoys a love affair with unbridled consumerism. This produces a large gulf between the values of a radical rights-based constitutional order combined with a battery of progressive laws, popular culture, and emotional attachments that dominate the public sphere. Practically this means that when radical actors invoke the histories of colonial dispossession and violence, there is not necessarily an affective resonance in society. Not that the past does not matter, it is just referenced and experienced in different registers imbued by beliefs in ancestors and transcendental resignation. Furthermore, the constitutional disposition allows for truncated forms of reparation, redistribution, and recognition, but is hemmed in by administrative law, limited resources, and an aversion to undo or contradict private land ownership (McKenna 2019). These sticky political-policy dynamics create a complicated curatorial imperative to excavate the palimpsests of the city, without an alien(ating) radical rhetorical repertoire. For working-class youth to acquire self-awareness, it is essential that programs are created to animate a desire for production of social narratives through social histories that are both personal (family trees) and spatial (neighborhood histories and circulations), expressed through contemporary genres of social media, podcasts, photography, and performance arts. The curatorial art lies in framing historical awareness as a precondition for futural imaginings and contemporary positionalities.

Draw on Cognitive (Data), Emotional (Narratives) and Affective (Aesthetics) Curatorial Strategies to Enroll Citizens and Visitors

In public-facing interventions the tendency is to conflate accessibility with simplicity. This means that communicators prefer to generate simplistic stories about the city and its facets to ensure the broadest possible appeal but at the expense of accuracy and fostering more authentic public discourse. Our experiences teach us that it is possible to synthesize large volumes of data through carefully crafted visualizations to convey trends, interdependent dynamics across the urban system, and provoke novel questions. These in turn create stepping stones to deploy narrative techniques to explore hidden (subaltern) histories and topics, which in turn can be rendered beautiful and arresting through artistic and design languages. Amidst deep complexity and contingency, there is a need for story building that spans data analytics, narratology, and beautiful representations to induce novel forms of questioning and joint exploration. An insistence on beauty in the lives of the most exploited is a lesson drawn from practices in social urbanism in Medellín, Colombia, and Torolab in Tijuana, Mexico.[5] These techniques are well placed to unpack the spiritual dimensions of the past, the present, and the future if they are embedded in the curatorial frame.

Always Combine Deconstruction and Proposition

A deeply ingrained habit of the left is to remain stuck in deconstruction and structural analysis on why things are in the unjust state they are in. This does not always correlate with a concomitant commitment to think prefiguratively, or to think propositionally in a grounded manner. Embeddedness demands the cultivation of a disposition that inhabits the tension between these two poles, and to use the inevitable confrontation with contradiction and uncertainty as a creative stimulus to invite multiple perspectives and experiences into the inquiry to arrive at fuller and more generative hunches. This descriptor of tentative proposition is appropriate because the history of intentional development reminds us that unintended consequences and nasty boomerang effects tend to almost always accompany policy actions. The best we can hope for is informed hunches that can inform delicate experiments that allow us the experience to formulate clearer concepts and institutional guidelines that will require further refinement through practice and reflection. Naming and honing these sensibilities are essential ingredients for the programming of the Edge Innovation Cluster.

Re-enchant the Sciences and Foreground the Power of the Arts

The Edge Innovation Cluster is a child of the University of Cape Town and part of a larger imperative to bridge the worlds of science, society, and policy. Science has lost its reputation as an obvious source of authority amidst the ascendency of populist authoritarianism. Yet, if we are to open public discourse and action around the regeneration of ecosystems, soils, water catchments, and air quality, that can galvanize citizen action and organization, we need to enchant the craft and findings of scientific inquiry. Knowledge animators who work directly on affect and emotional resonance tend to have a grounding in the arts and humanities. By deploying their repertoires new modalities of societal questioning, exploring, and celebration of knowledge can emerge, especially if the primary focus is the lifeworlds and passions of youth. Furthermore, the translational labor involved in such explorations can help scientists to see new questions and appreciate the relational nature of ontologies—itself a necessary cultural shift to bring conventional scientific institutions in closer step with societal currents (Bennett and Zournazi 2020).

Articulate Intimate Individual Narratives with a Metropolitan Perspective on Systems, Space, and Flows

Cities are inherently complex because they aggregate a multiplicity of systems that function on the basis of internal system logistics as well as rationalities that arise from their inter-dependency with other systems. Natural systems are driven by physical laws and social systems of governance or culture are propelled by more contingent and unpredictable dynamics, eliminating the possibility of prediction but demanding thoughtful anticipation (Karuri-Sebina 2020). Infrastructure systems are fascinating socio-technical systems that have physical, social, and institutional properties and evolve in highly particularistic forms over time. If an energy system, for example, is built around fossil fuel like coal, as is the case in South Africa, it is extremely difficult to alter the system because of path-dependency dynamics. Who will bear the cost of switching technologies from extractives to renewables? It is overwhelming for non-specialists to understand these knots of system interdependency, which is why it is curatorially important to connect systems dynamics with deep (political) histories to different forms of manifestation at different scales, including the most intimate, individual embodiments. When a system can be understood and felt corporeally, it creates the possibility for imagining alternative lineages and future trajectories. These dynamics are especially acute in urban systems.

Adopt a Curatorial Approach that Prioritizes Children and Youth

This principle is self-explanatory, but a few points of clarification are called for. Again, the intent is not to dumb down but to think deeply about affective resonance and curatorial enrolment. What are the passions of children and youth, especially those who come from tough, unrelenting neighborhoods where care, compassion, beauty, and emotional abandon are simply not available as routine experiences? How can such passions be worked with and extended to enter the thematic interests of the Edge Innovation Cluster at the intersections of history, scales, cultures, consumption (desire), production, value creation, and becoming? How does fun and play become an essential ingredient in all dimensions of learning and discovery? When scientists, entrepreneurs, and curators are confronted by these imperatives, they will inevitably rework their own habits and questions. Innovation will not be far behind such disruptions.

Treat Digital and Analogue Registers as Symbiotic and Essential

With the prolific uptake of digital devices and mediums there is a temptation to assume that curatorial strategies should confine themselves to digitally mediated programming. There is undoubtedly value in such moves, but it is even more important to appreciate that digital formats come into their full power when paired with analogue forms of engagement. In curatorial terms they foreground different experiences for questioning, exploration, and learning. However, if deployed with analogue methods that involve a fuller sensorial experience, they can become tools for pushing imagination and representation even further. If the Edge wants to explore the politics of memory, naming, memorialization, ancestorial care, and the forging of new cultural identities, for example, an intervention that focuses on street names could be generative. The administrative and social histories of street names would involve archival work and interviews with residents, which would generate a nuanced picture to deepen understandings of the effects of racialized regulation, but also open potentialities of working through the implications of such legacies. Part of such work could involve the deployment of digital tools to create digital twins of streets and neighborhoods in which various alternatives could be explored and tested without undermining bylaws and getting caught up in the practicalities of changing maps and street signs. However, the various forms of digital play would be impoverished without the more conventional forms of data collection and memory building.

Pinpoint and Amplify Economic Potential in Everything

In post-colonial cities like Cape Town, it is impossible to ignore the depth of economic distress. Amid the COVID-19 pandemic, unemployment reached 64 percent for youth between 15 and 24 years of age. This is in a context of long-term unemployment and low wages, triggered by a combination of premature deindustrialization in the early 1980s and a racialized labor market rooted in a racist education system. The economic crisis is amplified by the convulsions of a global economy undergoing contradictory transitions to internalize environmental externalities (e.g., carbon pricing), re-center away from the West to the East, and profound technological disruption impacting forms of work and the further devaluation of, especially, low-skilled labor. Given the psychological and social effects of large-scale unemployment and extreme inequality, it is an overriding imperative to return all questions that animate the various organizational components of the Edge Innovation Cluster to issues of value creation, employment, and the dignity of work. It is simply not possible to instantiate an innovation lab in Cape Town, in Africa, and not be obsessed with meaningful forms of economic expression, especially when there are ways of reframing the making of city, and citizenship in the image of sustainability, solidarity, and restoration of natural systems and indigenous lifeworlds as cultural goals for society.

These animating principles offer enough anchorage to allow experts, activists, scientists, citizens, entrepreneurs, and philanthropists to find common cause and always keep an eye on producing excellence for public-interest outcomes. They provide a basis for an ambition that the initiative becomes a recognized "thought collider"[6] in Africa, with global resonance. The animating principles can hold radical pluralism and diversity of approach without sacrificing a sense of purpose, a collective determination to confront the painful and intractable issues that plague the city. The principles are also broad enough to be enduring and open to a continuous stream of fresh and transgressive interpretations. That unsettled energy has to be nurtured at the very heart of the initiative.

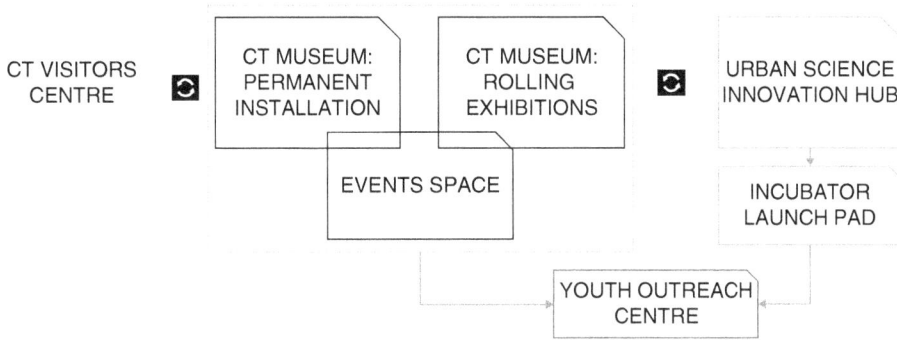

FIGURE 8.3 The Edge Innovation Cluster Program elements
*CT: Cape Town

At the core of the program is a City Museum with two synergetic parts. The first is a permanent installation that seeks to tell the multiple histories across temporalities of the city but in a fashion that provokes engagement, reflection, questions, and curiosity. Opening up questions about time and space is essential to deal with the silences of the past, and to create new discourses and imaginations about connections between the past, present, and future. The second component is a lot more flexible and open-ended: it will house rolling exhibitions structured around various themes and curated by (local) interdisciplinary teams. We envisage a competitive process to identify the most outstanding ideas to be let loose in the space. Given the endless combinations that various facets of the art world can team up with various configurations from the design and humanities fields, this will guarantee truly innovative and transgressive expressions. These elements of the Edge draw directly from long-standing engagements with the Centre for Contemporary Culture in Barcelona and a collective of designers and artists in Medellín, Colombia that draw heavily on exploring themes of urbanism through artistic exhibitions.

These two exhibition parts will form the basis for a series of public events that will enrich and enlarge vital public conversations in the city. In this vein, there are opportunities to enter into conversation and co-curation with other public, grassroots, and private art institutions in the city that share a desire to foster a more critical and dynamic public sphere. At all times, the events space will focus on various constituencies in the city and strive to draw in experts from the African continent and the Global South because the space will always serve to enrich larger global debates and deepen local, highly contextual discussions. In this domain we anticipate drawing on the experience and precedent of Go Down Arts Foundation in Nairobi, Kenya and C-Map in Port Harcourt, Nigeria. Existing relationships with these organizations will be deepened in the elaboration of the Edge. Both have deep experience of using the arts to draw in youth and animate complex urban planning debates. In Cape Town the challenge is to remain grounded in contextual issues but avoid parochialism, which inevitably results in factional chauvinism. However, if local debates are placed within larger pan-African and global circuits of ideas and explorations, it is easier to produce new insights beyond the conventional fault lines of intra-urban dialogues.

The fourth component of the overall program involves the establishment of a cutting-edge Urban Science Innovation Hub. It is a direct response to international calls for more holistic urban enquiry. A recent state of the art report, Science and the Future of Cities, suggests: "Contemporary city challenges require a step change in both scientific capacity and science–policy collaboration. This is a pivotal shift because urban systems are increasingly complex and multidimensional, and without a more synthetic and holistic enquiry, we run the risk of creating incomplete solutions. In order for "urban science" to be collectively greater than the sum of its parts it needs to draw from all the sciences—natural, engineering, and social, as well as the arts and humanities—while linking directly into practice and offering effective global assessments of the state of our planet's urban condition" (International Expert Panel 2018). Since its establishment in 2008, ACC has nurtured an intimate relationship of mutual learning and exchange with the Indian Institute for Human Settlements (IIHS), anchored in Bangalore, India.[7] This is one of the most radically interdisciplinary applied research and teaching centers in the world. This partnership will shape the detailed design of the urban science innovation hub.

Cape Town, South Africa and the Global South are confronted with the urgent need to develop systemic, land use, and economic solutions for growing urban populations, insufficient and inappropriate infrastructure (i.e., carbon intensive and fragile to climate change impacts), and extreme social pressures. Ideally, ACC will anchor this Innovation Hub and invite sister institutions and networks to colocate to amass a critical international node of urban expertise and testing of next generation solutions rooted in the knowledge and context of the Global South. There will be intentional cross-pollination between the scientific, artistic, and event components of the overall hub. Since the 2010s, ACC has developed a deep practice of coproduction of knowledge through an international platform called Mistra Urban Futures and various comparative research projects across the South (Parnell and Pieterse 2016). There is great potential to refine this practice through an engagement with the kinds of regulatory labs explored by the networks of "Legitimacies," which is a multi-scalar approach to transition pathways (Dark Matter Labs 2019).

To break with conventional approaches that delink scientific inquiry from economic application, the Edge Innovation Cluster will actively explore the incubation of new enterprises fit for the so-called fourth industrial revolution but rooted in a green economy. Furthermore, the enterprise incubator will unashamedly pursue black economic empowerment and excellence. The regional economy of the Western Cape remains largely untransformed and exclusionary. The urgency of economic transformation and inclusion will agitate the applied research and the curatorial priorities of the Edge Museum. There are a number of proto-initiatives in the regional economic and institutional system that can be drawn on to ensure that this element is robust. The government-funded agency, Green Cape, for example, has been pioneering identification of subsectors of the green economy and creating enabling support networks for regional businesses that can grow market share in these fields.

Finally, all the diverse components of the Edge Innovation Cluster will be translated and filtered to engage youth (15–24 years) in the city. A dedicated team will be assembled to bring to life a compelling public pedagogic approach that will strengthen narrative capacity. Again, there is a rich and diverse ensemble of organizations that focus on youth development and creative expression. We are convinced that unless we are able to surface and amplify the unique stories of the youth in the city, we will never be able to decipher the narrative of the African city writ large. This component will ground the overall program in the soil and passions of the city. Extra effort will be devoted to engaging these organizations and drawing upon their networks and practice to ensure that the outreach ambitions reinforce existing organizations with credibility and accountability.

Institutional Latticework

There is a very difficult problem that we have to inhabit: How to retain control of the curatorial intent of the initiative (as intimated above) while creating a genuinely open process that will allow diverse interest groups to co-design the program elements and the overall articulation of the Edge Innovation Cluster? Retaining control stems from an appreciation that the program has a global constituency and needs to rise above the deep and bitter internecine ideological battles that mark relationships between organizations in a city overdetermined by routine disappointment and anger. Generosity is not a public sentiment that comes to mind in thinking through how Cape Town addresses its stubborn problems. How to contemplate and undertake institutional design will be folded into the co-design processes that will, in the first instance, be anchored by the various programmatic elements of the Edge Innovation Cluster. Put differently, consultations and co-design will be clustered around each program area. A series of conversations and workshops will be mounted in 2022 (assuming a sufficient level of vaccination by the end of 2021) to interrogate and deepen the initial propositions of ACC. Thereafter, various international partners will be enrolled to share their practices, experiments, institutional models, and learning forged in the cauldron of "doing." The international partners include the various organizations mentioned in this chapter and others that may emerge through consultations.

Process as Catalyst

The dream is that we can shift the culture of engagement and listening, if we are able to curate a careful, challenging, and open process of engagement around the program elements with groups that have a direct interest and history in that domain. This will become Act One in the theater of innovation we hope to stage. Act Two will be exposure: various organizations that share a kindred spirit will be invited to share their respective experiences and learning with us with an eye on enriching the ideas that arise during Act One. Furthermore, Act Two will be essential to inoculate the initiative against parochialism and petty-minded organizational and ideological rivalries. It will, hopefully, instill a sense of wonder and urgency to realize the enormous potential that resides in Cape Town, untapped and unfulfilled. Act Three will involve the introduction of design-based exploration and testing to refine concept and business plans for each of the constituent elements and the overall Edge Innovation Cluster.

Of course, there will be a duty to conduct back-end technical feasibility investigations alongside to save time and energy but also to avoid a scenario where interest groups coproduce, completely disconnected from operating parameters. Furthermore, enrolling established organizations to start their planning to relocate into the site and its intentional commons will require careful and continuous discussions. The backdrop to these processual acts will be the architectural and land use implications of the vision. Thus, in close collaboration with the UCT School of Architecture and Planning, a cumulative set of student studios will experiment with design responses for the site, informed by the various consultative processes that will unfold in tandem.

If we are able to activate this groundswell of discussion and social imagineering (Mulgan 2020), the Edge Innovation Cluster will of course come to life even in the absence of buildings. This is the nature of true magic: to work toward a shared animating vision while the process of conjuring it into existence instantiates the very thing one is striving for.

Notes

1 The most recent public data on the socioeconomic profile of the Cape Town metropolitan area can be obtained from: COGTA & CCT. 2020. Profile: City of Cape Town. Pretoria: COGTA: www.google.com/url?sa=t&rct=j&q=&esrc=s&source=web&cd=&ved=2ahUKEwijleW JuJ7vAhWIRhUIHZHeCj4QFjABegQICxAD&url=https%3A%2F%2Fwww.cogta.gov.za%2Fddm%2 Fwp-content%2Fuploads%2F2020%2F11%2FCity-of-CT-September-2020.pdf&usg=AOvVaw0V tDV-IxMFU0o1rk66Oz7I.
2 The process, findings and provocations of the Integration Syndicate are documented here: Pieterse, E., P. Green, B. Knemeyer, A. Pulker, and A. Viviers, eds. (2019). *The integration syndicate. Shifting Cape Town's socio-spatial debate*. Cape Town: African Centre for Cities.
3 The exhibition has an afterlife here: https://cityscapesmagazine.com/projects/city-desired.
4 This draft integrated development framework was released for public comment in October 2019: City of Cape Town & Western Cape Government (2019) Two Rivers Local Spatial Development Framework (Draft October 2019). Cape Town: CCT & WCG.
5 This insight is based on my long-standing friendships with Raul Cardenas Osuna of Torolab in Tijuana and Alejandro Echeverri of URBAM in Medellín, Colombia.
6 I am indebted to Ravi Naidoo, founder of Design Indaba for the image.
7 For more information on IIHS, see: https://iihs.co.in/.

References

Bennett, J. and M. Zournazi, eds. (2020) *Thinking in the world. A reader*. Bloomsbury Academic.
Cape Town now ranks as the 8th most violent city in the world. (2020) *Business Tech*, June 11th, 2020: https://businesstech.co.za/news/lifestyle/407087/cape-town-now-ranks-as-the-8th-most-violent-city-in-the-world/.
City of Cape Town & Western Cape Government. (2019). Two Rivers Local Spatial Development Framework (Draft October 2019). CCT & WCG.
Cultural Atlas. (n.d.). South African culture. https://culturalatlas.sbs.com.au/south-african-culture/south-african-culture-religion.
Dark Matter Labs & Cities for People. (2019). *Legitimacities*. DML & Cities for People.
International Expert Panel on Science and the Future of Cities. 2018. *Science and the Future of Cities*. p. 4.
Karuri-Sebina, G. (2020). Urban Africa's futures: perspectives and implications for agenda 2063. *Foresight* 22(1): 95–108.
McKenna, L. (2019). Literature survey on urban land issues: South Africa. Centre for Affordable Housing Finance in Africa.
Manda, C. (2014). Becoming better humans in a world that lacks humanity: Working through trauma in post-apartheid South Africa. *Oral History Journal of South Africa* 2(2): 123–137.
Mogape, N. (2020). Overcoming trauma and woundedness for institutional and societal success. Trialogue: https://trialogue.co.za/overcoming-trauma-and-woundedness-for-institutional-and-societal-success/.
Mulgan, G. (2020). The Imaginary Crisis (and how we might quicken social and public imagination). UCL, Demos Helsinki and Untitled.
Parnell, S. and E. Pieterse. (2016). Translational global praxis – rethinking methods and modes of African urban research. *International Journal of Urban and Regional Research* 40(1): 236–246.

Pieterse, E. (2019). Urban governance and spatial transformation ambitions in Johannesburg, *Journal of Urban Affairs* 41(1): 20–38.

Pieterse, E. and Cirolia, L. (2016). South Africa's emerging national urban policy and upgrading agenda. In *Participatory informal settlement upgrading in South Africa*, edited by L. Cirolia, W. Smit, M. van Donk, T. Gorgens, and S. Drimie. UCT Press.

Pinnock, D. (1997). *Gangs, rituals & rites of passage*. African Sun Press.

Provoost, M. ed. (2015). *Cape Town: Densification as a cure for a segregated city*. International New Town Institute.

South Africa unemployment rate hits new record high. (2021). Business Tech, June 24th, 2021: https://businesstech.co.za/news/government/515388/south-african-unemployment-rate-hits-new-record-high/.

Stoltz, E. (2021). Shootings on Cape Flats claim 14 lives in less than a week. Mail & Guardian, March 2nd, 2021: https://mg.co.za/news/2021-03-02-cape-flats-shooting-week/.

9

RECONCILING RELATIONSHIPS WITH THE LAND THROUGH LAND ACKNOWLEDGEMENTS

Deborah McGregor and Emma Nelson

Introduction

One of the limitations of current Canadian conceptions of reconciliation is the underlying assumption that reconciliation applies, virtually exclusively, to relationships among peoples. There is no doubt that reconciliation among peoples, especially where conflict and violence have characterized (and continue to characterize) such relationships, is critical, as pointed out by Canada's Truth and Reconciliation Commission (TRC) (TRC 2015a). There are, however, other dimensions to reconciliation that are just as important from an Indigenous point of view. As Mi'kmaq Elder Augustine suggests, "other dimensions of human experience—our relationships with the earth and all living beings—are also relevant in working towards reconciliation" (TRC 2015a, 122). Elder Reg Crowshoe confirms this view, explaining that:

> Reconciliation requires talking, but our conversations must be broader than Canada's conventional approaches. Reconciliation between Aboriginal and non-Aboriginal Canadians, from an Aboriginal perspective, also *requires reconciliation with the natural world. If human beings resolve problems between themselves but continue to destroy the natural world, then reconciliation remains incomplete.*
>
> *TRC 2015a, 123, italics ours*

Indigenous conceptions of reconciliation extend beyond peoples to the natural world and are informed by direct relationships to the land. We must, the Elders say, reconcile with the Earth itself (TRC 2015a, 123).

This chapter has been written by an Anishinaabe scholar living and working in her own Lands (Deborah) in collaboration with a "settler" urban planner (Emma). In it, we explain how Land, spirit, and relationships with the natural world have endured through time and can

DOI: 10.4324/9781003199816-12

offer profound insights and knowledge. We choose to frame this topic through an examination of Land Acknowledgements. In so doing, we will address the following themes:

- **Land Acknowledgements:** their meaning and purpose, and how they are shared in practice;
- **Methodologies and Pedagogies:** re-centering land and relationships in education and planning teaching and practice;
- **Reconciling with the Land:** how relationships with, and *responsibilities* to, the land and future generations can be established through the process of acknowledgement.

Positionality

Deborah McGregor

Deborah McGregor n'dizhnikaaz (I am called). Wiigwaaskingaa n'doonjibaa (Birch Island, I am from). I am Anishinaabe from Whitefish River First Nation and currently I am Associate Professor and Canada Research Chair in Indigenous Environmental Justice at York University in Toronto, Canada. I have been teaching for three decades in areas relating to Indigenous knowledge systems, Indigenous environmental governance and Indigenous research methodologies. I have lived much of each year in Toronto since the early 1980s, and my life's work is to help ensure a sustainable future for human and all other life on our planet. My interest in Land Acknowledgements emerged out of efforts to facilitate student engagement with the Land, including developing relationships and assuming responsibilities with respect to it as well as to future generations.

Emma Nelson

I am the descendant of settlers from Scandinavia and the British Isles who arrived in so-called Canada and the USA sometime in the late 1800s. I moved to Tkaronto/Toronto (Haudenosaunee, Anishinaabe, Wendat, and Mississauga territory) in 2017 from Bozeman, Montana (Očhéthi Šakówiŋ, Apsalooke, Shoshone-Bannock, and Salish Kootenai territory) to complete a Master's degree in English and later a Master's in Environmental Studies. I have moved across the prairies all my life. I am interested in futures without capitalism and spend much of my time organizing with the Movement Defence Committee, a legal collective that provides support to progressive activists. For my Master's research, I produced a four-part podcast in which I interviewed settler planning-stream students about Land Acknowledgements after sensing a disconnect between the truths of those statements and the actions taken to address such truths. As a Queer and non-binary person, all of my writing, organizing, and creative work is imbued with my own experience of oppression and is done through an anti-colonial, antiracist, and anti-oppressive lens.

What Is a Land Acknowledgement?

In the public sphere, Land Acknowledgements are a relatively recent phenomenon which have already achieved widespread adoption in Canadian academic institutions (Daigle 2019;

Hewitt 2019). Such prevalence has led scholars such as Cree professors Jeffrey Hewitt and Michelle Daigle to point out that in many instances, Land Acknowledgements have become scripted spectacles, "performative acts" devoid of meaning with little or no effort to actually decolonize or achieve "right" relationships with Indigenous Peoples (Daigle 2019; Hewitt 2019).

As Hewitt writes, "I view the practice of land acknowledgments as good, necessary and important" (p.28). He adds, however, "the overwhelming majority of land acknowledgments are scripted. Typically, an organizer or host of a meeting will read from an institutional script approved by way of committee. Almost always the scripts read like a history in land occupation" (p.31). Daigle observes that Land Acknowledgements can be "respectful and meaningful as [long as] the people undertaking them—Indigenous and non-Indigenous—do so in a manner which activates the relational accountability that is embedded in this legal and political practice" (p.711). However, like Hewitt, Daigle writes that in many cases:

> Non-Indigenous peoples on campus seem to be more preoccupied with learning how to recite a territorial acknowledgment—"can you say that again so I can write it down properly?"—rather than learning about the place where they live and work, with all of the complexities of historical and ongoing colonial dispossession and violence.
>
> *p.711*

They become "hollow gestures and performances" (p.711). Hewitt emphasizes that Land Acknowledgements "should not make the reader or listener feel good" (p.40). If we are not careful, he warns, "land acknowledgments are in jeopardy of becoming part of the apparatus of colonial comfort that further displaces Indigenous Peoples" (p.40).

How then can we avoid reducing Land Acknowledgements to such platitudes? How can we as educators and planners work with Land Acknowledgements as a way to unsettle settlers, yet empower Indigenous Peoples? How can Land Acknowledgements be broadened to consider ontologically different relationships with the natural world as outlined by the Elders in the TRC report?

Different Perspectives on Land Acknowledgements

In 2016, I (McGregor) initiated a project at York University to develop a video that would offer deeper meaning and explanation of Land Acknowledgements from a variety of Indigenous perspectives, namely those of Indigenous faculty, administrators, staff, and students at York University. In the resulting video, "Understanding the Land Acknowledgment," Amy Desjarlais, a Knowledge Keeper with Aboriginal Student Services at York University, points out that Land Acknowledgments in academic and institutional settings are not necessarily for Indigenous People, but are rather tools to engage non-Indigenous people with the land and the active treaties to which they are subject (CASS yorku, 2019, "Understanding the Land Acknowledgement" [00:20]). For many non-Indigenous audiences, a Land Acknowledgement can be a call to begin a relationship with the land, the people, and the history of the land upon which they now reside, as well as with their own settler colonial identities. Land Acknowledgements have thus been touted as, "a small but essential step toward the reconciliation process" (Randy Pitawanakwat, in "Understanding the Land Acknowledgment" [3:40]).

Indigenous nations continue to "recognize each other often on the basis of clan, language, and nation … [and] engage in acknowledgment of each other [as] a cultural and political practice" (Wilkes, Duong, Kesler, and Ramos 2017, 91). Mary Bordeaux, a Sicangu Lakota person interviewed in the video "#HonorNativeLand," published by the US Department of Arts and Culture (2017), stated that when she heard a Land Acknowledgement read in a room "full of non-Native people," it was "like it pulled away this layer that's always there." She states that after hearing the acknowledgment of the Native history and culture of the land she was on, she was "relaxed" and felt more at ease ("#HonorNativeLand," [1:30–1:50]). Desjarlais also states that in her culture, Land Acknowledgements are done "when [they] wake up, when [they] breathe in and out, when [they] take care of [themselves]" ("Understanding the Land Acknowledgment," [0:00–0:26]). Land Acknowledgements can thus provide a chance to bring awareness of surroundings into a space which otherwise might not address them. Equally important, they bring settler colonialism to the forefront in spaces where it is unquestioned or normalized.

Finally, Land Acknowledgements are place-based announcements which draw audiences into thinking about the spaces they share with others. Larsen and Johnson (2017) state that "Place teaches coexistence, not consensus … Place is a 'scale of relation' that 'encompasses the infinite within the immediate,' and it is in these messy, agonistic scales of coexistence that [communities can] find themselves" (Hewitt, in Larsen and Johnson 2017, 9). Places are not equalizers, nor do they affect each inhabitant the same way. By understanding the "infinite" individual experiences within a community, "coexistence" becomes a show of respect, a central tenet of Indigenous–settler relations. "Native space must be constantly recognized and made visible through daily practices" (Barnd 2017, 15) so that it is not subsumed into the Canadian hegemony. Recitation and preparation of Land Acknowledgements are ways settlers can participate in disrupting this hegemony.

Reconsidering the Script

To help decolonize scripted Land Acknowledgements, the Native Governance Center (NGC 2019), based on an event they hosted on the topic, created a guide to assist organizations in avoiding the pitfalls described by Daigle and Hewitt. In response to the question "Why is the Indigenous Land Acknowledgement important?", they state:

> It is important to understand the longstanding history that has brought you to reside on the land, and to seek to understand your place within that history. Land Acknowledgments do not exist in a past tense, or historical context: colonialism is a current ongoing process, and we need to build our mindfulness of our present participation.
>
> *Northwestern University in NGC 2019*

As an outcome of this event, tips were shared for generating appropriate Indigenous Land Acknowledgements. Table 9.1 shows the suggestions of the organizers for people writing Land Acknowledgements.

In taking in the advice offered, we, the authors of this paper, begin with self-reflection. Both of us reside, work, and educate in an urban context, specifically in Toronto. In my teaching, I (McGregor) require students to engage with the York University Land Acknowledgement by engaging in self-reflection and walking methodologies. Students must then generate their

TABLE 9.1 Suggestions for writing Land Acknowledgements

Start with self-reflection

Before starting work on your Land Acknowledgement statement, reflect on the process:
- Why am I doing this Land Acknowledgement? *If you're hoping to inspire others to take action to support Indigenous communities, you're on the right track. If you're delivering a Land Acknowledgement out of guilt or because everyone else is doing it, more self-reflection is in order.*
- What is my end goal? *What do you hope listeners will do after hearing the acknowledgement?*
- When will I have the largest impact? *Think about your timing and audience, specifically.*

Do your homework

Put in the time necessary to research the following topics:
- The Indigenous People to whom the land belongs;
- The history of the land and any related treaties;
- Names of living Indigenous People from these communities;
- Indigenous place names and language;
- Correct pronunciation for the names of the Tribes, places, and individuals that you're including.

Use appropriate language

Don't sugarcoat the past.
- Use terms like *genocide, ethnic cleansing, stolen land,* and *forced removal* to reflect actions taken by colonizers.

Use past, present, and future tenses

Indigenous People are still here, and they're thriving. *Don't treat them as a relic of the past.*

[Understand that] Land Acknowledgements shouldn't be grim

They should function as living celebrations of Indigenous communities.
- Ask yourself, "How am I leaving Indigenous People in a stronger, more empowered place because of this Land Acknowledgement?"
- Focus on the positivity of who Indigenous People are today.

Source: NGC (2019)

own Land Acknowledgements based on lived experiences acquired by engaging with the natural world.

As a planning student in the Master of Environmental Studies (MES, now the Faculty of Environmental and Urban Change, or FEUC) program at York University, and in acting on this call to re-engage with Land Acknowledgements, I (Nelson) engaged in research on the statements, local history, and current movements, and possible paths forward for the planning profession. I prepared several Land Acknowledgements over the course of the research as a way to reflect on what I'd learned through the research process. We reflect upon these processes in the following pages.

Methodologies and Pedagogies: Re-centering Land and Relationships

Both Indigenous and non-Indigenous thinkers express the importance of understanding our relationship to each other through the land. Indigenous scholars refer to this as an Indigenous relational ontology (Daigle 2019; Todd 2016), whereas non-Indigenous planning scholars tend to call it "place-based" knowledge. Planning projects, especially in an urban context, while they may superficially engage with Indigenous perspectives of the land, often end up catering more to developers than to the community.

Styres and Zinga (2013) encourage researchers to think about "Land, not solely as a geographical and material place, but as a spiritual and relational place" (p.295). "Land", they write, "is a spiritually infused place that is grounded in interconnected and interdependent relationships, [and] cultural positioning" (p.301). They state also that:

> Land from an Indigenous perspective carries with it the idea of journeying, of being connected to, and interconnected with, geographic and spiritual space—in other words a deep sense of identification through a cosmological and ecological connection to both natural and spiritual worlds.
>
> *p.302*

Anishinaabek scholar Darlene Johnston adds, "Connecting people to place requires an exploration of how people understand themselves in relation to their place. For the Aboriginal peoples of the Great Lakes, there is both a physical and spiritual aspect to identity and landscape" (Johnston 2006, 3).

During a Zoom presentation for Dr. McGregor's "Indigenous Perspectives and Realities" course, I (Nelson) asked students to listen closely to their surroundings for several minutes, then report back to the class what they had heard. Many joked that they had had a hard time hearing at first, whether it be over a dog barking, a housemate watching TV, or loud appliances. They then realized, however, that these noises—originally being regarded as a din *covering up* the "natural" noises they *thought* they should hear—told them as much about their surroundings and how they related to them as the other sounds they strove to hear. One student, for example, mentioned being struck by the implications of the sound of their furnace: the privilege of a warm home, heating bills, the climate's impacts on our lives, the gas required to run the furnace, and so on. By reconnecting with other senses not privileged in academic spaces, students were able to reflect on the presence of the land within their lives at that (and every) moment.

Relationships and History Visible in City Design

Land Acknowledgements in particular help to unveil these connections as they call our attention to the world outside of the event or setting in which they're being presented. Especially in cities, concrete and glass buildings seem to hide connections to land and non-human beings, but these connections can be revealed if we look at the design of city layouts. Arterial roads now carrying vehicle traffic to and from Canada's largest cities were once deer paths, which became foot paths as hunters followed the animals, which were later retraced by travelers, and eventually became host to small shops and subsequent four-lane highways (Mills and Roque n.d.). The roads that provide patterns of human movement through urban space have their roots in Indigenous history and in the land.

In contexts where the land plays an active role in shaping planning or engineering decisions, such as in a mountainous area or near marshes or wetlands, the land can appear to be more present. Yet the myths of greatness propagated by colonialism are not able to contend with the fact that the land determines settling patterns. The Doctrine of Discovery[1] tells a story of unused and uninhabited lands, one in which settlers were capable of bending and working the land into what it was "meant to be," either through building cities or by attempting to conquer it. As places steeped in mythologies of supremacy (Tomiak 2016), cities can also be a major site of disruption of the myths upon which colonialism was built. Land Acknowledgements often provide the starting point for settlers in grappling with the colonial history of their presence and surroundings.

Education through Land Acknowledgements

Educators who take seriously the TRC of Canada's "Calls to Action" report (TRC 2015b) must begin to take an active role in teaching the importance of Indigenous history and perspectives. The TRC calls upon the Canadian Council of Ministers of Education to develop and implement a curriculum and resources on the history of Aboriginal people in Canadian history, as well as to build "student capacity for intercultural understanding, empathy, and mutual respect" (TRC 2015b, Section 63, i–iii). Their responsibilities therefore lie in both educating students about and aiding in self-reflection on their relationships to settler colonialism and the settler state of Canada. Janet Csontos' article (2019) and workshop on settler responsibilities places the onus on settlers to explore the privileges they are afforded by the state as well as the interventions they can make toward unsettling them. Csontos' call for "action beyond words" summarizes the TRC's recommendations and highlights the potential limits of practices, such as Land Acknowledgements and Truth and Reconciliation Commissions, as they exist today.

In decolonizing education, learning to re-engage with Land is referred to as "pedagogies of the land" (Haig-Brown and Dannemann 2002). Zoe Todd (2016, 90) writes that it is often a struggle to "situate the material we read in class within the physical realities that we inhabit as student–teacher–interlocutors moving through academic and civic spaces in Ottawa." Todd encourages her students to ground-truth their abstract, theoretical work by engaging with the natural world in the city in which she teaches.

In my own teaching, I (McGregor) refer to (and assign to every class) Darlene Johnston's seminal work *Connecting People to Place: Great Lakes Aboriginal History in Cultural Context*, her submission to the Ipperwash Inquiry. She sought to demonstrate that the "Great Lakes region is more than geography. It is a spiritual landscape formed by and embedded with the regenerative potential of the First Ones who gave it form" (Johnston 2006, 6). She also notes that,

> As a descendant of the Great Lakes Aboriginal Ancestors, I have been taught that our people come from the land and that we are shaped by the land. Aboriginal history and self-understanding is conveyed across generations by stories and teachings that are grounded in particular landscapes.
>
> *2006, 2*

I follow a similar logic and ask students to consider their own perspectives and knowledge in understanding their connection (or lack thereof) to place (in this case, Toronto). They each have a relationship with place, it just may or may not be recognized, and may or may not be positive. As such, self-reflection is critical. In Indigenous pedagogy, engaging with self is particularly important. Who you are, what motivates you, and what informs how you know—it all matters. Learning to position yourself, or explicitly stating your self-location and relationship to place, is an important way to begin this "coming to know." Within Indigenous, particularly Anishinaabek, knowledge, this means *acting* on your knowledge. An important part of Indigenous inquiry and pedagogy is therefore to understand the obligations and responsibilities that one assumes (i.e., the actions you must take) once you have come to "know"

TABLE 9.2 Deepening the Land Acknowledgement

Get outside	Reflect	Act
• Go outside and participate in the natural world (e.g., take a "self-reflection walk," "First Story" tour, etc.); • Describe the "experience(s)" undertaken to better understand their sense of place; • Specifically describe what they observed, how they felt, what they learned from the experience.	• Describe your relationship to place and with Indigenous Peoples of that place; • Describe Indigenous worldview, philosophy, intellectual/knowledge traditions and systems with an emphasis on relationship to place, land and language; • Identify your personal biases and positionality. Address how they might influence your experience, analyses and interpretations; • Reflect thoughtfully on how Indigenous presence is expressed or known in an urban setting; • Explain how your experiences as part of this class have deepened your understanding of the broader context of Canadian society and its institutions in relation to Indigenous Peoples.	Answer the following questions: • What does the Land Acknowledgement mean to you? • Who is the Land Acknowledgement for? • What responsibilities can be thought to derive from the Land Acknowledgement? • Having read a Land Acknowledgement, identify any responsibilities you feel you may have with regard to learning from place/people; • Prepare your own Land Acknowledgement for the Land/Place where you live; • Do you feel comfortable and ready to assume your role with the personal responsibilities you have identified? What factors/ considerations might inhibit or enable you?

something. It is during the "coming to know" process that one begins to appreciate these obligations and responsibilities.

Even entering into this process, of course, assumes a certain degree of readiness (McGregor, Sritharan, and Whitaker 2020). I expect students to begin their own process of inquiry. Learning about the "place" in which they live, study, and work, is an important step along this path. I ask students to formulate an understanding of their responsibilities to place/people/ land where they currently reside. As a starting point, they reflect upon York University's rather scripted Land Acknowledgement and the video *Understanding the Land Acknowledgment*, and are then asked to get outside, reflect on and share their insights, and asked to consider what actions they might take after the exercise.

Considering the Colonial Roots of Planning through Land Acknowledgements

Canada has yet to adequately address the ongoing impacts of settler colonialism on Indigenous communities. City planning has played a large role in land and societal development driven by settler colonialism in this country (Roy 2006; Stranger-Ross 2008). Planners, as counsel to private developers, employees of municipal or provincial governments, or practitioners at non-profit organizations, can and often do perpetuate unacknowledged tenets of settler colonialism. This is especially prevalent in the valuing and usage of land. As a planning student, I (Nelson) searched for a way to engage with the history of the land, knowing that the past uses of a particular plot of land determine its future uses (i.e., is it a "brown site"? Are there pre-existing structures with "heritage value"?). If planners are truly committed to responding to the TRC's recommendations (2015b), we must also explore how human history—settler colonialism in particular—can be considered in the development of land. Opportunities for such engagement within the planning field are few and far between, but recognition of an area's history often comes in the form of Land Acknowledgements.

When considering my Master's research subject, I became curious about the Land Acknowledgement's (in)ability to instill a sense that something must be done to reconcile—a word fraught with ambiguous expectations—Canada's history of genocide with its current self-image as a benevolent refuge. I wanted to study the impact Land Acknowledgements have had on both listeners and speakers, and, reflecting on these results, analyze how Land Acknowledgements are understood by settler-identified planning students as well as how their education and training within settler constructs influenced their understanding. In talking with other settlers and grounding my research in Indigenous scholarship, I expanded my own settler understanding of what it means to think with/through the land and how this informs "place-based" projects in the settler colonial state of Canada. This podcast project included an analysis of the colonial roots of planning alongside a discussion of the treaty-making process and a consideration of how planners reflect the shady history of Canada's development in their choices. I ended by suggesting that planning as a field, in its current iteration as a tool of organization by the Canadian state, must undergo immense change so that it does not perpetuate colonialism/capitalism/racism if it is to have real decolonizing potential. I also emphasized that planners who aspire to undermine colonialism through their work should also engage in decolonial activism.

Emma's Acknowledgements: An Ongoing Process

After moving to Toronto, I started to think less and less about the land, as I believed it wasn't really "here" anymore, having been long since covered up by concrete and streetcar tracks. But reading about place-based thinking (Barnd 2017; Larsen and Johnson 2017; and Walker, Jojola, and Natcher 2013) and exploring it through listening practice unveiled the possibilities for reconnecting with the land/Earth while in the city. These possibilities forefront the history of the land as being continuous and present.

In my experience, doing research and learning more about Toronto, about the unequal development of the Toronto Purchase, about the diversity of cultures and peoples living here before (during, and after) contact, and about the history of urban planning in the area, completely changed my relationship to the phrase "stolen land." I had known the statement to be true at some level, and I had already acknowledged that many treaties, and especially the ways in which they were implemented, were questionable at best, but learning about the area radically deepened my understanding of settler colonialism.

At the end of each podcast episode, I wrote a Land Acknowledgement to reflect on what I'd learned from the interviewee and how that had changed my relationship with my surroundings. The conversations led me to do further research on things like movements, planning history, and the development of Toronto. As a reflexive practice, Land Acknowledgements have become a methodology for exploring how I related to urban spaces on stolen land and where I could positively enact the privileges and responsibilities I have as a settler.

What Kind of Ancestor Will You Be? Reconciling with the Land

> In Anishinaabeg culture, there is an ongoing relationship between the Dead and the Living, between Ancestors and Descendants. It is the obligation of the Living to ensure that their relatives are buried in the proper manner and in the proper place. Failure to perform this duty harms not only the Dead but also the Living. The Dead need to be sheltered and fed, to be visited and feasted.
>
> *Johnston 2006, 24*

Anishinaabek relationships between the Living and the Dead tell us about "their connection to land and their ancestors, both human and other than human" (Johnston 2006, 24). In her research and understanding, Johnston notes that for the Anishinaabek "the remains of their Dead retained a spiritual essence which required ongoing respect" (p.27) and that "Human remains return to the earth with their spiritual essence intact, continuing the spiritual cycle of birth and re-birth" (p.28).

In my (McGregor's) role as a scholar and teacher, I am often asked to give presentations, serve on panels and facilitate workshops. Every time I give a Land Acknowledgement it is different. Like Johnston, I carry with me similar teachings, recognizing the continuity of the Living and the Dead and the importance of the Land in mediating this ongoing relationship. In my Land Acknowledgements, I like to remind all listeners to reflect upon what kind of ancestor they want to be for future generations. I spur them to recognize that they have ancestors and that they are in fact descendants, benefiting from a Land that is home, stolen, exploited, suffering, or healing. Recognition of the Living and the Dead in the Anishinaabek tradition is a recognition that we are all descendants and that we will all be ancestors: it is the Land that connects us.

Note

1 Starting with 15th-century Papal Bulls, or official letters regarding the future of the Catholic Church, the Doctrine of Discovery was a continuation of the same ideological, colonial underpinnings that spawned the Crusades. These official doctrines ordained new settlements as being divinely righteous, as was the colonization of Indigenous lands. They reinforced the racist myth that sites of settlement like North America were devoid of people and civilizations, which, when coupled with the perspective that man holds dominion over land, justified aggressive settler encroachment. The Doctrine is foundational to US property law and continues to be cited in legal cases (see, for example, *City of Sherrill vs. Oneida Indian Nation, 2005*; Miller and Ruru, 2009).

References

Barnd, N. B. (2017). *Native space: Geographic strategies to unsettle settler colonialism*. Oregon State University Press.

CASS (Center for Aboriginal Student Services) yorku. (2019). Understanding the land acknowledgement [YouTube video, January 2nd, 2019]: www.youtube.com/watch?v=qNZi301-p8k.

Csontos, J. (2019). Truth and decolonization: Filling the educator achievement gap darn it! *American Review of Canadian Studies* 49(1): 150–186. https://doi.org/10.1080/02722011.2019.1590430.

Daigle, M. (2019). The spectacle of reconciliation: On (the) unsettling responsibilities to Indigenous peoples in the academy. *Environment and Planning D, Society and Space* 37(4): 703–721. https://doi.org/10.1177/0263775818824342.

Haig-Brown, C. and K. Dannemann. (2002). A pedagogy of the land: Dreams of respectful relations. *McGill Journal of Education* 37(3): 451–468.

Hewitt, J. (2019). Land acknowledgment, scripting and Julius Caesar. *The Supreme Court Law Review: Osgoode's Annual Constitutional Cases Conference* 88(1). https://digitalcommons.osgoode.yorku.ca/sclr/vol88/iss1/2.

Johnston, D. (2006). Connecting people to place: Great Lakes Aboriginal history in cultural context. Ipperwash Inquiry: https://commons.allard.ubc.ca/cgi/viewcontent.cgi?article=1191&context=fac_pubs.

Larsen, S. C. and J. T. Johnson. (2017). Being together in place: Indigenous coexistence in a more than human world. University of Minnesota Press.

McGregor, D., M. Sritharan, and S. Whitaker. (2020). Indigenous environmental justice and sustainability. *Current Opinion in Environmental Sustainability* 43: 35–40. www.sciencedirect.com/science/article/pii/S1877343520300075.

Miller, R. J. and J. Ruru. 2009. An Indigenous lens into comparative law: The Doctrine of Discovery in the United States and New Zealand. West Virginia University: *The Research Repository* 111(3): 849–819.

Mills, S. and S. Roque. (n.d.). Land acknowledgements: uncovering an oral history of Tkaronto. *Local Love*. https://locallove.ca/issues/land-acknowledgements-uncovering-an-oral-history-of-tkaronto/.

Native Governance Center. (2019). A guide to Indigenous land acknowledgment. https://nativegov.org/a-guide-to-indigenous-land-acknowledgment/.

Roy, A. (2006). Praxis in the time of empire. *Planning Theory* 5(1): 7–29. https://doi.org/10.1177/1473095206061019.

Stranger-Ross, J. (2008). Municipal colonialism in Vancouver: City planning and the conflict over Indian reserves, 1928–1950s. *The Canadian Historical Review* 89(4): 541–580.

Styres, S. and D. Zinga. (2013). The community-first land-centred theoretical framework: Bringing a 'good mind' to Indigenous education research? *Canadian Journal of Education* 36(2): 284–313.

Todd, Z. (2016). An Indigenous feminist's take on the ontological turn: "Ontology" is just another word for colonialism. *Journal of Historical Sociology* 29(1): 4–22. https://doi.org/10.1111/johs.12124.

Tomiak, J. (2016). Unsettling Ottawa: Settler colonialism, Indigenous resistance, and the politics of scale. *Canadian Journal of Urban Research* 25(1): 8–21.

Truth and Reconciliation Commission, Canada. (2015a). Truth and Reconciliation Commission Reports: 1—History—Origins to 1939. https://archive.org/details/trcreport/1-1-History-Origins-to-1939.

Truth and Reconciliation Commission, Canada. (2015b). Truth and Reconciliation Commission Reports: Calls to Action. https://archive.org/details/trcreport/TRC--Calls-to-Action.

US Department of Arts and Culture. (2017). #HonorNativeLand [YouTube video, October 3rd, 2017]: www.youtube.com/watch?v=ETOhNzBsiKA&t=105s.

Walker, R., T. Jojola, and D. Natcher, eds. (2013). *Reclaiming Indigenous planning*. McGill-Queen's University Press.

Wilkes, R., A. Duong, L. Kesler, and H. Ramos. (2017). Canadian university acknowledgment of Indigenous lands, treaties, and peoples. *The Canadian Review of Sociology* 54(1): 89–120. https://doi.org/10.1111/cars.12140.

10

URBAN PLANNING OSCILLATIONS

Seeking a Tongan Way before and after the 2006 Riots

Yvonne Takau and Michelle Thompson-Fawcett

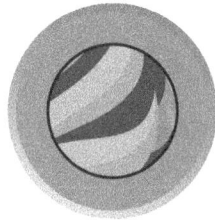

Introduction

> I wish we see the potential urban planning could play here in Nuku'alofa and Tonga
> as a whole, … I would like to see it well established, on its feet, having resources to do
> things and to make things work … that's my vision.
>
> *Quotation from interview with Tongan planner, 2019*

Although small by world standards, extensive transformation as a result of rapid urbanisation
in the mid-20th century has been particularly challenging for Pacific Island cities. In this
chapter, we reflect on the history, present state, and potential of urban planning in Tonga. The
chapter pivots around the calamity of the 2006 democracy riots in the city of Nuku'alofa.

As Indigenous planners and researchers—one Tongan and the other of New Zealand
Māori descent—we (the authors) have a commitment to exposing ongoing colonial legacies
and facilitating a future that better connects with place-specific sacred values and wisdom
derived from centuries of knowledge creation adapted into civic praxis. That perspective
underpins the analysis presented in this chapter.

The Kingdom of Tonga in the southwestern Pacific Ocean is comprised of four main
Island groups: Tongatapu, Ha'apai, Vava'u and the Niuas (Figure 10.1). Tongatapu contains
74 per cent of Tonga's total population of approximately 100,000 (Figure 10.2) and is home to
the Kingdom's capital, Nuku'alofa (Figure 10.3), the latter with a population of approximately
25,000. Whilst the total population of Tonga has declined in recent years, the population of
Tongatapu has increased, with internal migration from the outer islands on the rise. There
is considerable pressure, especially in terms of infrastructure, on Nuku'alofa. A majority of
Tonga's economic activity is concentrated in the city, and those living on Tongatapu—even
if not actually living in the city—commute to the city regularly for a range of work and daily
activities (Takau, 2019).

DOI: 10.4324/9781003199816-13

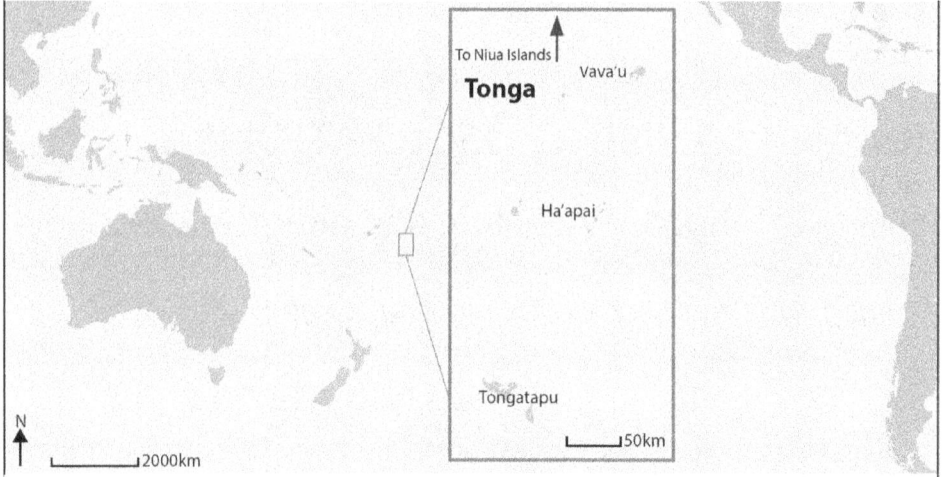

FIGURE 10.1 Location of Tongan islands (map by Daizy Thompson-Fawcett)

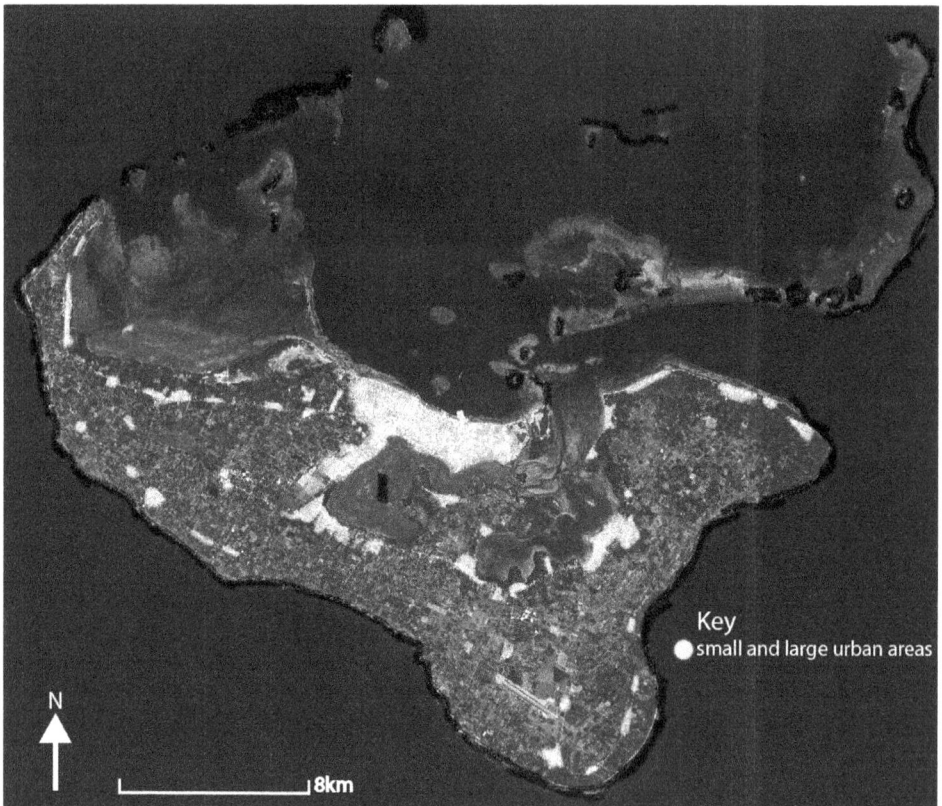

FIGURE 10.2 Main urban areas on Tongatapu (Source: adapted from European Space Agency—CC BY-SA 3.0 IGO)

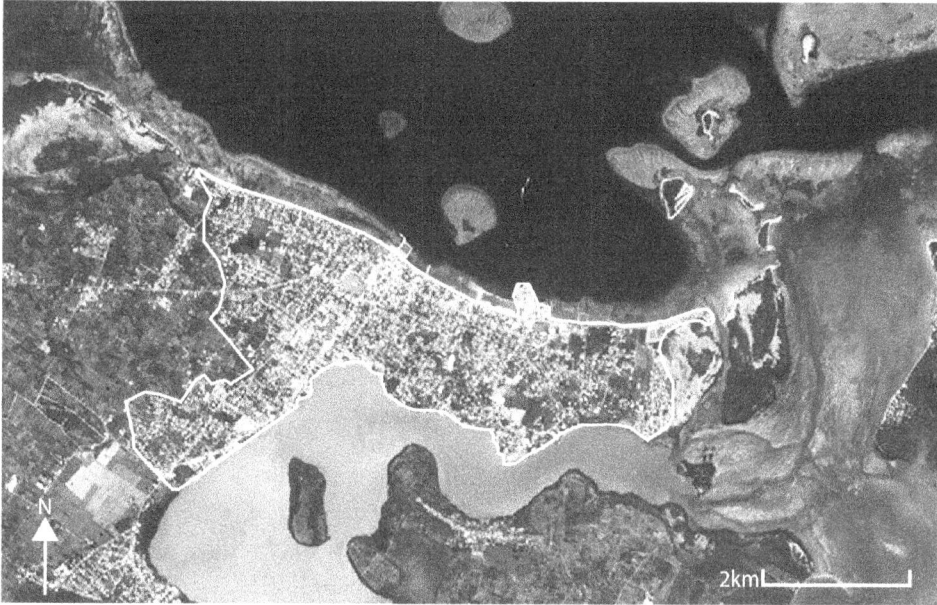

FIGURE 10.3 Contiguous urban development in Nuku'alofa (Source: adapted from European Space Agency—CC BY-SA 3.0 IGO)

In terms of governance, Tonga has been a constitutional monarchy for more than a century. However, pro-democratic movements began in the 1970s and their endeavours progressively led to the civil servants' strike in 2005. This transformation effort culminated in the riots of November 2006 in which 80 per cent of the Nuku'alofa Central Business District (CBD) was destroyed. To date, these events have been assessed predominantly in terms of the resultant constitutional reform. However, this chapter brings to light the resulting changes that urban planning in Tonga experienced when faced with the mass urban rebuild that ensued.

Early Planning and Context

Planning in the interest of wider society has long been practised in Tonga. Some 18th-century records describe a landscape that was immaculately managed including pathways lined with gardens of crops and plantations (Bott 1982). Queen Salote Tupou III indicated that this was due to the duty of the land occupants to ensure paths surrounding their plantations were well maintained (Bott 1982). Tongans had a system in place that—although not formally instituted as rules—confirmed an understanding of how property was to be kept in the public interest. At this time, people did not live clustered in villages, rather spread across the land, and they were known for their sustainable living practices (Beaglehole 1961). Tongan people have special and spiritual ties to their land and natural resources, which has inherently led to its careful management and preservation for future generations. This sense of stewardship is often tied to stories of creation and the divine world (Halatuituia 2002). In Tonga, the narrative of land being fished out from the ocean, or having been bestowed through divine intervention when Tonga was first created, has been passed down for generations (Halatuituia 2002).

Over centuries, people developed a detailed local environmental wisdom that has meant they tended land and the realm of nature with reverence.

However, European powers upturned Indigenous governance and planning procedures, and implemented Eurocentric regimes. Foreign exploration turned into exploitation at the turn of the 19th century, largely as a result of the expansion of the British empire. The British perspective was that Pacific traditions were a hindrance to advancement and that in applying their standard model of planning, they were imparting a "civilising influence" (Home 1997). Crucial to that model, was the idea of establishing a single town or place as the centre of a colony where all trade, commerce and government would be concentrated (Crocombe 1987). As such, the current planning regimes and the physical layout of many Pacific ports, towns, and urban centres were built on the ambitions of distant foreign societies, as opposed to the needs and aspirations of the Indigenous Peoples (Hibbard, Lane, and Rasmussen 2008).

Post-independence Era

Whilst Tonga remained independent during the colonial presence in the Pacific, its institutional and urban arrangements were directly impacted by and responsive to foreign interests and opportunities, and the threat of colonisation. A system was established that sought to protect pre-contact land management whilst at the same time introducing the potential for global exchange—as it turns out this was an unattainable ambition. Although subsequent efforts have been made to adapt foreign-influenced governance and planning processes better to the contemporary Tongan context, many incongruences still exist. The land tenure system has failed to regulate urban management and the successful provision of public services due to the limited rights to implement physical planning held by the government. There is, for example, high intrinsic value associated with land, and strong attachment to land that has been in the care of the same family for many generations. In an urban context, when city planning agencies seek to implement broader public amenity, environmental health, or climate resilience projects, negotiating through land tenure and potential compensation measures for acquiring family land is complex and expensive, and often unsuccessful (Jones and Lea 2007). This cultural sensitivity around land issues, and the constrained potential for projects to be realised, means that political commitment to planning and urban management is not always prioritised and limited headway is made on the planning front (Connell 2017). These externally influenced planning systems and processes are regarded with suspicion. However, with ever-increasing rates of urbanisation, like many Pacific nations, Tonga faces a plethora of issues that need to be addressed by more strategic and integrated planning.

Urbanisation

Following urbanisation instigated by foreign administrators, the popularity of urban lifestyles increased in the Pacific. By the mid-1990s, it was confirmed that the Pacific Islands were home to some of the most rapidly growing urban areas in the world (United Nations Development Programme 1996). By 2016, these same Pacific countries were experiencing urbanisation rates over three times the global average, and future projections only expect this trend to continue rising (United Nations 2018).

The burgeoning urban population has produced a number of challenges with which Pacific planning practitioners continue to grapple (Jones 2016). The principal challenges are summarised in Figure 10.4, although this is not an exhaustive list. In 1996, Jones asserted that one of the most crucial concerns of the 21st century for Pacific countries would be the development of effective urban management practices to address the impacts of urbanisation. In the 2020s, Pacific planners including those in Tonga still struggle to develop a system to safeguard against and alleviate these issues. Chief among the issues are the rise of informal settlements and the adverse impacts that urbanisation has had on the health of Pacific urban residents.

In response to these intensifying urban issues, since the early 2000s, Tonga has attempted to adapt the planning system to cater better to its own distinct cultural values. As with most Pacific Island countries the foremost obstacles are a general lack of resources, an institutionally fragmented approach to implementation, and a lack of political support. These

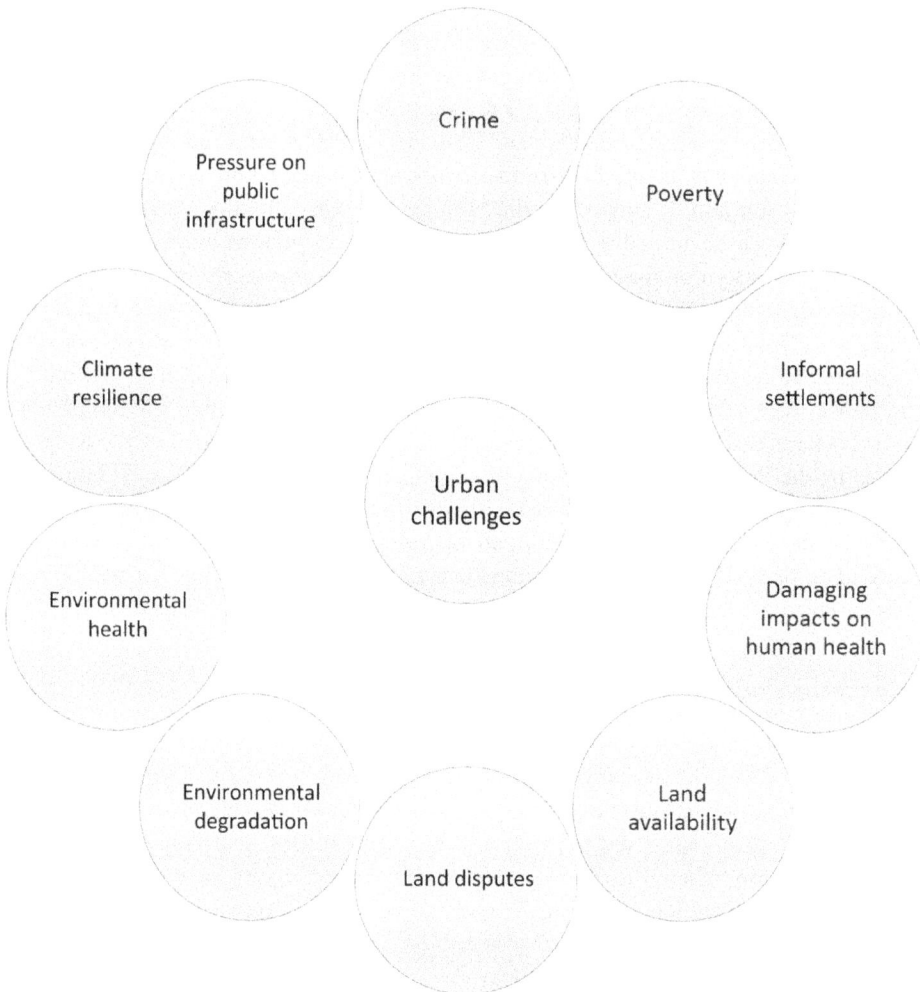

FIGURE 10.4 Key challenges for urban planning in Pacific Island countries (diagram by authors)

three barriers are interlaced. Connell (2017) cautions that for some Pacific communities, the memories of colonisation remain fresh and hence, such communities tend to have a deep-seated mistrust of any overarching authority. Therefore, it is important to foster a transparent environment where communities feel comfortable to engage in conversation with government officials.

Contemporary Planning in Tonga prior to the Riots

The Constitution and Land Tenure

The roots of contemporary planning in Tonga can be traced back to the 1875 Constitution. The Constitution has been a significant influencing factor in how planning has been allowed to develop (Halatuituia 2002). Its central purpose was to ensure that Tonga was safeguarded from the looming threat of colonisation. It had four main outcomes with specific implications for planning. Firstly, with regard to land, the Constitution gave power to the King, and from the King to the Minister of Lands. Secondly, it dealt with the registration of land. Thirdly, it ensured that the lines of succession for land rights were passed through the male heir; and finally, it instilled the duty to manage the land sustainably.

Tonga's Land Act was passed in 1903 and later superseded by the Land Act 1927 (and its subsequent amendments). It laid the legal framework for the land tenure system, giving effect to the 1875 Constitution by confirming the Minister of Lands' authority as the Crown's representative in all matters related to land. Part one of the Act opens with the declaration that all land of the Kingdom of Tonga belongs to the Crown. This means that no one except the Crown has freehold ownership over land in Tonga, thus establishing the foundation for the land tenure system. Of particular importance for planning, the Act gives the Minister of Lands the authority to reserve portions of Crown Land for public purposes, such as provision of roads, public ways, commons, cemeteries, school sites, playgrounds, and public health activities. It also states that land may be taken from any land holder if authorised by the King and approved by the Privy Council. In such a situation, the Minister of Lands would ensure the land holder is appropriately compensated, either financially or with an alternative parcel of land. However, given the almost sacred bond with their land, tenure issues place significant limitations on what, where, and how planning in the name of the "collective good" of Tongan society can be undertaken.

National Development Plans

Also of importance, and in light of the unprecedented growth that Tonga had been experiencing, during the 1960s the government recognised the need to formulate a national guidance document that would articulate a collective vision for future development in the nation. Development in this context did not just refer to urban development but to development in its broadest sense, where the improvement of all facets of society were considered. The resulting "Five-Year Development Plan," designed to be updated every five years, set out goals for key sectors and detailed strategies to accomplish those goals. It is important to be cognisant of scale in the Tongan context, whereby any national development plan will inevitably have significant implications for the management of the one major urban area in the country, Nuku'alofa.

It was not until the Sixth Five-Year Development Plan (DP6) (1991–1995) that environmental issues were brought to the fore as a matter of national significance. DP6 stated that effective resource management would also yield positive outcomes for employment opportunities, human health, and overall sustainable development. Nevertheless, by the new millennium, foreign profit-making motivations took precedence over environmental protection, causing the depletion of many of the country's natural resources. The new, more "strategic" seventh plan (SDP7) identified agriculture, fisheries, and tourism as its three priority sectors. Whilst the protection of the environment and physical infrastructure remained important, these goals were obscured by strategies rooted in achieving favourable economic outcomes. This was counterbalanced to an extent by the eighth plan in 2006, which recognised the deteriorating state of urban infrastructure. SDP8 highlighted the need for an urban planning and management strategy for Tonga. By the end of that year, this need was even more urgent.

The Riots

The pro-democratic movement that prompted the 2006 riots began during the 1970s with little immediate effect (Benguigui 2011). It was driven by different people over the years before it reached a critical highpoint in 2005 with the civil servants' strike, and with Tonga's late Prime Minister Akilisi Pohiva at the forefront. In 2006, pro-democracy demonstrations escalated to an uprising when demonstrators discovered that the Legislative Assembly was adjourning for the year without accepting the democratic and constitutional reforms they were demanding (Benguigui 2011). Rioting began in the afternoon of November 16th, initially targeting government premises then other organisations and shops, by throwing stones, looting, and setting buildings on fire. The government declared a state of emergency the next day, which was extended several times until finally being removed in January 2011 once the new Prime Minister took office after the 2010 elections.

The riots exhorted constitutional reform and in 2010, with the formalising of that change, the Monarch's privilege to appoint the Prime Minister and Ministers of Cabinet was removed. Under the reform, seats within the unicameral Legislative Assembly shifted from a majority designated for hereditary nobles to a majority of seats designated for parliamentary members chosen during general elections. This reform saw 17 of the 26 seats set aside for elected members and nine seats designated for the Kingdom's hereditary nobles, which they elected amongst themselves.

Whilst the riots accomplished a more inclusive approach to national governance, they had had horrific consequences for the Nuku'alofa CBD. This came in the form of USD $106 million in damages as 80 per cent of the CBD lay in ashes (*The Economist* 2006). It was these repercussions that highlighted the need for a body to coordinate the reconstruction of Nuku'alofa and thus bring planning to the fore.

After the Riots

Although it had previously been acknowledged that an holistic and more formal approach to planning was vital for improved urban management in Tonga, it was not until the 2006 riots that the significance of this became evident. Whilst a devastating event, in terms of planning the riots became an opportunity to put improved planning processes in place; construct a CBD that was appropriately resourced with infrastructure, services and amenities; and rebuild Nuku'alofa urban area in a way that was more cohesive and inclusive for the rapidly expanding urban population. Reconstruction also drew attention to a number of basic infrastructure needs beyond the scope of the rebuild itself that were shortcomings in the previous design of the Nuku'alofa urban area. Thus, not only did the outcome of the riots emphasise the importance of planning, it also facilitated the authorities in reassessing the physical design of the CBD and making broader adjustments during the rebuild efforts.

National Spatial Planning and Management

The lack of specific planning processes prior to 2006 obstructed reconstruction efforts, especially at the macro level. Whilst a Bill had been drafted prior to the riots, further work began in earnest after the riots to develop Tonga's first planning specific legislation. It was finally passed as the National Spatial Planning and Management (NSPM) Act in 2012, with the aftermath of the riots providing the incentive to push it through. The riots highlighted for decision makers the need for effective planning adapted for: the Tongan context; cultural institutions; interrelationships laid out in the Land Act; and, pea moe anga ae nofo fakakainga (the Tongan way of life as a family).

The Act has an emphasis on consultation for both the production of new plans and before new development projects commence. The creation of the Act itself involved the most extensive public consultation undertaken for a statute in Tonga. As a result, it incorporates deeply rooted Tongan values and norms in its operation. This aspect is not unexpected given that the Act developed in parallel with the political change taking place at the time. The resulting statute has now become a vehicle for democratic civic process via its requirements for consultation related to planning activities.

Planning and Urban Management Agency

The riots were also a persuasive event in leading to the establishment of a specific agency for managing planning in Tonga, which is now called the Planning and Urban Management Agency (PUMA). PUMA was first formed in 2007 as a small division called the Physical Planning Division under the Ministry of Lands, Survey and Natural Resources. Its primary role was to provide planning oversight during the rebuild efforts. Whilst the Physical Planning Division could have been a temporary arrangement, the government realised the value in having an agency to coordinate planning efforts for the country, thus launching PUMA in 2008 and expanding their initial mandate. Nonetheless, debate continues as various projects arise in regard to where they should be hosted: e.g. PUMA or Ministry of Infrastructure or Natural Resources Division, etc. thereby demonstrating an ongoing degree of fractured, siloed planning.

To assist in strengthening and building capacity within PUMA, the Sustainable Urban and Environmental Management Project ran from 2010 to 2012, with an emphasis on transportation, environment, climate change, and Geographic Information Systems in the Nuku'alofa Greater Urban Area. The project enabled a physical stocktake of the city, the delivery of evidence-based options for the city's future, and it quantified and legitimised urban planning activities (Takau 2019). The principal outcome was the completion of a 20-year Structure Plan for Nuku'alofa which provided guidelines, strategies, and proposed actions for future planning.

Strategic Development Framework

In terms of the overarching framework for planning, SDP8 was the national document providing strategic direction immediately after the riots and throughout the rebuild. Following SDP8, the government re-evaluated the approach and rebranded the national guidance documents as "Tonga Strategic Development Frameworks" (TSDF)—the first TSDF being enacted in 2011. All policies, plans, and projects, whether government, private or funded by foreign aid or investments, must be in line with the Strategic Development Framework. Like their predecessors, the Strategic Development Frameworks determine the direction of all development efforts in the country, with a new overarching vision in TSDF I of justice, equity, health, peace, harmony, and prosperity. Amongst other intentions, the TSDF I objectives included affirmation of the need for properly planned and well-maintained infrastructure; and cultural awareness, climate change adaptation, and environmental sustainability—aided by implementation of the Environmental Impact Assessment (EIA) process. However, the improvement in urban management, which was highlighted as fundamental in the previous SDP8, was no longer addressed in the TSDF I.

The TSDF II was released in May 2015. It is the current governing Strategic Development Framework until 2025. The TSDF II states that it is guided by the national motto "Ko e Otua mo Tonga ko hoku Tofi'a" (God and Tonga are my Inheritance), whilst seeking an overall outcome of a "more progressive Tonga supporting higher quality of life for all." It is clear that planning issues are prioritised in TSDF II to a greater extent than in any of the previous documents. The national outcomes acknowledge the importance of inclusive and sustainable urban development, with an emphasis on improving land use planning and urban management especially in light of urban growth and intensification. However, there is an absence of connectivity between the Framework and other planning mechanisms such as PUMA and the NSPM Act (Takau 2019).

Challenges for the Future

Subsequent to the seemingly overnight acknowledgement of planning and its subsequent development after the riots, numerous plans covering a range of different planning issues have been developed—especially in regard to the natural environment and climate resilience. And although it has been nearly 15 years since the riots and the establishment of a single planning authority, Tonga is still feeling the symptoms of transition experienced when a country has had a significant and impactful change to its usual institutional arrangements. The principal complexities stalling the implementation of integrated planning relate to ongoing fragmented sectoral planning; the political climate; the limited recognition that planning is not simply about resolving land disputes but involves action across government tiers and over economic, social, cultural, and environmental spheres; lack of financial, human, and natural resources; and the complications arising from the land tenure system (Takau 2019). So, where does that leave planning in Tonga?

Politics, Culture and Holistic Planning

Politics and Planning in Tonga

In order to understand why the development of planning in Tonga since the 2006 riots has not achieved an integrated approach, and in many regards has remained somewhat abstract, it is important to appreciate the critical role that politics—in the broadest sense—play in such a complicated historical setting. Even though the usual response to a singular catastrophic event resulting in such large-scale damage tends to be the dismissal of the conventional planning processes and democratic measures, this is not what happened in Tonga after the riots. The incident facilitated the acceptance of the first national planning framework and brought visibility to such activity, securing planning within the national agenda. However, politics has also been central in restricting its progress. As Jones (2016) and Connell (2017) explain, due to the elevated space within which planning operates in the Pacific, where planning decisions affect everyone and have policy implications at international, national, and local scales, approval is needed from the highest level. In Tonga, this includes the members of parliament and the Monarch. Although the Monarch is allowed a significant degree of autonomy, this is rarely applied, and even less so after the monumental constitutional reform that took place after the riots. Thus, although governance of the country in a sense became more inclusive, it also extended the decision-making process and has prolonged the establishment of many fundamental aspects of the Planning Act (NSPM). Because democratic processes are relatively new to Tonga, the country has also had to take time to adjust to the new regimen. Unfortunately, the switch to democracy was such a substantial change that it overshadowed the introduction of the new planning framework. Effectively, civil servants were preoccupied with adjusting to the constitutional reform and could not afford to be concerned with additional changes they deemed less of a priority—like planning. Yet Connell (2017) emphasises that effective planning outcomes cannot be achieved if the relevant agency is not afforded the room to carry out their responsibilities without interference. So there is a conundrum here.

Culture and Planning

Similarly, culture and planning will always be interlinked, whether it is through the worldview with which communities approach situations or the regulatory systems they design. The complex issue of land tenure is profoundly cultural, but also distinctly manipulated by historical experience. For planning in Tonga, the question of land tenure still confronts PUMA and relevant authorities in terms of any attempt to implement plans for shared amenities, housing, and other public projects. Such matters are deeply rooted in Tongan culture and are not easily dismantled or overruled by simply enacting legislation. Even with the recent attempts at democratisation, there is still an intense respect for hierarchy and authority, the epitome of which is the Tongan royal family. Thus, when systems that seem to disregard that authority are introduced, they are inevitably met with scepticism and some fierce opposition from certain quarters (Takau 2019).

Although the Land Act has indeed accounted for the cultural connection Tongan people have with their land, it has failed to accommodate the urban growth that has escalated since the early 2000s. All habitable land has been allocated and there is little potential for spatial planning to cater for urban growth, or for the maintenance or upgrading of infrastructure. For Tongans, land is symbolic and central to one's identity. In addition to this, the importance of family in Tongan culture is fundamental and many families wish to pass their land on and envisage that the land will be held by their family in perpetuity. Thus, it is important that planning agencies ensure that any future urban and national population growth will be debated and accommodated in a manner that upholds these cultural values. Mid-20th-century planning efforts were not created with Pacific values in mind. Nonetheless, the future of appropriate planning and urban management in Tonga necessitates that planning is consistent with local values in terms of structure, purposes, and processes.

Holistic Planning

Figure 10.5 is a visual depiction that models the four pillars—as espoused by planning officials and development plans (Takau 2019) of Tongan planning based on a fale (traditional house). In principle, the current planning system acknowledges all four of the pillars—but it does not do so evenly. It is evident that in the period immediately prior to the 2006 riots, the development and planning focus in Tonga prioritised the economic pillar seeking the economic benefits of development, whilst neglecting the other three pillars that hold the fale in place, weakening the integrity of the planning structure of the country. After the riots, more emphasis was placed on the environmental pillar and the protection of the natural environment, evident in such actions as the creation of several climate change-related agendas and the new Marine Spatial Plan. However, what is apparent in assessing planning activity and documents, is that the cultural and social pillars of the planning fale, whilst officially acknowledged in statute and frameworks, are not appreciated in any great depth nor actively prioritised in Tongan planning endeavours. Those provisions that do exist appear to hold

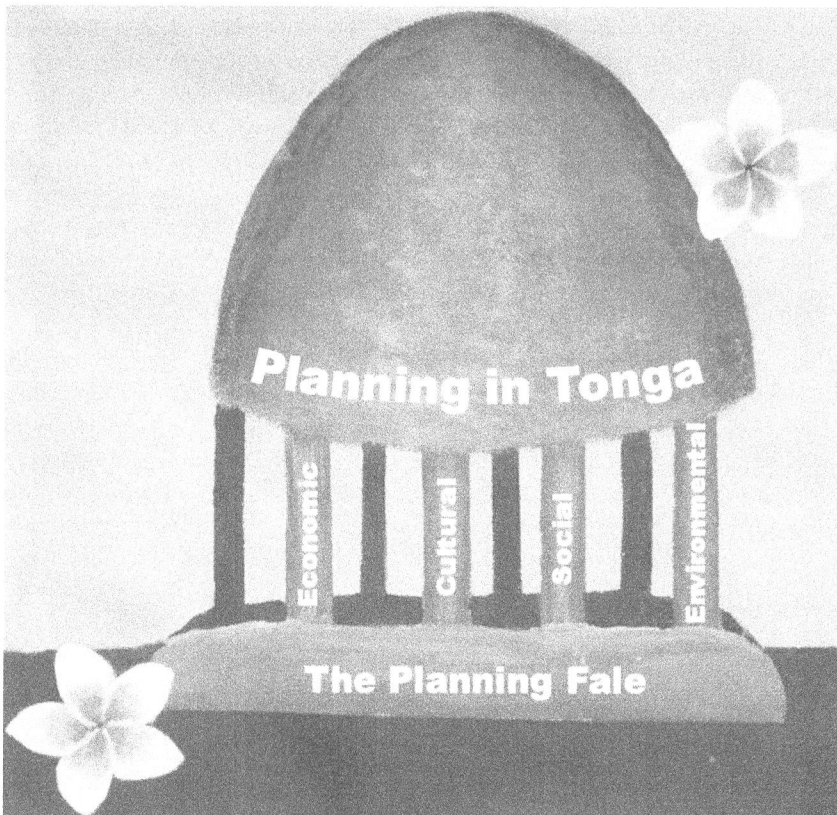

FIGURE 10.5 Tongan Planning Fale Model (artwork by Daizy Thompson-Fawcett)

limited weight in the uncoordinated planning decision-making processes. Whilst some intangible elements of culture are mentioned in planning documents, the lack of retention of heritage in the built environment is a clear example of the absence of translating cultural priorities in policy to manifestations in urban space. Similarly, whilst certain aspects of social planning are recognised in objectives for consultation and engagement processes, appreciation of the breadth of social planning and regard for assessing the social and health impacts of urban planning and development activities is weak. Planning related to transportation is a poignant example, where prioritisation of motor vehicle transit in recent transport and urban-form planning has overlooked and adversely impacted pedestrian and non-motorised activity and their health benefits.

The challenges are immense, and even when environmentally and economically sustainable options for development are pursued, they can "conflict with the cultural and social aspirations" of the local communities (Fernandes and Pinho 2017, 2). Although planning in Tonga has evolved into a more holistic form than existed prior to the 2006 riots, it is still in its infancy.

Conclusion

Developing tailored and effective planning systems in Pacific Island countries has proved particularly problematic due largely to the lingering adverse impacts of (and responses to) colonial interventions on administrative structures, Western-style planning and environmental management practices, cultural priorities, and processes of urbanisation. There is a highly complex and entangled web challenging urban prospects. Understanding the ongoing multi-dimensional effects of British interposition on working through aspirations for the future is critical to conceiving pathways forward and reasserting a locationally specific planning system.

Crucial advances that can be made in the Tongan context include prioritising conversations and capacity-building between government agencies, and between agencies and communities, about the wider trans-sectoral planning agenda for a rapidly urbanising and climate-resilient nation; working to overcome the fragmented and confusing share of responsibilities for planning-related activities between agencies; and taking an even-handed holistic approach to sustainable environmental, cultural, social, and economic planning. Certainly, there are major issues with regard to land resources, ecological fragility, economic markets, and isolation, but these cannot be adequately addressed until more fundamental changes are made to the overriding planning regime through concerted and culturally tailored processes of engagement and negotiation.

Acknowledgements

Many thanks to Daizy Thompson-Fawcett for her research assistance and preparation of graphics.

References

Beaglehole, J. C. (1961). *The journals of Captain James Cook on his voyages of discovery. Volume II, The voyage of the resolution and adventure, 1772–1775*. Hakluyt Society, Extra Series Number 35. Cambridge University Press.

Benguigui, G. (2011). Tonga in Turmoil. *Journal of the Polynesian Society* 120(4): 349–368.

Bott, E. (1982). *Tongan society at the time of Captain Cook's visits.* The Polynesian Society (Incorporated).

Connell, J. (2017). The urban Pacific: A tale of new cities. Special Edition: Urban Development in the Pacific, Crawford School of Public Policy, Australian National University. *Development Bulletin* 78: 5–10.

Crocombe, R. (1987). Overview: The pattern of change in Pacific land tenure. In *Land Tenure in the Pacific,* edited by R. Crocombe. University of the South Pacific.

(The) Economist. 2006. Turbulence in Tonga. The *Economist.* November 21st, 2006: www.economist. com/news/2006/11/21/turbulence-in-tonga.

Fernandes, R. and P. Pinho. (2017). The distinctive nature of spatial development on small islands. *Progress in Planning* 112: 1–18.

Halatuituia, S. (2002). *Tonga's contemporary land tenure system: Reality and rhetoric.* PhD thesis, University of Sydney.

Hibbard, M., M. Lane, and K. Rasmussen. (2008). The split personality of planning: Indigenous peoples and planning for land and resource management. *Journal of Planning Literature* 23(2): 136–151.

Home, R. (1997). *Of planting and planning: The making of British colonial cities.* 1st ed. Spon.

Jones, P. (1996). *The impact of the socio-cultural order on urban management in the Pacific Islands.* Unpublished PhD thesis, Department of Geographical Sciences and Planning, University of Queensland.

Jones, P. and J. Lea. (2007). What has happened to urban reform in the Island Pacific? Some lessons from Kiribati and Samoa. *Pacific Affairs* 80(3): 473–491.

Jones, P. (2016). *The emergence of Pacific urban villages urbanisation trends in the Pacific Islands,* Asia Development Bank, available: www.adb.org/sites/default/files/publication/201291/pacific-urbanvillages.pdf.

Jones, P. (2018). Pacific urban villages and village cities: Understanding town and city "as it is." Pacific Reflections: Personal Perceptions of Aid and Development. Crawford School of Public Policy, Australian National University. *Development Bulletin* 80: 109–114.

Takau, Y. (2019). *The development of planning processes in Tonga and the impact of the 2006 riots.* Master of Planning thesis, The University of Otago.

United Nations Development Programme. 1996). *Human development report 1996: Economic growth and human development,* available: www.hdr.undp.org/en/content/human-development-report-1996.

United Nations (2018). *2018 Revision of world urbanisation prospects.* www.un.org/development/desa/ publications/2018-revision-of-world-urbanization-prospects.html.

PART III

Agency

11

SOCIAL INFRASTRUCTURE FOR OUR TIMES

Building Participatory Systems that Value the Creativity of Everyone

Jayne Engle, Tessy Britton, and Pamela Glode-Desrochers

> Infrastructure, at its most fundamental level, is not about roads & bridges, cable and concrete. It's about who we are, what we value and what kind of society we want to create.
>
> *Eric Klinenberg*

Introduction

As societies awaken to cascading effects of the COVID-19 pandemic and climate and inequality crises, there is increasing recognition that the infrastructure we build for the future needs to be different from the infrastructure that got us to where we are. Infrastructure building has aimed primarily to optimize efficiency in ways that have benefited financial interests of the few, and it has rarely taken into account implications for the health and well-being of all people and life, and the underlying ecosystems on which we depend. If we are to rise to the challenges of this age, we will need to redefine what constitutes infrastructure, so that the trillions invested in it during the crucial 2020s' decade will lay the foundations for a renewed civilization.

Political debates about infrastructure are growing. In the context of the US infrastructure proposal of 2021, Secretary of Transportation Pete Buttigieg stated that "physically robust infrastructure is not enough if it fails to foster a healthy community; ultimately, all infrastructure is social." Increasingly countries are counting social infrastructure as critical and seeing that it needs to be complementary to natural and built physical infrastructure as well as institutional infrastructure. There is also growing recognition by courts that governments and businesses must do more to address the climate crisis, which has infrastructure implications.[1] Consistent with the spirit of sacred civics, every infrastructure decision ought to apply lenses of climate, equity, and health of people and planet, and for at least seven generations into the future.

DOI: 10.4324/9781003199816-15

This chapter is about social infrastructure and emphasizes a particular subset that we call participatory social infrastructure, which is place-based and takes a long-term, systemic, and radically inclusive approach. It is based on a vision to create conditions in the fabric of everyday community life that invite creativity and collaborative action and that enable transition to local wellbeing economies that are regenerative, circular, and inclusive of everyone. We are currently involved in building and testing a participatory social infrastructure called the participatory city approach, in locations in the UK and Canada. Our positionality sets out briefly how we came to be doing this work.

Jayne Engle. I was born on Susquehannock Peoples' homelands, in an area also known as Pennsylvania, USA, a descendant of settlers from Europe. I left those territories in adulthood and went on to live and work in a diversity of contexts and countries, including places of deep societal transition and multiculturalism, often engaging at the intersection of transformative community development, participatory urban planning, and social and civic infrastructure building. Core to my worldview are participatory values of social and environmental justice and reconciliation between Indigenous and all peoples, and with the land, and through time. I came to be working with the Participatory City Foundation in my role leading Cities for People at the McConnell Foundation, one of the partners behind Participatory Canada.

Tessy Britton. I was born in Zimbabwe and spent a large portion of my childhood in apartheid South Africa where I experienced first hand the effects of racial segregation. These experiences convinced me that if we can design societies for keeping people apart, we can design them for bringing people together. My work since 2010 has focused on designing and testing new systems that build connectivity back into the everyday lives of people living in urban areas. Learning from citizen innovators from across the world the Participatory City Approach has aimed to discover what essential new participatory systems are needed to support a new way of living together for greater collective agency and all the public tools we need to co-create and act on all the challenges we face as a society.

Pamela Glode-Desrochers. I was born on the ancestral lands of the Mi'kmaw people in a place called Kjipuktuk—Great Harbour. Today these lands are known as Halifax, Nova Scotia by those who have settled here. I am an L'nu (The People) woman and a member of Millbrook First Nation community in Truro, NS. I have lived my life within an urban setting and have had the privilege to work for my urban Indigenous community through the Friendship Centre Movement for 30 years. It is this work that has helped bring me to this point in time, where Friendship Centres are recognized and supported for the work of Truth and Reconciliation that they have been doing since the beginning. I have seen how this work is able to bring Indigenous and non–Indigenous Peoples together. I see the value in how society can be, should be, and will be for everyone. The importance of social infrastructure is not just about bricks and mortar; it is about belonging, acceptance, the environment, capability development, and self-determination. It is a living, breathing system that needs to be nurtured to see its full potential.

This chapter argues that communities where people live are critical sites of local and societal transformation, and that building adaptive and scalable social infrastructure is a key part of that. We make the case that a holistic systems approach is needed that centres a participatory dimension in order to unlock the agency and creativity of people to produce collaborative action in neighbourhoods. We explore learnings about the potential of the participatory city approach as a critical social infrastructure, with examples from the UK and Canada, where the larger vision is to demonstrate what societal change can look like when we build a regenerative, circular, wellbeing economy from the neighbourhood up. Both barriers and benefits are discussed, as well as intentions for future research and scaling.

Social Infrastructure: What Is it and Why Is it Important?

Social infrastructure is increasingly discussed in academic, policy, and public discourses as a distinct and vital form of infrastructure. It provides the foundations of social life and conditions for civic engagement and relationship building between people, including from different backgrounds. Sometimes referred to as "soft" infrastructure, it is that which we rely on to hold society together when "hard" infrastructures collapse, as they sometimes do in crises, such as terrorist attacks, climate disasters, and pandemics.

The term "social infrastructure" came into more frequent usage in civic contexts with sociologist Eric Klinenberg's book, *Palaces for the People: How social infrastructure can help fight inequality, polarization, and the decline of civic life* (2018). Many fields reference social infrastructure,[2] and increasingly, governments are talking about it. The City of Vancouver, for example, developed a ten-year Social Infrastructure Strategy,[3] and the Government of Canada committed CAD $25 billion over a decade to support social infrastructure investments in Indigenous communities; early learning and childcare; affordable housing; home care; and cultural, community, and recreational infrastructure.[4] Following are some definitions of social infrastructure, starting with a strong place-based grounding.

Klinenberg (2018, 5) defines social infrastructure as "the physical places and organizations that shape the way people interact." This includes the libraries, playgrounds, parks, sports pitches, schools, swimming pools, and other public institutions, as well as sidewalks, community gardens, and other green spaces in the public realm. Civic associations and community organizations provide social infrastructure when they have physical spaces where people can get together, such as food or art markets youth centres, and wellness and healing centres (City of Vancouver 2021). Businesses such as bookshops and cafés may be part of social infrastructure, especially when they constitute "third spaces"[5] where people can hang out. Congregation spaces for people of varied backgrounds can create conditions for building trust, co-operation, and a sense of belonging in city life.

Other definitions focus more on creating conditions for relationship building and organizational arrangements.

> Social infrastructure refers to the social environment. It includes formal groups and networks that cater to all sorts of social, professional, and life stage interests or needs. It also includes non-specific or incidental infrastructure that encourages informal social interaction.
>
> *Williams and Pocock 2010, 76*

> Social infrastructure refers to the organizational arrangements and deliberate investments in society's systems, relationships and structures that enable society to create a resilient, just, equitable and sustainable world. It includes social, economic, environmental and cultural assets.
>
> *Strandberg 2017, 6*

Our synthesis definition of social infrastructure for the purpose of this chapter is:

> The publicly accessible systems, amenities, physical places, spaces, platforms, services, activities, organizations, networks and movements that shape how people interact, and which can support collective life. These infrastructures have the potential to foster civic interactions and enable individuals, families, groups, and communities to meet their social and collective needs, maximize their potential for flourishing, and improve community wellbeing, vitality, and resilience, now and into the future.

Social infrastructure is at least as essential as other forms of infrastructure, and when designed well, can be mutually reinforcing and add value to other infrastructures. When it is neglected, however, it can often go unnoticed, because it does not typically collapse all at once, as physical infrastructure might. Rather, it can weaken slowly over time. Evidence can include increases in people feeling isolated and excluded, drug addiction, crime, and distrust; and signals also include decreases in civic participation, weakening of social networks, and reduced time that people from a diversity of backgrounds and interests spend in public spaces.

The Need for a Participatory Dimension in Social Infrastructure

Social infrastructures are typically more robust if they embed a participatory dimension or culture. This means designing with an explicit intent of building systemic support that enables agency of people: inviting their creativity to build projects alongside their neighbours that contribute to better life outcomes for themselves and their communities. We call this *participatory social infrastructure*. "Participatory" here is not primarily about consultative or ameliorative approaches. It constitutes a culture and a systems practice for engagement and co-creation, and it is a transformative concept that represents a way of seeing and being in the world and a way of life that is not value-neutral: it strives for social and environmental justice for everyone.

Participation became widely acknowledged in the early 1970s as an essential, transformative concept and practice in community development, strongly influenced by the pedagogy of Paulo Freire (1972). Consistent with Freirian tradition, a participatory culture holds an "ideology of equality," in which dignity, respect, co-operation, trust, reciprocity, and mutuality are fundamentally valued and strengthen the validity, effectiveness, and integrity of work (Ledwith and Springett 2010). The links between participation, bridging social capital, and community resilience building are strong (e.g., Putnam 1993; 2000; 2001), and critical in contexts of disaster (Aldrich 2012). Participation is seen as well as mutually reinforcing with the "capability approach" (Sen 1999; Nussbaum 2003) where development of human capabilities, agency, freedom, justice, and participation are fundamental to human wellbeing.[6]

In civic realms, social infrastructure that lacks a participatory dimension risks erosion over time, as it may be less visible, less tangible, and less outcome-oriented than that which can be accomplished through people working shoulder to shoulder on collective action projects. Without participation, social infrastructure risks being seen as non-essential, which can contribute to disinvestment, as has been seen in parks and libraries in many countries. On the other hand, as Klinenberg argues, social infrastructure that supports participatory, collective action is more likely to build social cohesion which "develops through repeated human interaction and joint participation in shared projects, not merely from a principled commitment to abstract values and beliefs." (Klinenberg 2018, 11). Participatory social infrastructure can also provide a means to strengthen creating the city as a commons (Foster and Iaione 2016; 2018) and a sharing cities ethos (McLaren and Agyeman 2015), as well as a means for collective intelligence and wisdom building (Peach and Smith 2022).

Participation, though, is not a panacea, and it has valid critiques and barriers. Cooke and Kothari (2001) call participation the "new tyranny," and caution that it can be captured as a buzzword to serve interests of power in order to maintain the status quo. They argue that participation must be transformative and not ameliorative, which requires demonstrating outcomes in relation to social cohesion, environmental sustainability, and collective well-being. Barriers that prevent participation from being transformative include short-termism with too-little investment, overly top-down approaches, and conflating participation with service delivery.

Participatory Social Infrastructure for our Times Requires Holistic System Innovation

So how to design and build participatory social infrastructure commensurate with the challenges and complexities of our time? It requires innovating holistic systems-based approaches that go beyond short-term, one-off interventions that have little to no lasting impact. It must be designed for multiple co-benefits,[7] with a long-term view, and it must be designed to scale in communities anywhere. Foundationally, it requires a learning architecture so that communities build on and learn from each other with continuous feedback loops, and so that each iteration involves drawing on multiple aspects of learning both within and between communities who are practising.

As Leadbeater and Winhall (2020) point out, better and different systems are needed for people to live sustainably in socially inclusive societies—a need heightened by the COVID-19 pandemic, and that building systemic opportunities means creating new operating models for new goals that make new ways of life, possible. Such systemic opportunities take time to unfold, because they are generative and create new value, socially and economically, and they require imagination, courage, and a willingness to take radical leaps, not just small steps.

> Society needs system innovation to tackle deep seated social challenges, meet emerging, growing needs and to open up systemic opportunities to support new ways of life. While a lot of innovation is going on in public and social fields, it usually falls short of innovating new systems. That means there is a huge gap between the kind of innovation society needs and the kind that is produced. To act more deliberately and effectively to change systems the people involved need to see and think about systems in different ways: to understand both the depth of the challenge and the scale of the opportunity; as well as the dynamic, collaborative processes of system innovation.
>
> *Leadbeater and Winhall 2020, 46*

So what are possible system innovations for participatory social infrastructure, and how could they be built in ways that are appropriate for our times and adaptable to a wide variety of contexts? Such innovations would need to invite creativity of people in their everyday lives, and to foster multiple individual and collective outcomes. In the next section we present one promising systems approach with these aims.

The Participatory City Approach: Vision, Components, Experience

In the London Borough of Barking and Dagenham, UK, the Participatory City Foundation is working with thousands of neighbourhood residents to build networks of friendship and co-create a new kind of large-scale, fully inclusive, practical participatory ecosystem—an infrastructure of sorts. Together with residents, the team are collectively building the spaces and creating the conditions for people to work together, side by side, for a better life for everyone, and for the planet. This system-building approach is intrinsically adaptive in its design, enabling neighbourhoods and communities in multiple contexts to co-create with the talents, ideas, assets, and resources they all have locally.

The participatory city approach is a combination of systems, methodologies, platforms, and strategies that have created a unique method of building and co-creating inclusive local participation. Founder Tessy Britton and the team, along with thousands of neighbourhood residents, have developed this approach to building practical participation into the fabric of everyday life. The approach places people and their capabilities at the centre of co-creating a different way of living together. Research to date on the impact of repeated and ongoing participation in the flagship Every One Every Day platform shows that individual and collective agency is born and nurtured through action—people doing everyday, practical, and useful activities together.[8]

Building new practical participation systems is different from copying off-the-shelf projects or programs. The participatory city approach is not a model to be copy-pasted; it involves learning how to facilitate the co-creation of opportunities that allow every person, every family, and every organization to contribute to building cohesive and regenerative ways of living. It involves knitting together every idea and every space into a vast and diverse network of participation opportunities where everyone can find a place for their creativity. The approach involves embedding a learning, unlearning, and relearning social infrastructure deeply into neighbourhoods. It is a dynamic co-creation process that constantly adapts to the changes of people and ideas that make neighbourhoods and cities vibrant. This adaptive, creative, and evolving process facilitates a living, breathing environment that is highly responsive to challenges and opportunities as they continually present themselves.

Figures 11.1 and 11.2 show the systems of the participatory city approach, which requires building two interconnected systems—the support platform and the participatory ecosystem, each with different elements and design principles (Figure 11.1). Figure 11.2 represents the practical participatory ecosystem as an evolving network of people, projects, and businesses which create thousands of inclusive opportunities for local residents to participate in practical, enjoyable activity in their neighbourhood. The participatory ecosystem is a living, breathing ecology, in which project ideas and activities are continuously being designed, tested, grown, paused, discarded, or replicated. Similar to ecosystems in nature, it develops organically, is unpredictable, and is rooted in the shifting interrelationships of many diverse and distinct parts (multiple residents joining and leaving, and projects emerging, thriving, replicating, and stopping on a continual basis).[9]

Case: Participatory Canada

Based on the success, evidence, and early outcomes in London, teams in Halifax, Montreal, and Toronto wanted to test the approach. Participatory Canada, a joint venture of the

Inclusivity design principles

Make it easy for many people to
participate regularly in practice projects
that fit with their daily everyday lives.

Low time and commitment
No or low cost
Simple and straightforward
Many opportunities with wide variety
Nearby and accessible
Opportunities from beginner to expert
Promote directly and effectively
Introduce and accompany
Tangible benefits to people
Attracting talents not targeting needs
Fostering inclusive culture
100% open—no stigma
Build projects with everyone
Welcome children

Participatory Ecosystem

A collection of many and varied practical
projects and businesses

Essential Living
Co-operatives

Clothing   Home

Food   Platform   Services
        co-op

Tomorrow Today Streets
Mini-platforms & mini
eco-systems

Organizational
Member network

Co-creation
Design
Process

Co-creation
design
principles

Essential
Living Lab

Support platform design
principles

Trained support
team

Essential
Universal
Inclusive
Open Source
Simple
Circular
Co-created
Affordable
Regenerative

Operations &
Logistics

Warehouse
makerspace &
network of shop
spaces

Make it easy for many people to
participate regularly in practice
projects that fit with their daily
everyday lives.

Support Platform

A collection of co-ordinated
shared infrastructure

A system of practical support
Supports collections of projects
Works quickly to prototype
Reduces and shares personal risk
Co-design and/or Co-creation
Many people as co-builders
Many organizations collaborate

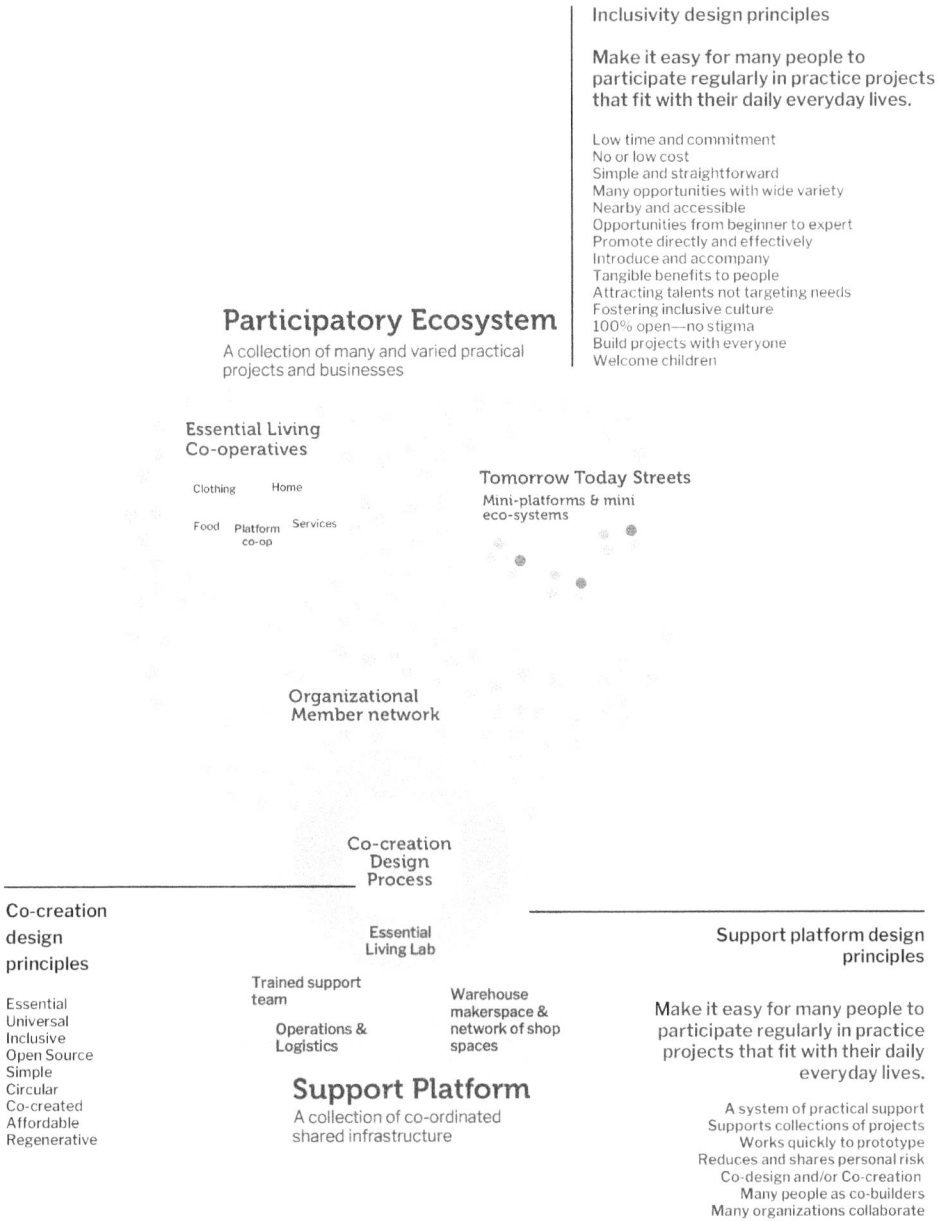

FIGURE 11.1 Two systems of the participatory city approach

Source: Participatory City Foundation (in Participatory Canada (2021, 219))

McConnell and Participatory City Foundations, was born, and received additional support
from the Employment and Social Development Canada's Investment Readiness Program.[10]

Participatory Canada prototyped the participatory city approach and explored feasibility
with partners in three city neighbourhoods. The social research and development (R&D)
phase was designed to build partnerships and share knowledge and practices between cities. It

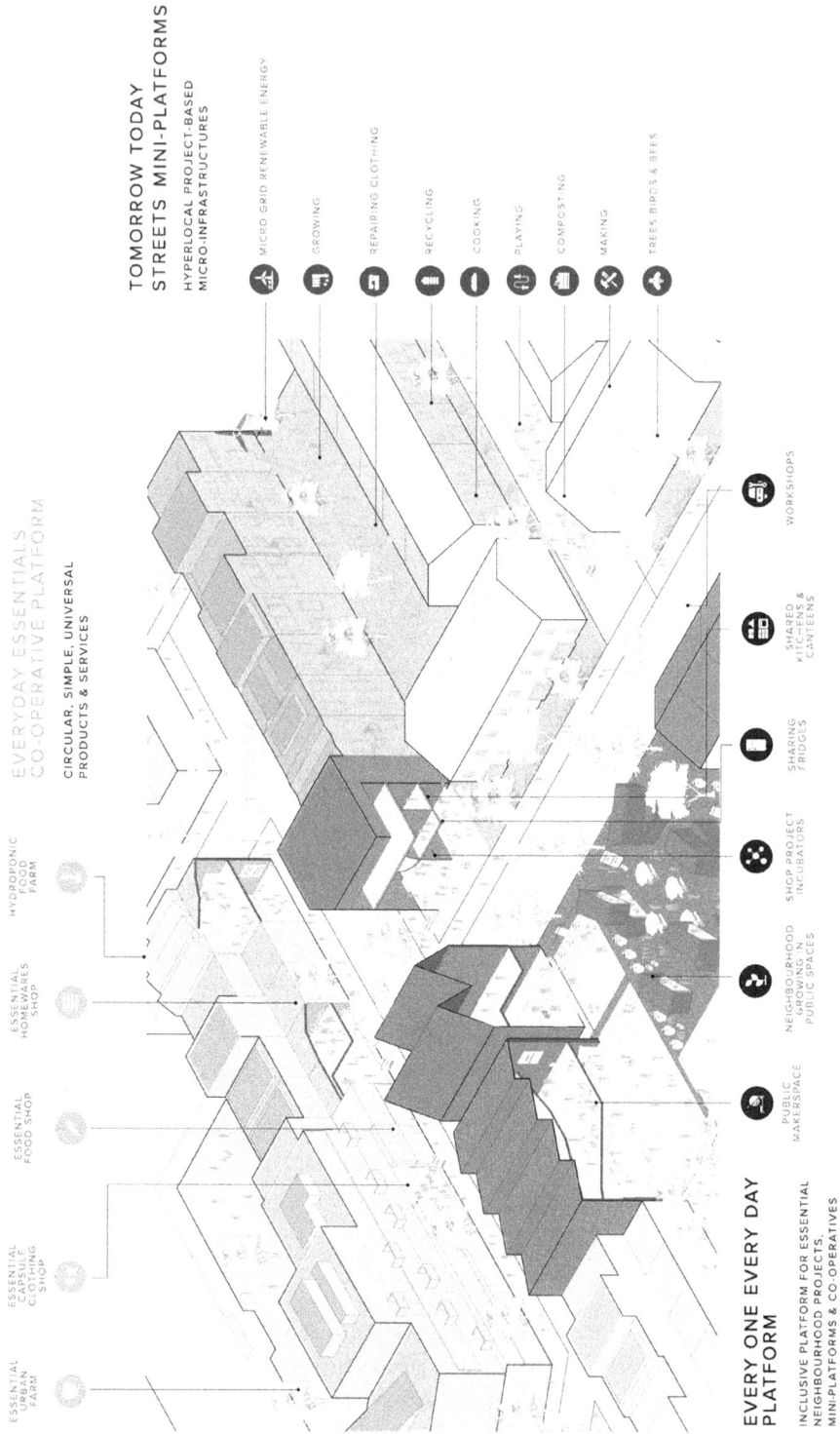

FIGURE 11.2 Practical participatory ecosystem

Source: Participatory City Foundation (in Participatory Canada (2021, 52–53))

was also a chance to test local responses to strengthened participation culture and assess emerging opportunities for building participatory social infrastructure in these communities for the long term. Findings from this phase suggest that the participatory city approach to building large-scale participation is feasible, highly adaptive, creates value for neighbours, and generates radical inclusion in a variety of contexts. And one of the most promising early results shows it can be a critical infrastructure for making reconciliation manifest in people's everyday civic interactions.[11]

Key Findings, Insights, and Limitations

We used developmental evaluation methodology to assess feasibility, inclusivity, value creation, and viability for each of the three prototype cities as well as for the initiative as a whole, engaging with a range of qualitative and quantitative data.[12] The emergent learning process revealed the following key insights.

Overarching learnings
1. Participatory City is not a "UK model" to replicate, but rather, a "systems approach" to learn from and then adapt to local contexts.
2. The participatory city approach is viable in varied contexts and able to integrate into existing ecosystems of local programs, community assets, and businesses.
3. The participatory city approach can be a platform for Truth and Reconciliation.
4. Diverse resources are needed to reach minimum viability of the participatory city approach.
5. The prototypes suffered when and where it was not possible for people to get together in physical spaces due to the COVID-19 pandemic, though where it was possible, results show great potential for the approach to be part of pandemic recovery strategies.

Local learnings
1. Coaching support by the Every One Every Day team in London to local teams in Canada was critical to learning the approach, including nuanced and systemic aspects, and adapting it wisely to quite different contexts.
2 Neighbours from widely diverse backgrounds took part in the prototypes, and they built networks that brought together individuals and communities that were not connected previously.
3. The participatory city engagement approach and venue in neighbourhood "third spaces" and "fourth spaces" provided for community members to come together, overcoming usual barriers and cultural divides.
4. Among what community residents found most valuable was their increased connections to neighbours they did not know before and getting to know their community better.
5. Community residents showed strong desire to co-create the future of the participatory platforms, and demand is growing from local neighbours in the prototype cities, and from other communities across Canada.

A key risk is under-resourcing the work and falling into a trap of being one among a plethora of underfunded, short-term programs which, despite great efforts, often fail to create systemic change. Based on experience in the flagship London Every One Every Day campus, it is increasingly evident that substantial and long-term commitment of support and resources is required to make visible possibilities for transformed ways of life that the platform opens up.

Regulatory restrictions and time horizons of policy and funders are also ongoing challenges. The obstacles underline the need for funding models that support social R&D for large-scale social change prototyping in live contexts. Given the emphasis on whole systems rather than working on problems one at a time, and of being radically inclusive rather than targeting population groups, it takes longer to develop evaluation tools and measure progress and outcomes.

Focus on Halifax: Creating a Platform that is Indigenous-led, Reconciliation-centred and Inclusive of Everyone

> Even though we are so close together, there's a lot we don't know about each other.
>
> *Tony Thomas, Mi'kmaw Native Friendship Centre Board Chair*

The Participatory Canada prototype in Halifax, called Every One Every Day Kjipuktuk, was led by the Mi'kmaw Native Friendship Centre (MNFC), an Indigenous organization based in the North End of the city.[13] Over the course of seven months 2020–2021, MNFC worked with North End neighbours, and alongside Participatory City Tutors, to create a participatory platform and program of activities.[14] The vision was to inspire new connections and friendships through everyday participation in useful and enjoyable activities, designed to make life better and to help foster a sense of togetherness.

The overarching ethos was to build an Indigenous-led, reconciliation-centred participatory platform that was inviting and inclusive of everyone. That involved people learning about Indigenous culture and history and sharing across cultures, including with African Nova Scotian communities and newcomers to Canada. Early evidence is compelling that the approach planted seeds of transformation for changing local culture and practices. MNFC Executive Director Pam Glode-Desrochers remarked: "This platform gave us the opportunity to move reconciliation in Halifax so much further ahead than I ever thought."[15]

The approach of creating everyday participatory practices that centre Indigenous reconciliation in neighbourhoods is increasingly important as a means to build social cohesion and strengthen community resilience. In 2021 there have been horrific unearthings of mass and unmarked graves of Indigenous children who died while attending "residential schools."[16] There are renewed calls and commitments to reconciliation and reckoning, along with growing societal recognition that colonization is not merely part of history, but that it continues to manifest throughout our systems, cultures, and infrastructure in ways that are oppressive and discriminatory. Society cannot reckon merely through policies; for reconciliation to be deep and meaningful, it must manifest in everyday life between everyday people in neighbourhoods.

The experience of centring the initiative in Indigenous reconciliation in Halifax involved a Two-Eyed Seeing[17] evaluation approach and aimed to embed Truth and Reconciliation at all levels of the initiative. This led to the governance group agreeing to solidify and maintain the commitment to reconciliation throughout every phase of the project and to educate all involved in the history, culture, and traditions of Indigenous Peoples and create awareness of the legacies of colonialism. The team developed guiding principles to integrate the Seven Sacred Teachings and Euro–Canadian practice in order to help draw insights around how the teams worked together as a critical indicator of success (see Figure 11.3).

STRATEGIC GROUP PRINCIPLES

The following principles were created using the Mi'kmaw teaching of Etuaptmumk, "Two-eyed Seeing", introduced by Elder Albert Marshall of Eskasoni First Nation, in the district of Una'ma'ki. This teaching asks us to take the strengths of both a colonized world and an Indigenous world, and, through both lenses, build greater capacity and success for all. These principles integrate Euro-Canadian practice with the Seven Sacred Teachings of the Mi'kmaq through a process of co-learning and an exchange of stories.

LOVE & OPENNESS
Through the teaching of love, we approach our tasks with an open heart and steep our work in love so that we always remain welcoming and inclusive.

COURAGE & BRAVERY
Through the teaching of courage, we unleash the tenacity we carry inside to overcome fears that prevent us from advancing in our worwwk by acknowledging our discomfort and facing it with bravery and integrity, together.

RESPECT & HARMONY
Through the teaching of respect, we acknowledge the existence of multiple truths and give equal consideration to all perspectives. We accept differences and do not judge or dismiss but work together to establish a mutual understanding that will sustain a harmonious environment for all to thrive.

HUMILITY & RECIPROCITY
Through the teaching of humility, we recognize that we are a part of something greater than our individual needs. We honour our interconnectedness – Msit no'kmaq, "all my relations," by exploring beyond words, to the essence of ourselves and our existence on this earth. We appreciate our inter-dependence by supporting working relationships that are both reciprocal and steadfast.

WISDOM & REFLECTION
Through the teaching of wisdom, we utilize our individual gifts in ways that promote wellness and equity. We realize that our work is dynamic and always changing and we intentionally create space to reflect on the past and present to prepare for the path ahead.

TRUTH & TRANSPARENCY
Through the teaching of truth, we adhere to these principles and are purposeful in our work and intentional in our actions. We are aware of our personal truths and recognize the multiple lenses that influence how we see and act in the world so that we remain accountable and transparent in everything we do.

HONESTY, LEARNING & UNLEARNING
Through the teaching of honesty, we remain true to ourselves, our community, and each other by always speaking from the heart. We create a safe space to learn, grow, and develop alongside each other and lead with curiosity, questioning what is, and why things are the way they are to surface our shared history.

❝ The principles are beautiful. They depict that there needs to be vulnerability present to be in practice. ❞

- Strategic Group member

FIGURE 11.3 Evaluation principles of Participatory Canada in Halifax: Two-Eyed Seeing integrating Seven Sacred Teachings of Indigenous Peoples with Euro–Canadian practice

Source: Every One Every Day Kjipuktuk-Halifax (in Participatory Canada, 2021, 123)

Looking forward, and in response to growing demand and early compelling evidence from Participatory Canada Social R&D, partners aspire to create a deep demonstration learning campus in Halifax. Every One Every Day Kjipuktuk will continue to centre Indigenous reconciliation and be inclusive of everyone.[18] The Halifax learning campus will also provide a training ground for other communities as part of developing a national platform of support. An essential learning architecture for the participatory city approach, the Here&Now School of Participatory Systems Design (recently created by the Participatory City Foundation), will connect the various communities and learning campus nodes with research partnerships and communities of practice, and on a global level.

Essential Components for Scaling the Approach

Based on experiential learning, research, and development in London, Halifax, Montreal, and Toronto, in early 2021 partners explored together possibilities for scaling, building learning architecture, and developing novel approaches to finance participatory platforms for the long term, such as outcomes-based financing. Knowledge generated from the R&D highlighted essential components for growing the practical participatory ecosystem within cities and as part of a larger global network. The lead team envisions building the network through a phased approach over a decade-long horizon. Each phase would focus on supporting and growing people's capabilities, as well as on identifying and mobilizing sustainable financing sources, and strategically scaling across geographies using a strong network and relationship approach (see Figure 11.4).

Coordination, relationships, and communication. Strong coordination of resources and networks across local and global programming, continuous development of relationships

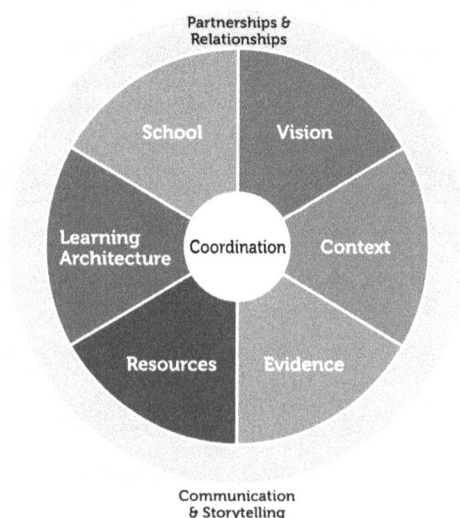

FIGURE 11.4 Essential components for scaling the participatory city approach

Source: Participatory City Foundation (in Participatory Canada, 2021, 24–25)

with partners and advocates, and a range of creative and unique communication assets are additional elements that will support the growth and evolution of the participatory city approach.

Vision. The vision for Participatory Canada must be co-developed with the partners to align with the ambitions unique to each city and community.

Context. Local conditions determine the development of practical participation systems. Financial implications affect costs for social infrastructure and core assets while social factors impact the types of activities.

Evidence. Robust research and measurement and collection of data and stories will be crucial in understanding outcomes, improving continually, and developing financial sustainability through strong business cases for practical participation ecosystems within cities.

Resources. The Participatory Canada vision requires well-trained teams and resources coordinated across the scaling phases and at both national and local levels.

Learning architecture. Participatory Canada will focus on curriculum and learning programs ranging from experiential and immersion to digital experiences to build capabilities with partners in building the participatory city approach.

School. Full-scale implementation of the approach in one city (Halifax) will act as a deep demonstration learning campus in Canada. This school will connect the growing set of hubs, share learnings and adaptations of the approach, build skills for local teams and communities, and support data collection and impact measurement.

Why This Matters: Participatory Social Infrastructure to Harness Community-created Value

When well designed and carried out, participatory social infrastructure can provide a social R&D platform for people to share, grow, and test their ideas and to connect with others in their civic environments, thereby creating collective value and resilience. The need for resilience at community level is growing and has direct relationship with three broader societal trends that represent opportunities for change: (1) opportunity to redefine infrastructure so that we build to meet the increasing challenges of this age; (2) opportunity to strengthen collective capabilities so that communities can think, learn, and act together with wisdom; and (3) opportunity to innovate financing in order to value what matters while building community wealth and a wellbeing economy. Each of these trends can be addressed and embedded at local level so that communities have agency, tools, and systems to strengthen resilience and play an active, ongoing role of collective value creation.

Redefining infrastructure. The notion of infrastructure is changing, both in civic discourse and governments.[19] Recent recovery budgets of many governments reveal stronger emphasis on social infrastructure to improve community wellbeing. At local level, infrastructure needs to be more adaptive to enable people living in proximity to mobilize collectively in times of crisis. Building such civic infrastructure requires strengthening social capital and community resilience. Well-designed and tested participatory social infrastructure can provide an effective platform and accessible public good to do just that.

Strengthening collective capabilities. If communities are to transition to socially equitable and ecologically healthy environments, they will need to strengthen collective capabilities to think and act together and to continually learn as conditions change. And they will need to learn from other communities about what works. Learning architecture to facilitate adaptive capabilities within and between communities is an essential part of robust participatory social infrastructure and can benefit from research partnerships and communities of practice.

Innovating financing. The COVID-19 pandemic revealed that financing resilience in local communities is more rapid and responsive when decisions are made closer to the ground. The current model of governments determining how community recovery should occur is increasingly inadequate as governments are slow to act and it takes time for on-the-ground information to inform policy change.

To respond to future shocks and chronic problems, communities need better financing tools at their disposal beyond the traditional grants, loans, and equity investments available. Newer social and community finance tools exist, such as impact bonds, impact investments, outcomes-based financing, and participatory budgeting. They are, however, not yet at the required scale, and a greater range of instruments for community wealth building is needed. In short, there is a need to innovate community-resilience financing. While several community wealth labs and initiatives are underway, and new economy models such as circular, doughnut, and wellbeing economy frameworks are increasingly being applied at local levels, they have not yet attracted substantial investment from governments or philanthropy. There is opportunity to integrate such frameworks within participatory social infrastructure, and to innovate impact and outcomes measurement tools that can redefine value when it comes to long-term community resilience. Participating in influencing these trends together through place-based systems will be crucial to developing investment-ready ideas from a social R&D base, which community members themselves will have shaped.

Regarding the specific case of the participatory city approach, evidence from London is compelling. Every One Every Day has enabled creation of an open, fertile ecosystem from which great and investable ideas can be seeded by local people to grow and flourish, thereby creating new forms of community wealth. The Participatory City team and neighbourhood residents have expanded the R&D into community business incubators, and supported the growth of local collaboratives and cooperative business models. Early signs from the Canada prototypes show promise for similar trajectories.

Conclusion

As we move further into an era of increasing volatility, inequality, and more frequent crises locally and globally, the need for community resilience and social cohesion is more evident than ever. Social infrastructure will become more critical to everyday neighbourhood life, so that people have the means, supports, and tools to work together on collective action projects, and to build better lives, together. This chapter has defined social infrastructure, demonstrated the need for it to include participatory and systems dimensions, and provided an example of the participatory city approach and Canada case as promising social infrastructure for our times.

The social infrastructure that we need to build from here must be different from that which got us to this point in history. Centuries of colonization and an extractive economic system have contributed to social fragmentation, isolation, and in some cases, breakdown. Critical questions to address in assessing how to build forward include:

- What does decolonized, emancipatory social infrastructure look like?
- What participatory social infrastructures show promise to address the growing challenges of our times?

- How could systemic approaches of social infrastructure for community transition be scaled anywhere?
- What learning, scaling and financing architectures are needed to build more robust social infrastructure?

There are many more questions to ask and address in coming years, and much more transdisciplinary research on emerging social infrastructures will be needed in order to learn from and scale those with greatest transformative potential.

This time of societal reckoning opens the possibility to question basic assumptions about how we live and work together in our neighbourhoods. It is time to build social infrastructure and create conditions that invite creativity, innovation, and participation of everyone, to improve the long-term health of Mother Earth, to centre reconciliation among peoples, and to embed the Seven Sacred Teachings of many Indigenous traditions. Let's move forward together with love, respect, courage, honesty, wisdom, humility, and truth. And let's imagine and build the social infrastructure needed so that children in future generations will thrive in equitable, regenerative communities.

Notes

1 In May 2021 a Dutch court made a historic ruling ordering Shell Oil to reduce emissions by 45 percent by 2030: www.forbes.com/sites/davidrvetter/2021/05/26/shell-oil-verdict-could-trigger-a-wave-of-climate-litigation-against-big-polluters/?sh=640ac8a41a79. In April 2021, a German court ruled that the government must do more for future generations: https://fortune.com/2021/04/29/germany-climate-court-ruling-emissions-targets-2030-2050-radical-abstinence-fridays-for-future/.

2 The term "social infrastructure" is discussed in many fields and academic disciplines. Some examples: sociology (Aldrich & Meyer 2014; Flora & Flora 1993; Putnam 2000); community development (Williams & Pocock 2010); geography (Latham & Layton 2019; urban planning (Davern et al. 2017); educational technology (Bielaczyc 2006); higher education (Strandberg 2017); and ecology (Flitcroft et al. 2009).

3 City of Vancouver (2021) 10-year Social Infrastructure Strategy: https://vancouver.ca/people-programs/social-infrastructure-strategy.aspx.

4 Government of Canada (2021) Social Infrastructure funding stream: www.infrastructure.gc.ca/plan/si-is-eng.html.

5 Coined by Ray Oldenburg (1999) "third places" refer to social surroundings that are separate from the two social environments of home (first place) and workplace (second place). Examples include cafes, clubs, public libraries, bookstores, community centres, churches, and parks. Third places are critical for community vitality and local democracy. The term "fourth place" has recently emerged, in part due to the COVID-19 pandemic, to describe the "intangible digital environments that have proven to be spaces of connection, or spaces of reprieve from social isolation." (Ogundele, A. 2020. The Fourth Place and Re-imagining the City. *Urbanarium Journal*. https://urbanarium.org/journal/fourth-place-and-re-imagining-city. July 16th.

6 Amartya Sen's *Development as Freedom* (1999) and the "capability approach" laid the ground for the UN's establishment of the Human Development Index (HDI). The 2020 Human Development Report is here: http://report.hdr.undp.org/.

7 "Co-benefits" means recognizing interdependencies of issues and working across sectors to achieve multiple benefits simultaneously; this can be linked to a "multi-solving approach": www.tamarackcommunity.ca/library/changing-how-i-think-about-community-change-multisolving (article by Sylvia Cheuy). Co-benefits are also called "compound outcomes," as in page 31 of the Tools to Act report of Participatory City Foundation: www.participatorycity.org/tools-to-act.

8 The approach and experience of the Every One Every Day flagship demonstration campus is documented in its year two report, *Tools to Act*: www.participatorycity.org/tools-to-act.

9 For further explanations of Figures 11.1 and 11.2, see *Tools to Act* (Participatory City Foundation year two report, pages 22–27): www.participatorycity.org/tools-to-act; and specific reference to Figure 11.2 is in Tessy Britton's blog, Universal Basic Everything: Creating essential infrastructure for post-Covid 19 neighbourhoods: https://tessybritton.medium.com/universal-basic-everything-f149afc4cef1.

10 The full report for Participatory Canada Social R&D 2020–2021 is here: www.participatorycanada.ca/y1report.

11 Reconciliation refers to repairing relationships between Indigenous and non-Indigenous Peoples, and involves raising awareness about colonization and its ongoing effects on Indigenous Peoples. Reconciliation is part of the Truth and Reconciliation Commission (www.trc.ca/) and efforts to address harms caused by deliberate policies and programs of colonization, such as residential schools. For some, the word "reconciliation" represents an opportunity and commitment to reflect on the past, to heal, and to work in the present for decolonized futures. The term is also problematic for some, who view current gestures of reconciliation as merely performative and lacking in meaning and action to address harms of past and ongoing colonization.

12 COLAB was the developmental evaluation partner. The evaluation assessed feasibility, inclusivity, viability, and value creation, and for the Halifax case, a fifth dimension was added: reconciliation. Evaluation report: www.participatorycanada.ca/y1report.

13 See Every One Every Day Kjipuktuk-Halifax site: https://halifaxiseveryone.ca/. The initiative was developed with a strategic group, including Develop Nova Scotia (provincial crown corporation), Inspiring Communities, United Way Halifax, Engage Nova Scotia, Community Sector Council of Nova Scotia, and the Halifax Regional Municipality (Mayor's Office). An excellent blog by Aimee Gasparetto and other members of the team provides further insight into outcomes and evaluation as well as lived experiences: https://agasparetto.medium.com/insights-from-the-ground-on-developing-a-platform-approach-to-inclusive-participation-and-9ee0fa1994de.

14 The activities including collective cooking, tea and bannock with Elders, building benches, planting window gardens, making flutes and dream catchers, taking community-led walks, and more. Full program here: https://bit.ly/2VzQKci.

15 The Participatory Canada four-minute video has a focus on reconciliation and interviews with Mi'kmaw Native Friendship Centre Executive Director, Pam Glode-Desrochers and Program Director, Aimee Gasparetto: https://vimeo.com/548126695.

16 In 2021, hundreds of unmarked graves of Indigenous children who attended "Indian Residential Schools" were found: www.cbsnews.com/news/canada-indigenous-children-school-bodies-unmarked-graves-2021-06-30/.

17 Two-Eyed Seeing explores the integration of multiple perspectives (i.e., Indigenous and settler worldviews) to create a holistic understanding of multifaceted relationships, experiences, content, and processes. Tammy Mudge led on this evaluation work.

18 Every One Every Day Kjipuktuk-Halifax is part of the vision of the Mi'kmaw Native Friendship Centre to build Wije'winen (meaning "come with us"), a proposed new facility as a place to gather, learn, celebrate culture, and support reconciliation. It will be the city's first Indigenous-inspired and -informed building.

19 A number of governments are setting up national infrastructure assessments and commissions, for example in Canada: www.infrastructure.gc.ca/nia-eni/index-eng.html, and in the UK: https://nic.org.uk/.

References

Aldrich, D. (2012). *Building Resilience: Social capital in post-disaster recovery*. University of Chicago Press.

Aldrich, D. P. and M. A. Meyer (2014). Social capital and community resilience. *American Behavioral Scientist* 59(2): 254–269.

Bielaczyc, K. (2006). Designing social infrastructure: Critical issues in creating learning environments with technology. *Journal of the Learning Sciences* 15: 301–329.

Canada, Government of (2020). *Investing in Canada plan funding stream: Social infrastructure.* www.infra-structure.gc.ca/plan/si-is-eng.html.

Cooke, B. and U. Kothari, eds. (2001). *Participation: The new tyranny?* Zed Books.

Davern, M., L. Gunn, C. Whitzman, C. Higgs, B. Giles-Corti, K. Simons, K. Villanueva, S. Mavoa, R. Roberts, and H. Badland. (2017). Using spatial measures to test a conceptual model of social infra-structure that supports health and wellbeing. *Cities & Health* 1(2): 194–209.

Flitcroft, R. L., D. C. Dedrick, C. L. Smith, C. A. Thieman, and J. P. Bolte. (2009). Social infrastruc-ture to integrate science and practice: The experience of the Long Tom Watershed Council. *Ecology and Society* (2)36.

Flora, C. B. and J. L. Flora. (1993). Entrepreneurial social infrastructure: A necessary ingredient. *The Annals of the American Academy of Political and Social Science* 529(1): 48–58.

Foster, S. and C. Iaione. (2018). Ostrom in the city: Design principles and practices for the urban commons. In *Routledge Handbook: The study of the commons*, edited by B. Hudson, J. Rosenbloom, and D. Cole. Routledge.

Foster, S. and C. Iaione. (2016). The city as a commons. *Yale Law and Policy Review* 34: 281.

Freire, P. (1972). *Pedagogy of the oppressed.* Penguin.

Klinenberg, E. (2018). *Palaces for the people: How social infrastructure can help fight inequality, polarization, and the decline of civic life.* Crown.

Latham, A. and J. Layton. (2019). Social infrastructure and the public life of cities: Studying urban soci-ality and public spaces. *Geography Compass* 13:e12444.

Leadbeater, C. and J. Winhall. (2020). *Building better systems: A green paper on system innovation.* The Rockwool Foundation. October. www.systeminnovation.org/green-paper.

Ledwith, M. and J. Springett. (2010). *Participatory practice: Community-based action for transformative change.* Policy Press.

McLaren, D. and J. Agyeman. (2015). *Sharing cities: A case for truly smart and sustainable cities.* MIT Press.

Nussbaum, M. A. (2003). Capabilities as fundamental entitlements: Sen and social justice. *Feminist Economics* 9(2–3): 33–59.

Ogundele, A. 2020. The fourth place and re-imagining the city. *Urbanarium.* https://urbanarium.org/journal/fourth-place-and-re-imagining-city. July 16th.

Oldenburg, R. (1999). *The Great Good Place: Cafes, coffee shops, bookstores, bars, hair salons, and other hangouts at the heart of a community.* Da Capo Press.

Participatory Canada (2021). *Participatory Canada: Social Research and Development Report and Roadmap 2020–2021.* www.participatorycanada.ca/y1report.

Peach, K. and L. Smith. (2022). Participatory futures: Reimagining the city together. In *Sacred Civics: Building seven generation cities, edited by* J. Engle, J. Agyeman, and T. Chung-Tiam-Fook. Routledge.

Putnam, R. D. (2001). Social capital: Measurement and consequences. *Canadian Journal of Policy Research* 2, no. 1: 41–51.

Putnam, R. D. (2000). *Bowling alone: The collapse and revival of American community.* Simon & Schuster.

Putnam, R. D. (1993). The prosperous community: Social capital and public life. *The American Prospect:* 13, Spring, Vol. 4.

Sen, A. (1999). *Development as freedom.* Alfred A. Knopf.

Strandberg, C. (2017). Maximizing the capacities of advanced education institutions to build social infra-structure for Canadian communities. Commissioned by the J. W. McConnell Foundation and Simon Fraser University. April. https://re-code.ca/wp-content/uploads/2018/12/Background-Paper.pdf.

UNDP (2020). *Human Development Report. The next frontier: Human development and the Anthropocene.*

Vancouver, City of. (2021). Social infrastructure strategy (in process as of September 2021). https://vancouver.ca/people-programs/social-infrastructure-strategy.aspx.

Williams, P. and B. Pocock. (2010). Building "community" for different stages of life: physical and social infrastructure in master planned communities. *Community, Work & Family* 13(1): 71–87.

12

THE CEREMONY OF RECLAIMING AGENCY THROUGH WONDER

Catherine Tàmmaro

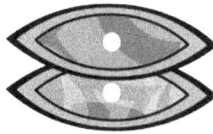

FIGURE 12.1 The Red Canoe

DOI: 10.4324/9781003199816-16

uⁿdawaʔ—Riding the Currents

On the shore of "Niwa'ah Onega'gaih'ih"[1] or "Little Thundering Waters," also known as the Humber River on the western edge of Toronto, Canada, lies a brilliant red canoe made by the Brothers Bastien in the middle of the 20th century in Wendake, Québec; the home of the Huron Wendat First Nation. The surface of the vessel is made of soft canvas covering the skeletal struts and gunwales hardened by layers and layers of carmine paint, brilliant against the muddy brown river water on this dull autumn day. The rich reddish brown cedar innards gleam with old varnish … the light just catches the struts, as reminders of our MoonWater Song.

We're both; canoe and I, waiting to travel to a place between the worlds on this day of honouring the death of the year. My two companions are young and able-bodied, the canoe and I, relatively the same age. It is October 31, 2020. We are all in semi-lockdown, following new protocols for social distancing, masked, gloved, and coated with antiseptic gel; protected too, from even this river-infused atmosphere. This transitional day marks the end of the agricultural year when the harvest had been completed and stores laid in for the coming winter months. Here in the Great Lakes region, it is a full Moon—the Blood Moon.

My young friends, two spirited world-bridgers, are there to help carry me across. Quiet, I have gone deep inside to a seeming timeless place of the renewal of my relationship with water, into the beautiful space of preparedness for ceremony. We are three, young, older, and oldest; birth, life, and death and we are there to honour this beautiful red canoe which has come to the homeland. I climb stiffly in and immediately feel both sadness and love for my older body and remember my first step into Lily the Red Canoe, some 29 years ago, in 1992, in Frontenac County, Ontario and the countless reasons this red canoe means so very much to me.

The pull into Spirit is powerful and my consciousness begins to shift just as it did then; at the time in my life, I began to realize that I may have Indigenous blood. I know there is a connection to Ancestral memory here but I couldn't begin to articulate how I know this. It is part of what I *now know to be true* and then, was not something I could be certain of. Suffering the recent loss of my dear husband, I want to connect with him as a newly made Ancestor, which is part of the reason I am on the water. Before we even depart the shore, into timeless rivers of moments, moons, and seasons I've gone, as if I might have taken some tincture designed to carry me to embracing spaces and I instantly feel soothed and at peace in this beautiful watercraft. I am quietly empowered; held within immediate upward surges of grief and release; bodily memories of water; swimming and swimming all the way, moment to moment through my life. Water is life, water is the Matrix (the Mother) of my being.

I sit within both the canoe and myself. Heart centering, coming to balance in the subtle stabilizing movements. My hips loosen and rock along with the water rhythms. I feel her begin to make headway like just … nothing. Managing herself almost, with ease; the paddlers sensitively caressing this beauty along the soft river, responding to upswellings and troughs as the green-brown waters allow us forward. The Wendat had created her with great skill and abundant connectedness with the spirits of water. I feel the makers' water-wonder and both canoe and I meet with the Niwa'ah Onega'gaih'ih. I go deeper to my heart's centre and the tears flow as we make our journey to the places which silence one with reverence. The rhythmic movements of paddle strokes are like the pulsation of blood inside the body, almost as if one is indeed the river. I feel as if I am entering the flow through the mandorla-shaped canoe, the entry point into the feminine. On the heart-shaped deck of the canoe sits a small tobacco offering, soon also to be released. I see the red heart against the reflective waters. Sanguine. Sacred.

The Goddess of the Lake

Some 29 years ago, in 1992, I walked down the woodland path from the beautiful Buddhist House in the forest in Frontenac County, Ontario, through the sharply descending twists and turns of the trail. I climbed over the Canadian Shield, all pinky-grey granite, jutting up out of the earth and finally propelled by the downward slope to the lake, heavily strode onto the dock and managed to stop moving before being pitched into the water. I loved the sounds my footfalls made on the wood and how the dock rode the waves my weight created. The scent of pine and cedar and the gorgeous colour of the water were like blood to the bone! The immersion into the varied greens and the movement of everything; clouds, water, tree limbs, medicines, water guardians; what bliss! I took my otter tail paddle in hand and put myself into the old red canoe with my dear friend. In old Cataraqui Territory, down the lake we paddled, hugging the shoreline, heading toward the beautiful shallow bog, thick with budding waterlilies. There were strange yet familiar feelings surfacing at every stroke of the paddle. Travelling through the deeper waters along the way, under pine arches and smiling cedar trees—freshness all and everywhere; those greens echoing across the water in 27 million shades and hues. Taking our sweet time, feeling the tipping back and forth of the canoe as waves broke close to us along the shore. Moving through patches of light down by the strange Triangle Rock, The Collapsing House, and SHE, the Goddess of the Lake. We stopped at the large Earth Mother rock formation to look up at and honour her. We felt the need to make an offering; a spirit plate but had no food in the canoe.

We had named her; we revered her. My dear friend spontaneously took the bubble gum out of his mouth, jumped out of the canoe onto the rocky base there and quickly made a large pink vulva to stick to her front, at the foot of this immense 80-foot-tall rock formation. We laughed with glee at our bubble gum Lake Goddess's new adornment, placed there in reverent and somewhat comical fashion. A very creative ceremony honouring the Earth Mother, the Lake, and all life therein, the diatoms and the duckweed, the bladderwort and the water snakes. We were delighted by our own laughter too. There, I began to home in on who I really was and so many childhood mysteries began to unravel.

Clan and Clay/Surface Tension[2]

When one asks what Clan are you in Wyandot, one essentially asks what fire are you from? "What chimney?" Clan and clay have the same root stem in our language. Think about that for a moment. My Clan is known as Keeper of the Heavens and the Carriers of the Fire— The People of the Little Turtle. The spots on her back were thought by our Ancestors to represent the stars in the night sky, thus she is part Wonderworker in our Stories of Origin. Our cosmogony.

The story goes like this … the Great Turtle held a Council, and all the animals came together to give Sky Woman a place to live on its back, afloat on the surface of the waterworld.

It was She, the Little Turtle, who made the heavenly bodies for Aataentsic by rubbing bolts of lightning together. It was She who moved through the heavens creating the heavenly orbs. She was speckled and splendid with stars and went about her business carrying the fire for the Young Woman Fallen from Above. Aataentsic had fallen through a tear in the celestial ceiling; perhaps descending within a great beam of light from the Sky World. Little Turtle moved through the heavens and her back reflected the cosmos that she helped create.

After Grandmother Toad brought mud from the ocean floor, her sister and brother animals readily swam to assist Aataentsic to prepare the back of the Snapper for the planting of seeds in her hand, which were to sprout the corn and berries, to nourish the People and provide the tobacco for their ceremonies. They danced in ancient patterns, moving the earth on the Turtle's back; an activation of love and community; of kinship. The deep waters cradled the great Moss Back Turtle as the waterfowl had cradled Aataentsic, down onto the blue-green island within the vast primordial sea.

In this new-to-me, yet much-earlier-made, red vessel on the water, through the early evening fading light, I move through the vast cosmic ocean of stars and waves in my mind's eye. Out of the abyss I emerge, out of the dark womb into the most profound realization of my own existence. The cosmos is reflected upon my back as I move through the night sky and over the indigo waters. I have been reborn as the small speckled one; I keep the heavens, I carry the fire. Before me, are the faces of those yet to be born; generation upon generation—along the great trail of Turtle Time. Behind me, my Ancestors. I have planted the stars in the great night sky—and we are all of one mind. I glide on the river and traverse the twilight sky. This is why I needed this canoe. This wonder of wonders, this sacred vessel of rebirth. The Ancestors know my Clan name—I spark into the night and I, too, am filled with love.

Lily and the Snapper

We set out again in old Lily in the middle of the night under a brilliant full moon. The starscape is incredible in the blackness of the night. Fire over water. I feel such nourishment, I am star-starved in the city. This blackness is deep and endless, the heavenly orbs fill me in indescribable ways—I might have come from there, I may return. They may be long gone but their light has only just arrived. Little did I know my own Wyandot cosmogony and the journey along the Milky Way the spirits travel to the Village of the Dead out of the Western Gate. We are all connected. We are made of carbon; both the stars and us.

On another trip to that same lake, my friend found a large dead Snapping Turtle down in the bog. I needed the shell although I wasn't sure just why. In my upswelling of Ancestral memories, my paintings were adorned with bone and natural animal parts. We paddled down to the bog, and I lifted the huge dead animal out of the water on the end of my paddle. She was so heavy! We placed her in a rock cairn and waited for three years, checking several times every summer, until she had been stripped of flesh by time, scavenger beasts, and insects of the forest. I brought her shell back to the city. Some 28 scutes around the edge; one for each lunar day and 13 in the middle of her back, one for each Moon. A total of 39 Moons had come and gone.

Time is so deliciously good at breaking things down and turning them into other things, into ceremony, grey hairs, rattles, and stars. I kept the shell for many years, it was a Snapper. Huge. Just like Turtle Island, I painted pictures of it with Hawk Feathers all before I knew of my Indigenous blood. I eventually let go of it … like other talismans in my life, they are markers of change and they come and go. Time is medicine.

Ceremonies for the Dead/Ceremonies for the Living

I went back to the sacred site for our People; the place where the Jesuit Brebeuf made first contact with the Wendat who were engaged in preparations for the Great Kettle Feast; The Feast of the Dead as has been illustrated and written about in the Jesuit Relations. This was my first visit to the homeland after the death of my husband. He allowed himself to let go of this life with graciousness and lack of fear, but I needed the comfort of that space to grieve. I sat with the Ancestors and as I unwrapped the bundle and made preparations to smoke, I could feel the presence of my Ancestral Sisters there, as they circled me, like the smoke rising and curling around my head, washing over my crown, penetrating my consciousness. It was such a wonderfully comforting ceremony of heart and mind, that warm slow tears began to track their way down my cold cheeks that crisp day. I drove south, back to the city thinking about time, as I always do … is time reversible, I wondered? Could I regain lost time—or even penetrate the Multiverse, the land of love and dreams—to be with my husband again not only in my unconscious or memory but in actual time? Could the grief-worn lines etched into my skin suddenly vanish? Could I reclaim the disruption in my own life and experience the world anew, as Aataentsic must have?[3] Could I be "anywhen" in the great Multiverse?

I took the Big Turtle shell home finally and worked at it, peeling away any leftover flesh, painting the underside with red ochre to mark it as sacred. I had no knowledge of such practices at the time, other than for the entombed dead. I was acting on impulse. I put it in the garden. I honoured that death with incense and flowers. It was a beacon, a ceremonial item with special significance. Part of my ceremonial bundle, now long gone.

In 2013 I attended one of the most momentous experiences of my life. The reinterment of some 1,700 Wendat Ancestors in the Greater Toronto Area, graciously hosted by The Huron Wendat Nation, Ontario Heritage, and the University of Toronto. Protocols prevent descriptions of events that took place during those days but at that moment in my history, so much was locked into place. My 90-year-old mother among her kin, finally. Our Ancestors are literally and figuratively imbued in the land. How, therefore, can we not see that every Wendat or Wyandot(te) foot stepping into a canoe sparks a resonant memory of time and place? That every pipe sparked and smoked, every water drum filled, every pot coiled and every shuffle dance, is not a reactivation of ceremonies in time. We are the continuum; we have survived and reunited as one large collective of Clans and families. We are the land.

Through all the transformative change, the deep loss, and the re-cognition of my life, I have reconnected with the ground of my being. My connection to my mother's birth peoples has been riveting and container shaking, in ways I have felt, explored, and resolved. It was a huge expansion of my identity as a mixed-race person. Something I had always intuited but had no proof of. It has been 12 years of forging a new awareness in and of the world. With this understanding comes hope for the future. Like Aataentsic, falling into the consciousness of consciousness, of becoming—being held by the true governing body of this body, the Earth herself and all our beautiful kin whose memories rest therein. This is the ultimate truth of who I am and where I love, in downtown Toronto.

Ontario is a Wendat Word

The Great Lake, Ontario is cold today in steely blue-grey winter light. We see her gorgeous and turbulent, being whipped around by the wind as we zip westward from downtown on the Gardiner Expressway on this first day of winter. We are at the Solstice (Sun Stands Still), the longest night of the year. I am determined to get to High Park to honour the ancient mounds before nightfall. There are many sacred sites in this space, to the millennia-old inhabitants of the western dale of the park … We are heading that way to check on them and to leave tobacco, to hold space for them and turn the mind toward peace for the Ancestors, for their sleeping time, their dreaming time, in this city-designated space.

What is called High Park, as I understand it, was bequeathed by John Howard in 1873, to the City of Toronto on the condition that the old Indigenous trails and pathways be maintained. Animal paths became the walkways of Indigenous trade and connection. The space is spiritually presided over by many EarthWorkers and FaithKeepers and maintained by a society of caring people: volunteers, scholars, and settlers who support the Indigenous restorying of these lands. Not everyone agrees of course about what lies therein. Arrowheads have been found, chert, and natural gifts from other places, signifying trade and sacred spaces. Our shared history in the Dish With One Spoon Wampum Belt Covenant Territory is echoed in settler place names and streets. Indian Road, Indian Road Crescent, Indian Grove, Indian Trail, Algonquin Road, and Indian Valley Crescent. None of them are that far from Thunderbird Mound, Bear Mound, and Watersnake Mound. We hold sacred fires and ceremony in the park; we earthwork, we plant seeds, we nurture, feast, and sing to them as we feasted, and sang, and welcomed the canoe into the waters in Toronto. We sing with children: yawastih!

Owls on the Wing

Many years ago, I was asked to caretake Owl Mound because of my family's connections to Owls and it is still part of my sacred responsibility. We honour our sacred connection to the lands and waters in their mystery and sovereignty. Practising the Honourable Harvest and teaching children that they can embody their understanding of the spirits of the land, that they are indeed united with, not separate from all living and non-living; seen and unseen beings that surround them. They revel in the spring thaw, the summer heat, the autumn leaves and the winter snows. We are youth, Elders, and visitors. I carry Deer Horns everywhere I go because little Turtle and the Deer have a special relationship, you see.

Living in the city and watching over Indigenous spaces can be daunting. Regulations, permits, restrictions, chemicals … the grief of stewardship taken away and the sometimes challenging relationships between Indigenous Peoples and settlers regarding who has what rights, where and why. Most of the time, for me, it involves sussing out campers and the unhoused; picking up cigarette butts, and alerting the park stewards to piles of human waste. I always leave conspicuous offerings of cedar and tobacco to signal to other humans that this space has significance, even if it is not made clear exactly what it is. The Grandmother Tree who has fallen there is doing her job obstructing the paths on beautiful Owl Mound. The incidences of outdoor living folks camping there are fewer and fewer despite the city's growing need for more affordable housing. My clan name connects me to that land and I believe that signifying your relationship with it through art and ceremony, acts as a resonant *energetic signature*.

I believe that the land remembers the languages that have been spoken there, just as the seeds hold those secrets. Reconciliation is needed for the trees as much as the people. When we put through the ceremonies there, I believe that we are reconnecting with those memories and therefore activating our relationship in a deeper way to what is all around us. It is how we are on the land. If you want to know something, just ask the old oak in the Savannah, but be prepared to feel its grief for the wounds to its community. Phragmites are also people. This place, this city, is filled with our Ancestors entombed in the land. Witnessing all we do, every seed we plant and every healing salve we remember, every ceremony we put through, every Mother Tree's child we hug.

Constellations and Ossuaries, the Aurora Borealis

We map out the Fisher Constellation on the gentle slope of a snow-covered rise in Thomson Memorial Park, in sweet small tea lights at Scarborough Museum, in the very eastern end of the city. Volunteers are helping me set up for ceremony as my cousin and Fire Keeper, Two Crows, lights the fire following strict Indigenous protocols. The night is cold and the snow is crunchy beneath our feet. We are surrounded by Victorian farm buildings, charming and quaint in this lovely winter scene. The central square is jammed with people.

Not far from here, is one of the many Wendat sites in Greater Toronto. Tabor Hill, is a very well-known ossuary holding within its earthen womb several hundred Ancestors. The scent of medicines and woodsmoke rises and fills the air as the crowds begin to lean into the space. Closer and closer they get to the table with medicines on it, a silver fox tail, a beaver pelt, tobacco, cedar, sage, sweetgrass, my water drum, and of course water. The children's hands reach out, I caution them gently but firmly. "No." They pull away quickly as if scolded by Mother. They want and need these teachings and are fascinated by the nature they so need. I push out against the energy a little, protecting myself from their hunger, establishing boundaries, and claiming my personal space. They relax a little. Authority is something they understand.

This Solstice night, the Museum is unveiling the third of four panels that I created for them, marking the cycles of the astronomical world. Spring Equinox, Summer Solstice, Autumnal Equinox, and Winter Solstice. The 4-foot x 6-foot panel reflects the heavens in the depiction of the Aurora Borealis. True North. It is rendered in metallic copper, bronze, interference green, which turns pink in the changing light and white. It is entitled "ⁿdekyukǫtáhkwih yarí:waʔ The Law One Has Begun With" or, "Original Instructions." It is dancing in the firelight, just as the Borealis would. The atmosphere is charged with anticipation. Many Indigenous folk are interspersed with people from all nationalities. Scarborough has many communities of different origins and they are out in full force this evening. What a joy to see faces of people from this metropolis, one of the most cosmopolitan cities in the world!

The Museum host offers a lovely welcome and one of our quartet offers the audience a very political and extensive land acknowledgement. It's a good one, including all the painful historiography. Things that are most often left out. It is a tough way to begin the ceremony: treaty violations, white supremacy, colonial oppression, residential schools, stolen land, wars and alliances, missing and murdered Indigenous girls, two spirited, trans and cis women, disease and abuse. People are uneasy, feet stamping the snow to stay warm, or dealing with nervous energy. Some feel settler guilt, some shame, some genuine pitiless grief, some awaken to new knowledge about the depths of hurt Indigenous People carry and interestingly, hearing it from a white academic settler carries a certain weight. The speaker rests and I begin the "yanǫrǫhkwányǫhk"—the Thanksgiving Address—and people are quieted, plugging into the reverence and gratitude-guided tones in my voice. The rhythmic formality of The Address is comforting and humbling, it seems, or maybe people are just paying attention. I relax a little and roll into the ceremony. I see the odd tear in an eye here and there, people's expressions soften and their hearts open. The Address sends out greetings and thanks to many components of the Natural World. We start by greeting each other as people. I invite them to look at each other, to make eye contact with their neighbours. A strange and not habitual practice these days in a big city of almost five million humans. Most respond in a good way and some shake hands—one or two even embrace. Thinking about it now makes me long for those hugs. One by one we greet them, we thank them: The Ancestors, the Stars, Elder Brother Sun and Grandmother Moon, the fishes, the grasses and mighty trees, the waters, the plant life, the medicines, and the keepers of the medicines. Our Enlightened Teachers, the Great Mystery: *the unknown and unseen*, the forgotten. We thank them all and together— we are of one mind. Into the ceremony we go, singing and inviting people to join us in a friendship dance … and the mural is unveiled to "oohs" and "ahhs". I have asked them to "sakahkwah šra:wíʔ! Look up!—(to the stars)!" and hope they continue to do so as this simple ceremony connects them to the Heavens. Little Turtle Business.

Talismans and Fetishes. Gifts of the Earth

As a multidisciplinary artist, I am faced daily with the notion of how to unleash my mind from the constraints of traditional European image-making and let go into pure abandoned expressionism. I also actively try to unteach the colonization of the natural world, in the forms of debunking the idea of the so-called supernatural. We are born into this world with clusters of cell memory, sense consciousness, inherited trauma, or gifts, or both, and so much more and the capability to be in touch with the Natural World in the deepest ways. The beauty of being held in that most sacred of spaces for a period, our mother's wombs. Like ley lines, sacred energetic hot spots, or tombs in the earth, marker trees, and spiral rock formations, great henges, and even temples—creativity is about connecting to earthly, cosmic, and internal messages. Being an urban dweller, I have always made assemblages with broken car window glass, broken mirror shards, pieces of leather, or painted micaceous iron oxide, bits of my photos, and red ochre. Light shards reflected in the city depict the harshness of urban life, but these reflections offer the magic that transcends concrete canyons and steel towers. Arrowheads can be found almost anywhere in Toronto gardens. I wear one around my neck in my medicine bag. It is apparently thousands of years old. *The earth in my palm, makes me think of you.*

Fire over Water

I am organizing an installation for Crawford Lake, an early Wendat site within the Greater Toronto Area; a show in collaboration with Professor Kathryn Magee Labelle honouring several of our Ancestral Sisters. It is my favourite place to hang out, amid Longhouses and Indigenous planted spaces. For the installation I am planning, I send one of my students out to find a red canoe just like the one I entered all those years ago in Frontenac County. I want to create a video installation called Fire Over Water. It will float on the meromictic lake, a fire bowl within the canoe sent out into the middle of the mist-covered lake, as temperatures drop in the autumn sunset. This lake has little oxygen at the bottom. One that acts as a time capsule to corn seed. One that honours human occupation of the area surrounding it for at least 500 years. One that seems a portal to other places and marks the Anthropocene Epoch. People lived in the Village in layers, just like the core sediment taken from the bottom of the lake. One village on top of the next. All in all, 11 Longhouse footprints have been found next to the lake. Wolf Clan, Deer Clan, Turtle … perhaps 11 layers of clans, families, deaths, burials, children, infants, stewardship. Women tending the cornfields, horning and dehorning Chiefs. I want to honour them all with music, images, and installations showing some personal interpretations of lifeways among the People—My student was lucky! Three friends and I bought the canoe, sharing costs. This afternoon we are trying desperately to get it into Evergreen Brickworks where my studio is. It won't fit. Up and down, around the stairs, trying this way and that to guide it into the elevator without nicking the precious surface or scratching the sides. No punctures please! As they approach me to let me know we will have to find another solution, my friend extends their left hand. In it is a red cardinal feather, something I have been searching for, like my Mother's lost family, for 50 years. I am stunned! This is another solution. A token, a red flash in a blue sky—a found canoe, a red cardinal feather from the place I sought comfort. The woodland spaces in exurban Ohio where the Wyandot lived, where I remember discussions about my Mother's absent heritage. After the Snowy Owl appeared and Indigenous art started making its presence known in the house we lived in, where I first recognized and loved Cardinal calls—it's almost as if the Natural World was alerting me to the Ancestors' presence. Toronto was where I was born, in Old Wyandot territory I began to realize myself within the Natural World. While falling asleep one night I heard a little voice … that didn't seem to come from me. A dream voice that said, "Cathy go home!" I came home.

Jouskeha and Tawihskarǫʔ[4]

Aataentsic, in various versions of our Creation Story gave birth to—or was the grandmother of the twins … Tižuskáʔah and Tawihskarǫʔ. In our rich Narratives, it appears that the Twins, to avoid conflict, divided the land, half to each. As they are called in different versions of the story; Johskeha or Tižuskáʔah, secured the East and Tawihskarǫʔ the Western lands, wherein they were both to utilize their creative powers. The "good" twin, Tižuskáʔah made the surface of the earth smooth and the "bad" one, Tawihskarǫʔ, corrupted his beautiful work, covering the surface of the earth with flint, boulders, and mountains—and placed brambles, vines, and thorns into the lush woodland forests Tižuskáʔah had created.

Tižuskáʔah, brought the Wendat and Wyandot People down from The Sky World but in some versions, they created the People together, perhaps explaining why humans have such complex behaviours. Twins are referred to in other Indigenous Peoples' creation stories as well—Glooscap the "Man [created] from only speech" and his twin brother Malsumis "who seeks evil to this day" (Wabenake).

The Twins might stand as a heroic metaphor for the challenges we face in re-establishing our traditional life and death ways in this new urban world. After contact—foreign systems were imposed upon our perception of the natural order of things. The overturning of old insights and observations, practices of living in relationship with the Earth, which we had understood for millennia, brought a resilient people havoc and adversity—punishing us for embracing our lifeways and language, creating discord and dispersal, and casting our agency and self-determination into "every man for himself" models of civilization and commodification, rather than the stewardship of nature: never all, never too much, never the first and always offering gratitude. The honourable harvest. The oldest teachings.

Our strong, resilient Clan Mothers; decision makers and leaders, were oppressed by Eurocentric models of female subservience. Aataentsic was declared a witch. Eurocentric religious world views, imposed notions of shame and degradation into the Indigenous, holistic bodymind, thus intergenerational grief and trauma became the legacy of generations; the illness contained within Ancestral memories. How then were we to overcome the punitive and destructive forces of an unequal, non-circular society? How could we revitalize our Ancestral birthright and repair and honour our Ancestors, in service of the People? Our teachings contain metaphors for opportunism, survival, and balance but also pragmatism or expedience; death and rebirth *and the reason unseen things are given their proper place in this world*. Something that was originally holistic, and relationship-focused, was co-opted; holism became dualism and "power-over" nature was used as a device to turn our lifeways into superstitious fetishism. Circular became linear, pressing for advantage, perhaps born from suffering.

In the Longhouse, the Clans sit together divided into different kinship groups of Clan animal. They sit in circular awareness, as community—like a beautiful, embroidered flower. At Green Corn our Ancestors are revitalized and remembered—in their language and honoured, and thanks are given for the first fruits of the harvest.

To attain the balance The Twins represent, we must overcome our trained resistance toward practising our very own traditions, as they are the earth from which we spring. Our land-based pedagogy; life and death ways celebrate our passion for the truth of what is observed and how we are to be; the changing seasons, the first fruits, the dark, sleeping winter, the re-empowerment of our Clan Mothers and FaithKeepers—without fear, growing within the womb of Mother Earth and looking onward to the Star Ancestors … and in acknowledging these cycles and enlivening these beautiful practices, we allow ourselves to continue in their ways—and they in ours. Newly challenged city governance must release old notions of inequality and strive for that same balance.

Grandmother Toad and Futurity

Which ceremonies count? Who establishes the rules of conduct in the natural world? Policy makers or Earthworkers? Mother Nature herself? Who and where do we turn in moments of climate crisis despair and how can we practise the Honourable Harvest when our kin are so distressed? How does one hold that balanced state of reciprocity when burdened with intergenerational grief and trauma? How can we maintain life not much less, living with all we need? How can we rectify this horrendous loss with healing and recovery? Is a simple Address enough to start that activation of intentionality toward shifting our understanding of the Natural World within the urban landscape? Can we rely on Indigenous teachings to take us where we need to be? Are we aware of the scientific *and* spiritual base of Indigenous lifeways? Can we start privileging Indigenous reworlding instead of settler legacies (for non-settler and Black, Indigenous, and People of Colour (BIPoC) Communities?) How do we reworld this space and all spaces in time, to save what we hold so dear? Can you imagine life without Turtles? Without plant medicines? Without those enlightened teachers? Without ceremony to honour them? It would not be long before we would all perish and yet responsibilities and obligations to decolonize this land are largely unknown by most settler folk. There is active resistance toward Indigenous bodies taking up space in white dominant paradigms of privilege. It is hard to shake loose that perception of "power-over," when no one wants to give up what little or large power they perceive they have. "Power-over" nature is a fraudulent and erroneous concept. Indigenous Peoples also struggle with these notions in attempts to decolonize themselves and relieve themselves of internalized racism and grief. Some never will. It is a long road heading toward that new and better world for all beings. Do we even dare to dream city-civics can be built on a foundational understanding of Sacred Natural law?

Like Grandmother Toad we must rise with that rich black earth in our little fists. That handful of good earth, we cannot let stream through our fingers and wash away. We must hold on tight to raise that vision of reworlding in the newly born Sacred Civics Movement. We must plant the seeds in our governmental bodies and foster them, carry them through to harvest to be put through like ceremony in the next cycle of growth. Policies must be rewritten; compassion must guide us. We must shift the collective mindset from taking all into being thankful, from war into peace and from commodification into resonance and reverence. We must forgo selfishness, greed, and destruction and not set humans against each other. We must renew our capacity to wonder. Speaking truth to power, in one great Friendship Dance we must circle round until we get it right; before all we have is lost to us. This is old news, and these are ancient teachings. We all have something to offer in the path we're forging into new understandings of very old knowledges for the world we must fashion for ourselves and our kin. Grandmother Toad, the Ancestors, and the Clan Mothers from All Nations will be our guides.

Notes

1 Linguistic assistance for this chapter was provided by Dr. Craig Kopris.
2 Adapted from an original reflection piece entitled *Dreaming Creation* by Catherine Tàmmaro (2021), in Magee Labelle, K., the original *Daughters of Aaetentsic: Life Stories from Seven Generations*, McGill-Queen's University Press.
3 Recollet, K. (2019). Personal communication.
4 Adapted from the original conference presentation by Tàmmaro, C. (April 11th, 2018). *47th Symposium on the American Indian* at Northeastern State University, Tahlequah, Oklahoma.

References

Recollet, K. (2019). Personal communication.
Tàmmaro, C. (2021). Dreaming Creation in Magee Labelle, K., the original *Daughters of Aaetentsic: Life Stories from Seven Generations*, McGill-Queen's University Press.
Tàmmaro, C. (2018). *47th Symposium on the American Indian* at Northeastern State University, Tahlequah, Oklahoma. April 11th.

13

FEMINIST, ANTIRACIST VALUES FOR CLIMATE JUSTICE

Moving beyond Climate Isolationism

Jennie C. Stephens

Centering Feminist, Antiracist Values for Transformation

To resist the continued concentration of wealth and power, and to transition toward a more just, healthy and sustainable future, feminist antiracist values need to be centered in decision-making at every level to allow for different forms of wisdom and knowledge. To respond to the intersecting crises of health, housing, and economic precarity, structural racism, and climate change, a transformation away from exploitative and extractive processes toward regenerative and renewable systems must be prioritized. Transformation will only be possible if and when feminist, antiracist values are prioritized and more different forms of knowledge and wisdom are integrated into decision-making to broaden beyond the narrow technocratic lens that currently dominates climate discourse.

I have been working on climate and energy issues for the past 25 years. My professional experiences as a woman in this male-dominated technical field have taught me that the inadequacy of our efforts to respond to the climate crisis—our inability to end fossil fuel reliance and transition to a renewable-based society—is not due to a lack of technological innovation or scientific expertise. Rather, our ineffectiveness results from a lack of investment and attention to social innovation and social justice. A narrow technical focus on climate and energy, a male-dominated dangerous belief that technology will somehow save us, has resulted in so many missed opportunities to invest in people and communities. Instead, I believe we need an inclusive approach to climate and energy policy with antiracist, feminist leadership that prioritizes the needs of all people. We need diverse leadership to advocate for social innovations that center climate action and the renewable energy transformation on social justice, racial justice, and economic justice.

From my perspective, feminist, antiracist values involve constant consideration of power dynamics, i.e., paying attention to who has power and privilege, who is being excluded or

DOI: 10.4324/9781003199816-17

marginalized, what legacy processes and priorities are perpetuating discrepancies in power, and ultimately whether and how power is being concentrated or distributed (Stephens 2020). Vigilant and transparent analysis and assessment of power, including understanding the multiple ways that social, economic, and political power shape institutions and social change (Kashwan, MacLean, and García-López 2019), are fundamental to the transformations that are needed for a more just, equitable, healthy, and prosperous future. Recognizing that social change and innovation can disrupt or reinforce existing and legacy power dynamics, explicit and continuous attention to different forms of empowerment and disempowerment are critically important (Avelino 2021). Given the disruptive time and the human suffering exacerbated by the COVID-19 pandemic and the climate crisis, elevating feminist, antiracist values is a central priority for societal transformation.

To understand the term "antiracist" I refer to Ibram X. Kendi's powerful 2019 book *How to Be an Antiracist*. In his book, Kendi explains that anyone who declares that they are not racist is signifying neutrality, but, he points out, in the struggle with racism there is no neutrality (Kendi 2019). Kendi explains that the opposite of "racist" isn't "not racist" but it is "antiracist"—whenever we ignore issues of race, we are inadvertently perpetuating racism. Given the deep legacy of racial injustice embedded in our culture, in our institutions, in our communities, in our economy, and in our policies, those who do not actively resist racism are in fact supporting it. Embracing antiracist values requires continual recognition and active resistance to racism in all its many legacy forms and structures.

A similar argument can be made regarding patriarchy, misogyny, and gender discrimination (Manne 2018). Like racism, sexism is deeply rooted in our society, and many of our institutions, norms, and values will continue to reinforce gender discrimination unless we are continually and actively resisting. Unless we are actively resisting racism and patriarchy, we are actually perpetuating these systems of oppression.

According to Chimamanda Ngozi Adichie, author of *We Should All be Feminists*, many men say that they don't think much about gender or notice gender disparities (Adichie 2012). Similarly, many white people say that they don't think much about race or notice racial disparities. Those with privilege who consider themselves successful within current systems are generally less aware of the structural oppression that stratifies society.

This is why antiracist, feminist values are so critical in society's efforts to confront the interconnected crises facing humanity. If we continue to rely on climate solutions proposed by those who are unaware of or indifferent to racism and sexism, we are guaranteed to reinforce those inequities. And, if we don't embrace antiracist and feminist values, we are unlikely to succeed in designing inclusive and effective responses to the climate crisis.

It is important to note that anyone can embrace antiracist and feminist values. Every human being has the capacity to learn, understand, and have empathy for other human beings, so all of us can resist systems of oppression regardless of where we are positioned within those systems. Ultimately, everyone is negatively impacted by racism, misogyny, and other forms of oppression. So, everyone, regardless of gender, race, or any other identities, can be encouraged to embrace and prioritize feminist, antiracist values.

The Inadequacy of Climate Isolationism

As the climate crisis worsens and continues to reveal stark injustices and inhumane inequities in society, the evidence suggests that our decision-making and policy processes have resulted in ineffective and inadequate responses in both climate mitigation (UNEP 2019) and climate adaptation (Kuhl 2021). The systemic, transformative changes that are needed to end fossil fuel use and to invest in supporting the most vulnerable people and communities have not yet been prioritized. A key contributor to the insufficient actions taken so far toward a more just and sustainable future is the fact that climate decision-making has been all-too-often constrained within a narrow technocratic lens which I call "climate isolationism" (Stephens 2020). Climate isolationism refers to the common framing of climate change as an isolated, discrete, scientific problem in need of technological solutions. Decision makers working within a lens of climate isolationism often focus in a quantitative way on carbon reductions, greenhouse gas emissions, and temperature changes while inadvertently ignoring the societal complexities associated with these quantitative measures (IPCC 2018).

This narrow technocratic lens is prevalent in decision-making around both climate mitigation and climate adaptation. When climate isolationism is applied to climate mitigation, decarbonization is usually the goal (Geels, Sovacool, Schwanen, and Sorrell 2017), carbon accounting is the primary metric, and incentives and costs of a variety of different mitigating technologies are often projected and compared (Auel and Cassady 2016). When climate isolationism is applied to climate adaptation, a disproportionate focus on investing in technical infrastructure (i.e., sea walls and drought-resistant crops) often detracts attention and investment from social innovation and social changes that could enhance climate resilience (Rodima-Taylor, Olwig, and Chhetri 2012).

The narrowness of climate isolationism results in limited opportunities for people to connect and engage (Peterson, Stephens, and Wilson 2015). The technocratic focus limits public discourse because it excludes people for whom these abstract, scientific terms or the technological details may not be meaningful and it makes the challenge seem distant and unapproachable (Stephens 2020). Not only does this very technical way of discussing climate change resonate with only a small subgroup of society, it also often projects the need for sacrifice and hardship rather than highlight benefits and opportunities (Peeters, Diependaele, and Sterckx 2019). Climate isolationism is also exclusive because many proposed technological "solutions" are also expensive and perceived as options that are only accessible to the rich (Biermann and Möller 2019). Driving a Tesla electric vehicle, for example, is not an option for most people, so the focus on this technological innovation results in many people feeling disempowered and disengaged (Stephens and Surprise 2020).

This disempowerment is compounded by science and engineering—being fields that continue to be dominated by white men (Woolston 2020). Despite efforts to diversify science and engineering, persistent racial, gendered, and economic injustices of our economy and our educational systems perpetuate exclusive access to science and engineering (Valantine and Collins 2015). Participating in science continues to be a selective activity only accessible to a privileged few (Lee 2016). The lack of diversity within the fields of science and engineering limits the scope of inquiry and constrains the types of connections that are made among science, technology, and society (Stephens 2020). As we move to incorporate innovative responses that promote social justice to climate change beyond technological justifications for energy transformation, there is a need to include other kinds of expertise, experiences, and perspectives.

The technical focus of climate isolationism also obfuscates and diminishes the potential for transformative social change (Anderson and Peters 2016) and it limits the possibilities for investing in social innovation, social infrastructure, and social justice (Stephens 2020).

When the climate crisis is framed as a scientific problem with a possible technological fix, the systemic societal and economic problems, including the concentration of wealth and power among those profiting from maintaining fossil fuel reliance, are all-too-often ignored (Stephens 2020). The prevalence of climate isolationism has encouraged too many leaders to be blind to the important opportunities for improving people's lives and strengthening communities as we transition away from a society reliant on fossil fuels (Stephens 2019).

The narrow technocratic approach of climate isolationism has not only been ineffective in mobilizing transformative change but it has also resulted in climate and energy programs and policies that exacerbate inequities and perpetuate injustice (Jenkins, Stephens, Reames, and Hernández 2020). Because the social dimensions of climate and energy have not been adequately considered, we have ended up with policies that further exclude and disadvantage low-income communities, women, and communities of color (Reames 2016). The quantitative technocratic tendency of climate isolationism reinforces a dubious technological optimism (Basiago 1994), which has led to growing interest and funding for technological fixes to the climate crisis (Stephens and Markusson 2018).

While technology is an essential part of a transition toward a more just, equitable and climate stable future, investments in science and technology have not yet been balanced with investments in social science, social infrastructure, social innovations, and social justice. This lack of investment in social infrastructure and social innovations has weakened our social ties and reduced our societal resilience (Aldrich 2012). For decades, strategic governmental responses to the climate crisis have been focused almost exclusively on investments in science and technology (Stephens 2009), while very little has been invested in social innovation.

The Dangers of Climate Isolationism: Concentrating Wealth and Power

By focusing almost exclusively on technological innovation, climate isolationism obfuscates the potential for transformative social change and diminishes the priority of investing in climate-resilient innovations that simultaneously advance social justice (Jenkins 2018). The persistence of the narrow climate isolationism perspective has been beneficial for the polluter elite, those wealthy individuals and organizations that do not want transformative change because they are profiting from fossil fuel reliance and exploitative corporate business practices (Kenner 2019). Climate denialism, which has been supported by fossil fuel interests and the polluter elite, has also required climate decision makers to spend a lot of time and energy defending what is known about the science of climate change (Oreskes 2019). The polluter elite's decades-long strategic misinformation campaign to confuse the public about the science of climate change has been an effective delay tactic (Frumhoff, Heede, and Oreskes 2015). The prevalence of climate denialism has confined climate discourse to the scientific realm and limited options for non-scientific discourse about how to respond to the climate crisis and reduce climate vulnerabilities.

Continuing to increase investment in technological innovation while underinvesting in social innovation is preventing the transformative changes that are required both for stabilizing the climate and for reducing social injustice. So not only does climate isolationism result in missed opportunities to advance social and economic justice, but it also results in insufficient environmental protection (Jenkins 2018).

One example of the dangerous implications of climate isolationism and how it contributes to concentrating wealth and power is the recent increased interest in investing in solar geoengineering research (Surprise 2020). The National Academies recently released a report providing recommendations for advancing research on solar geoengineering, which is a technological intervention in the climate system that involves spraying aerosols into the atmosphere to block incoming solar radiation (NASEM 2021). Once on the fringes of climate policy, solar geoengineering is gaining traction, particularly in the USA, where some are calling for substantial public investments in solar geoengineering research (NASEM 2021). The ultimate "technical fix," this approach does nothing to address the cause of climate change, and the social and political risks of advancing this cannot be understated (Stephens and Surprise 2020).

During the past five years, the US has become the global leader in solar geoengineering research, with multiple philanthropic efforts funding research at major universities, with the largest solar geoengineering research program at Harvard. Harvard's Solar Geoengineering Research Program is funded by philanthropic gifts from individuals and foundations including Bill Gates (Stephens and Surprise 2020). Solar geoengineering is also fraught with ecological and governance risks and investing in this approach is detracting from efforts for transformative social change (Frumhoff and Stephens 2018). The imagined potential of solar geoengineering has created a new pathway for the rich and powerful to establish additional control over everybody else as climate impacts worsen (Stephens and Surprise 2020). Advocacy for solar geoengineering research continues to be dominated by white-male scientists from the global north funded by tech-billionaires and elite philanthropy (Biermann and Möller 2019). More diverse voices are needed to expand public discourse beyond the narrow technocratic narrative that limits authentic deliberation about the risks of advancing solar geoengineering.

The stark contrast between this narrow perspective of climate isolationism and a more holistic, feminist, antiracist perspective including Indigenous knowledge and Indigenous wisdom about the earth's systems became international news in spring 2021 when Harvard's Solar Geoengineering Research Program collaborated with the Swedish Space Corporation intending to conduct solar geoengineering experiments in Kiruna, Sweden. The Indigenous Saami Council resisted the proposal for the Stratospheric Controlled Perturbation Experiment (SCoPEx) designed to gather data on the cooling effect of aerosol particles in the upper atmosphere; the Harvard researchers were planning to first test the equipment to inject aerosols and then actually inject the aerosols to analyze the effects. After successfully resisting the experiment, the Saami Council and leading Swedish environmental organizations wrote an open letter to Harvard asking them to cancel SCoPEx. This international conflict and the successful efforts of a coalition of Indigenous and environmental activists to resist this solar geoengineering experiment demonstrate the collective power and potential of feminist, antiracist values and Indigenous wisdom (Fountain and Flavelle 2021). From the values of Indigenous knowledge, those resisting the Harvard researchers were holding the Western scientists accountable and calling them out, preventing them from acting on their belief that they can somehow engineer and control nature.

Toward Climate Justice: Redistributing Power

Moving beyond the lens of climate isolationism, climate justice provides a more productive, complex and holistic framework within which to assess and prioritize responses to the climate crisis (Robinson 2018). Climate justice requires recognizing that: (1) many policies, processes, and practices of wealthy elite institutions and individuals are the drivers of climate change;

(2) the impacts of climate disruptions and the capacity to adapt are distributed unequally among and within local and global communities; (3) equitable climate adaptation and strengthening climate resilience requires new transformative investments, innovations, and actions to rectify the disproportionate burdens on those who are most vulnerable to ongoing and future climate impacts (Harlan, Pellow, and Roberts 2015). Decision-making within a climate justice frame involves striving for transformative systemic changes that integrate technological and social innovation while prioritizing equity and social, racial, and economic justice.

Just as there is no such thing as neutrality when it comes to considering systemic racism (Kendi 2019), there is no policy that is neutral on climate justice. Policies and decisions at every level are perpetuating climate injustices if they are not intentionally and explicitly trying to reduce climate injustices. Given the racial and economic injustices associated with fossil fuel reliance (Healy, Stephens, and Malin 2019) and fossil fuel combustion (McKibben 2016), a societal transformation toward a renewable-based society needs to be prioritized. The case for keeping fossil fuels in the ground can be made from a climate isolationism lens. However, the case becomes so much more compelling and practical when the social justice opportunities are also explicitly called out (Lenferna 2018).

To move beyond climate isolationism toward climate justice, feminist, antiracist values need to be elevated and centered, and different forms of knowledge, including sacred and spiritual knowledge, need to be integrated. Climate decision-making must focus more explicitly on problematic power dynamics by advancing social innovations and practical wisdom in order to redistribute power to people and communities who are most vulnerable. Climate decision-making needs to explicitly consider how policies, practices, and priorities either reinforce or disrupt the systems that are currently concentrating wealth and power. For less powerful groups to gain a foothold in decision-making processes, renewed attention to the multiple ways that social, economic, and political power shape social change must be acknowledged (Kashwan, MacLean, and García-López 2019). Because feminist theory offers established frameworks for the study of power (Bell, Daggett, and Labuski 2020), embracing a feminist lens is one valuable approach to moving away from climate isolationism toward climate justice.

The social science literature on socio-technical transitions has been critiqued for minimizing the role of power (Avelino 2017), and a recent contribution by Avelino (2021) identifies seven specific ways to consider power in decision-making, processes of change, and innovation: (1) power *over* versus power *to*; (2) centered versus diffused; (3) consensual versus conflictual; (4) constraining versus enabling; (5) quantity versus quality; (6) empowerment versus disempowerment; and (7) power in relation to knowledge (Avelino 2021). As jurisdictions around the world grapple with the interconnected crises of housing and food insecurity, climate disruptions, and economic precarity, narrow efforts to reduce greenhouse gas emissions or control the global average temperature are likely to cause more harm than good. New ways of strategically integrating climate action into other social policies, in the way that the Biden/Harris administration was attempting to "quietly" integrate their climate agenda in 2021 into pandemic recovery and infrastructure investments, provides an empirical example of the practical valuable potential of moving away from climate isolationism (Osaka 2021).

An example of advancing climate justice in the urban context by making space for community knowledge and feminist, antiracist values can be seen in Providence, Rhode Island where the city's climate justice plan demonstrates what is possible when equity and racial justice are prioritized in climate action (Providence 2019). The first city in the USA with a climate justice plan, Providence has prioritized in its planning process frontline communities, environmental justice communities, and the communities bordering industrial areas exposed to multiple sources of pollution with the highest levels of poverty, asthma, and lead poisoning in the state (Fitzgerald 2020). By embracing what Mary Robinson, the Former President of Ireland and international climate justice leader, calls a "peoples first approach" (Robinson 2018), the City of Providence designed a participatory process intended to shift the decision-making power to frontline communities. This planning process and the resulting climate justice plan which prioritizes community health, collaborative governance and accountability, strengthening a local and regenerative economy, and green justice zones for priority action, in addition to clean energy, transportation, and buildings, is unique and serves as an example of an alternative climate justice approach based on feminist antiracist values.

Who is Perpetuating Climate Isolationism?

To move mainstream climate decision-making beyond climate isolationism toward climate justice, it is helpful to understand how climate isolationism is being perpetuated. The prevalence of climate isolationism can be attributed to multiple factors including the limited experiences and perspectives of many climate experts whose knowledge is limited to climate science and technology. White men have made up the majority of climate and energy experts (Kempe 2021), and the systemic exclusion of diverse voices in mainstream climate decision-making has contributed to climate isolationism (Stephens and Surprise 2020). Since the climate crisis was first recognized as an emerging problem in the late 1970s and early 1980s (Keeling, Bacastow, and Bainbridge et al. 1976; Marchetti 1977; National Research Council 1983), a technocratic, reductionist, top-down approach to climate policy has dominated. Large investments have been made in technological innovations to mitigate climate change (Gallagher, Holdren, and Sagar 2006; Holdren 2006), but minimal attention has been given to social innovation, power dynamics, and how climate and energy policy could leverage change toward social justice (Webler and Tuler 2010).

One prominent and influential privileged white man who is perpetuating climate isolationism is Bill Gates. His 2021 book *How to Avoid Climate Disaster* focuses exclusively on technological innovations demonstrating the inadequacy and dangers of climate isolationism (Gates 2021). In this book, Gates openly acknowledges that he does not "have a solution to the politics of climate change." Rather he professes that new and existing technologies can solve the climate crisis; all that is needed is more investment in technological innovation to speed up the pace (Gates 2021). Gates also describes solar geoengineering as a "cutting edge, 'Break Glass in Case of Emergency' kind of tool" that is valuable to have in case things get so bad that there are few other options. He says, "There may come a day when we don't have a choice. Best to prepare for that day now." Gates's singular focus on technological innovation is characteristic of climate isolationism and represents a trend of privileged tech-savvy men, the so-called "climate dudes" who think they can swoop and solve complex problems that others have spent decades attempting to address (Jones 2021).

The prevalence of climate isolationism can also be attributed to a male-dominated climate and energy leadership that continues to prioritize scientific and technological expertise to inform climate policy (Fraune 2015; Pearl-Martinez and Stephens 2016). Like many other aspects of society, the science, politics, and economics of climate and energy have been dominated by privileged white-male leadership which has tended to be technocratic, reductionist, patriarchal, and top-down (Faber, Stephens, Wallis et al. 2017; Sorman, Turhan, and Rosas-Casals 2020). The technological optimism that is characteristic of climate isolationism is also linked to masculinity as the colloquial phrase "boys and their toys" represents (Lohan and Faulkner 2004).

Climate Isolationism and Climate Fundamentalism

Climate isolationism is characterized by a narrow, technocratic way of considering the climate crisis—as an isolated threat that is separate from other issues. Within this framing, the dire impacts of climate change justify a simplistic and targeted approach that ignores many societal complexities—including the distributional justice issues of who is benefiting from climate action and inaction, and who is being harmed most. In energy policy, a similar, related concept of "climate fundamentalism" has been defined and introduced by Shalanda Baker in her book *Revolutionary Power: An Activist's Guide to the Energy Transition* (Baker 2021). Baker defines climate fundamentalism as "the narrow focus on advancing climate and clean energy policy while failing to account for justice concerns or, more insidiously, deliberately delaying justice considerations." In her book, Baker describes how a climate fundamentalism approach to the energy transition replicates and reinforces structural inequality and she calls for ambitious clean energy policies grounded in equity (Baker 2021).

To counter the prevalence of both climate isolationism and climate fundamentalism, social justice, economic justice, and racial justice need to be centered in all climate and energy policy. Conversely, to respond effectively to the crises of social injustices, renewable energy and resisting fossil fuels has to be integrated into all social policies. Appreciating the value of this kind of integrative thinking is a critical part of moving beyond narrow climate decision-making.

Reframing for Transformation

Climate justice leader and human rights attorney Colette Pichon Battle calls on all of us to reframe our understanding of the problem (Battle 2020).

> Climate change is not the problem; climate change is the most horrible symptom of an economic system that has been built for a few to extract every precious ounce of value out of this planet and its people, from our natural resources to the fruits of our human labor. This system has created the crisis.
>
> *Battle 2020*

This perspective is shared by multiple scholars who have critiqued how climate experts and sustainability transitions researchers have failed to engage in any significant critiques of capitalism (Markusson, Dahl Gjefsen, Stephens et al. 2017; Feola 2020). Until more climate experts and key climate decision makers with power and influence over climate policy are able to reframe their own understanding of the crisis, and move beyond climate isolationism, societal responses will continue to be inadequate and both climate risks and social injustices will continue to worsen. Without this essential reframing, well-intentioned climate decision makers will continue to inadvertently perpetuate inequities and exacerbate disparities in health, wealth, and opportunity.

One example of reframing the problem beyond climate isolationism is energy democracy, a growing social movement that envisions a fossil fuel-free future in which individuals, households, and communities rely on a regionally appropriate diverse mix of renewable energy with local ownership, local control, and local benefits (van Veelen and van der Horst 2018). Highlighting all the social justice benefits of redistributing power, literally and figuratively through the renewable transformation, energy democracy is centered on social justice and investing in vulnerable communities. The climate crisis is often not even mentioned within energy democracy discourse (Sorman, Turhan, and Rosas-Casals 2020). Climate mitigation and the decarbonization that results from moving to a renewable future are co-benefits of energy democracy decision-making rather than the primary driver for change. Energy democracy connects the renewable transformation with redistributing political and economic power, wealth, and ownership to create a more just and equitable world (Burke and Stephens 2018). The energy democracy frame recognizes the social potential for co-creation and co-ownership of a renewable future that is much more than a simple substitution of energy technologies (Doukas, Nikas, Stamtsis et al. 2020). Rather, the renewable transition provides an opportunity to reverse the economic oppression associated with concentrated wealth and fossil fuel reliance by empowering local energy production and control (Burke 2018).

Three kinds of innovative activities are central to the energy democracy movement: *resisting* the legacy energy agenda that continues to support fossil fuels, *reclaiming* energy decision-making so that the public interest is prioritized over corporate interests, and *restructuring* energy systems to maximize distributed local and regional benefits (Burke and Stephens 2017). A key feature of energy democracy is the critical recognition that "how" renewable energy is deployed—that is, who is included, who is excluded, and how the benefits are distributed—matters a lot. To leverage the interconnected social justice benefits, renewable energy has to be explicitly linked to investments designed to meet the needs of families and communities rather than large corporate interests (Stephens, Burke, Gibian et al. 2018). Doing so requires moving beyond climate isolationism, the narrow carbon accounting, and the technological framing that has dominated climate policy so far.

Energy democracy is an alternative way to frame society's response to the climate crisis as an opportunity for investing in communities and redistributing power literally and figuratively. Energy democracy is a growing social movement that resists the concentrated power and influence of fossil fuel energy companies and recognizes that ownership of energy resources and a more equitable distribution of profits from renewable energy infrastructure would redistribute political and economic power. The social changes resulting from investments in a new distributed renewable economy has huge potential to be politically and economically transformative. Investing in a future powered by renewables including wind (both onshore and offshore), solar power (utility scale, household scale, and community solar), as well as geothermal and maybe micro-hydro, wave and tidal—allows more people, communities, and organizations to benefit and be involved—and could bring widespread benefits by allowing for local and community-owned energy. The reasons renewable energy has this revolutionary potential is because every community and region of the world has access to renewable resources—resources that are perpetual, abundant, reliable, and free. It is not just solar and wind, but coastal communities that can also leverage wave, tidal, and offshore wind energy, while inland communities can rely on geothermal energy as well as wind and solar at multiple different scales. A renewable future is fundamental to the transformation from an exploitative and extractive society to a more compassionate and regenerative society.

The transformative principles of energy democracy provide a valuable lens to guide participation, governance, and leadership in other areas related to climate decision-making. Distributing the power to expand who is involved in climate decision-making to better connect with other social priorities will enable the development of more integrated transformative policies like the Green New Deal (Boyle et al. 2021; Galvin and Healy 2020). Building and fostering multiracial, multiethnic, gender-balanced coalitions of ambitious and optimistic advocates of transformative change requires expanding expertise and engagement in climate-decision-making. With this expansion, opportunities are possible for a more just, sustainable, and equitable future with prosperity for all. Only when substantial investments are made in social innovations that redistribute power to the people by linking climate decision-making with critical social justice issues including equitable access to jobs, education, health care, housing, transportation, and food, will the transformative changes that are needed be possible (Stephens 2020).

References

Adichie, C. H. (2012). *We should all be feminists*. Anchor Books.

Aldrich, D. P. (2012). Social, not physical, infrastructure: the critical role of civil society after the 1923 Tokyo earthquake. *Disasters* 36(3): 398–419.

Anderson, K. and G. Peters. (2016). The trouble with negative emissions. *Science* 354(6309): 182.

Auel, E. and A. Cassady. (2016). The costs of climate inaction. Center for American Progress. www.americanprogress.org/issues/green/reports/2016/09/22/144386/the-costs-of-climate-inaction/.

Avelino, F. (2017). Power in sustainability transitions: Analysing power and (dis)empowerment in transformative change towards sustainability. *Environmental Policy and Governance* 27(6): 505–520.

Avelino, F. (2021). Theories of power and social change. Power contestations and their implications for research on social change and innovation. *Journal of Political Power* 14(3): 425–448.

Baker, S. (2021). *Revolutionary power: An activist's guide to the energy transition*. Island Press.

Basiago, A. D. (1994). The limits of technological optimism. *Environmentalist* 14(1): 17–22.

Battle, C. P. (2020). An offering From the Bayou. In *All we can save*, edited by Johnson, A. E. and K. K. Wilkinson. One World.

Bell, S. E., C. Daggett, and C. Labuski. (2020). Toward feminist energy systems: Why adding women and solar panels is not enough☆. *Energy Research & Social Science* 68: 101557.

Biermann, F. and I. Möller. (2019). Rich man's solution? Climate engineering discourses and the marginalization of the Global South. *International Environmental Agreements: Politics, Law and Economics* 19(2): 151–167.

Boyle, A. D., G. Leggat, L. Morikawa, Y. Pappas, and J. C. Stephens. (2021). Green New Deal proposals: Comparing emerging transformational climate policies at multiple scales. *Energy Research & Social Science* 81: 102259.

Burke, M. J. (2018). Shared yet contested: energy democracy counter-narratives. *Frontiers in Communication*: www.frontiersin.org/articles/10.3389/fcomm.2018.00022/abstract.

Burke, M. J. and J. C. Stephens. (2017). Energy democracy: Goals and policy instruments for sociotechnical transitions. *Energy Research & Social Science* 33: 35–48.

Burke, M. J. and J. C. Stephens. (2018). Political power and renewable energy futures: A critical review. *Energy Research & Social Science* 35: 78–93.

Doukas, H., A. Nikas, G. Stamtsis, and I. Tsipouridis. (2020). The green versus green trap and a way forward. *Energies* 13(20): 5473.

Faber, D., J. Stephens, V. Wallis, R. Gottlieb, C. Levenstein, P. CoatarPeter, and Boston Editorial Group of CNS. (2017). Trump's electoral triumph: Class, race, gender, and the hegemony of the polluter-industrial complex. *Capitalism Nature Socialism* 28(1): 1–15.

Feola, G. (2020). Capitalism in sustainability transitions research: Time for a critical turn? *Environmental Innovation and Societal Transitions* 35: 241–250.

Fitzgerald, J. (2020). Transitioning from Climate Justice Planning to Climate Justice Action. *Planetizen*. www.planetizen.com/blogs/110144-transitioning-climate-justice-planning-climate-justice-action.

Fountain, H. and C. Flavelle. (2021). Test flight for sunlight-blocking research is canceled. April 2nd, 2021. *New York Times*.

Fraune, C. (2015). Gender matters: Women, renewable energy, and citizen participation in Germany. *Energy Research & Social Science* 7: 55–65.

Frumhoff, P. C., R. Heede, and N. Oreskes. (2015). The climate responsibilities of industrial carbon producers. *Climatic Change* 132(2): 157–171.

Frumhoff, P. C. and J. C. Stephens. (2018). Toward legitimacy in the solar geoengineering research enterprise. *Philosophical Transactions of the Royal Society A* 376(2119).

Gallagher, K. S., J. P. Holdren, and A. D. Sagar. (2006). Energy-technology innovation. *Annual Review of Environment and Resources* 31: 193–237.

Galvin, R. and N. Healy. (2020). The Green New Deal in the United States: What it is and how to pay for it. *Energy Research & Social Science* 67: 101529.

Gates, B. (2021). *How to avoid a climate disaster*. Penguin Random House.

Geels, F. W., B. K. Sovacool, T. Schwanen, and S. Sorrell. (2017). Sociotechnical transitions for deep decarbonization. *Science* 357(6357): 1242–1244.

Harlan, S. L., D. N. Pellow, and J. T. Roberts. (2015). Climate justice and inequality. In *Climate Change and Society: Sociological Perspectives*, edited by Dunlap, R. E. and R. J. Brulle. Oxford

Healy, N., J. C. Stephens, and S.A. Malin. (2019). Embodied energy injustices: Unveiling and politicizing the transboundary harms of fossil fuel extractivism and fossil fuel supply chains. *Energy Research & Social Science* 48: 219–234.

Holdren, J. P. (2006). The energy innovation imperative, addressing oil dependence, climate change, and other 21st century energy challenges. *Innovations, Technology, Governance & Globalization* 1(2): 3–23.

IPCC. (2018). *Summary for Policymakers. In: Global warming of 1.5°C. An IPCC special report on the impacts of global warming of 1.5°C above pre-industrial levels and related global greenhouse gas emission pathways, in the context of strengthening the global response to the threat of climate change, sustainable development, and efforts to eradicate poverty*. World Meteorological Organization**:** 32.

Jenkins, K. (2018). Setting energy justice apart from the crowd: Lessons from environmental and climate justice. *Energy Research & Social Science* 39: 117–121.

Jenkins, K. E. H., J. C. Stephens, T. G. Reames, and D. Hernández. (2020). Towards impactful energy justice research: Transforming the power of academic engagement. *Energy Research & Social Science* 67: 101510.

Jones, P. N. (2021). The rise of the climate dude. *New Statesman*, February 17th, 2021. www.newstatesman.com/bill-gates-avoid-climate-disaster-michael-mann-new-climate-war-review.

Kashwan, P., L. M. MacLean, and G. A. García-López. (2019). Rethinking power and institutions in the shadows of neoliberalism: (An introduction to a special issue of World Development). *World Development* 120: 133–146.

Keeling, C. D., R. B. Bacastow, A. E. Bainbridge, C. A. Ekdahl, P. R. Guenther, L. S. Waterman, and J. F. S. Chin. (1976). Atmospheric carbon dioxide variations at Mauna Loa Observatory, Hawaii. *Tellus* 28(6): 538–551.

Kempe, Y. (2021). Who's talking about climate change on TV? Mostly white men. *Grist*. March 12, 2021. https://grist.org/justice/whos-talking-about-climate-change-on-tv-mostly-white-men/.

Kendi, I. X. (2019). *How to be an Antiracist*. One World.

Kenner, D. (2019). *Carbon inequality: The role of the richest in climate change*. Routledge.

Kuhl, L. (2021). Policy making under scarcity: reflections for designing socially just climate adaptation policy. *One Earth* 4(2): 202–212.

Lee, J. J. (2016). Is science only for the rich? *Nature* 537(7621): 466–470.

Lenferna, G. A. (2018). Can we equitably manage the end of the fossil fuel era? *Energy Research & Social Science* 35: 217–223.

Lohan, M. and W. Faulkner. (2004). Masculinites and technologies. *Men and Masculinity* 6(4): 319–329.

McKibben, B. (2016). Why we need to keep 80 percent of fossil fuels in the ground. *YES!*, February 15th, 2016. www.yesmagazine.org/issues/life-after-oil/why-we-need-to-keep-80-percent-of-fossil-fuels-in-the-ground-20160215.

Manne, K. (2018). *Down girl, the logic of misogyny*. Oxford University Press.

Marchetti, C. (1977). On geoengineering and the CO_2 problem. *Climatic Change* **1**(1): 59–68.

Markusson, N., M. Dahl Gjefsen, J. C. Stephens, and D. Tyfield. (2017). The political economy of technical fixes: The (mis)alignment of clean fossil and political regimes. *Energy Research & Social Science* 23: 1–10.

NASEM (2021). *Reflecting sunlight: Recommendations for solar geoengineering research and research governance*. NASEM.

National Research Council. (1983). Changing climate: Report from the Carbon Dioxide Assessment Committee. Carbon Dioxide Assessment Committee, Board on Atmospheric Sciences and Climate, Commission on Physical Sciences, Mathematics, and Resources, National Research Council.

Oreskes, N. (2019). *Why Trust Science*. Princeton University Press.

Osaka, S. (2021). Why Biden's climate agenda might be very, very quiet. *Grist*. May 23rd, 2021. https://grist.org/politics/why-bidens-climate-agenda-infrastructure-package-might-be-very-very-quiet/amp/?__twitter_impression=true.

Pearl-Martinez, R. and J. C. Stephens. (2016). Toward a gender diverse workforce in the renewable energy transition. *Sustainability: Science, Practice and Policy* 12(1): 8–15.

Peeters, W., L. Diependaele, and S. Sterckx. (2019). Moral disengagement and the motivational gap in climate change. *Ethical Theory and Moral Practice* 22(2): 425–447.

Peterson, T. R., J. C. Stephens, and E. J. Wilson. (2015). Public perception of and engagement with emerging low-carbon energy technologies: A literature review. *MRS Energy and Sustainability* 2(e11): 1–14.

Providence, R. I. (2019). *The City of Providence's Climate Justice Plan*. www.providenceri.gov/wp-content/uploads/2019/10/Climate-Justice-Plan-Report-FINAL-English.pdf.

Reames, T. G. (2016). Targeting energy justice: Exploring spatial, racial/ethnic and socioeconomic disparities in urban residential heating energy efficiency. *Energy Policy* 97: 549–558.

Robinson, M. (2018). *Climate justice: Hope, resilience, and the fight for a sustainable future*. Bloomsbury.

Rodima-Taylor, D., M. F. Olwig, and N. Chhetri. (2012). Adaptation as innovation, innovation as adaptation: An institutional approach to climate change. *Applied Geography* 33: 107–111.

Sorman, A. H., E. Turhan, and M. Rosas-Casals (2020). Democratizing energy, energizing democracy: Central dimensions surfacing in the debate. *Frontiers in Energy Research* 8(279).

Stephens, J. C. (2009). Technology leader, policy laggard: Carbon capture and storage (CCS) development for climate mitigation in the U.S. political context. In *Caching the carbon: The politics and policy of carbon capture and storage*, edited by Meadowcroft, J., and O. Langhelle. Edward Elgar Publishing**:** 22–49.

Stephens, J. C. (2019). Energy democracy: Redistributing power to the people through renewable transformation. *Environment: Science and Policy for Sustainable Development* 61(2): 4–13.

Stephens, J. C. (2020). *Diversifying power: Why we need antiracist, feminist leadership on climate and energy*. Island Press.

Stephens, J. C., M. J. Burke, B. Gibian, E. Jordi, and R. Watts (2018). Operationalizing energy democracy: Challenges and opportunities in Vermont's renewable energy transformation. *Frontiers in Communication* 3(43). https://doi.org/10.3389/fcomm.2018.00043.

Stephens, J. C. and N. Markusson. (2018). Technological optimism in climate mitigation: The case of carbon capture and storage. In *Oxford Handbook of Energy and Society*, edited by Gross, M. and D. J. Davidson. Oxford University Press.

Stephens, J. C. and K. Surprise (2020). The hidden injustices of advancing solar geoengineering research. *Global Sustainability* 3, E2.

Surprise, K. (2020). Stratospheric imperialism: Liberalism, (eco)modernization, and ideologies of solar geoengineering research. *Environment and Planning E: Nature and Space* 3(1): 141–163.

UNEP. (2019). Emissions gap report 2019. United Nations Environment Programme.

Valantine, H. A. and F. S. Collins. (2015). National Institutes of Health addresses the science of diversity. *Proceedings of the National Academy of Sciences* 112(40): 12240–12242.

van Veelen, B. and D. van der Horst. (2018). What is energy democracy? Connecting social science energy research and political theory. *Energy Research & Social Science* 46: 19–28.

Webler, T. and S. P. Tuler. (2010). Getting the engineering right is not always enough: Researching the human dimensions of the new energy technologies. *Energy Policy* 38: 2690–2691.

Woolston, C. (2020). White men still dominate in UK academic science. *Nature* 579(622): www.nature.com/articles/d41586-020-00759-1.

PART IV

Togetherness

14

PARTICIPATORY FUTURES

Reimagining the City Together

Kathy Peach and Laurie Smith

Introduction

In November 2020 residents of the London borough of Hounslow asked the UK's High Court to reverse recent changes to traffic management on Chiswick High Road—claiming that even the Queen had got stuck in the resulting gridlock (Lydall 2020). The controversy concerned a new cycle lane that was introduced as part of the London Street Spaces programme, an initiative to rapidly transform the city's streets to accommodate more cycling and walking after the first UK COVID-19 pandemic lockdown (Mayor of London 2020). The programme, which has added 89km of new or upgraded cycle lane across London, like the one in Chiswick, has polarised views amongst residents: 120 health professionals wrote to London's Mayor in support, yet over 2,000 people signed a petition criticising the scheme (Bhaskaran et al. 2020; Shaw 2020). The strong reactions on both sides illustrate the challenges city leaders face when tackling messy, long-term problems like transport and air pollution.

In this chapter, we argue that overcoming the complex issues that cities face requires new approaches to public engagement—going beyond the extractive surveying of needs and wants that often characterise most traditional consultation processes. As social innovation researchers and practitioners, we have spent the last three years studying a range of approaches that we call "participatory futures" methods (Ramos et al. 2019).[1] What these methods have in common is an ambition to mobilise large numbers of people in thinking about the future—rather than just relying on experts.[2] They also harness the arts and digital technologies to help people diagnose change and develop collective images of the futures they want. It is our view that to help unblock decision-making around big, controversial topics, cities should make more use of participatory futures.

We also argue that it is time for cities to reimagine themselves and their purpose. The COVID-19 pandemic has forced people to shift away from offices, and few now desire a return to full-time commuting. Cities must also grapple with the urgent need to decarbonise

DOI: 10.4324/9781003199816-19

if we are to avoid climate catastrophe—a major transition that will require the upending of many existing behaviours as well as large investments in new infrastructures. With the future of cities in flux, we highlight the importance of enabling residents to reimagine new futures for themselves and the places they live—the wider benefits that will be felt, and the risks of failing to do so. Throughout the chapter we showcase examples of the cities and people that are already using participatory futures methods, and set out some practical ways city leaders can use these new methods within traditional decision-making processes.

From "Used Futures" to Democratised Futures

At the heart of the debate around cities is a question about their purpose and who decides what that is. Discussions about this have been dominated by economic growth—after all, half of the world's GDP comes from the largest 300 metropolitan areas (*The Economist* 2020). But this view has been contested by groups from Reclaim the Streets to the Bloomberg Foundation and even some cities themselves (Yost 2014). The dynamic, complex, and conflicting factors at work amongst cities, exacerbated by the COVID-19 pandemic, now makes their future even more uncertain. Concerns are rife that city centres may become hollowed out as people permanently adopt remote working, and we may see a new kind of urban sprawl as people move further away. City leaders are increasingly acknowledging that the city itself needs to be reimagined. Before the pandemic Anne Hidalgo, the Mayor of Paris, made the idea of a "15-minute city" a centrepiece of her re-election campaign. Interest in the concept; where residents can meet all their needs within a 15-minute walk or bike ride, has exploded since COVID-19 shut down city centres (Sisson 2020).

But trust in politicians is declining almost everywhere. In the US, for example, 48 per cent of people say they don't have confidence in politicians to deal with future challenges (Parker et al. 2019). This trend of declining trust makes it much harder and also more critical to engage people constructively in tough public choices. There is no one solution to this growing crisis of democracy, but opening up people's ability to engage with the future must be part of the remedial work. Not just through voting once every few years, but through regular and sustained opportunities for people to wrestle with the challenges their city faces and to shape plausible and desired alternative futures. Most municipal governments know that they alone do not have sufficient power or knowledge to influence the changes they wish to see in communities. The goal instead must become one of building constituencies for long-term change.

A battle for the future of the city is underway. And with it, there is a danger that cities adopt "used futures" borrowed from someone or some other place, rather than allowing communities to forge their own. Sohail Inayatullah gives the example of Asian cities which for years mimicked the used futures of Western urban development—leading to sprawling megacities rather than liveable communities (Inayatalluh 2007). Growing trends make it increasingly clear that if residents are not given a platform to reimagine and reshape their cities, then big tech will try to fill the void. For what this might look like we can consider the lessons of commercially driven smart cities, which have often focused on technology rather than the problems that matter to people (Baeck and Saunders 2015). Kenya's flailing Konza smart city project illustrates the pitfalls: dreamed up by McKinsey and announced by government in 2008, few attempts were made to gain the support of the local population. Nearly 13 years later the project remains nowhere near completion (Baraka 2021). In 2020, Alphabet's Sidewalk Labs finally abandoned its Toronto smart city project citing economic uncertainty (Gibson

2020). But from the start the initiative faced a sustained local opposition who objected to the company's sensor-laden vision for the city's waterfront (Hawkins 2020).

Big tech has also shown it is willing to exploit local democracy to cement its preferred future. Silicon Valley companies spent an estimated USD $200 million on the Proposition 22 campaign in California—roughly ten times as much as the organised labour groups who opposed them (Times Editorial Board 2020). Whilst Proposition 22 has now been struck down, it initially meant these gig economy companies could continue to classify their workers as contractors, which meant they had no access to employee rights such as minimum wage and unemployment benefits. Meanwhile, China's Digital Silk Road initiative is bringing Chinese technology and tech companies to countries across Africa, the Middle East, and beyond which desperately need to expand internet and mobile phone coverage. But many worry that China is using the Digital Silk Road initiative to help other governments adopt its own model of technology-enabled authoritarianism, or to set "data traps" to leverage further Chinese political influence (Kurlantzick 2020).

In some ways this is not new. Elite interests have long competed to influence and engineer our collective imaginations of the future. From the nation-building projects of the 19th century's great exhibitions to corporate futurism with its technologically determinist agenda and consumerist values. Today, however, we are facing what Professor Geoff Mulgan calls an "imaginary crisis." Many people are finding it hard to picture positive futures yet mainstream culture finds it easy to conjure apocalypses from artificial intelligence (AI) enslavement to climate chaos. This lack of desirable yet plausible futures often leads to a sense of fear, impotence, and malaise (Mulgan 2020).

Even before the COVID-19 pandemic struck, people were feeling overwhelmed by the pace of change and pessimistic about the future. Just 34 per cent of people in advanced economies, and 42 per cent in emerging economies, believed their children would be financially better off than them when they grew up (Stokes 2019). The uncertainty experienced by individuals from rapid change has been linked to support for nationalism and religion, as people search for a collective identity to provide security and answers (Kinvall 2004).

Helping people feel a sense of agency over their future is critical for maintaining social cohesion to avoid societies fracturing along ethnic, cultural, and historical lines (Demneh and Morgan 2018). And making progress in how we think and act together for the future is critical to our ability to solve the complex challenges that cities face, whilst we still have time. Giving people agency over their future means democratising knowledge about the future, and the opportunity to shape alternative futures based on shared values and preferences. To avoid purchasing a "used future" we must democratise the process of developing our futures. This is where participatory futures methods can help.

Participatory Futures Approaches

The emerging field of participatory futures offers a range of approaches that can help unblock decision-making and action on contentious, long-term challenges by involving people in exploring or shaping potential futures. They both build on, and are part of, a range of other collaborative and community-driven approaches to planning, design, research, democracy, and innovation. It is, however, the crossover with the field of futures studies that helps distinguish participatory futures from other approaches. Typically, they aim to build collective intelligence by helping people to diagnose change over the long term, draw out knowledge and ideas about how the future could be, and develop collective mental images of the futures people want.

Participatory futures exercises have been around since at least the 1960s.[3] A prominent early example was Hawaii 2000—a project launched by the newly elected Governor of Hawaii in 1970 to explore public opinion on what the state should look like in the year 2000 (Dator et al. 1999). The year-long exercise involved thousands of residents and blended public engagement with scenario-based futures methods.

For a long time, participatory futures methods relied on group workshops, interviews, and in-person discussions. Since 2000, however, this has begun to change. Conventional futures methods are now being combined with emerging digital technologies and new players are getting involved, such as artists, designers, and psychologists. Since the 2010s, this has led to an explosion of new ways of thinking about or experiencing the future—phenomena that can be described as "mutant futures" because of the combination of approaches involved (Ramos 2020).

As part of our research into participatory futures we catalogued over 300 exercises from around the world. Many included elements of *play* and gaming. After a major earthquake destroyed Christchurch in New Zealand, for example, the city council created a Massive Multiplayer Online Roleplaying Game called Magnetic South (Institute for the Future 2011). It was played by almost 1,000 people over two days and involved players generating ideas and strategies for rebuilding the city, with 8,889 micro-forecasts.

Participatory futures approaches often use *immersive* physical or virtual environments, allowing people to place themselves in a future world and experiment with new values or behaviours. One well-known example is Block by Block. It uses the Minecraft platform (an easy-to-learn 3D digital modelling game) as a community participation tool for visualisation and collaboration to actively engage neighbourhood residents who don't typically have a voice in the spatial planning and design of cities. Once project ideas are completed in Minecraft, stakeholders from local government, the mayor's office, planners, and architects listen to presentations by people who were part of the design process. In the Gaza Strip, the programme allowed the incorporation of women and girls' ideas in reconstructing key public spaces that have since benefited around 100,000 people (Harrouk 2020). So far, Block by Block has helped the renewal of urban neighbourhoods in more than 30 countries (Block by Block n.d.).

The techniques also encompass *sensing* initiatives that harness digital technologies to engage people in scanning, exploring, or forecasting the future. One example of this was Futurecoast—a storytelling project about possible climate-changed futures where anyone could participate by voicemail. The game generated a range of perspectives on climate change from peoples' imagined futures.

Another approach involves *creating* or engaging with physical objects that represent the future. This has been used in an exhibition conceived in 2019 called *Carbon Ruins* which is set in 2053 and tells an imagined story of how Sweden became the first nation to achieve net-zero emissions in 2045. Based on current climate models and research, it demonstrates how scientific data can be translated into various physical artefacts aimed at creating awareness and stimulating thought on transformative action at a global scale.[4]

Many participatory futures exercises also involve *deliberation*. In Germany, Finding Places brought together Hamburg residents to identify optimal locations to provide housing for a predicted influx of refugees in the city. The participants were engaged through a combination of colour-coded Lego bricks, augmented reality, touch feedback and geographical simulation algorithms, which allowed people to understand urban land use patterns and propose housing sites. The project helped to successfully identify 160 accommodation locations that were widely accepted by Hamburg's residents, 44 of which were approved by the authorities.[5]

Five Ways to Use Participatory Futures to Reimagine the City

The flexibility of participatory futures approaches means they can operate across many countries and cultures. They can also be local and place-based. They can be driven initially by the state or institution, civil society, or by the energy of individuals. Some exercises are very broad—mapping out the options for a whole place (for example, between food, energy, city design, and lifestyles). Others are more specific, dealing with a narrow issue.

Our research shows that commissioning or designing participatory futures exercises requires careful consideration of a number of different design variables, but perhaps the most important is to be clear on the type of strategic impact desired and to provide clarity on how any activity will connect into the decision-making process. Understanding the different roles of participatory futures can help make this connection more concrete. Below we describe these five main roles, provide a description of the methods used, and illustrate with an example in practice. This is intended to help guide city leaders about how participatory futures can be used in practice, including in the context of more traditional decision-making processes.

Role 1: Mapping Horizons

In this role, participatory futures can be used to deepen awareness of changes on medium- and long-term time horizons. These activities involve members of the public in identifying signals of change, emerging issues, and the factors driving them. They can also involve exploration of different ways these changes may play out and their potential impacts through the creation or use of alternative scenarios.

A tangible demonstration of this was the Future Energy Lab—a United Arab Emirates (UAE)-based event to help decision makers and businesses engage with the implications of climate change on the region's future. Participants were taken through five different future worlds that expressed the consequences of different energy policies (from the implementation of renewable energy technologies to peer-to-peer energy trading). For each future, objects and experiences were designed to simulate that particular future urban environment. In the "Business as Usual" future where fossil fuel use continued, participants could inhale a series of polluted air samples from the years 2020, 2028, and 2034, based on climate and fossil fuel emission projections. The event is credited as having created actionable insights towards the goal of achieving the UAE's National Energy Strategy 2050 (Superflux 2017).

Role 2: Creating Purpose

In this role, participatory futures can be used to develop a sense of meaning and direction. These activities explore people's values, needs, and aspirations that lead to a vision of a preferred future. They can also involve examining and reframing deep-seated cultural or organisational assumptions.

A practical illustration of this comes from the Dutch Caribbean nation of Aruba. In 2008, the government initiated a deliberative exercise to chart a *2025 vision* for the island that would also deal with the existential challenges it faced—such as fragile ecosystems and vulnerability to volatile global energy markets. It used a structured process of appreciative inquiry to generate positive visions for the future, and scenario building—creating stories about different futures. More than half the island's 100,000 residents were involved, which enabled the exercise, and the national strategy that came from it, to outlast the vagaries of the political cycle and a change of government.

Role 3: Charting Pathways

In this role, participatory futures can be used to help create high-level strategies and socially acceptable pathways for desired change. They often involve people in generating novel ideas to realise a vision or collaboratively setting priorities and milestones.

The population of Mexico City had for decades been politically disenfranchised because, like many federal districts, it had no status as a state and citizens were not given the opportunity to vote for local representatives. In 2016, the Mayor of Mexico City decided to address this by crowdsourcing a citywide constitution from local residents. He appointed a 28-person drafting committee made up of Mexico City residents, supported by technical staff. Local people's visions for the city were gathered through a survey called *Imagina tu Ciudad* (Imagine Your City), and student volunteers, armed with tablets were deployed to gather responses from residents in public spaces. People could also set up online petitions for specific articles to be included in the constitution. The Imagine Your City project received over 34,000 survey responses, and 278,000 signatures were collected through the online petition system. The constitution was formally approved in February 2017 with crowdsourced components providing an important influence on policy, including on LGBTI rights and the right to mobility, the first time such a right was ever enshrined in a city constitution (Cities of Service n.d.).

Role 4: Acting Together

In this role, participatory futures can be used as a process to mobilise collaborative action and distributed innovation across a community to realise a desired future. They might involve supporting individuals and a wider range of organisations to initiate and drive social innovations, community enterprises, or change campaigns.

A "transition management" process in Ghent, a city in Belgium, offers a demonstration of this in practice. The aim was to address major sustainability challenges, particularly climate change. The process first developed a long-term vision that provided the overall context to guide newly involved actors in piloting social innovations. The approach saw participants "learn by doing" and showed how residents could be signposts of change, building enthusiasm, and driving more public participation. A total of 100 highly motivated people initially attended a launch event. They joined working groups, which included people from various backgrounds, to develop projects. This group initiated and drove a number of projects, experiments, and social innovation processes. This included: an energy efficiency project working with small and medium enterprises; a network of cultural organisations monitoring their CO_2 emissions and a project to use sewage water to produce heat, biogas, nutrients, and water. All but one initiative was deemed successful (Roorda et al. 2014).

Role 5: Testing Ideas

In this role, participatory futures can be used to generate feedback and learn about a specific idea of the future, a scenario, or prototype. They can produce novel insights as people interact with scaled experiments that enable them to interrogate the desirability of that future, to stress test it and consider potential unintended consequences.

As cities become more congested and seek out creative ways to reimagine mobility, they are increasingly using large-scale events, as well as small-scale prototypes, to inspire and test alternatives. Reimagine London exemplified this. As part of World Car Free Day, the Mayor of London announced that on September 22nd, 2019, 20km of roads in and around the city would be closed. From skate ramps to treasure hunts, Greater London featured a variety of "festivalesque" activities, including special programming for young people. The organisers explicitly sought to include people of all ages and from all backgrounds, with residents and visitors able to participate. What makes Reimagine London compelling is that it showed how local governments can provide freedom for people to experiment with, and create new future visions for, their car-free areas. Reimagine London has echoes of an older London-based people-powered movement, Reclaim the Streets, which has a shared ideology of community ownership of public spaces (Mayor of London 2019).

"Powerful Time Bombs"

For Fred Polak, one of the founding fathers of futures studies, images of the future were "powerful time bombs," which when exploded release masses of concentrated energy (Polak 1973). In this section we set out why participatory futures are different to other types of engagement, and the benefits participation in them can bring—including as powerful time bombs to catalyse new thinking and behaviour.

Participatory futures exercises stand in contrast to many traditional public engagement techniques, which regularly fail to enthuse people to participate and can be seen as tokenistic rather than leading to real change. Conventional surveys offer some insights but when used alone are rarely the best way to understand how people think about the future, as participants often haven't had the space to sufficiently develop their ideas and offer meaningful answers. Workshops allow richer dialogue but frequently require considerable time and resource, so in practice can only involve very few people.

Despite the hype around citizen's assemblies, they cannot deliver the scale of public engagement needed to democratise futures thinking. The national Climate Assembly UK, for example, with 108 participants had a level of participation of *0.0002 per cent* of the voting population of the UK. Instead, these should be considered primarily as tools for providing diverse and representative inputs into tricky and often well-defined policy problems.

Conversely, one of the potential strengths of participatory futures exercises is the ability to help groups of people build collective images and stories of the future. Throughout history people have used mental images in the form of myths and legends to organise themselves. As Polak points out, religion has often employed this device: *The Bible's Book of Genesis*, for example, tells us that God created man in his image (Polak 1973). The author Yuval Noah Harari explains that storytelling is a uniquely human ability that has allowed us to co-operate by convincing millions of others to believe shared narratives (Harari 2018).

Participatory futures approaches help people unlock their collective imaginations by creating shared public images of the future that can provide a "destination identity"—acting as a motivating force to turn the "imagined" into the real (Slaughter 1991). Like Martin Luther King's "I have a dream" speech, or John F. Kennedy's "Moon speech." positive images help pull us towards the future helping to catalyse social change and overcome cultural obstacles to it. Brain research shows that collective images offer orientation in times of uncertainty or when the necessity of reshaping our environments becomes apparent (Hüther 2010).

In some ways perhaps participatory futures exercises can also help fill or replace the gap created by growing secularism—by bringing together a community to achieve a particular goal. The functionalist view of religion sees its purpose as uniting strangers around a task such as building a temple, performing charitable acts, or supporting a political party. Behind many participatory futures approaches, there is often a desire to unite communities to build or demand more sustainable, equitable, and inclusive futures. And like religion, participatory futures can help change mental models and social norms—in part through the adoption of new shared rituals (Appiah 2016).

Japan's "Future Design" movement involves the shared rituals of roleplay where participants take the perspective of residents from 45 years in the future—dressing up in ceremonial robes to aid this imaginative leap. Using generational thinking, similar to the seven generation perspective employed by Native American peoples, Future Design integrates long-term thinking into local planning and policy discussions. It emphasises the perspective of those "not yet born" to shift typical conversations on policy from wants and their costs to how decisions today can and might benefit future generations. The Future Design process has been run across numerous prefectures in Japan with residents of various backgrounds and ages, and in 2019, the town of Hamada officially adopted the approach as its basis for long-term planning (Krznaric 2020). Multiple studies have shown that the process results in far more radical and progressive city plans (Krznaric 2020). It also changes the way individual people think, and this continues well after their participation has ended (Sakura and Saijo 2019).

Participatory futures approaches offer us an opportunity to both switch from our current present bias and incorporate new ways of knowing and seeing. Take the example of Future Dreaming, an immersive virtual reality (VR) film allowing audiences to join four Aboriginal youths in their futures. Inspired by Australian Aboriginal Dreamtime storytelling, the project uses a mental visualisation technique to see your spirit move through the past, present, or future.[6] People frequently report leaving participatory futures exercises feeling inspired—a state often associated with greater creativity and progress towards goals, as well as increased levels of spirituality and meaning (Kaufman 2011).

Einstein famously said that the world as we have created it is a process of our thinking. It cannot be changed without changing our thinking. This is the power of participatory futures.

Realising the Potential of Participatory Futures

The ultimate success of participatory futures exercises will be the extent to which they increase the likelihood that the decisions we take today will turn out to be collectively wise decisions—not just for the here and now, but for generations after us.

The COVID-19 pandemic has shown us starkly that the world can change. From the rapid adoption of remote working to online health care, the plasticity of the future has been exposed. As we begin to realise that many of the constraints of the pre-COVID-19 world existed only in our heads, novel futures come into focus. Governments furloughed millions of their citizens, effectively introducing a (temporary) universal basic income, an idea that was previously considered politically impossible by many. Yet already these futures are being colonised by big business, consultancies, and governments. Employees, for example, have expressed concern about increasing digital surveillance of remote workers, now made more common by the pandemic (Solon 2021).

As the effects of the pandemic continue to widen inequality and change the cities where we live, the opportunity to engage people is now. In a potentially precarious future, city leaders and voluntary organisations can help make imagining the future a right, rather than a luxury (Candy 2016). Funders for instance have a key role in supporting bottom-up initiatives such as the Emerging Futures Fund, a GBP £1 million programme from the UK National Lottery Community Fund to help communities and civil society draw on their creativity and move towards recovery and renewal after the impact of the COVID-19 pandemic.[7]

City leaders, too, should harness participatory futures to think beyond the present and engage with their constituents. Following the lead of some governments which have appointed ministers responsible for the future, cities should make a Deputy Mayor responsible for future generations whose role would include commissioning, experimenting with, and evaluating participatory futures exercises. These positions should come with resources, staff, legal mandate, status, clear goals and be integrated with other work across the city. They should also be at the forefront of plans to regenerate cities after the pandemic.

As the world continues to struggle with the impact of the pandemic, increasing polarisation, and immobilised decision-making on our most complex challenges and emerging risks from new technologies, we must build the capability of many more members of the public to think long term and shape the futures they want for the benefit of people we might never live to see. We call on city leaders, national governments, public institutions, funders, and civil society to spearhead the adoption of participatory futures techniques and help us reimagine our cities together.

Notes

1 This chapter draws on research carried out by the authors with Jose Ramos and John Sweeney which was published by Nesta in 2019.

2 We define participatory futures as a range of approaches for involving citizens in exploring or shaping potential futures. It aims to democratise and encourage long-term thinking, and inform collective actions in the present.

3 Examples from the USA in the 1960s and 1970s can be found in Bezold, C. (ed) (1978) Anticipatory democracy: People in the politics of the future. Random House, New York and examples from around the world can be found in academic futures journals such as *Futures, Foresight, Journal of Future Studies, Technological Forecasting and Social Change, World Futures Review, World Futures, European Journal of Futures Research* and *On the Horizon.*

4 For further information see: www.climaginaries.org/carbon-ruins.

5 For further information see: https://urbact.eu/finding-places.

6 Further details are available from: www.sutueatsflies.com/art/future-dreaming.

7 Further details are available from: www.tnlcommunityfund.org.uk/funding/programmes/emerging-futures-fund.

References

Appiah K. A. (2016). Creed. *The Reith Lectures*. BBC. www.bbc.co.uk/programmes/b07z43ds.

Ardern J. (2017). The future energy lab. *SUPERFLUX*. https://superflux.in/index.php/work/futureen ergylab/#.

Baeck P. and T. Saunders. (2015). Rethinking cities from the ground up. *Nesta*. www.nesta.org.uk/report/rethinking-smart-cities-from-the-ground-up/

Baraka C. (2021). The failed promise of Kenya's smart city. *Rest of World*. https://restofworld.org/2021/the-failed-promise-of-kenyas-smart-city/

Bhaskaran S., et al. (2020). 120 doctors and nurses urge continuation of low traffic neighbourhoods and cycle lanes schemes. www.pgweb.uk/planning-all-subjects/quieter-neighbourhoods/2847-120-doctors-and-nurses-urge-continuation-of-low-traffic-neighbourhoods-and-cycle-lanes-schemes.

Block by Block (n.d.) www.blockbyblock.org/.

Candy S. (2016). Foresight is a right. *the sceptical futuryst*, April 30th, 2016. https://futuryst.blogspot.com/2016/04/foresight-is-right.html.

Cities of Service (n.d.). http://citiesofservice.jhu.edu/resource/crowdsourcing-a-constitution-mexico-city/.

Dator J., M. Hamnett, D. Nordberg, and W. S. Pintz. (1999). Hawaii 2000: Past, present and future. www.futures.hawaii.edu/publications/hawaii/HI2KDBEDTReport1999.pdf.

Demneh M. and R. Morgan. (2018). Destination identity: futures images as social identity. *Journal of Futures Studies* 22(3): 51–64.

Devlin K. and A. Connaughton. (2020). Most approve of national response to Covid-19 in 14 advanced economies. *Pew Research Center*, August 27th, 2020. www.pewresearch.org/global/2020/08/27/most-approve-of-national-response-to-covid-19-in-14-advanced-economies/#coronavirus-has-changed-many-lives-throughout-14-nations.

(The) Economist. (2020). Centres of Excellence. Covid-19 challenges New York's Future. *The Economist*, June 13th, 2020. www.economist.com/briefing/2020/06/11/covid-19-challenges-new-yorks-future.

Gibson E. (2020). Sidewalk labs abandons Toronto smart city during pandemic. *dezeen*, May 7th, 2020. www.dezeen.com/2020/05/07/sidewalk-labs-abandons-toronto-smart-city-coronavirus-pandemic/

Harari Y. N. (2018). Yuval Noah Harari extract: "Humans are a post-truth species." *The Guardian,* August 5th, 2018. www.theguardian.com/culture/2018/aug/05/yuval-noah-harari-extract-fake-news-sapiens-homo-deus.

Harrouk, C. (2020). UN-Habitat promotes inclusive planning and gender equitable cities using technology. *ArchDaily*, January 2nd, 2020. www.archdaily.com/931217/un-habitat-promotes-inclusive-planning-and-gender-equitable-cities-using-technology.

Hawkins, A. J. (2020) Alphabet's Sidewalk Labs shuts down Toronto smart city project. *The Verge*, May 7th, 2020. www.theverge.com/2020/5/7/21250594/alphabet-sidewalk-labs-toronto-quayside-shutting-down.

Hüther (2010), quoted in D. Wilhelmer. (2016). Society in need of transformation. Citizen-Foresight as a method to co-create the future. *Public Philosophy & Democratic Education* 5(2): 51–72.

Inayatalluh S. (2007). Six pillars of futures thinking for transforming. *foresight* 10(1): 4–21. www.benlandau.com/wp-content/uploads/2015/06/Inayatullah-2008-Six-Pillars.pdf.

Institute for the Future. (2011). A foresight engine collaborative forecasting game. *Magnetic South* www.iftf.org/our-work/people-technology/games/magnetic-south/.

Kaufman S. (2011). Why inspiration matters. *Harvard Business Review*, November 8th, 2011. https://hbr.org/2011/11/why-inspiration-matters.

Kinvall C. (2004). Globalization and religious nationalism: Self identity, and the search for ontological security. *Political Psychology* 25(5): 741–767.

Kurlantzick J. (2020). China's Digital Silk Road Initiative: A boon for developing countries or a danger to freedom? *The Diplomat*, December 17th, 2020. https://thediplomat.com/2020/12/chinas-digi tal-silk-road-initiative-a-boon-for-developing-countries-or-a-danger-to-freedom/.

Krznaric R. (2020). The good ancestor: How to think long term in a short-term world. *The Experiment*: p. 181.

Lydall R. (2020). Cycle lane wars: Row over Covid traffic scheme as fight heads to High Court. *Evening Standard*, November 23rd, 2020. www.standard.co.uk/news/london/cycle-lane-row-chiswick-ltn-transport-for-london-b75072.html.

Mayor of London/London Assembly (2019) Mayor launches plans for London's biggest Car Free Day celebrations. www.london.gov.uk/press-releases/mayoral/londons-biggest-ever-car-free-day.

Mayor of London/London Assembly. (2020). Mayor's bold new Streetspace plan will overhaul London's streets. www.london.gov.uk/press-releases/mayoral/mayors-bold-plan-will-overhaul-capitals-streets.

Mulgan G. (2020). The imaginary crisis (and how we might quicken social and public imagination). *Demos Helsinki*. https://demoshelsinki.fi/julkaisut/the-imaginary-crisis-and-how-we-might-quicken-social-and-public-imagination/.

Parker K., R. Morin, and J. Menasce Horowitz. (2019). Looking to the future, public sees an America in decline on many fronts. Pew Research Center, March 21st, 2019. www.pewsocialtrends.org/2019/03/21/public-sees-an-america-in-decline-on-many-fronts/.

Polak F. (1973). The image of the future. Jossey-Bass Inc. Publishers. http://en.laprospective.fr/dyn/anglais/memoire/the-image-of-the-future.pdf, pp. 1–11, 24.

Ramos J., J. Sweeney, K. Peach, and L. Smith (2019) Our futures: by the people, for the people. *Nesta*. www.nesta.org.uk/report/our-futures-people-people/.

Ramos J. (2020). Messy grace: The mutant futures program. In *Phenomenologies of grace: The body, embodiment and transformative futures*, edited by M. Bussey. Palgrave Macmillan.

Roorda C., J. Wittmayer, P. Henneman, F. van Steenbergen, N. Frantzeskaki, and D. Loorbach. (2014). *Transition management in the urban context: guidance manual*. Dutch Research Institute for Transitions. https://drift.eur.nl/wp-content/uploads/2016/11/DRIFT-Transition_management_in_the_urban_context-guidance_manual.pdf.

Sakura O. and T. Saijo. (2019). Discussion between Professor Sakura Osamu and Professor Saijo Tatsuyoshi. *Discuss Japan*. www.japanpolicyforum.jp/society/pt20190109210522.html.

Shaw A. (2020). Petition launched against Harrow Council's Streetspace LTNs. *Harrow Times*, October 22nd, 2020. www.harrowtimes.co.uk/news/18815186.petition-launched-harrow-councils-streetspace-ltns/.

Sisson, P. (2020). How the "15-minute city" could help post-pandemic recovery. *Bloomberg CityLab*, July 15th, 2020. www.bloomberg.com/news/articles/2020-07-15/mayors-tout-the-15-minute-city-as-covid-recovery.

Slaughter (1991), quoted in Demneh, M. and R. Morgan. (2018). Destination identity: Futures images as social identity. *Journal of Futures Studies* 22(3): 51–64.

Solon, O. (2021). Big tech call center workers face pressure to accept home surveillance. *NBC News*, August 8th, 2021. www.nbcnews.com/tech/tech-news/big-tech-call-center-workers-face-pressure-accept-home-surveillance-n1276227.

Stokes, B. (2019.) A decade after the financial crisis economic confidence rebounds in many countries. *Pew Research Center*, September 18th, 2018. www.pewresearch.org/global/2018/09/18/a-decade-after-the-financial-crisis-economic-confidence-rebounds-in-many-countries/.

Superflux (2017). The future energy lab. http://superflux.in/index.php/work/futureenergylab/#.

The Times Editorial Board. (2020). Editorial: Prop. 22 just showed tech companies how to write their own labor laws. *Los Angeles Times*, November 4th, 2020. www.latimes.com/opinion/story/2020-11-04/editorial-prop-22-just-showed-tech-companies-how-to-write-their-own-labor-laws.

Yost, C. (2014). reinventing cities for an age of purpose. New Cities. https://newcities.org/can-reinvent-cities-age-purpose/#:~:text=Just%20as%20a%20%E2%80%9Ctypical%E2%80%9D%20city,choose%20a%20more%20meaningful%20lifestyle.

15

BASQUE CIVICS

Gorka Espiau and Itziar Moreno

Context and Positionality

We write this chapter from the experience lived during the last ten years trying to understand more deeply the Basque civics and share these learnings globally. We are both Basques and, thus, conditioned by the way of seeing the world from the perspective of one of the oldest cultures in Europe. In our imagination, we carry the torch of an identity that has been enriched by and survived the most powerful civilizations of this continent thanks to their ability to adapt without losing a particular way of seeing the world. We are both journalists with different backgrounds. Itziar worked for the Bilbao Guggenheim Museum and now coordinates innovation programs for the United Nations in more than 15 countries around the world. Gorka actively participated in the peace movement that brought an end to the violence in the region ten years ago and was a special advisor to the Presidency of the Basque Government.

The Basque case presents a unique case of civic transformation under extreme circumstances. This experience involves the urban renewal of the city of Bilbao, the Mondragon cooperatives, the large-scale social economy ecosystem, an intensive cluster strategy, the local advanced manufacturing and technology alliances, a 20-year-old basic income policy, the recovery of the ancient pre-Indo-European Basque language, and the highest concentration of Michelin Guide-awarded restaurants per square meter, among many other interconnected initiatives (Ibarretxe 2015).

Since the end of the Spanish dictatorship in 1975, self-government has been a key driver of the socioeconomic transformation for the Basque society. The recovery of a democratically elected Basque Parliament and other local institutions that have been preserved in the area since Late Middle Ages (9th–11th centuries) took control over health, education, security, and economic planning; and local governing bodies were re-established with the capacity to collect and allocate taxes. The strategies and specific initiatives promoted by these self-governing institutions helped to design and implement a sustainable human development strategy, rooted in economic growth and social cohesion.

The local taxation policies are similar to European standards but the area has enjoyed high income equality rates for decades, since the recovery of self government (1978) until today.

DOI: 10.4324/9781003199816-20

The situation is far from perfect, but this data allows us to think that it is possible to comple-ment the necessary distribution of wealth through taxes aimed at generating capital and value. A more egalitarian salary policy and strong solidarity mechanisms can provide real and large-scale "pre-distribution" of wealth.

When the social, institutional, and business protagonists of this civic transformation are questioned about the key elements to understanding the extraordinary responses to very negative circumstances in a very short period of time, they highlight the importance of respecting the local culture and ancient identity and a "values-based strategy." While current innovation and competitive models are built on instrumental rationality (Weber 1993; Flyvbjerg 2006), the Basque experience demonstrates that large-scale interventions can be interconnected by a civic "software" that is based on Indigenous culture and a deeper aspirational goal.

Compared to similar post-industrial situations, the key factor of this transformation seems to be associated with a particular way of understanding social progress. Extensive research conducted by the Agirre Lehendakaria Center for Social and Political Studies (University of the Basque Country) indicates that the initiatives associated with the Basque experience share a common value system expressed by transformative narratives. As mentioned, they took a very different form (cooperatives, museums, restaurants, and public policies) but they were responding to an ancient way of interpreting Basque identity. Things that didn't make sense to an external observer were described as normal for the local stakeholders.

The cultural dimension of an innovation process can be, therefore, interpreted as the set of values and beliefs shared by a particular community and the way they are expressed in col-lective narratives, ultimately conditioning strategic decisions and their implementation. The stories that we tell ourselves about what is possible and what is not need to be better under-stood and incorporated into the core strategy when working to transform communities, cities, or regions.

We need to identify what stories we are telling about ourselves. Are those limiting or amplifying existing opportunities and challenges for civic transformation? And most import-antly, what is the transformational narrative that can connect ancient societies like the Basque people? In the Bilbao case, for example, it is crucial to deconstruct why local institutions even considered it possible to convince the Guggenheim Foundation to locate their new flagship museum in a city that was devastated by industrial collapse, rampant unemployment, and weekly terrorist attacks. It would also be helpful to understand the driving force powering the Mondragon cooperatives that is successfully competing with the most advanced industrial corporations applying a totally different rationale in regards to decision-making (one worker, one vote), salary policy (1:7 pay differential instead of 1:300 in similar size companies), and inter-solidarity mechanisms (in 2013, Mondragon relocated 2,000 workers in 24 months). This icon of the social economy needs to be understood as the Basque way to interpret what sacred civics mean in action.

In contrast to decisions based on an exclusively instrumental rationality, Mondragon applies a value-based decision-making process. There is vast evidence of the "Culture Lever" and the strong correlation between corporate financial performance and the way values are practiced. Carucci (2017) expresses this idea in a beautiful way by saying that "values hold the power to drive meaningful differences in performance by shaping a culture, and when misused, can undermine performance with toxic force." In the Basque case, we have been able to verify that multiple narratives can build a transformative way of interpreting culture.

Self-responsibility

The value of self-responsibility is shared by most of the key initiatives associated with the Basque transformation. Although most transformative values appeal to the collective, research conducted by Agirre Lehendakaria Center (ALC) shows that the success of this process is associated with the need for each individual to take ownership of "his or her share of responsibility" (Espiau 2022) as an indispensable condition for collective action.

The narratives and discourses identified with ethnographic tools highlight this issue and the fact that due to the emergency context of the social and economic crisis of the 1980s, it was not possible to appeal to an external institution or force from which to request external help. The devolution of institutional, social, and economic powers to the Basque Government implied acceptance that no external actor to whom the main responsibility for finding a solution to the situation could be transferred. The centrality of the value of self-responsibility is, therefore, one of the keys to understanding the capacity for endogenous innovation (Eizagirre and Udaondo 2020) developed in Basque society, in contrast to other similar situations that have not been able to develop a process of systemic transformation.

In the case of the Mondragon cooperatives, this principle of self-responsibility is present even in the organizational model of the cooperatives. Instead of creating a corporation or business group in the traditional style, in which the different divisions are managed by a centralized Board of Directors which assumes responsibility for strategy, coordination and, where appropriate, controls the profits generated, a model of independent cooperatives (each of which has its own legal personality and total freedom of decision) united by a system of voluntary strategic collaboration has been chosen. In other words, each cooperative in the Mondragon Group is totally independent from a legal and operational point of view. On the basis of this self-responsibility (which must guarantee the business viability of each unit), cooperation and solidarity mechanisms are established with the other cooperatives on a voluntary basis. Any cooperative in the group can leave the corporation whenever it wishes and there have been cases, such as that of the Irizar cooperative (Nuño 2006) in which this decision was taken in a period of high profits after having received solidarity funds from the rest of the cooperatives.

This principle of self-responsibility is shared by the narratives expressed by the organizations that play a leading role in the recovery of the Basque language (each one is organized autonomously), the companies dedicated to generating employment for people with functional diversity, or those in charge who subsequently develop collective action strategies. This value of self-responsibility may be related to the way in which the Basque farmhouse was historically managed since the Middle Ages and the importance that this imaginary continues to have in society. The strategies of solidarity and collective action described in Basque language as "auzolan" (neighborhood-based collective labor) developed to deal with the tasks that the farmhouse couldn't carry out on its own (road repairs, management of common land, support for families in emergency situations, etc.) combined solidarity with self-sufficiency. According to the Basque way of interpreting the civics, it is not possible to appeal to solidarity and collective action without self-responsibility.

This narrative also helps to explain many of the extraordinary initiatives generated by the Basque society since the 1980s. From the local perspective, there was no alternative to collective action because no one "from the outside" was going to come and solve the problems, and differs greatly from other narratives that demand external support to transform complex situations.

In the case of the "Bilbao Effect," the revenue-raising capacity of the Basque provincial treasuries (Agirreazkuenaga and Alonso 2014) is perceived as one of the key instruments to generate agency. Collecting more money meant a greater capacity for local investment and spending, while economic activity weighed down by the industrial crisis meant taking on the responsibility of offering top-quality services without the income to finance them.

In the narratives linked to the Mondragon cooperatives, the value of self-responsibility is also interpreted as personal "sacrifice." This value is expressed by the members of the cooperative as the ability to make certain concessions or efforts for the collective good, for the community. The way in which it is expressed has an obvious religious connotation, which can be explained by the convictions of the people who founded the cooperatives but which is shared by a much broader sociological spectrum.

This value is not understood in the traditional way, but as a collective way of "sacrificing" personal gain for the common good. It is an organizational commitment to sacrifice certain short-term benefits for the sake of survival and the common good in the medium and long term. The most obvious examples include decisions to cut salaries to cope with difficult situations and to invest in technology, training, research or solidarity with other cooperatives. The response to long working hours and even the provision of capital is also mentioned by cooperative workers.

Most analyses of ecosystems or large-scale egalitarian societies fail to explain how large-scale transformations can develop without external financial knowledge or human resource support. It is known that grassroots initiatives can have an impact on policy and even transform national and international systems (Seyfang and Smith 2007) but it is not known why in some similar contexts this is possible and in others it is not. Further research on this topic would be extremely useful.

The Common Good

Solidarity and collective action are often mentioned in the way local actors describe the transformation experienced by the Basque society. The narratives collected within the Basque ecosystem speak of an emergency situation (systemic crisis) to which no one could respond individually. The challenge was too great and too complex for a particular response. In this situation, solidarity and collective intelligence were naturally perceived as more effective alternatives (Malone 2004; Mulgan 2018).

This narrative and its associated value are substantially different from the way in which other societies have tried to respond to similar systemic crises (Hodgson 2017). In these cases, although public narratives may have been linked to these same values of solidarity and collective action, they concealed underlying narratives of individual response and even meta-narratives that did not see systemic change possible.

The traditional concept of collective action or "auzolan" (Douglass 1989) discussed in relation to the value of self-responsibility is also associated with collaboration. It is an action-oriented value born of community life. The interpretation given to this concept by the people and initiatives we have investigated is that working for the common good "is morally more just than the pursuit of personal profit" (Hodgson 2017). The value of solidarity and collective action give a very specific and differential content to what is understood by the "common good" in Basque society. This common good (Ostrom 1990) is interpreted as the will to work for mutual benefit. It is "the way of joining forces to respond to a hostile environment."

However, some of the narratives identified question whether this value is still present in the same way in Basque society. To the extent that the quality of life has improved significantly, the sense of need and urgency to respond together has diminished. If the "auzolan" is interpreted only as the collective effort to respond to basic needs, it would no longer make as much sense as in the past. In general terms, the research conducted by ALC found a great deal of concern about whether this model of solidarity and collective action can be sustained in situations where there is not such a deep crisis to respond to.

Competitiveness

Since the 1990s, regional competitiveness systems have tried to emulate the experience of California's Silicon Valley. This approach to competitiveness combines radical individualism, neoliberal economics (Friedman 1962) and techno-utopianism (Fernandez 2017). Advocates of such regional competitiveness strategies understand that in a post-industrial economy, information and knowledge drive growth favoring those who can benefit most from the use of information technologies (Castells 1996). This interpretation of regional competitiveness has been referred to as the "Californian ideology" (Bartbrook and Cameron 1996). This highly individualistic approach to competitiveness has strengthened the power of corporations over the individual, has increased social stratification, and remains distinctly American-centric. Barbrook and Cameron (1996) argue that this ideology masks a form of reactionary modernism, "American neoliberalism seems to have achieved two contradictory goals: economic progress and social immobility."

However, the narratives identified in the case studies linked to the Basque experience challenge the idea of an individualistic competitiveness model (Collier and Kay 2021), such as that of Silicon Valley. The Basque model of innovation and competitiveness is founded on equality; "they need to know that all voices count, that they have meaning … In light of these findings, the idea that innovation is unique, rather than shared, and that it is born of exceptional individuals squeezed under conditions of coercion, rather than a mutually empowering collectivity taking relative risks, sounds rather strange" (Glucksberg 2017). The keys to this Basque model of competitiveness for Glucksberg would be: "close social networks, a strong commitment to equality as a shared experience, self-reliance and cooperation, a strong work ethic, openness and a firm belief in the power of education."

The narratives identified show us that collective action narratives can be compatible with successful models of competitiveness in the market (Arizmendiarrieta 1999). In fact, the narratives of Mondragon's cooperative members show that they consider themselves to be more competitive because they have principles of collective action and social practices that guide their work (Eizagirre and Udaondo 2020). The values and social practices that have been the focus of this study are not a peripheral element of their work. These practices are fully integrated and are key to the decision-making process, allowing decisions to be coherent with the needs of local populations and their values.

The narratives described have allowed us to discover institutions that are lived by most of their members as an "experience" that transcends business projects. The stories used to tell this experience are not limited to highlighting the results obtained for the groups with the greatest difficulties in finding employment, or the number of new speakers of the oldest language in Europe, but rather they speak of a true "movement" of social transformation that has tried to combine the generation of quality employment with an integral way of understanding human development.

Despite building a hybrid model of action between the social and the entrepreneurial, when there were no structured frameworks for social innovation in the European context, the narratives described do not understand it as something extraordinary.

The experiences described are examples of large-scale social innovation (Mulgan and Leadbeater 2013) and are naturally integrated into the regional competitiveness system (Morgan, Navarro, and Valdaliso 2020). These public entities, companies, and social organizations naturally integrate the technological, entrepreneurial, and social dimension in their interventions. This evolution of the most advanced innovation approaches responds to the complex nature of the challenges facing contemporary international society. It is a fundamental question for understanding the value we attach to the different elements and agents that constitute the processes of value creation and innovation (Mazzucato 2019), and their impact on the model of society and human development.

As of the 2010s, we understand increasingly that a company or territory that is not able to offer innovative solutions to challenges such as the climate crisis, population aging or inequality is not truly competitive (Raworth 2012). More traditional strategies that separate social and business objectives still make it possible to present a positive bottom line in line with traditional market indicators. However, from a global sustainability perspective, not including the social or environmental dimension in all innovation processes generates much higher risks.

Resilience

In the case of the urban transformation of Bilbao, the way in which local institutions built a collaborative strategy in an extreme situation allows us to visualize a large-scale process of adaptation and transformation. This value occupies a central space in the narratives identified in the territory of Gipuzkoa, the Mondragon case, the recovery of the Basque language, or the new Basque gastronomic scene.

The narratives linked to the Mondragon cooperative experience stress that the idea of adapting to difficulties forms part of the original discourse of its founder: "the aim of Mondragon is not to survive, but to adapt" (Arizmendiarrieta 1999). It is not therefore a complementary value, but central to the cooperative model.

The case of the Gureak group is particularly significant as it interprets the way in which a company made up of workers with disabilities organizes itself to develop manufacturing processes. Traditional business management processes look for professional profiles that can develop the necessary tasks for a given process. In the case of Gureak, the production process is organized on the basis of the capabilities of each person.

This same model can be applied to the process of revitalizing the Basque language. Grassrooted organizations were born in a very complicated context due to the impact of Franco's dictatorship, the scarcity of resources to invest in a minority language, and a globalization process that demanded prioritizing the use of languages with a greater number of speakers. Despite all these factors, they managed to establish a collaborative ecosystem, agility to adapt to the legislation of each stage and influence its modification, as well as to generate resources adapted to the personal reality of the families themselves.

Equality

As we have seen, the value of equality can be considered central or transversal to almost all the initiatives studied. The experience of the Mondragon cooperatives and the commitment to basic income are the most obvious cases, but all the discourses incorporate the need to generate equality mechanisms as a way of creating a fairer society. At the end of the 1980s, the key was to integrate the economy and welfare ("economic growth, yes, but for everyone"). By working on our own, we would not achieve a transformation.

The narratives identified speak of a vision of the economy that is doomed to failure if it is not built on a solid foundation of equality. This is not only a question of social justice but also of effectiveness, competitiveness, and impact. The former President of the Basque Government, Juan José Ibarretxe, refers to this understanding of the centrality of equality with the mantra: "All together, or not at all."

In the case of Gureak, the described narratives tell us about a company that has been able to develop because local citizenry considers that all people should have the same rights and opportunities, whether they have intellectual disabilities or not. This principle of equality is the one that allows the building of a different and interconnected response that is coherent with the whole system of values of the territory. In this sense, Gureak's story "is the same story as that of the cooperatives" (Barandiaran et al. 2020, p.50).

The ethnographer Gluckberg highlights the value of the community practices that are built in the Basque territory on the principle of equality (Glucksberg 2017). This researcher highlights the fact that this way of understanding reality generates the trust and support necessary to promote innovation processes. Unlike the narratives of individual innovation (coming from the technological imaginary), the ancient imaginary in the Basque case links society's capacity for innovation to equality and collective action. This way of understanding innovation influenced, among other related initiatives, the extraordinary gastronomic transformation and it was described as the main reason for the Guggenheim Foundation to select Bilbao rather than Venice or Salzburg as their next European flagship initiative.

Conclusions

In the Basque case, collective narratives were used to express local values as a mechanism of self-definition, informing attitudes, behaviors and ultimately, taking countercyclical strategic decisions. Identity building is a human process that combines local culture and values with historical facts in a non-objective way. Local communities and territories identify themselves with a certain set of values that can be found in those historical facts, but many other values and facts that could also be interpreted as part of their local identity are left aside. Identity building is therefore a social construction and an evolving process that can be positively or negatively channeled through cooperative action.

More effort needs to be made in order to understand why certain strategic decisions are taken and why territories like the Basque Country have responded in a very different way to the same challenges that many struggling ancient communities are facing, such as climate change, aging and inequality. This experience also suggests that those cities and territories that have been able to associate themselves with transformative values like equality, solidarity, self-responsibility, radical democracy, and resilience can become socially sustainable and more competitive. On the contrary, those for whom a negative narrative has emerged face much more serious problems in dealing with the current global challenges.

Urban communities and 21st-century citizens are demanding practical solutions to their growing, complex needs but if given the opportunity, joining a civic transformation movement would allow them to be part of a much more ambitious and mindful enterprise. A civic movement can only be co-created by generating a new narrative of transformation capable of connecting the ancient cultural identity of a particular territory with a "collective decision" to build a new future that local communities are proud to be associated with, and proud to be living in.

The Basque case needs to be understood as a movement rather than the result of an expert-driven strategy. Leadership was shared and spread out, and there was no single person, institution, or organization controlling the process. Many apparently disconnected initiatives were structurally linked in terms of the principles, values, and vision of the transformative goal. Operating as a civic transformation movement allowed Basque organizations, companies, and institutions to work together without setting up rigid or complex legal structures. They were a wide range of projects sharing a collective narrative of transformation. In other words, an extensive spectrum of individuals and organizations creating alternative narratives about their community and the possibility for change.

The Basque experience, by positioning fighting inequalities at the core of the transformation process, differed profoundly from the neoliberal competitiveness processes dominated by new forms of illustrated despotism. It is not a new phenomenon. In 1957, Michael Young explained the negative effects of welfare policies in London's East End because they were disconnected from the real needs and aspirations of the people they were supposed to help. The new urban planning projects broke up—unintentionally—the social networks of solidarity of the communities that had emigrated to the area; networks that had been established over generations.

Current models of civic innovation applied to community transformation are still influenced by theories of change based on this type of despotism and the search for individual talent. Following the experience of large-scale technology companies, territorial innovation is supposed to be conditioned to the generation of the so-called "black swans." Applied to urban transformation, we look for the unexpected solution brought by a person or organization that should have an extraordinary talent or knowledge. Occasionally, this way of operating can contribute to identifying interesting initiatives. Most of the time, it is rare to document systemic change (Breznitz 2021).

Current innovation models thus tend to reinforce individuals and organizations that were previously empowered, and they do not show evidence of large-scale and structural impact. We should invest more resources and efforts in understanding how local communities and institutions perceive their capacity for innovation and change. In poorer neighborhoods, people do not usually feel empowered to play this role. The narrative imposed on them emphasizes negative elements and the perception that change is not possible. At an individual level, it takes the form of a powerful meta-narrative: "Who am I to act in a different way?"

The Basque experience indicates that systemic change only comes about when the entire community feels empowered to act innovatively. These narratives of collective change can be found in ancient cultures, but also in other places that have undergone very positive civic transformations. Instead of looking for rare "talent" in exceptional individuals, ancient and modern advanced forms of civic transformation set out to empower an entire community so that everyone can act in an innovative way.

References

Agirreazkuenaga, J. and E. Alonso. (2014). *The Basque fiscal system. History, current status, and future perspectives*. University of Nevada.

Arizmendiarrieta, J. M. (1999). *Pensamientos*. Otalora.

Barandiaran, X., G. Espiau, and M. Larraza. (2020). *Narrativas y sistema de valores en Gureak*. Agirre Lehendakaria Center.

Barbrook, R. and C. Cameron. (1996). The Californian ideology, *Science as Culture*, 6:1, 44–72

Breznitz, D. (2021). *Innovation in real places: Strategies for prosperity in an unforgiving world*. Oxford University Press.

Carucci, R. (2017). How corporate values get hijacked and misused. *Harvard Business Review*. https://hbr.org/2017/05/how-corporate-values-get-hijacked-and-misused.

Castells, M. (1996). *The rise of the network society*. Oxford, Blackwell.

Collier, P. and J. Kay. (2021). *Greed is dead*. Penguin Economics.

Douglass, W. (1989). *Essays in Basque social anthropology and history*. University of Nevada Press.

Eizagirre, A. and A. Udaondo (2020). *Eraldaketa globalari neurria hartzen*. Mondragon Unibertsitatea.

Espiau, G. (2022). *Normas, valores y narrativas de la innovación social*. PhD Dissertation, University of the Basque Country.

Fernandez, M. (2017). *La Smart City como imaginario socio-tecnológico*. Cuadernos Ciur.

Flyvbjerg, B. (2006). Making organization research matter: Power, values and phronesis. In *The Sage Handbook of Organization Studies*, edited by S . R. Clegg, C. Hardy, T. B. Lawrence, and W. R. Nord. Sage.

Friedman, M. (1962). *Capitalism and freedom*. University of Chicago Press.

Glucksberg, L. (2017). *Exploración etnográfica de la transformación socio-económica del País Vasco*. Agirre Lehendakaria Center.

Hodgson, M. (2017). *Humanity at work*. They Young Foundation.

Hogdson, M. (2016). A story of Leeds. Changing the world everyday. Amplify Leeds, The Young Foundation.

Ibarretxe, J. J. (2015). *The Basque case. A comprehensive model for sustainable human development*. CEINIK.

Malone, T. (2004). *The Future of Work: How the New Order of Business Will Shape Your Organization, Your Management Style, and Your Life*. Harvard Business School Press.

Mazzucato, M. (2019). *El valor de las cosas: quién produce y quién gana en la economía global*. Taurus, pp. 353–357.

Morgan, K., M. Navarro, and J. M. Valdaliso. (2020). Economic governance in the Basque country: balancing continuity and novelty. *Ekonomiaz* 35(2): 170–201.

Mulgan, G. and C. Leadbeater, C. (2013), Systems Innovation Discussion Paper, Nesta. https://media.nesta.org.uk/documents/systems_innovation_discussion_paper.pdf.

Mulgan, G. (2018). *Big mind*. Princeton University Press.

Murry, R., J. Coulier-Grice, and G. Mulgan. (2010). *The open book of social innovation*. The Young Foundation, NESTA.

Nuño, R. (2006) ¿Caos y Excelencia? el caso de Irizar S. Coop.

Ostrom, E. (1990). *Governing the commons: The evolution of institutions for collective action*. Cambridge University Press.

Raworth, K. (2012). A safe and just space for humanity: can we live within the doughnut? Oxfam Policy & Practice. *Climate Change and Resilience* 8(1): 1–26.

Seyfang, G. and A. Smith. (2007). Grassroots innovations for sustainable development: Towards a new research and policy agenda. *Environmental Politics* 16(4): 584–603.

Weber, M. (1993). *Economía y sociedad*. Fondo de Cultura Económica de España.

16

COMMONS ECONOMIES IN ACTION

Mutualizing Urban Provisioning Systems

Michel Bauwens, Rok Kranjc, and Jose Ramos

Commons

We start this chapter by defining two key concepts—the commons and peer-to-peer production—and outlining a vision for a contributive economy based around them. Following the research by Elinor Ostrom, we define "the commons" as a set of shared resources that are maintained, created, or cared for by a situated community or group of stakeholders.[1] While the first part of the definition proposes that commons are something objective, the second adds a subjective element: commons are constituted by human beings, it is a choice a "we" makes as to how they manage a resource (natural or otherwise) and the allocations it can provide. The third stresses self-governance: around the commons, specific rules and norms are created. This clearly distinguishes it from the "dominium" principles of private property, but also from public goods that are managed by an external agent, i.e., the State.

Here we should stress that post-anthropocentric discourses question the definition of natural resources in terms of its ontological dualism between nature and culture. The definition of commons can meaningfully be deepened here by borrowing the notion of "web of life"[2] as an extension of the resources, their governance, and the (multi-species) communities involved. A key issue today is to move from the idea of human commons that manage "external" resources, to the idea of commons as an alliance or partnership between human and non-human communities and entities as interdependent agents and subjects. Many Indigenous cultures, more conscious of their interdependencies in the web of life, often achieved this through the sacralization of the forces of life and nature, and by declaring certain zones off limits to human exploitation. Today we could reinterpret this as a form of "sacred property." The commons, as a modern form of inalienable property, can be seen as a reiteration of that insight. Alan Page Fiske (1993) and Kojin Karatani (2014) both conclude that the commons was the primary mode of exchange in indigenous civilizations, and that it kept an important role in the subsequent scaled-up tribal federations, when gift exchange became a more

DOI: 10.4324/9781003199816-21

important modality of exchange. What is clear is that, historically speaking, the commons has been the primary regenerative human institution, able to balance and restore the harm done by market and state institutions, which have historically been extractive.[3]

It should be stressed that commons and commoning as normative claims to resources and their governance, already shared by many communities and struggles around the world and known under different names, are at their core a pluralist, or rather, *pluriversal* vision, which presupposes that many worlds, ways of knowing, being, and doing can coexist in both locally situated and planetary-scale interdependence. This last dimension is reiterated in this chapter through the idea of cosmolocalism, discussed later. This also means that the position we take in this chapter is not one of replacing every other economic form with a purely commons-based one, but rather that we advocate rearranging the relative priority, and hence the associated dominant institutions, of the various forms of governing and allocating resources.

Peer-to-peer Dynamics

Understanding contemporary commons also requires an understanding of the emergence of peer-to-peer dynamics. The term "peer-to-peer" (P2P) was popularized by the emergence of a new type of digital network, where computers can interact with any other computer, bypassing the need to go through centralized servers. To a substantial degree, the early liberatory ideology of the internet was inspired in its design by such principles. But more fundamentally it is a social dynamic, i.e., any dynamic where humans can freely connect, interact, and create value together, can be considered a P2P system, sometimes despite the fact that such a network can be privately owned. P2P has led to the emergence of global open-source and design communities that lie at the heart of new industries, such as free software and the shared designs of new electronics, but also self-management of mutualized urban resources (Bauwens and Niaros 2017). Citizens and private and public actors now have access to open collaborative ecosystems that are active at different scales. Commons can emerge from P2P interactions as contributors co-create and co-develop shared resources that need to be co-managed for common benefit.

Our vocabulary for this transformation, building on these P2P dynamics, therefore emphasizes the notion of a "contributive economy," composed of productive communities that create shared value around shared resources. A contributive economy sees people and communities co-creating shared resources, based on open-source or open-design principles; while people, teams, and communities create livelihoods around these. When we imagine this contributive and collaborative logic applied to cities, we are talking about the urban commons.

The Urban Commons

The praxis of the urban commons builds on these two ideas, the commons and the potential of P2P interaction and co-creation, to reimagine what a city is and can be. Sheila Foster and Christian Iaione, two of the foremost pioneers in the idea of the urban commons, provide this definition of what an urban commons is:

> The concept of urban commons is based on the idea that public spaces, urban land, and infrastructure ought to be accessible to, and able to be utilized by, urban communities to produce and support a range of goods and services important for the sustainability of

those populations, particularly the most vulnerable populations. The founding principles of this movement include sharing, collaboration, civic engagement, inclusion, equity, and social justice. Urban commons are created and managed by civic collaborations including participants from local communities, government, business, academic, and local nonprofit organizations. In this way, the city is a platform utilized and optimized by citizens from all backgrounds and social statuses.

Foster and Iaione 2020

Work on the urban commons is thematically diverse, e.g., shared mobility, housing, food and energy projects; many also feature open-source protocols, designs and infrastructures targeting the provision of specific services or service nexuses at the urban level, broadly understood. However, they can also be considered, as proposed by Foster and Iaione (2016), as a governance model for cities themselves, to the degree that a city can be considered as a kind of commons.

The emergence of a commons-centric urban ecosystem, i.e., the "commonification of public services" (Fattori 2013), necessitates a specific interface between the public sector and a new civic/citizen sector, which can take the form of "public-commons partnerships" or, potentially, public-commons–private partnerships (Ibid.; Milburn and Russell 2019). Foster and Iaione (2016) have proposed a "quintuple helix" model for urban collaborative governance which includes (1) businesses or similar entrepreneurial forces; (2) knowledge institutions such as universities; (3) government; (4) official civic organizations (NGOs); and (5) citizen-commoners themselves. As suggested in the introduction, the circle of moral obligation here can be meaningfully expanded to include non-human perspectives and concerns.[4]

At different scales, urban commons can take the form of hybrid property or governance arrangements, but it can also take the form of concrete "commons accords." The primary aim is to reinforce the capacity for the autonomy of citizens in driving commons-centric projects, and to provide them with resources and capitalization. Ideally, it strengthens the autonomy of projects, while the alliance with public actors injects the elements of the wider common good that individual projects cannot necessarily carry on their own. In terms of governance, they often combine a public authority agent, joined by a commons or civic association which represents the "commoners"—those citizens working in the common interest.

A recent commons transition initiative for the city of Ghent,[5] as well as examples of urban commons in Barcelona and a number of other cities, give substance and further contours to the case for contributive, commons-based institutions and economies. The following examples provide already running and prefigurative examples of these.

Partner Cities: Lessons from Ghent and Bologna

In 2017, members of the P2P Foundation research network were commissioned by the city of Ghent in Belgium to map local urban commons, conduct conversations with founders of pioneering projects, and advise city authorities on adaptations of the city in favor of the commons-centric citizen initiatives. Figure 16.1 shows the underlying "value logic" of urban commons, which in Ghent grew from 50 to 500 projects in ten years.[6] These urban commons are most often grassroots efforts that create open contribution-based communities, i.e., they are not market, state, or even NGO models.

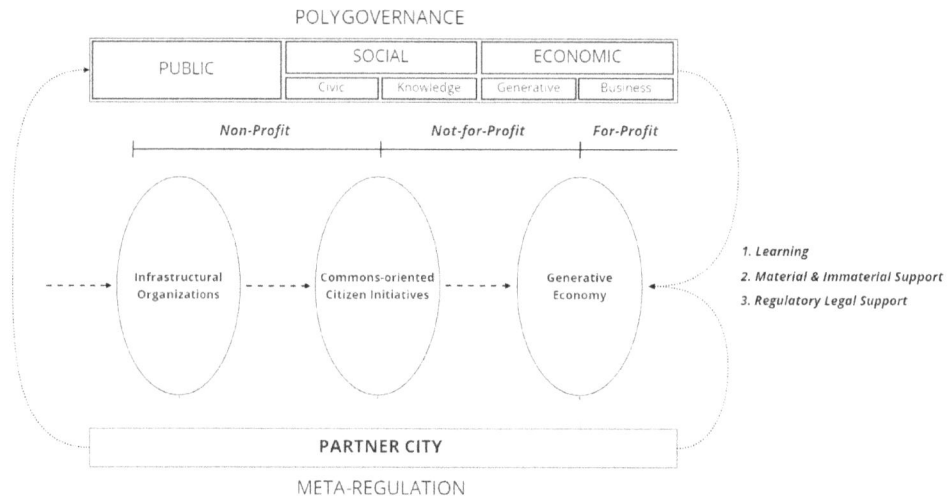

FIGURE 16.1 Synthetic overview of the urban contributive economy (Bauwens and Onzia 2017).

Another finding is that even without formal policy from the city, public agents and other forms of support were present during all phases: infrastructural organization, incubation and functioning of commons projects, incubation of economic projects, and support for commons-centric economic activities. Therefore, in many cases city authorities must first of all recognize that they are already involved in supporting urban commons, but may want to develop a more coherent support of what is at once a newly emerging value regime, one that is based on contributions and not on either pure market activities nor as planned public projects. These projects advance the sustainable wellbeing of the urban populations, but may not always be directly measurable by Gross Domestic Product (GDP), to the degree that they do not involve the monetization of some or all of these activities. This highlights the importance of introducing new types of metrics (such as sustainable wellbeing[7] and local doughnut economics[8]) as well as redefinitions of work (e.g., to recognize and include socially and ecologically regenerative and reproductive labor).

Referring back to Figure 16.1, governance in this model is often polycentric, combining public, social–civic, and economic institutions and organizations, as well as non-profit (no profit allowed), not-for-profit (profit must be reinvested in a social goal), and even for-profit models, which can consist of networks of freelancers, small and big companies, or entities from the ethical, impact, cooperative, and solidarity economy. At the bottom, we place the "Partner City" model, where the city acts as a meta-regulator of the whole system. Figure 16.2 shows the new logic of cooperation that may emerge, once the existence of the commons, and of the public-commons relationships, are recognized. This takes the form of what we call "public-commons cooperation protocols." The first more sophisticated form of such cooperation likely originates in Italian cities, more precisely in the city of Bologna. The Bologna Regulation for the Care and Regeneration of the Urban Commons is based on a specific model that has been emulated in more than 250 other Italian cities and has by informed accounts mobilized around one million Italian citizens to take care of their urban commons.[9]

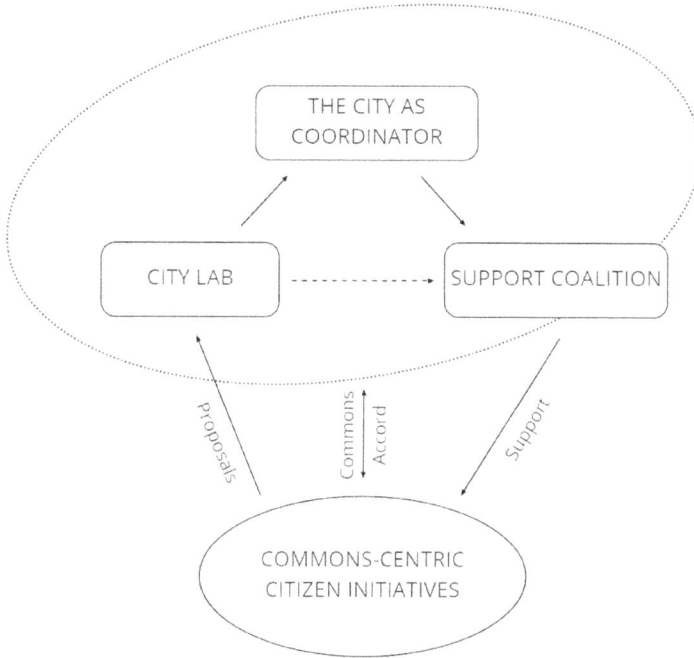

FIGURE 16.2 Public-commons cooperation protocols (Bauwens and Onzia 2017)

A marker of this movement is a recognition of a right of initiative of the citizens, who can claim a commons, a "right to care." Many of these cities also initiate a "Commons City Lab," an institution where citizen-commoners can seek validation and legitimation for their projects. This is then formalized through a "Commons Accord," a mutual agreement between the citizen groups and the city, which specifies mutual duties of support.

This model also has very strong economic implications in the context of a potential new value regime that integrates the presently excluded externalities. First of all, in this model, what is primary is not the commodity value of goods/services or labor power, but "contributions," as defined and experienced by that particular community. Commodity prices and income may be involved, but they exist in hybrid arrangements around the core contributive logic of the specific community. As we found in a study[10] of 300 peer production communities, nearly three-quarters of them were involved in or have experimented with "contributive accounting," a way of keeping track of the variegated contributions that comprise a commons. This usually involves creating a membrane distinguishing the inner logic of the community from the outer logic of the existing market or governmental forms (prices and subsidies). In other words, the project may seek classic funding from external sources, but combine this with innovative forms of internal value definition and distribution. Second, these commons-oriented projects may seek the type of income and funding that maximizes their freedom of action and value regime. This is why we speak of an "ethical economy" or a generative economy surrounding their projects. This may take the form of an entrepreneurial coalition which has specific usage and reciprocity arrangements with the peer production communities.

Urban Commons and Contributive Democracy

Urban commons prefigure a new political contract, in the dynamic multi-actor agreements for collaborative governance and the co-constitution of a city. Urban commons thus express an emerging logic of "contributive democracy" (see Figure 16.3). Democracy can exist in different forms such as representative democracy, in which people choose representatives, and participatory democracy, in which public institutions actively seek direct input from citizens. Contributive democracy functions differently. It recognizes that citizens that already contribute to vital tasks in active ways, must have their voices heard in active ways, and this can be done, for example, by including such engaged and contributive citizens, into the transition councils that determine policy in the context of ecological transformation.

Urban commons are neither pure representative democracies, nor participatory democracies, as these modes are not sufficient to carry forward the transformational dynamics of polycentric governance and multi-actor commoning. Representatives are highly sensitive to their sources of funding and financial support, while so-called participatory models are often top down and seek the opinion of citizens, but not transformative citizen contributions. (A merely representational model based on existing civil society dynamics may invite in the municipal actors whose main goal is actually to slow down required transformative actions). This, then, is what contributive democracy brings to the table; a necessary counterweight of already transformative agents. In the case of the city food council "*Ghent en Garde,*" it integrated not only citizen participation, but invited in civic actors who were already successfully carrying out transformative activities that the city needed. In other words, the legitimacy

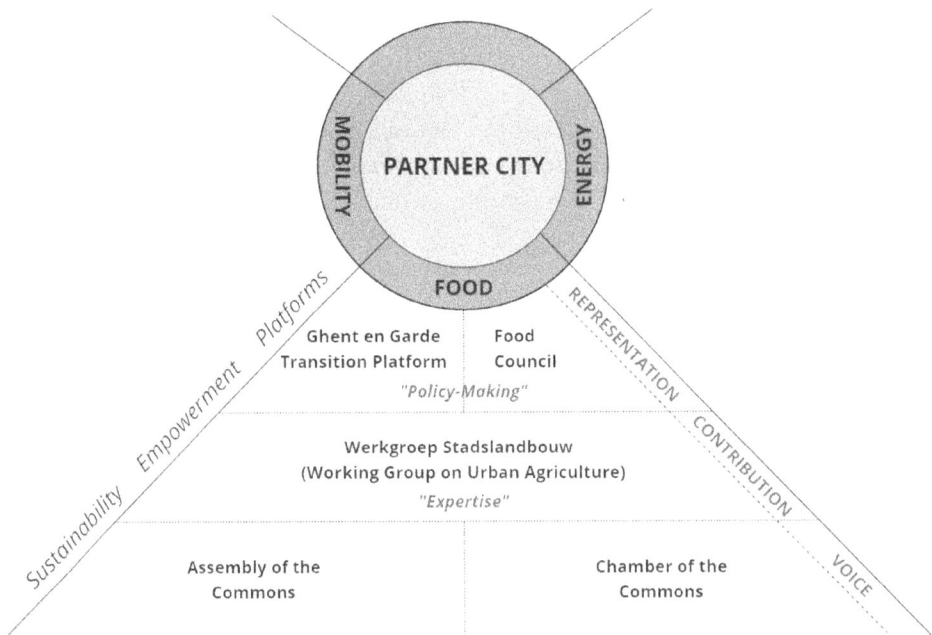

FIGURE 16.3 An example of contributive democracy: the food transition council in Ghent (Bauwens and Niaros 2017)

comes from citizens already expressing in practice the legitimate political goals of the representative regime. This is indicated, in Flemish, as "Working Group on City Agriculture" which represented these new actors.

Figure 16.3 shows the institutional arrangement that the city created to facilitate the food transition efforts in line with climate objectives, with some of the extra proposals that were forwarded to the city administration. The figure also refers to "Assemblies" and "Chambers" of the Commons. These are not public-commons institutions but proposed autonomous institutions of the Commons. The Assemblies of the Commons federate citizens that are actively engaged in the creation and protection of urban commons in a particular city or region, while the "Chambers of the Commons" is a proposal for creating links with the generative enterprises that work with commoners and commons. An Assembly of the Commons was pioneered by Lille in northern France and has been informally operating for several years, a model that is being emulated under various names (e.g., *Fabrique des Communs*). The city of Grenoble has been supporting a permanent assembly of this type. One of the outcomes has been the presentation of public policy proposals to candidates in the municipal elections of France in May 2020. The initiative Remix the Commons has compiled a *Politiques des communs: Cahier de propositions en contexte municipal*,[11] an overview of commons-oriented policies proposed for the municipal level.

Contributive Democracy and *Patrimoni Ciutadà*

One of the best examples of contributive democracy in an urban commons comes from Barcelona, where the city has initiated a so-called communitarian management framework called *Patrimoni Ciutadà*. This regulation enables citizens and neighbors to manage citizen heritage projects, mostly referring to old urban voids (vacant land and dis-used buildings) and important historical buildings.

After the major social mobilizations of 2011 and the election of a commons-oriented coalition, the city of Barcelona created new urban institutions to support the development of a commons-oriented economy. This entailed the collaboration with a knowledge coalition of experts with a focus on the commons (BarCola29), new communication platforms (Procomuns) as well as experiments with in-depth forms of citizen participation (Decidim. barcelona). The city created an open-source Municipal Action Plan which relates to the local commons-based collaborative economy, specifically recognizing it and supporting it with an ambitious investment plan (Impetus Plan30). Using the urban commons and the logic of contributive democracy, Barcelona has generated significant innovations and achievements, including:

- Becoming the first European city to implement a Solar Thermal Ordinance (STO), making it compulsory to use solar energy to supply 60 percent of running hot water in all new buildings, renovated buildings, and buildings changing their use (Puig 2008);
- The Open Digitisation Programme from Barcelona City Council's Office for Technology and Digital Innovation, a government measure for open digitisation, free software, and agile development of public administration services (see Bria, Rodríguez, and Bain 2017);
- The Barcelona City Data Commons initiative raised the question of how citizens can make the most out of data by putting the digital right of the citizen at the core;

- The creation of Barcelona Activa, a new department inside the local development agency which aims to encourage alternative economies;
- The Barcelona Commissioner for Cooperative, Social and Solidarity Economy and Consumption is tasked with promoting and visualizing the social and solidarity economy in order to create new commons-oriented policy directions in the City Council;
- The Impetus Plan for the Social and Solidarity Economy in Barcelona;
- Barcelona Initiative for Technological Sovereignty (BITS).

A similar participatory framework was voted on by the Lisbon City Council in 2010 in order to promote neighborhood preservation and improvement, which benefits 77 Priority Intervention Neighborhoods and Zones. These and other notable examples are collated in the European policy brief prepared by Generative European Commons Living Lab (2020).

Reimagining Urban Agentic Variety

How can diverse socioeconomic, ethno-cultural and newcomer communities have equal access to engaging in and benefiting from these commons? Contributors to commons-centric citizen initiatives are not exclusively reserved to legal citizens, but often involve all inhabitants of a city. Nevertheless, local commons are not necessarily entirely mixed and many factors can have effects on the willingness and capacities of inhabitants to cooperate, the shapes this cooperation takes, and how open or exclusive these spaces are. In our observations in the case of Ghent, there were two types of commons that emerged in that context.

The first type of civic commons observed is theoretically open to everyone, but they might in practice be led by the longer-established populations, and especially by the so-called urban elite, which may lead to a reluctance of more recent migrant communities to participate. The second type of commons are ethnic and religious commons, which are theoretically closed but may in practice be better able to attract poorer inhabitants of the city.

This contradiction is not easy to resolve but public policy and framing may play a role in creating more hybridity in their cooperation. Geneviève Perrin, a French doctoral researcher, has written about how to converge the commons governance orientation of Elinor Ostrom with the capacity-building orientation of Amartya Sen. She proposes the idea of "commons of capabilities" as one of the duties of the "partner cities" that are interested in promoting and assisting the expansion of urban commons (Perrin 2019). Some approaches may be conducive to fostering intercultural cooperation. In Ghent, for example, a project by the non-profit Wervel, aimed to provide organic food to the five million public school meals needed annually. This system brought together the local organic farmers, the zero-carbon cargo bike transport solution, the hiring of cooks in the school, cooperation with the parents and, in addition, the use of technically savvy experts to maintain the technical infrastructure. In this way, the various sectors of the population were brought together as contributors in an integrated system.

Contributive democracy suggests a transformation of the role and indeed definition of "citizen," as the urban commons generates agentic complexity and dynamism far beyond traditional notions of the citizen:

- At the core of this new value regime is an active value-creating (and diverse in itself) civil society, which actively participates in commoning, and cares for the shared resources that it needs for the common good;

- Around this core civil society exists an ethical and generative market system, which creates livelihoods for the citizens, but acts in a generative capacity toward the human communities and the web of life in which they are embedded;
- Facilitative common-good institutions, the *res publica* acting as the "commons of the commons" defend the integrity of the whole system in a "partner state" configuration which augments the capability of its citizens to participate fully in the creation of common value;
- The more-than-human—as embedded in the web of life and validating the critical idea of urban planetary boundaries, the variety of other species and non-human agents that are required to co-generate the common good.

Urban Commons and the Cosmolocal Shift

Cities are not just nested into the context of the global neoliberal economy, but are active creators of it. Cities are where economic and political power have consolidated from the time of great empires to the present. Many cities have historically expressed an imperial core-periphery dynamic (Homer-Dixon 2006). Thus, while we contend with a climate crisis that requires urban transformation, the perverse logics of neoliberal growth are seemingly "baked into" the DNA of many cities.

The new dynamics of urban commoning, which involve the characteristics of being open collaborative systems and contributive democracies, allow us to finally introduce an important concept, that of cosmolocal production. Cosmolocal production is the planetary mutualization of knowledge, in which localities benefit from and contribute to all other localities through open design, open hardware, open technology, and open knowledge, which can transform the logic of cultural, digital, and material production. Two key purposes of cosmolocal production are:

1. To open up opportunities for the majority world (those most in need) to generate livelihoods from a global knowledge/design commons;
2. To create the conditions for a sustainability revolution whereby we, the people of the Earth, are solving our mutual sustainability problems.

A cosmolocal mode of production can exponentially accelerate our ability to address the great sustainability challenges of our era, as one locale solves a problem (e.g., reducing its carbon footprint), by keeping the solution open, it potentiates any other locale to do the same. Likewise, as designs and ideas circulate in an open collaborative system, it allows projects and enterprises to access these to generate livelihoods. These ideas already have proof of concept in dozens of examples (see Ramos, Bauwens, Ede et al. 2021). While the cosmolocalism described here focuses on a new mode of production, the project of cosmopolitan localism more broadly crucially brings in post-colonial, post-development and pluriversal perspectives (Manzini 2015; Escobar 2015).

Cosmolocal production in urban settings presents obvious and important synergies. Cities have scale: large populations, professional expertise, markets, and the proximity needed to produce complex goods and services. We can envision urban citizens harnessing the potential of cosmolocal production to support transitions toward sustainability goals as well as generate jobs and livelihoods. The Fab City Global Initiative is a network of cities that aim to produce everything they consume, thereby dramatically reducing waste and eliminating a large proportion of transport in goods.[12] The emerging ecosystems for urban commons may also have a natural affinity with cosmolocal production. Research conducted by Bauwens and Onzia (2017) on the city of Ghent discovered a proto-cosmolocal ecosystem there with production based on an open contributive system already mature in substantial and diverse niches. Every provisioning system in Ghent already offered a choice in public, private, and commons-oriented ecosystems.

Frontiers in Cosmolocal Value Accounting

A key challenge cities face, as nexuses of dynamic flows and exchanges, is a transition from competition of closed entities that prioritize their own survival and dominance to open ecosystems that operate on a cosmolocal basis. In this new model, material production is maximally localized based on the principle of subsidiarity of material production, thus minimizing the matter–energy expenditure. However, the knowledge cooperation becomes trans-territorial and flows through the ecosystem as a whole, wherever the entities are located. In the old system, the role of regional and national authorities is to attract financial capital. In the cosmolocal economy, the role of territorial authorities is to attract global knowledge flows, so that they can enrich and support local territorial development.

Such new models of production will require wholly new systems of accounting, bringing into the foreground not just territorial fiat moneys but an ever-evolving diversity of intelligent tokens that express the new requirements to respect ecological boundaries. We see a possibility here for scientific bodies and public-science collaborations to evolve to determine these "thresholds and allocations," whereby accounting gains the capacity to represent actual material realities (see Bauwens and Pazaitis 2019). Perhaps the most interesting work being done in this direction, next to Amsterdam's Doughnut Coalition, is the "global threshold and allocations infrastructure" proposed by the Global Commons Alliance and R-30.org.[13] In this system, a global "magisterium of the commons," i.e., a council of scientists would keep track of all commodities, identify their negative pivots, and set annual limits to their usage, which would be embedded in globally accepted accounting ledgers.

Emerging post-blockchain distributed ledger technologies may actually represent an essential infrastructure for this leap in modes of planetary accounting and potentially, a global coordination of production, spanning not only digital but also physical production of value (Fritsch, Emmett, Friedman et al. 2021). With the establishment of an internet of transactions, accounting models become concerned about actual resource dynamics in terms of physical flows and thermodynamics. In this new model, the so-called "externalities" are fully accounted for, both the contributions of many participants who are presently uncounted, but also the negative impacts that such production entails for the web of life.

Concluding Reflections on Activating Urban Commons

Cities will require models at different scales that can draw on the institutional cooperation of various partners. Cities interested in the mutualization of their provisioning systems, for example, could set up a four-layered system of collaboration, as outlined below.

The idea of the urban commons opens the city to a new ontological reality for those who can engage creatively in shaping the city, and for whom a city is shaped. The underlying and implicit nature of cities is both diverse and complex, but this creative groundswell often gets marginalized or ignored. The first "layer" to consider in activating urban commons is to acknowledge the rich existent collaborative complexity that is already engaged in commoning, and to develop the meta-networks and prefigurative meta-formations that can begin to mutualize and extend what is latent.

The second layer in activating urban commons is, as discussed earlier, to bring together the coalitions of support (e.g., the idea of the quintuple helix), which can be supported by a (Partner) city. Accords and agreements play a critical role in formalizing the relationship between a city and "commoners," establishing a new sociopolitical contract. This contract mobilizes legitimacy, public resources, and establishes a new narrative context for action/agency.

The third layer in activating the urban commons is in a city explicitly creating a synergy between a global open design, knowledge collaborative process (cosmolocalism) where a city uses open design to transform its own cultural, digital, and material production, and where what a city creates remains open to any other locale (e.g., other cities) to use for their benefit, creating a virtuous cycle. As mentioned, the Fab City global initiative is pioneering such city visions and experiments.

Finally, a fourth layer in activating the urban commons is, more hypothetically, creating alliances or leagues of cities that can practice city-to-city mutualization, yoking multiple urban commons into synergies where urban commons in various parts of the world work for each other's benefit; addressing the challenge of scale and the inherent competition with capitalist globalization.

Notes

1 There is no singular agreed-on definition of the commons, but many authors acknowledge the tri-partite definition listed here. For a comprehensive study of competing definitions of the commons and the social practice of commoning, see Euler (2015). We have collected various definitions of the commons at https://wiki.p2pfoundation.net/Commons.
2 "Web of life" is described as a succession of organisms in an ecological community that are linked to each other through the transfer of energy and nutrients. See the book-length treatment in Capra (1997); on the web of life, capital accumulation and human non-human co-production, see Moore (2015).
3 The dynamic between expansive market–state systems, leading to resource exhaustion, and the peri-odic revolts of local popular alliances with spiritual reformers that advance a return to commons-based institutions, is documented by Mark Whitaker, who presents various case studies from ancient China, medieval Japan to post-Roman Europe; see Whitaker (2010).
4 For important work on "post-human" urban commons and economies, see, for example, Metzger (2015) and Schönpflug and Klapeer (2017).
5 Further details on the case study may be found in the report by Bauwens and Onzia (2017).
6 This figure comes from our own mapping exercise and the associated timelines of founding dates. The database is privately available in Timelab, Ghent and was previously accompanied by a public wiki.
7 See, for example, Gough (2017) and Buchs and Koch (2017).
8 See the Doughnut Coalitie (https://amsterdamdonutcoalitie.nl/) and the implementation of the doughnut economy in Amsterdam, the Netherlands.
9 The figures come from a conversation by one of the authors with LabSus (www.labsus.org/) members.
10 See P2P Value, https://p2pvalue.eu/.

11 See platform Politiques des communs (https://politiquesdescommuns.cc/).
12 See https://fab.city/.
13 See www.r3-0.org/gtac.

References

Bauwens, M. and V. Niaros. (2017). Changing societies through urban commons transitions. P2P Foundation in cooperation with Heinrich Böll Foundation Berlin. Available at: http://commonstransition.org/wp-content/uploads/2017/12/Bauwens-Niaros-Changing_societies.pdf.

Bauwens, M. and Y. Onzia. (2017). Commons transition plan for the city of Ghent. http://base.socioeco.org/docs/commons_transition_plan_-_under_revision.pdf.

Bauwens, M. and A. Pazaitis. (2019). P2P accounting for planetary survival: Towards a P2P infrastructure for a socially-just circular society. A joint publication between the P2P Foundation, Guerrilla Foundation and Schoepflin Foundation. https://p2pfoundation.net/wp-content/uploads/2019/06/AccountingForPlanetarySurvival_def.pdf.

Bria F., P. Rodrıguez, M. Bain, et al. (2017). *Barcelona city council digital plan: A government measure for open digitization. free software and agile development of public administration services.* Ajuntament de Barcelona.

Brumas, A. and Y. Tarinski. (2017). The future is a "pluriverse"—An interview with David Bollier on the potential of the commons. Towardsautonomyblog. https://towardsautonomyblog.wordpress.com/2017/05/01/the-future-is-a-pluriverse-an-interview-with-david-bollier-on-the-potential-of-the-commons/.

Buchs, M. and M. Koch. (2017). *Postgrowth and wellbeing: Challenges to sustainable welfare.* Palgrave Macmillan.

Capra, F. (1997). *The web of life: A new scientific understanding of living systems* (2nd ed.). Cultrix.

Escobar, A. (2015). *Designs for the pluriverse: Radical interdependence, autonomy, and the making of worlds.* Duke University Press.

Euler, J. (2015). Defining the commons: the social practice of commoning as core determinant. Presented at The City as a Commons: Reconceiving Urban Space, Common Goods and City Governance, 1st Thematic IASC Conference on Urban Commons, in Bologna, Italy, November 6th, 2015. http://hdl.handle.net/10535/9950.

Fattori, T. (2013). From the Water Commons Movement to the Commonification of the Public Realm. *South Atlantic Quarterly* 112, 2: 377–387.

Fiske, A. P. (1993). *Structures of Social Life.* Free Press.

Foster, S. R. and C. Iaione. (2016). The city as a commons. *Yale Law & Policy Review* 34, 281.

Foster, S. R. and C. Iaione. (2020). Urban commons. *Oxford Bibliographies Online.* www.oxfordbibliographies.com/view/document/obo-9780190922481/obo-9780190922481-0015.xml.

Fritsch, F., J. Emmett, E. Friedman, R. Kranjc, S. Manski, M. Zargham, and, M. Bauwens. (2021). Challenges and approaches to scaling the global commons. *Frontiers in Blockchain* 4:578721.

Generative European Commons Living Lab. (2020). European policy brief. https://generative-commons.eu/wp-content/uploads/2020/08/policy-brief_last-version-post-round-table.pdf.

Gough, I. (2017). *Heat, greed and human need: Climate change, capitalism and sustainable wellbeing.* Edward Elgar.

Homer-Dixon, T. (2006). *The upside of down: Catastrophe, creativity and the renewal of civilization.* Alfred A. Knopf.

Karatani, K. (2014). *The structure of world history: From modes of production to modes of exchange.* Duke University.

Manzini, E. (2015). *Design, when everybody designs: An introduction to design for social innovation.* The MIT Press.

Metzger, J. (2015). Expanding the subject of planning: Enacting the relational complexities of more-than-human urban common(er)s. In *Space, power and the commons: The struggle for alternative futures,* edited by S. Kirwan, L. Dawney, and, J. Brigstocke. Routledge, 133–159.

Milburn, K. and B. Russel. (2019). Public-common partnerships: Building new circuits of collective ownership. *Common Wealth*. www.common-wealth.co.uk/reports/public-common-partnerships-building-new-circuits-of-collective-ownership.

Moore, J. W. (2015). *Capitalism in the web of life: Ecology and the accumulation of capital*. Verso.

Perrin, G. (2019). *Les communs de capabilités: une analyse des Pôles Territoriaux de Coopération Economique à partir du croisement des approches d'Ostrom et de Sen*. PhD thesis, University of Paris-Est. www.erudite.univ-paris-est.fr/fileadmin/public/ERUDITE/erudph/2019_Perrin.pdf.

Puig, J. (2008). Barcelona and the power of solar ordinances: Political will, capacity building and people's participation. in *Urban energy transition: From fossil fuels to renewable power*, edited by P. Droege. Elsevier, pp. 433–449.

Ramos, J., M. Bauwens, S. Ede, and J. G. Wong, eds. (2021). *The Cosmolocal Reader*. Clreader.net.

Schönpflug, K. and C. M. Klapeer. (2017). Towards a posthumanist economics: The end of self-possession and the disappearing of homo oeconomicus. In *Varieties of alternative economic systems: Practical utopias for an age of global crisis and austerity*, edited by R. Westra, R. Albritton, and, S. Jeong. Routledge.

Whitaker, M. D. (2010). *Ecological revolution: The political origins of environmental degradation and the environmental origins of axial religions; China, Japan, Europe*. LAP.

17

RADICLE CIVICS—UNCONSTITUTING SOCIETY

Building 21st-Century Civic Infrastructures

Fang-Jui "Fang-Raye" Chang and Indy Johar

In the Paiwan language (a native language of Taiwan), the closest word to "citizen" is "adidan" which rather metaphorically means "root," "foundation" and reflects the essence of "Radicle" Civics.

In botany, a radicle is the embryonic root of a plant and the first part of a seedling to emerge from the seed during germination.

Introduction

Today's Planetary Challenges Cannot Be Solved Using Centralised Frameworks

Over the past 5,000 years, we've evolved from small intimate clans or tribes forming larger and larger groups until we created large nations, corporations, and meta-national structures composed of millions of strangers. For all their scaling innovation, these societal structures have largely operated under a theory of boundaries, in- and out-groups, us and them.

Whilst today's nations, and major corporations, attempt to take on bigger challenges than a small tribe ever could, many of today's planetary challenges cannot be solved within their frameworks—without in turn creating new hegemonies.

In the age of increased uncertainty, we're accepting outdated approaches, opting for reductive or centralised responses to complex, interconnected challenges. City administrators, for example, plant trees in neat rows, and—rather than recognising them as living beings— count, measure, and reduce them to statistics (Scott 2020). Corporate algorithms, however sophisticated, continually overlook diversity. Mass surveillance in cities could provide safety, but centralised data makes information vulnerable to attack and breaches in privacy. Centralised systems are proving limited—many global problems such as pandemics, climate

DOI: 10.4324/9781003199816-22

change, growing inequality, and rising precarity, inadequate proxies for societal wellbeing and prosperity (e.g. GDP), colonisation, and the increasing concentration of power, cannot be solved by one nation, or even a few nations, corporations, or philanthropists, no matter how strong and powerful they are.

As people flee war zones, authoritarian regimes, or environment crises, several European politicians have stoked nationalisms based on difference and division. But to take on global challenges, we need to think beyond the borders of the nation state. Through Radicle Civics, we're proposing the possibilities of new means of organising—fit for a newly networked, interdependent world, in which we more equitably share responsibility.

New or Newly Re-understood Technologies Can Help

Despite utopian ambitions, many advances in technology have exacerbated the concentration of wealth, power, and influence. But technological advances can always create new opportunities for democratising, liberating practices.

The wheel (transportation) and the printing press (information distribution) helped to facilitate the development of civic infrastructures. We could similarly embrace traditional ecological knowledge (TEK) (Houde 2007), or cutting-edge digital tools, and also learn from non-human "technologies," such as photosynthesis in plants[1] or stigmergy among ants.[2]

New or newly re-understood technologies can help facilitate the development of civic infrastructures and liberated civic spaces (see Figure 17.1); enabling open, decentralised and scalable ways of organising. These distributed ways of organising have the potential to make the positive structural changes we need to challenge power imbalances and bypass existing limitations.

In the age of interdependency, we'll need new frameworks for how we relate to each other and our environment, how we recognise value beyond markets and money, how we organise across differences at an unprecedented scale, and how we nurture democratic agency beyond election cycles and reimagine the possibility of genuine civic spaces. Whilst exploring these opportunities, we are asking ourselves:

- What can we learn from genuinely liberated civic spaces without sectorial attachment to either the public, private, or traditional third sector?
- Could actors from across the private, public, and third sectors (as well as individuals, families, streets, and many other constellations) find shared consciousness and agency, and create new ways of "commoning" to address the shared needs and deep risks of our time? And could this be achieved without subordinating to any authority, internally and externally, or being manipulated by an information ecosystem?
- Could we arrive at new hybrid institutions that move beyond the power imbalances in both state and market behaviours?
- Could this civic space provide humans and non-humans with new freedoms in ways that are overlooked by current, polarising debates and interests?

In the following section, we'll begin to look at some of the emerging principles and technologies that lie behind these alternative models and establish a vision for commons-centric, equitable societies.

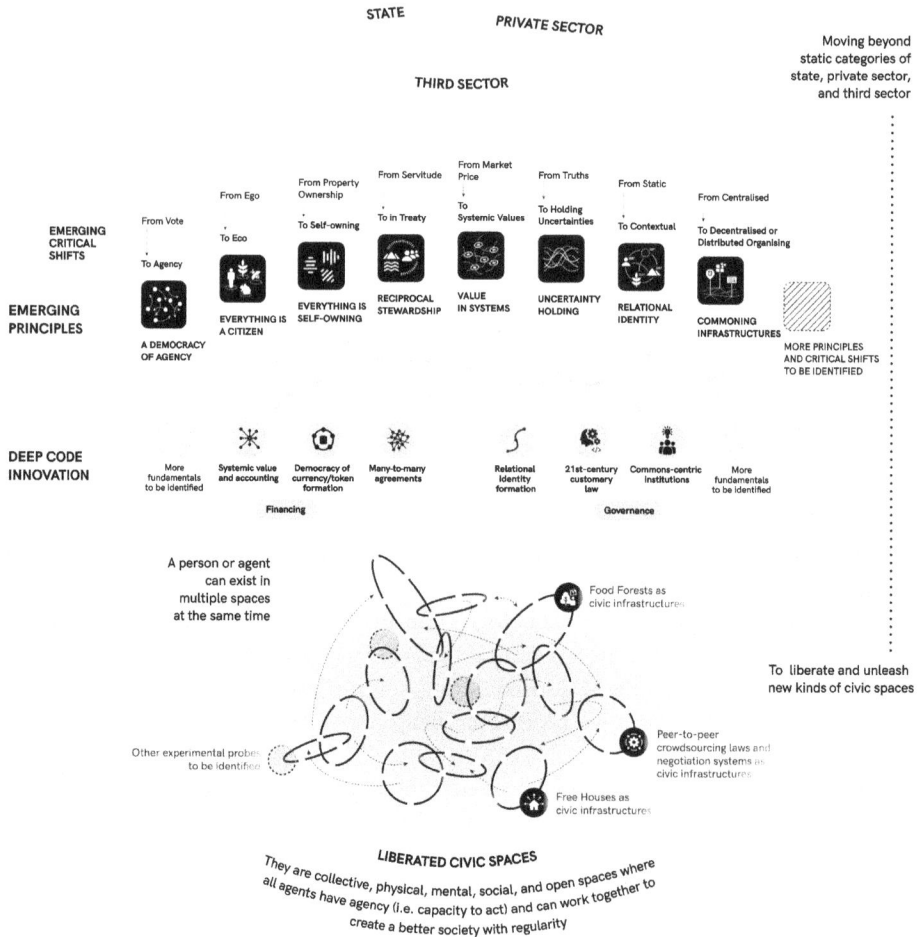

FIGURE 17.1 Overview

Emerging Principles

We've attempted to distil some principles from trends and critical shifts that are enabling the emergence of possible futures—embryonic shoots that will require deep roots and become the foundations of future civic infrastructures.

1. **A Democracy of Agency: From vote to agency**

    Representative democracy—in which enfranchised citizens cast votes every 4–5 years— are reaching a point of crisis. In response, we need to expand our understanding of democracy beyond election cycles, tokenistic focus groups, or intermittent

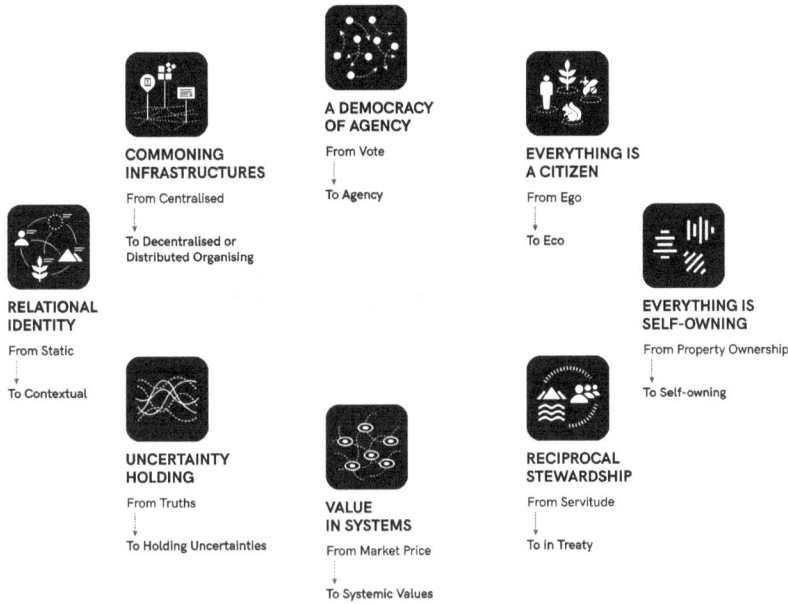

COMMONING INFRASTRUCTURES
From Centralised
↓
To Decentralised or Distributed Organising

A DEMOCRACY OF AGENCY
From Vote
↓
To Agency

EVERYTHING IS A CITIZEN
From Ego
↓
To Eco

RELATIONAL IDENTITY
From Static
↓
To Contextual

EVERYTHING IS SELF-OWNING
From Property Ownership
↓
To Self-owning

UNCERTAINTY HOLDING
From Truths
↓
To Holding Uncertainties

VALUE IN SYSTEMS
From Market Price
↓
To Systemic Values

RECIPROCAL STEWARDSHIP
From Servitude
↓
To in Treaty

FIGURE 17.2 Emerging principles and critical shifts

public consultations, increasing collective ambition for what it can become, and reconsidering the ways we distribute power, whether through co-creation or participatory deliberation.

We'll require dynamic decision-making practices that allow us to adjust in a complex and changing world. We therefore advocate that different opinions should be allowed to coexist in continuous negotiation, exploration, and adjustment. This is not just about developing shared perspectives, but also decentralising and redistributing societal responsibilities—creating a "democracy of agency," shared caring and genuine participation, rather than "democracy by representation." Those with opposing views are not bitter enemies, but co-creators, we see their co-creative capacities as a core component of democratic legitimacy. Together, co-creation and representation need to be expanded across space and time, as civic behaviour should not just benefit the here and now, but other places and future generations.

For this "everyday-yet-long-term democracy" to be fair and inclusive, we'll have to invest in growing shared capabilities (e.g. tools and settings for sense-making of the present and imagining the future), which will in turn require foundational infrastructures such as a long welfare (Dark Matter 2020b) system (e.g. a guaranteed basic income). If we invest in such capabilities and infrastructures, we could cultivate dynamic (and joyful) environments for co-creation, in which people experienced fairer power distribution, increased autonomy, and the agency to make positive change in their daily lives.

EXAMPLE:

Permanent Citizens' Assemblies (Patriquin 2019) establish a continual dialogue between individuals and their governments; forcing politicians to constantly pay attention to "the people." Larry Patriquin argues for creating permanent citizens' assemblies, which would be charged with examining issues of public concern and giving advice to governments.

2. Everything Is a Citizen: From ego to eco

So who participates in our democracies? How do they participate? Who is enfranchised to have their voice and needs acknowledged? What is the scope of their enfranchisement?

We see "citizenship" as inclusive, beyond its currently narrow and exclusionary legal logic that creates hostile environments for "other" people, and incorporates a broader array of "agents," including under-represented humans, future generations, and non-humans. This challenges us to develop new relationships, but to invite new citizens to participate in conversations we'll need to develop a hybrid approach, for which we can take inspiration from models already in existence.

To transition from a human-centric to an ecocentric perspective, we need to embrace a more-than-human notion of agency. Indigenous wisdom (alongside the rights-of-nature movement [Burgers and den Outer 2021]) often grants great stature to nature (such as rivers, mountains, animals) or future generations, and finds ways to speak on their behalf. In his theory of the Parliament of Things (Latour 1993), Bruno Latour argues that we need to give rights to non-humans and quasi-objects and enable their democratic participation; Christopher D. Stone argues that we should recognise the rights of nature (Stone 2010). We could also harness emerging technological capacity for monitoring and representing non-human or future-human voices, through a mixture of data and sensors held in civic data trusts.

EXAMPLE:

A new policy-making system for future generations is: a participatory policy-making workshop, in which participants are divided into two distinct groups: one where participants speak to a future issue from the present, the other speaking to a future issue from the future. Facilitators found that when participants assumed the roles of future generations, they felt more empathy for the potential realities those people might face, which motivated them to advocate for more radical, effective solutions (Capozzi and Dubé 2021).

3. Everything Is Self-owning: From property ownership to self-owning

We'll also need to create a new theory of self-ownership; attributing autonomy to the animate and inanimate agents around us.

Western law allows us to become property owners and therefore gain property rights. Then, we may use the land or other "object" as we see fit within our rights, which means that we can manage, sell, exploit, abuse, and extract from these objects, all of which are thus considered commodities. In *Contract and Domination* (Pateman and Mills 2007), Carole Pateman shows how such arguments were used to justify the colonisation of land.

For many Indigenous cultures, the idea of ownership is envisaged more like stewardship, with rights as responsibilities towards the land, river, or other non-human actor.

Adopting a similar mindset, or attributing personhood (Frow 2019) to agents, would require us to give such non-human actors an autonomy and stronger voice in our legal and cultural frameworks.

To allow for self-owning civic assets to exist, we would also need to redefine identity and how we relate to each other, which are expanded in principles 4—Reciprocal Stewardship and 7—Relational Identity.

A self-owning, autonomous civic infrastructure such as Free House (please refer to experimental probes) could be one of the ways to respond to the accumulation of wealth and growing inequality as no one could acquire it as a property; we may have temporary rights over such beings, but they are accompanied by obligations around its care and upkeep.

In an everyday environment, parents would care for (and exercise their guardianship over) their minor-aged children without owning them. We could adopt similar thinking when forming relationships around the civic infrastructures we build and what surrounds us more generally; presenting an opportunity for emancipation (away from extraction and exploitation) for both "non-humans" and "humans."

EXAMPLE:

The Whanganui River is a legal person: In New Zealand, control of rivers was taken away from the tribes during colonisation. In 2017, following decades of depletion, the river was granted personhood thanks to the efforts of the native Māori people. This represents a shift from government ownership and centralised control to self-ownership. Although "granting" a river personhood can be seen as a condescending or human-centric approach, the legal shift is still valuable as it demonstrated how our current problematic legal system could be more in accordance with Indigenous worldview.

4. **Reciprocal Stewardship: From servitude to "in treaty"**

Transcending our habit of organising the world according to a theory of property requires us to embrace new ways of being "in relationship with" or "in treaty with" the world around us.

Human existence is hugely dependent on a thriving environment, creating a persistent, shared responsibility and requiring us to hold ourselves accountable for each decision we make. The stability of our food systems is hugely dependent on pollinators with around one-third of our food production relying upon them. If we don't take the responsibility to care for the environment, then it won't be able to care for us.

A river is not a thing but a living process as Robin Wall Kimmerer explored in *Braiding Sweetgrass*:

> A bay is a noun only if water is dead. When a bay is a noun, it is defined by humans, trapped between its shores and contained by the word. But the verb wiikwegamma—to be a bay—releases the water from bondage and lets it live. "To be a bay" holds the wonder that, for this moment, the living water has decided to shelter itself between these shores, conversing with cedar roots and a flock of baby mergansers. Because it could do otherwise—become a stream or an ocean or a waterfall, and there are verbs for that, too.

Recognising that we are all related to each other, and to all life on Earth, requires not merely contractual shifts, but further shifts in the way we recognise ourselves, our relationship with the world around us and the institutional frames which scaffold these relationships. Rather than reducing interactions to contracts, can we collaborate in a dynamic treaty, building on mutual care as opposed to fear of violence or the exclusion of others? Could machine learning be shaped by care and kindness, rather than *homo economicus*-era thinking? Through deep consideration of these questions, we can begin to recode ourselves and our being-in-the-world.

EXAMPLE:
All my relations (Dark Matter 2020c): As the Mohawk phrase "Akwe Nia'Tetewá:neren" (all my relations) expresses, Indigenous worldviews often have a philosophy of interconnectedness and belonging, an understanding that we are all related to each other and to all life on Earth.

5.   Value in Systems: From market price to systemic values

Our environment, ancestry, memories, and relationships are all deeply valuable, live at the heart of our existence, and shape our daily decisions—yet our mechanisms of understanding and operationalising such value are extremely reductive. We need a theory of value that recognises entanglement and multiple values beyond the abstraction of price.

The standard economic model considers the making of singular "rational" profit maximisation decisions to be "efficient" and requires that every good, or more broadly "everything we care about" can be privately owned and traded in markets, with prices reflecting "worth." But clearly many things we value are impossible to buy or sell directly—no one can go to a store and purchase a good reputation, shared memories, or one's ancestry.

To help bridge this gap, we first consider retaking the non-market approach of gift-giving, be it through straight physical goods or through stewarding things we care about. Gift exchange can signal mutual trust, interconnectedness, and regard for principles and values, or specifically for one another. The gift economy (see Give It Away [Graeber 2008] and Gifts [Yan 2020]) allows for a revaluing of goods and resources by not putting a monetary value at the centre of its thinking but adding other dimensions of value like social cohesion, cultural identity, and the natural environment whilst improving the overall wellbeing of the system.

The notion of interconnected self-ownerships (see principle 3—Everything is Self-owning) forms a foundation that asks us to rethink value.

A thriving mycelium network is integrally connected to the soil, trees, aquifer, birds, and more. Currently, most accounting systems struggle to go beyond putting, for example, a city's trees on the balance sheet (and usually as a liability rather than as a multiple-benefit asset). But rather than seeing (or even ignoring) them as separate entities, they should be seen as a network of interconnected agents, and relationships among them are where the value lies. Without the mycelium—which often goes unaccounted for—lots of things that are important to us struggle to survive.

To better assess and share the real values of the whole system and its complexity, we need to better calculate the cost of resources and goods the market prices of which often fail to reflect environmental damage or human harm caused by their supply chains. The work by Michael Bauwens in P2P Accounting for Planetary Survival (Bauwens and Pazaitis 2019) starts to critically explore the needs of new accounting practices necessary for a relational world.

This also sets the foundations for a "capability approach" (Robeyns 2006), which considers that the primary focus of understanding value should be to allow effective opportunities for every being in the system to achieve wellbeing.

It's not simply a matter of recognising and adequately pricing negative externalities but challenging the normalisation of uncivic, environmentally degradational behaviours within our economies; recognising that all externalities affect us, whether now or later.

EXAMPLES:
New Zealand's Happiness and wellbeing metrics, the Sustainable Development Index, Bhutan's Gross National Happiness Index or the Better Life Index of the Organisation for Economic Co-operation and Development (OECD) Better Life Index are some current attempts to capture systemic values.

6. **Uncertainty Holding: From truths to holding uncertainties**
In most parts of the world, human history has created a long legacy of control, classification, and documentation practices which aim to create single registries of truth. Governments, or other grand institutions, are typically single guardians of that truth—citizen identity records, land registries, and housing registries are all examples of centralised record-keeping, and are critical mechanisms for how societies organise.

Categorisation and classification can be inherently problematic—who does the classification? And who therefore defines the spaces of operation, possibility, and impossibility? Targeted zoning laws like Home Owners' Loan Corporation (HOLC) in the USA, for example, which have all played a role in isolating minority populations whilst simultaneously privileging white residents.

Scientific method (constructing hypotheses and experimenting) is a framework for holding uncertainties, not truths. As societies, we need to create robust frameworks for holding uncertainties, recognising that many "truths" may evolve and we needn't try to cling to them forever. We approach truth as Mikhail Bakhtin put it—"Truth is not born nor is it to be found inside the head of an individual person, it is born between people collectively searching for truth, in the process of their dialogic interaction" (Bakhtin and Booth 1984)—which places emphasis on relationality.

To move towards a genuinely civic future, we need to recognise that distributed, decentralised knowledge production provides an approach to holding uncertainty. We need to move beyond single holders of truth and classification as David McConville beautifully puts it, "the ability to view the world from multiple perspectives is essential for tackling complex, interconnected challenges." We need to "expand the subject/object dichotomy to include intersubjective, interobjective, and nondual perspectives" (McConville 2014).

EXAMPLE:
Wikipedia is a civic knowledge infrastructure that focuses on the benefit or interests of all people. Unlike traditional encyclopaedias or corporate publishers, it strives for less direct control and ownership of knowledge. It replaces the conventional model by providing

stewardship of knowledge and facilitation of resources such as self-checking mechanisms through citation and peer review. It's part of our everyday, web-browsing lives, but also presents a glimpse; a poem of a different future.

7.   Relational Identity: From static to contextual

In principle 6, we explored some of the difficulties surrounding categorisation by others, but we are often co-constituted by other beings. As books like *I Contain Multitudes* (Yong 2016) show, the self is anything but self-contained. How do we build frameworks of identity which neither statically and universally capture us, nor perpetuate the myth of total autonomy, but instead help us evolve in an understanding of our interconnectedness?

One such perspective is that of relational identity, which reflects the idea of "a person is a person through other persons" (Birhane 2017)—an identity is contextual, depending on many others (e.g. family, friends, culture) and is formed through interactions, relationships, and experiences over time. Some Indigenous People embrace the worldview, "I'm the land and the land is me." This depicts a different relationship with nature, emphasising relationality and reciprocity (as opposed to the worldview that sees land as a commodity) allowing identity formation to be contextual. Building a new theory and praxis of identity will be fundamental to engaging and unleashing a deep praxis of freedom.

EXAMPLE:

Proof of Existence: The power of single verifications of truth is challenged by emerging technological revolutions. San Francisco-based entrepreneur Santiago Siri, for example, registered the birth of his daughter, Roma, using the blockchain-based verification service Proof of Existence which is a statement that declares her primarily a citizen of Earth rather than of a nation state (an arbitrary piece of territory controlled by centralising power). Whilst states tend to rely on closed bureaucracies to support their institutional belief systems, the world has the Internet and the blockchain (Bello Perez 2015). (We recognise however that prevalent ledger systems are still at a beta stage and need much more work in terms of impact validation, trust, and decentralised structures.)

8.   Commoning Infrastructures: From centralised to decentralised or distributed organising

Trust in our current intermediaries, particularly conventional financial institutions or corporate utilities, is all-too-often an illusion, as exposed by the 2007–2009 financial crisis and the ensuing European sovereign debt crisis, the abdication of responsibilities by the UK's privatised water companies, or the sudden collapse of energy providers.

If we give these conventional intermediaries more trust and responsibility then we give them more power, leaving us unprotected. So we need to reimagine the role of the intermediary, be it for transactions, wealth redistribution, rule-making or code creation from a centralised holder towards a *new network of peers and infrastructures of economic democracy*.

"Commons" provide a remarkably effective (Ostrom 2009) alternative model for governing shared resources and redistributing trust, but many commons are limited to in-groups (excluding outsiders). "Commoning" seeks greater inclusivity, it is both an ancient practice and a contemporary way to rethink how we can fulfil everyday needs and ensure the thriving of all. It describes a social practice related to production, sharing, maintaining, and distribution through the facilitation of resources and elimination of barriers, rather than through direct control or ownership.

Commoning ("becoming in common" [Nightingale 2019]) might describe a more open-ended exploration of a new class of civic, institutional, self-owning, autonomous, yet shared infrastructures. A whole range of civic "things" such as identity systems, monetary, and land registry could build on this new commoning infrastructure beyond the realm of both markets and the state.

EXAMPLE:
Distributed ledger technology (DLT) provides a secure and trustless framework hoping to improve collective efforts through peer-to-peer verification and without intermediaries who hold monopoly power. We can build a system with decentralised cryptography without relying on third-party auditing, by moving trust from the auditors to the software infrastructures and mechanisms.

Deep Code Innovation

Radicle Civics are the emerging, entangled roots whose growth and nurture are vital for commons-centric civic infrastructures. To enable their development—and encourage cultures of equity, freedom, safety, and sustainability—we require a series of deep code innovations, so let's now shift our focus towards systems change.

Money, markets, laws, and contracts make up seemingly immutable cornerstones of our societies, but they're based on narrow, centralised definitions of value, and encourage extractive, competitive behaviours. Through a time of transition and large-scale reorganising, we need inspiration from compelling and diverse stories requiring imaginative capacities so often overlooked in our understanding of how change happens.

Some design questions related to these fundamentals include:

1. What if we actively sought new ways of accounting for multiple values that considered the diverse relationships between system elements such as trees, air, bees, humans?
2. What if currencies and tokens (i.e. mediums of exchange) were formed based on how different actors across society create environmental and social goods, rather than on debt? What if their formation were decentralised allowing for values to be understood more pluralistically?
3. What if we created new types of agreements and treaties to establish perpetual positive promises to care for the wellbeing of all agents?
4. What if humans were able to manage their own identity and data without being exploited by private corporations or data management infrastructures? What if civic assets/agents such as forests, rivers, schools could be self-owning and be free from financially driven extraction through rethinking how we view their identity and registry?
5. What if we could actively learn from Indigenous and other traditional practices to inform and shape our laws through our lived experiences, stories ("an Indigenous legal

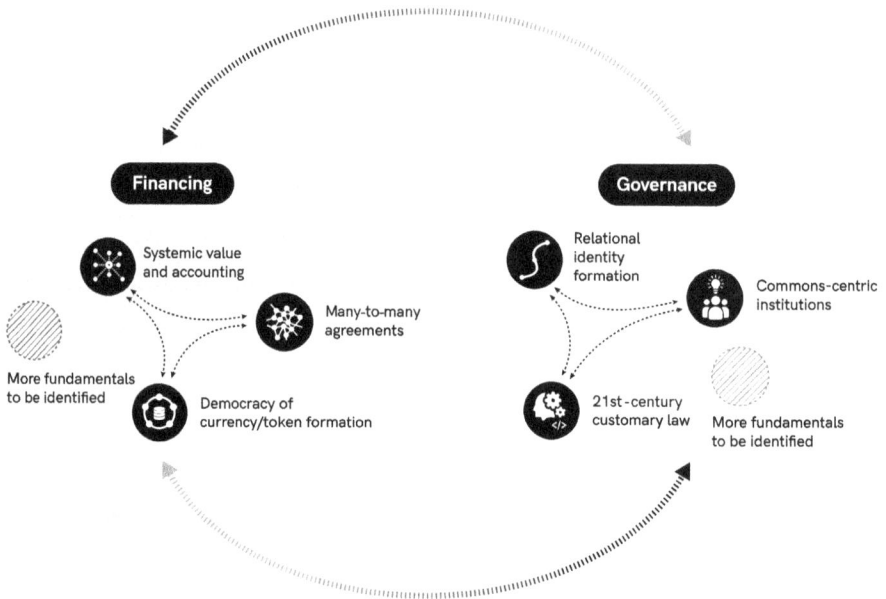

FIGURE 17.3 Emerging fundamentals

perspective emerges from the literacy of nature. Water, plants, animals are our legal archives and professors. The beauty the world conveys is filled with stories, teachings, procedures and principles" [Dark Matter 2020a]) and enforce them through peer-based mechanisms?

6. What if existing and new institutions (like public interest trusts and grassroots democratic structures) could form a new type of relationship with civic assets which was not based on property ownership but better stewardship and care?

Experimental Probes

Experimental probes are future-imagining devices that let us explore deep code innovations with a great practical tangibility. We've illustrated three examples of civic, self-owning, autonomous, yet shared infrastructures and outlined how emerging principles and deep code innovation could be applied to different contexts.

1. Food Forest 2.0: A self-owning civic infrastructure providing social, environmental, and economical security based around the interactive, interdependent ecology of an urban forest, requiring new types of civic asset stewardship through public interest trusts and an economy of gifting. (See Figure 17.4.)

2. Free House: A near-future self-owning house, built as a piece of local civic infrastructure, sitting at the crossroads of a new circular biomaterial economy, open distributed manufacturing capabilities, and a new relationship between home and human, based on reciprocal care and stewardship. (See Figure 17.5.)

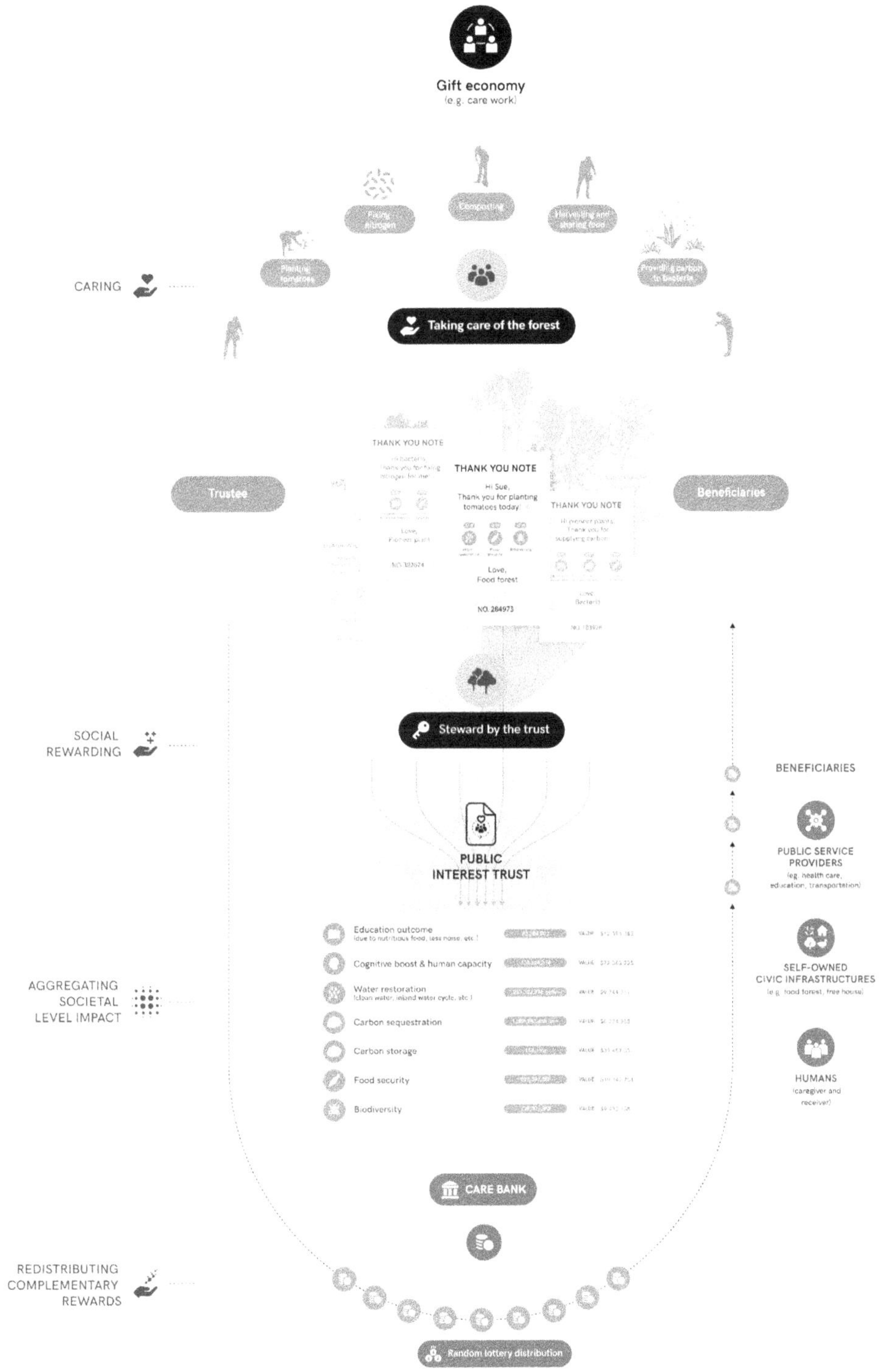

Gift economy
(e.g. care work)

CARING

Taking care of the forest

Trustee

THANK YOU NOTE

THANK YOU NOTE
Hi Sue,
Thank you for planting
tomatoes today.

THANK YOU NOTE

Love,
Food forest

NO. 264973

Beneficiaries

SOCIAL
REWARDING

Steward by the trust

BENEFICIARIES

PUBLIC SERVICE
PROVIDERS
(e.g. health care,
education, transportation)

PUBLIC
INTEREST TRUST

AGGREGATING
SOCIETAL
LEVEL IMPACT

Education outcome
(love to nutritious food, less noise, etc.)

Cognitive boost & human capacity

Water restoration
(clean water, inland water cycle, etc.)

Carbon sequestration

Carbon storage

Food security

Biodiversity

SELF-OWNED
CIVIC INFRASTRUCTURES
(e.g. food forest, free house)

HUMANS
(caregiver and
receiver)

CARE BANK

REDISTRIBUTING
COMPLEMENTARY
REWARDS

Random lottery distribution

FIGURE 17.4 Food Forest 2.0

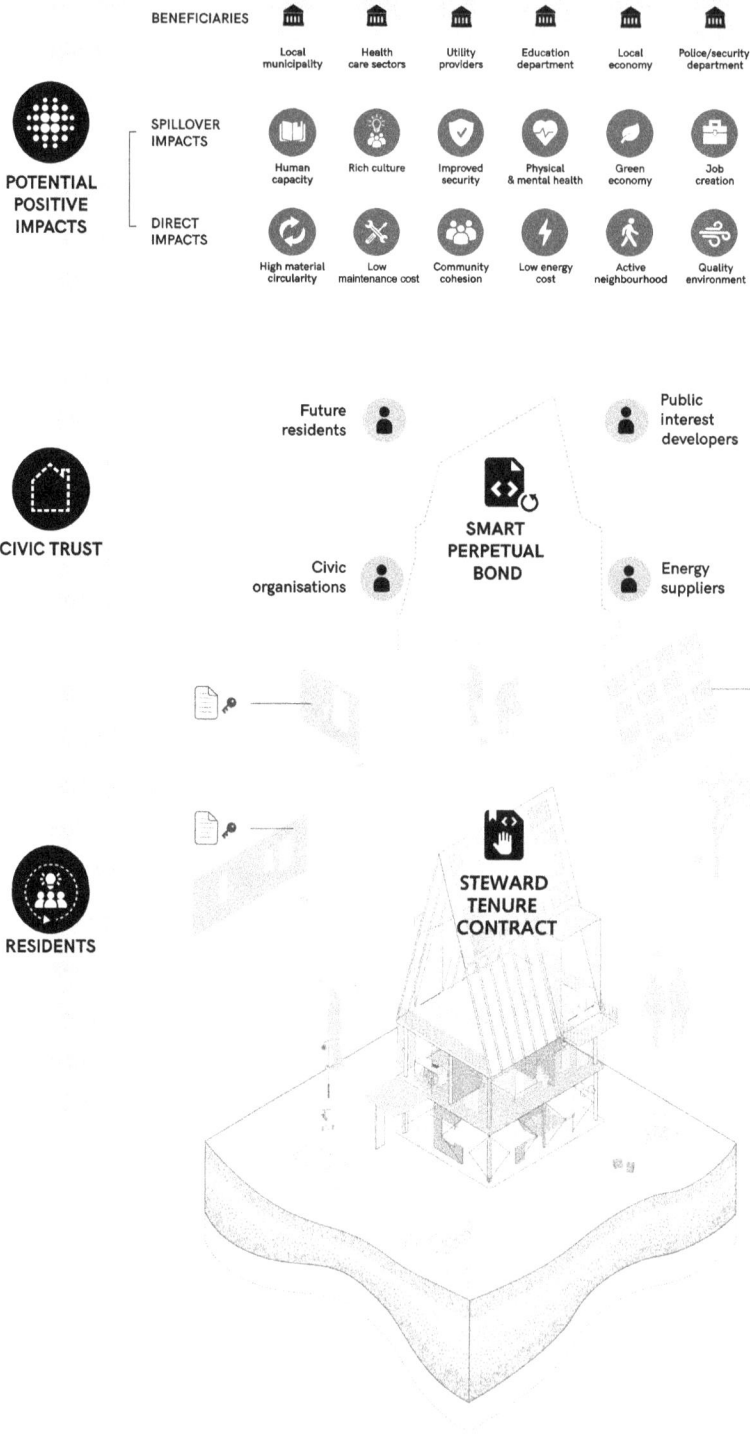

BENEFICIARIES

Local municipality · Health care sectors · Utility providers · Education department · Local economy · Police/security department

POTENTIAL POSITIVE IMPACTS

SPILLOVER IMPACTS

Human capacity · Rich culture · Improved security · Physical & mental health · Green economy · Job creation

DIRECT IMPACTS

High material circularity · Low maintenance cost · Community cohesion · Low energy cost · Active neighbourhood · Quality environment

CIVIC TRUST

Future residents · Public interest developers · Civic organisations · SMART PERPETUAL BOND · Energy suppliers

RESIDENTS

STEWARD TENURE CONTRACT

FIGURE 17.5 Free House

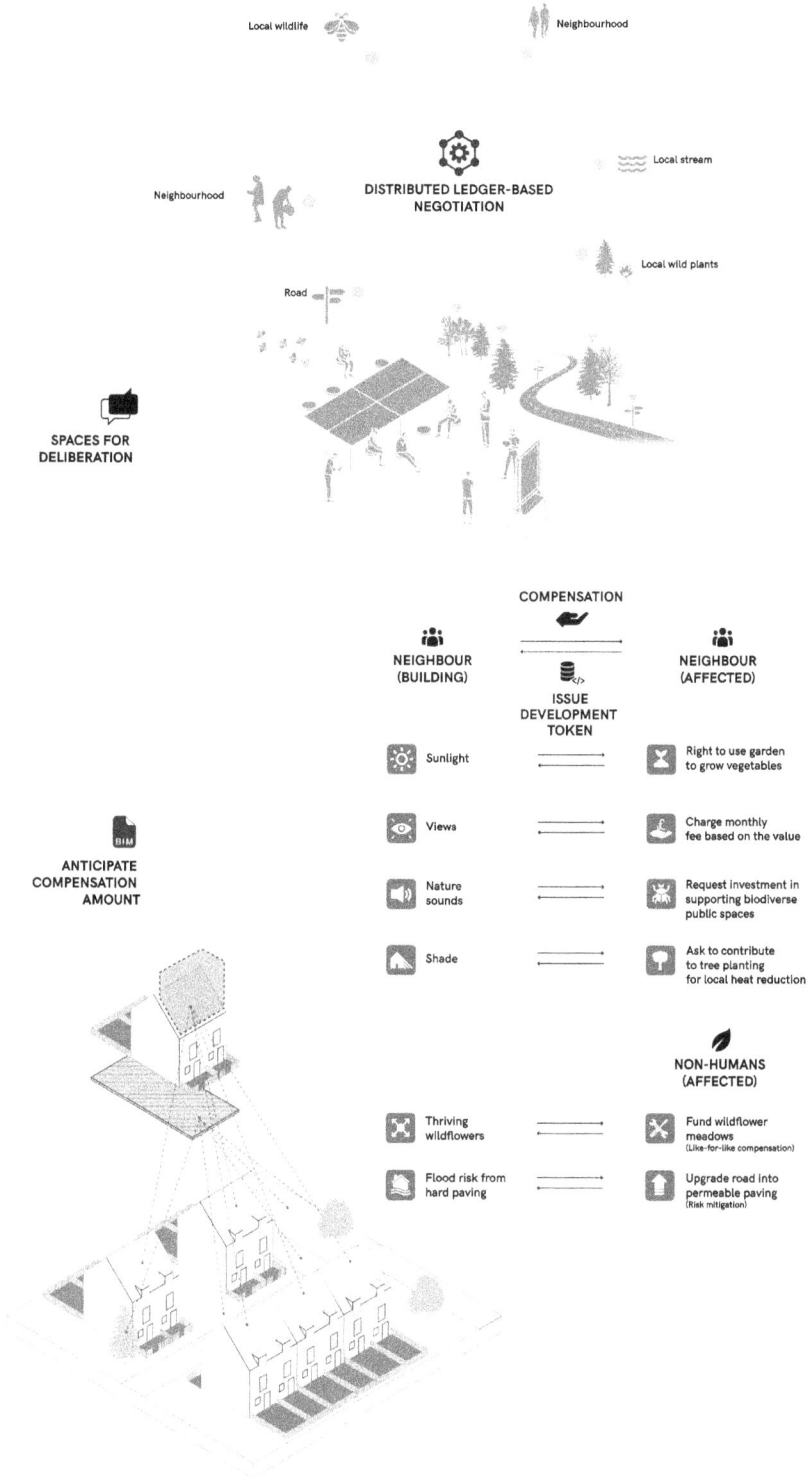

Local wildlife

Neighbourhood

DISTRIBUTED LEDGER-BASED NEGOTIATION

Local stream

Neighbourhood

Local wild plants

Road

SPACES FOR DELIBERATION

COMPENSATION

NEIGHBOUR (BUILDING)

ISSUE DEVELOPMENT TOKEN

NEIGHBOUR (AFFECTED)

Sunlight — Right to use garden to grow vegetables

Views — Charge monthly fee based on the value

Nature sounds — Request investment in supporting biodiverse public spaces

Shade — Ask to contribute to tree planting for local heat reduction

ANTICIPATE COMPENSATION AMOUNT

BIM

NON-HUMANS (AFFECTED)

Thriving wildflowers — Fund wildflower meadows (Like-for-like compensation)

Flood risk from hard paving — Upgrade road into permeable paving (Risk mitigation)

FIGURE 17.6 P2P planning

3. P2P Planning: An accessible, transparent way of negotiation and dispute resolution in regulating development through networks of peer-to-peer relations, modelled as a free market exchange of "development rights tokens." It proposes new types of agreement creation and processes for enforcement. (See Figure 17.6.)

Moving Forward

Dark Matter Labs[3] is part of the 00[4] family, who have a long history focusing on democratising individual and collective agency. 00 talked about the role of civic entrepreneurship in the book *Compendium for the Civic Economy* (Ahrensbach et al. 2012), and co-developed platform infrastructures in the civic domain such as for democratising home design and construction through WikiHouse,[5] and distributed an ethical furniture supply chain through Open Desk.[6] Through the endeavours we came to a realisation that we need institutional "roots," not just projects.

The principles and deep code innovations previously covered are the "roots"; they start to show how autonomous yet interdependent agents can work towards commons-centric futures and build 21st-century civic infrastructures. All of the questions and provocations are the beginning of an exploratory journey looking into different ways of organising the future. This is an open invitation to have conversations, experiments, and make different ideas of the future; it is also a call for a new scale of societal funding instruments for a new class of civic, self-owning, autonomous, shared infrastructures as well as partnerships and allies for building real-world experiments. We need such experiments to learn and exercise an enriched social imagination that embodies interdependency, shared responsibility, open contribution, and participation in a more ambitious way than we might be able to envision at this moment of social and environmental crisis across the world.

Please visit radiclecivics.cc to read about details of experimental probes that demonstrate plausible futures and to find further ideas about how we could realise them in years to come.

Acknowledgements

The work is (partly) reviewed by: Alberto Hernández Morales, Calvin Po, Eunsoo Lee, Gurden Batra, Jack Minchella, Jonathan Lapalme, Joost Beunderman, Nick Stanhope, Raj Kalia, and Thomas Theodore. The visuals are designed by: Fang-Jui "Fang-Raye" Chang, Hyojeong Lee, and Juhee Hahm.

Notes

1 Most people of course would argue that photosynthesis in plants is nature—not technology, but that's the exact point we are trying to make. We don't see technology as just cutting-edge electronic/digital elements and we would like to give it a broader definition by including nature and Indigenous wisdom. The technologies humans created can be seen as replications/inspirations of the "real nature technology."

2 Stigmergy is indirect communication in which individuals communicate with one another by modifying their local environment. It was first observed in social insects such as ants. They adapt their

responses or start new activities without centralised command and control. In that way, they collectively develop a complex network of trails, connecting the nest in an efficient way to locate food. We consider all collaboration and future imagining needs to become stigmergic. "Stigmergy." Wikipedia. https://en.wikipedia.org/wiki/Stigmergy.

3 *Dark Matter Labs*, https://darkmatterlabs.org/.
4 *Zero Zero*, https://www.project00.cc/.
5 *WikiHouse*, https://www.wikihouse.cc/.
6 *Opendesk*, https://www.opendesk.cc/.

References

Ahrensbach, T., J. Beunderman, A. Fung, I. Johar, and J. Steiner. (2012). *Compendium for the civic economy: What our cities, towns and neighbourhoods should learn from 25 trailblazers*. Trancity Valiz.

Bakhtin, M. and W. C. Booth. (1984). Acknowledgments. In *Problems of Dostoevsky's poetics*, edited by C. Emerson. University of Minnesota Press, pp. vii–x. https://doi.org/10.5749/j.ctt22727z1.3.

Bauwens, M. and A. Pazaitis. (2019). *P2P accounting for planetary survival. P2P Foundation*. https://commonstransition.org/wp-content/uploads/2019/09/AccountingForPlanetarySurvival_defx-2.pdf.

Bello Perez, Y. (2015). Meet the dad who registered his daughter's birth on the blockchain. *CoinDesk*, November 14th, 2015. www.coindesk.com/meet-the-dad-who-registered-his-daughters-birth-on-the-blockchain.

Birhane, A. (2017). Descartes was wrong: A person is a person through other persons. *Aeon*, April 7th, 2021. https://aeon.co/ideas/descartes-was-wrong-a-person-is-a-person-through-other-persons.

Burgers, L. and J. den Outer. (2021). *Rights of nature. Case studies from six continents*.

Capozzi, M. and J., Dubé. (2021). *Inviting Future Generations into Present Negotiations*. Concordia University Seminar. www.concordia.ca/cuevents/offices/provost/fourth-space/programming/2021/04/13/office-hours--inviting-future-generations-into-present-negotiati.html.

Dark Matter. (2020a). Civic-Indigenous 7.0. *Dark Matter Laboratories*, January 27th, 2020. https://provocations.darkmatterlabs.org/civic-indigenous-7-0-459436b6f60.

Dark Matter. (2020b). Property rights/property wrongs: Micro-treaties with the Earth. *Civic-Indigenous 7.0*, September 14th, 2020. https://provocations.darkmatterlabs.org/property-rights-property-wrongs-micro-treaties-with-the-earth-9b1ca44b4df.

Dark Matter. (2020c). Long welfare. *Climate-KIC*, February 21st, 2020. https://medium.com/futures-in-long-termism/long-welfare-3476004d2e00.

Frow, J. (2019). Personhood. *Oxford Handbooks Online*. www.oxfordhandbooks.com/view/10.1093/oxfordhb/9780190695620.001.0001/oxfordhb-9780190695620-e-48.

Graeber, D. (2008). *Give it away. The Anarchist Library*. https://theanarchistlibrary.org/library/david-graeber-give-it-away.

Houde, N. (2007). The six faces of traditional ecological knowledge: Challenges and opportunities for Canadian co-management arrangements. *Ecology and Society* 12(2).

Latour, B. (1993). *We have never been modern*. Harvard University Press.

McConville, D. (2014). *On the evolution of the heavenly spheres: An enactive approach to cosmography*. Plymouth University.

Nightingale, A. (2019). Commoning for inclusion? Commons, exclusion, property and socio-natural becomings. *International Journal of the Commons* 13(1): 16–35.

Ostrom, E. (2009). *Beyond markets and states: Polycentric governance of complex economic systems*. www.nobelprize.org/uploads/2018/06/ostrom_lecture.pdf.

Pateman, C. and C. W. Mills. (2007). *Contract and domination*. Polity.

Patriquin, L. (2019). *Permanent citizens' assemblies: A new model for public deliberation*. Rowman & Littlefield Publishers.

Robeyns, I. (2006). The capability approach in practice. *Journal of Political Philosophy* 14(3): 351–376. https://onlinelibrary.wiley.com/doi/abs/10.1111/j.1467-9760.2006.00263.x.

Scott, J. C. (2020). *Seeing like a state: How Certain Schemes to Improve the Human Condition Have Failed.* Yale University Press.

Stone, C. D. (2010). *Should trees have standing? Law, morality, and the environment.* Oxford University Press.

Yan, Y. (2020). Gifts. *Cambridge Encyclopedia of Anthropology.*

Yong, E. (2016). *I contain multitudes: The microbes within us and a grander view of life.* Random House.

INDEX

For Product Safety Concerns and Information please contact our EU
representative GPSR@taylorandfrancis.com
Taylor & Francis Verlag GmbH, Kaufingerstraße 24, 80331 München, Germany

www.ingramcontent.com/pod-product-compliance
Lightning Source LLC
Chambersburg PA
CBHW080131270326
41926CB00021B/4435